ENCOUNTER:
Love, Marriage,
and Family

SECOND EDITION

ENCOUNTER:
Love, Marriage, and Family

Ruth E. Albrecht
E. Wilbur Bock

The University of Florida

HOLBROOK PRESS, INC.   BOSTON

Library of Congress Cataloging in Publication Data

Albrecht, Ruth E 1910- comp.
    Encounter.

    Includes bibliographies.
    1. Family life education. I. Bock E. Wilbur, joint comp.
II. Title.
HQ10.A5   1975   301.42   74-34405
ISBN 0-205-03402-0

Contributors

Jack O. Balswick, Ph.D., is an Associate Professor, Department of Sociology, University of Georgia, Athens, Georgia.

Inger Becker is a journalist and social observer who lives in Stockholm, Sweden.

Robert R. Bell is a Professor of Sociology at Temple University, Philadelphia, Pennsylvania.

Miriam E. Berger, M.S.W., is Emotional Health Consultant, Jamaica, New York.

Jessie Bernard, Ph.D., is a research scholar, Honoris Causa. She retired from teaching in the Department of Sociology, Pennsylvania State University, University Park, Pa. and now devotes herself to writing and research. She is the author of many books and articles on the sociology of sex roles, marriage, and family topics.

Jerry Bigner, Ph.D., is Assistant Professor, Department of Home Economics, Indiana University, Bloomington, Indiana.

Paul Bohannan, Ph.D., is Professor of Anthropology at Northwestern University, Evanston, Illinois.

Jordan T. Cavan was Professor Emeritus from Rockford College, Rockford, Illinois.

Ruth Shonle Cavan, Ph.D., is Adjunct Professor of Sociology, Northern Illinois University at DeKalb. She is the author of many outstanding books and articles dealing with the family.

Jay E. Chaskes, Ph.D., is an Assistant Professor in the Department of Sociology, Glassboro State College, Glassboro, New Jersey.

Phillips Cutright, Ph.D., is teaching in the Department of Sociology, Indiana University, Bloomington, Indiana.

Duane Denfeld, Ph.D., is an Assistant Professor in the Department of Sociology, University of Connecticut, Storrs, Connecticut.

Robert F. Drinan, S.J., LL.B., LL.M., Dean of the Boston College of Law and former Chairman of the Section of Family Law of the American Bar Association.

Evelyn M. Duvall, Ph.D., is a consultant and writer in the areas of human development and sociology of the family. She has worked with family specialists throughout the world and is the author of leading books on family concerns.

Dana L. Farnsworth, M.D., is Director, University Health Services, Harvard University, Cambridge, Massachusetts.

Michael Gordon, Ph.D., is an Associate Professor in the Department of Sociology at the University of Connecticut in Storrs.

Susan O. Gustavus, Ph.D., is now an Assistant Professor of Sociology at the University of Cincinnati, Cincinnati, Ohio.

George J. Hecht is Chairman and Publisher, *Parent's Magazine* and *Better Family Living*, 52 Vanderbilt Avenue, New York.

James R. Henley, Jr., Ph.D., is an Assistant Professor, Department of Sociology, Texas Christian University, Fort Worth, Texas.

Lura F. Henze, M.A., is an Assistant Professor in the Sociology Department of Arizona State University in Tempe, Arizona.

Reuben Hill, Ph.D., is a Professor and Director of the Family Study Center, University of Minnesota, Minneapolis, Minnesota.

John W. Hudson, Ph.D., is a Professor, Department of Sociology, Arizona State University, Tempe, Arizona.

Jerome Kagan, Ph.D., is in the Department of Social Relations, Harvard University, Cambridge, Massachusetts.

Judson T. Landis, Ph.D., is Professor of Family Sociology and Research Associate, Institute of Human Development, University of California at Berkeley.

E. E. LeMasters, Ph.D., is in the School of Social Work, University of Wisconsin, Madison, Wisconsin.

David R. Mace, Ph.D., is Professor of Family Sociology, Behavioral Science Center, The Bowman Gray School of Medicine, Wake Forest University, Winston-Salem, North Carolina.

Eleanor D. Macklin, Ph.D., is a Lecturer, Department of Human Development and Family Studies, Cornell University, Ithaca, New York.

Edith G. Neisser is a freelance writer and lecturer in family relations and lives at 239 Hazel Street, Highland Park, Ill.

David H. Olson, Ph.D., is Professor of Family Studies, Family Social Science Department, University of Minnesota, St. Paul, Minnesota.

George C. O'Neill, Ph.D., is Associate Professor of Anthropology, City College of New York, New York.

Nena O'Neill is a graduate student in the doctoral program in Anthropology, City University of New York.

Charles W. Peek, Ph.D., is Assistant Professor, Department of Sociology, University of Georgia, Athens, Georgia.

Sharon Price-Bonham, Ph.D., is an Assistant Professor in the Department of Child and Family Development at the University of Georgia, Athens, Georgia.

Alfred J. Prince was Head of the Department of Sociology, Eastern Washington State College, Cheney, Washington.

Norman Robbins is an Attorney-at-Law, 2206 Commonwealth Building, Detroit, Michigan.

Vicki Rose, N.I.M.H. Trainee, Department of Sociology, Washington State University, Pullman, Washington.

Benjamin Schlessinger, Associate Professor, School of Social Work, University of Toronto, Toronto 5, Canada.

Penelope Shankweiler, M.A., was at the University of Connecticut in Storrs, Connecticut.

Charles E. Smith made the study of Negro-White Intermarriages as part of his doctoral studies and dissertation at Columbia University, Teachers College, New York, New York.

Elizabeth M. Smith, M.S.W., is Assistant Professor, Department of Psychiatry, Washington University School of Medicine, St. Louis, Missouri.

CONTENTS

PREFACE

Young people are constantly raising issues about modern life. These include things with which they have to cope, things they have to consider and points they want settled. The term "issues" as used here seems to be appropriate in focusing on many of the problems confronting youth and in zeroing in on the tenor of the "now" generation.

The purposes of this book are:

to raise issues with which young people are dealing and to supply appropriate studies or reading which will help deal with them;

to make available relevant reading material not always found in libraries;

to supply reading material which supplements texts in courses dealing with marriage and the family; and

to produce a reader which is selective, relevant, short, and inexpensive.

During all the years we have been teaching these courses, we have felt the need for a reader at this level. We used other readers and a variety of source material, but found that the students were not as responsive as we desired. They were assigned topics and had to evaluate studies which related to these, but this technique had only moderate success. Our next step was to select journal articles and portions from books which students evaluated. We discarded about half of these because the students did not like them. The most common reasons for rejection were that the articles were too technical, complicated, statistical, simplistic, or irrelevant, as far as the issues which concerned them most.

We used another set of studies, some rather old, some "far-out" and others which the students themselves had chosen. Again, we were sometimes surprised the students liked certain articles and rejected others, but we let their interests override our own biases.

The students were representative of all parts of the academic world. Some had a background in sociology, psychology, and other people-centered courses; others were majoring in technical or natural science fields. They were people ages 18 to 30 and over; some were married, some engaged, but the majority were in the dating stage. As a result, we had a cross-section of students and their opinions.

The book is divided into sections for convenience in covering issues, but there is nothing sacred about these. Some articles might fit into one of three sections. Many issues are not covered here, but we tried to point out some of the most salient ones within the limits of the present book. Questions are interspersed in the introductions to the various sections, and others are concentrated at the ends of the parts.

Readers are invited to suggest other articles or references from books they find interesting and helpful so they may be incorporated in a future edition.

Issues of Change

Social changes usually come about gradually even though each generation may be aware of some differences in the mode of life, certain behavior patterns and of attitudes. Don Martindale, a professor of sociology and a keen observer of the social system, examined recent history to see what changes have been made and how they can affect the family. He noted that rugged individualism gave way to the influence of urbanization, and that outer-directed individuals learned to take directions from their peers. Among the social forces that shaped the lives and emotions of family members were the great depression of the thirties with its deprivations, followed by World War II with its great movement of people from one part of the country to another. In one decade there were no jobs available, while in the next one there were not enough people to fill the positions available. Parents moved from poverty to relative affluence but remembered the hard times and were apt to give their children all of the things they felt they missed, and gave them too much. Martindale emphasized the search for identity in the modern world—pressures of city living, the lack of social and occupational outlets forcing the individual who wants a close relationship to try to find it at home. Hence, the spouse, children, and other relatives may become more important in providing a person with intimate, satisfying relationships that help him maintain his identity.[1]

David R. Mace's viewpoint, in the first article in this section, is an optimistic one. He discusses most present issues and refers briefly to the future of the family, dealing with equality in marriage, sex stereotypes, sex standards, and stability in modern marriages. There are many kinds of marriages throughout the world, and husbands and wives have to fit into the type of marriage that is generally expected in their particular society. Several kinds of marriages have existed in the United States, but

[1] Don Martindale, "Timidity, Conformity, and the Search for Personal Identity," *The Annals of the American Academy of Political and Social Science*, Vol. 378 (July 1968), pp. 83–89.

the predominant one has been the patriarchal form, imported from
Europe, in which the husband is head of the household. This form suited
a rural society but also existed in cities, especially when the man was the
chief wage-earner. Dr. Mace outlines changes, including those in individual sex roles, that have led to greater equality and companionship between
husband and wife. The changes are neither complete nor uniform, and
many issues raised by the changes are still to be settled. The present
family structure is moving with the pressures of our times; in the future,
families will need to be creative.

David H. Olson gives facts and figures in the second article to show
that old predictions about the demise of the family do not hold up. He
covers the dating-mating game and shows how young people are searching
for meaningful relationships. He looks at myths regarding marriage and
considers the possibility that the sex revolution may have evolutionary
qualities. With modern alternative styles of living and experiments in
group relationships, he sees the need for the series of recommendations
he gives regarding marriage and suggests methods of meeting current
problems associated with the family.

1 *David R. Mace*

Contemporary Issues
in Marriage

You have given me a nice, broad subject, with plenty of space to move about in; and this I appreciate. I shall take the liberty of putting what I have to say in a large frame of reference. I shall begin by saying something about marriage in the past, so that we have some historical background. I shall then spend most of my time discussing marriage in the present. Finally, I shall venture to say a few words about marriage in the future.

MARRIAGE IN THE PAST

The archaeologists now tell us that we have had at least a million years of man. They are not able to report with equal confidence that we have had a million years of marriage; but I strongly suspect that we have. We can be certain that, during those million years, the continuity of the race was provided for by the fact that women had babies. We know that they couldn't have had babies without first having had sexual intercourse with men. We know that the experience of motherhood makes a woman vulnerable, and in the grim struggle for existence we can assume that the woman whose man stayed with her and supported her through the experience of motherhood would have a better chance of survival than the woman left to fend for herself. The search for food and shelter and safety was probably most successfully carried out by small groups of people cooperating with one another; and the most natural nuclear grouping, in terms of mutual needs and mutual service, is a man, a woman, and

David R. Mace, "Contemporary Issues in Marriage." Address given at the annual meeting of the Southeastern Council of Family Relations, February 26, 1968, Charleston, South Carolina. Unpublished material printed by permission of the author.

5

their children. So it is a reasonable supposition that marriage of some sort has existed throughout the entire period of human history.

This was the view of Edward Westermarck, who wrote the classical three-volume *History of Human Marriage* nearly eighty years ago. One of his major conclusions was that marriage is a universal human institution and has been part of the social structure of all settled societies; but that it is also a very flexible institution, and has existed in many forms. He defined marriage as "a relation of one or more men to one or more women which is recognized by custom or law and involves certain rights and duties both in the case of the parties entering the union and in the case of the children born of it."

Another of the major findings of Westermarck was summarized in his famous dictum that "marriage is rooted in the family, and not the family in marriage." What he meant was that human survival depends upon providing the best possible conditions for the birth and upbringing of children, that experience has shown these conditions to be best provided in family life, and that therefore marriage must be controlled and safeguarded by the community in order to ensure the continuity of the family.

This concept of marriage as subsidiary to the family, and therefore subservient to it, has dominated human history and has never been seriously challenged until our own time. But we are living today through an era of tremendous cultural change, in which all our institutions are being severely shaken; and marriage is no exception. In fact, marriage is changing so much that it is literally being turned inside out. If you think this sounds like dramatic exaggeration, let me assure you that I mean it quite literally; and let me explain what I mean.

In the entire sweep of human history, there have been only two major changes in our way of life—changes so vast that I prefer to call them "social mutations." The first was when man stopped being a wandering hunter and food-gatherer, a puny pigmy fighting against the enormous forces of a hostile nature, and learned to cooperate with nature by growing his food and taming wild animals and enlisting them in his service. This was the change from the nomadic to the agricultural way of life. It led to a long period of relative prosperity, with people living on the land in comparative security. The family was the basic unit of society, and it was generally a large or "extended" family of one kind or another, in which the kinship groups were united in cooperating with one another for the common good. The family was a very rigid institution, resisting all change and dedicated to maintaining the *status quo* from generation to generation.

Then came what we call the Industrial Revolution, which led to the second major social mutation in human history. We are in the midst of this now, and there has never been anything like it before. It began in

England with the building of the first factories, and the flocking of the people from the land to the cities. We know all about this change, because we are part of it. The enormous advances of science and technology have now given man power over nature, so that its great forces are more and more coming under his direct control. This is changing radically the entire pattern of human living. Because it is happening gradually, we are not aware how profound the change is. It is almost as if the human race were being transferred from one planet to another, and having to adapt to almost entirely new conditions.

What is important for us is that our new environment is breaking up all our traditional institutions and forcing us to create new ones of quite a different kind. Professor J. K. Whitehead, the English social philosopher, expressed this very well when he said that before the Industrial Revolution, an institution could survive only if it had rigidity and stability; whereas since the Industrial Revolution, the qualities needed for survival are the opposite, namely flexibility and adaptability. These were in fact qualities that the traditional type of marriage could not tolerate. Consequently, marriage and the family as we have known them in the past, throughout most of human history, are breaking down, and must break down. There is absolutely no possibility that they will survive, in the new urban-industrial culture that is taking shape everywhere in the world today.

Many people take alarm at this, because they assume that marriage and the family are themselves breaking down. It is very important to stress the fact that this is not so. The disintegration of the old rigid patterns is not something unhealthy, but something healthy. It is the inevitable prelude to the establishment of new patterns that will be much more appropriate to our new way of life. The family is changing, not breaking down. And, as Clark Vincent pointed out in a speech at a N.C.F.R. Conference, the family is showing its fundamental health by proving, after long centuries of rigidity, that it is actually capable of considerable adaptation to our new environment.

In the process of this adaptation, marriage is being turned inside out. In the old days, the central goal in marriage was that it must fulfill certain social and familial obligations—the continuation of the family line, the family inheritance, the family tradition—while somewhere out on the periphery there was a pious hope that the couple might get along harmoniously together. But so long as the familial obligations were met, nobody cared very much whether the couple were happy or unhappy in their interpersonal life. That was quite secondary.

Today, however, the central goal in marriage is personal fulfillment in a creative relationship, and the traditional familial and social obligations have moved out to the periphery. The mood of today is that if your marriage doesn't turn out to be happy, you quit, because finding happiness in marriage is the fulfillment of its fundamental objective.

Some people consider this change of goal as a manifestation of selfishness and irresponsibility. But the change of goal actually corresponds with the change of environment. In the old rural-agricultural society, the major business of life was economic survival and physical safety, and marriage had to conform to these requirements. But in an affluent society, economic survival is taken for granted; and the police, though they have troubles, do their best to assure us of physical safety. In our urban-industrial society, many of the traditional functions of marriage and the family—education, economic production, recreation, and many others—have been taken over by the state. And now our deepest need is for *emotional* security, for the survival of our sense of personal worth and individual significance in a vast world of people in which the individual often doesn't seem to count for anything. By shifting its focus, marriage has now become the primary means by which this individual need for comfort and support and love and understanding can be met. Gibson Winter calls this the "quest for intimacy." In our study of the Soviet family, my wife and I found that in the days of Stalinist terror, marriage was sometimes the only means by which people could keep sane. Surrounded by insecurity, they found their security in the openness and the cathartic communication they could enjoy as husband and wife, when they were alone together. There is a sense in which this kind of need, though not in the same extreme sense, is pervading the whole of modern life. And if marriage can meet that need, it will simply be manifesting one of its dormant potentialities which was almost totally neglected in the past, but is highly relevant today.

MARRIAGE IN THE PRESENT

This brings us to the point at which we can look at contemporary issues in marriage. There are so many of these that it is hard to choose; but for this discussion I have selected four:

1. Marriage as companionship. You will remember that Ernest Burgess, who might be called the father of family sociology, summarized the fundamental change that is taking place today in the title *Marriage: From Institution To Companionship.* So our focus today is upon marriage as a relationship. This is what we are concerned about, this is what more and more of what we are writing about marriage focuses upon, this is what marriage counselors are working with and trying to facilitate. So I would say that the primary issue in modern marriage is how we can make it a really creative relationship for husband and wife.

When we think of marriage in these terms, however, we begin to realize that husband and wife enter not into one relationship, but into two relationships, which coexist and interact, and yet can be clearly distinguished from each other. There is the relationship between two persons living together as partners, sharing life on an equal basis; and there is the relationship between a man and a woman, which is not equal at all, but reciprocal and complementary. In simple language, married couples have to contrive to be both good partners and good lovers. Failure in one of these areas will not compensate for success in the other. There must be a reasonable measure of satisfaction in both.

The concept of husband and wife as equal partners, sharing life in openness and intimacy, represents a radical break with tradition. Of course there have always been marriages in which good partnership was achieved; but there has never before been a time in which this was a primary criterion of success applied to *all* marriages. Indeed, traditional societies devised two means by which the concept of equal partnership, and of the two-vote marriage, was carefully avoided. First, a hierarchical distinction was made between husband and wife, the husband being acknowledged as having almost all the power, and the wife being compliant and obedient. Second, the spheres of influence of husband and wife were rigidly segregated, so that there was the minimum chance that they might compete or clash with one another. These devices were highly developed, and there is no doubt that they were based on the discovery that attempts to make marriage a relationship of close sharing led to explosive consequences that must be avoided in the interest of family stability.

But in our modern world we have deliberately given a central place to this concept of the shared life; and the explosive possibilities are very much with us! It would not be too much to say that interpersonal conflict, far from being an extraneous element in modern marriage, actually represents the raw material out of which an effective marital partnership has to be shaped. Unless we clearly recognize this, and deliberately teach young people to expect conflict in marriage, and to cope with it adequately, we simply doom large numbers of them to inevitable disillusionment and even disaster. Conflict in marriage is simply the emotional manifestation of disagreement, which is an inevitable consequence of difference. And difference cannot be avoided between two people who live in continuing intimacy, because it is unreasonable to imagine that two different people would always want to do the same thing in the same way at the same time. By insisting on homogamy as a primary condition for successful marriage, we have contrived to minimize interpersonal conflict. But I am not at all sure that the marriages of people with a minimum of difference are necessarily the best marriages. There are enormous potentials for creativity and growth in two people who begin with a good deal of difference, but have the maturity to resolve it and grow together.

When we consider the other relationship in marriage, that of husband and wife as lovers, we encounter at once the fascinating but baffling question of masculine-feminine interaction. For long centuries this has been rather naively interpreted in terms of dominance and submission, or even as superiority and inferiority. One of the somewhat bizarre side-effects of the emergence today of the idea of marriage as companionship is the open revolt of youth against the extreme stereotypes of masculinity as hairy-chested male aggressiveness on the one hand, and docile female compliance on the other. Modern youth has dramatized this protest in the long-haired boy who is not ashamed to identify himself with femininity by looking like a girl, and the modern girl who does not feel any loss of womanhood when she engages in activities that hitherto were reserved exclusively for men.

2. *Marriage and sex.*   There is an argument going on at the present time as to whether there is a sexual revolution or not. I am in no doubt whatever about this question. There is, emphatically, a sexual revolution. But the confusion is caused by the fact that people are arguing not about the revolution, but about the consequences of it. In my judgment, a revolution is by definition a complete change, a reversal of what previously was believed. But a revolution also, in my view, always takes place in the realm of ideas, and then is gradually translated into changed patterns of living. In these terms, we can say emphatically that the sexual revolution is not only here; it is now almost complete. It began about three-quarters of a century ago, and has resulted in a total change in the way we think about sex. Beginning with an attitude that considered sex essentially negatively, as unwholesome and regrettable though perhaps an unavoidable necessity, we have moved to an attitude which sees sex positively, as something essentially good and creative, though of course capable like everything else of misuse. If a change of this magnitude is not a revolution, I can think of no other radical change in human thinking that is worthy of the name.

However, this revolution has led to many consequences, and one of them concerns the relationship between sex and marriage. In the older cultures, where sex was officially recognized only as a means of procreation for married people, and unofficially as a clandestine pastime in which men exploited women with little regard for the interpersonal implications, a state of uneasy equilibrium could with a little difficulty be maintained.

But our new attitude to sex has broken this up completely, and forced us to reevaluate the total situation.

What has precipitated the crisis is the change in our concepts of mate selection. So long as the parents or village elders chose your husband or wife for you, there was no need for boys and girls to be exposed to the risks of meeting socially and forming friendships. Indeed, Confucius insisted that after the age of seven a boy and girl must never even sit together in public! But once the principle was established that young people could choose each other, they naturally wanted to do so on a basis of personal compatibility, and personal compatibility has to be tested out in a period of friendship. Once this has been conceded in any culture, the flood gates are open to the free association of unmarried men and women. This means that it is henceforth impossible to confine sex to marriage by the appeal to force or fear, and sexual morality becomes a question of conscious and deliberate choice based on an acceptance of certain values, which all men and women will not necessarily accept.

Once a principle is established that a man and woman who are unmarried may respond to each other emotionally, and carry that response as far as they personally choose, it becomes impossible to exclude married people from the same privileges. Once premarital chastity has become a matter of conscious choice, marital fidelity follows suit. The consequences of infidelity for the married are of course generally more serious, and this introduces restraints, but we should not be realistic if we did not recognize that one of the major issues in marriage today, in an era where increasingly effective contraceptives are available, is the question of how far married couples generally will accept the principle of sexual exclusiveness, and what is likely to happen to marriage if they don't.

3. *Marriage and parenthood.*   We all recognize that there has been a radical change in our pattern of marriage, but we are not so ready to see that there has been a corresponding change in parenthood. The societies of the past were rigidly structured, and had little use for individualists who refused to accept the roles allocated to them. The son was expected to follow in his father's footsteps, or to go in whatever direction the family decided was appropriate for him. The task of families was therefore to bring up children to be obedient conformists, who would do what they were told without expressing individual preferences or asking awkward questions. Parenthood was therefore essentially a task of molding human beings to accept their lot without resistance or complaint.

Today, in our open society, obedient conformists become social misfits. In a world where the individual must stand on his own feet and shape his own destiny, qualities that are desirable are the opposite of those needed in the past—namely, autonomy and self-reliance, and the capacity to handle a degree of personal freedom seldom experienced in the past. To prepare children for living in this new world, parents have to accept completely new roles. Their task now is not to mold the child into conformity, but to cooperate with him flexibly in learning to use freedom with wisdom and restraint. This is a much more difficult task, and puts a heavy strain on modern families.

One aspect of this strain is the need for a child to see in his parents the effective exercise of freedom in good relationships and cooperation. We used to accept, without critical examination, the principle that one of the child's primary needs was to be brought up in a home where his father and mother were both present. But the question is now being asked, whether the mere presence of father and mother is enough, if their relationship is vitiated by destructive conflict. We would all agree with the principle that a warm, loving relationship between husband and wife creates the perfect emotional climate for the healthy development of the child. But we have been less willing to examine what the atmosphere created by a bad marriage does negatively to the emotional life of the child. In the close and confining atmosphere of the nuclear family, a continued state of unresolved marital conflict might well be a breeding-ground of psychopathology. In the old extended family, this was unlikely to happen, because there were always other family members in whom the child could find emotional compensation when his immediate parents caused him anxiety and distress.

4. Marriage and stability. We have seen that in the past the continuity of the family was absolutely essential, and everything else had to be sacrificed to it. Today, our values are different. In the old days, the married couple were shut up in a box together and had to get on with the familial tasks that were committed to them, whether they were happy together or not. I once asked a group of Indians what an Indian wife could do if she found herself in an intolerable marital situation. Quite seriously, I was told that the correct solution for this problem was suicide! This was true throughout the Orient, and there are plenty of illustrations that it was resorted to on occasions. The stability of marriage was the primary value, and nothing else mattered in comparison.

Today the emphasis has shifted, and I believe the shift is permanent. We must face realistically the fact that in the future it will be impossible to hold marriages together by coercion from outside. They will only be held together by cohesion from within. What this means is that the principle that an unhappy marriage must be tolerated for the sake of the stability of the institution, which is an article of Catholic dogma, will be less and less readily accepted in the future. People who consider their marriages unhappy will get out of them, either to remarry or to abandon marriages as a way of life. I think we are moving to the point at which the primary value in marriage will no longer be stability, but creativity. We may not like this, or approve of it. But we can hardly suggest that the difference between stability and creativity in marriage can be equated to the difference between good and evil.

What seems to be clear from our discussion is that the case for a good marriage is overwhelming. A good marriage results in the kind of companionship that marriage is ideally fitted to provide in our modern world. A good marriage finds its own satisfactory solution of the sexual needs of the partners, and provides the atmosphere for happy and successful parenthood. But a bad marriage, or a poor marriage, or a mediocre marriage, poses problems for the persons involved, and for the society to which they belong, which can no longer be avoided or neglected.

What is clear is that marriage in contemporary culture raises all kinds of problems and questions which simply did not bother our ancestors. Those of us who are workers and specialists in this field have been facing these problems and questions. As I perceive the situation, there are three basic tasks that confront us. The first is study and research, so that we may identify the true nature and dimensions of the problems. The second is a massive program of education to enlighten people concerning what is happening to marriage today, and to give them some intelligent understanding of the task they assume when they get married. The third is to develop counseling services to tide married people through the crises that are inevitable in the close and intimate kind of relationship they are asking marriage to provide. The programs we have developed have been on the right lines, and we have made considerable headway with them. What we now need is the widespread support of the community, and the money to provide the services that are needed. This will come only when the community and the nation recognize that good marriages are their most precious asset, and that bad marriages lead to costly and destructive consequences.

MARRIAGE IN THE FUTURE

I have tried to indicate that the changes that are taking place in marriage are a healthy adaptation to the new functions marriage must serve in the altogether different environment in which our children and our children's children will have to live. In the vast, impersonal world of the future, technology will achieve miracles in ministering to human need. But what technology cannot do is to provide for that deep need in all of us that can only be met through intimate relationships in which we know ourselves to be loved and cherished, supported and sustained. There are many ways in which this need can be met, but none that can compare with the experience of a really happy marriage. None of us can predict what life will be like on this planet for distant future generations. But in the foreseeable future, I believe men and women will seek to enter marriage not less eagerly, but more eagerly, than in the past. And as our knowledge increases, and as we learn to make it available and assimilable through sound education and effective counseling, I think the chances are that people will become more mature and more creative, so that they are able to enter into the relationships in depth that make marriages truly happy and successful. In short, as I look into the future of marriage I feel rather optimistic. I do not share the gloomy forebodings that I often hear expressed by those around me. As I look ahead, my feeling is that the potentialities of marriage have not been exhausted. On the contrary, they have not yet begun to be fully developed. I think there is a good chance that what the children of today will see, in their lifetime, is not marriage sinking ignominiously into obsolescence, but blossoming and flourishing as it has never done before in human history.

2 *David H. Olson*

Marriage of the Future: Revolutionary or Evolutionary Change?*

The land of marriage has this peculiarity, that strangers are desirous of inhabiting it, whilst its natural inhabitants would willingly be banished from thence.—Montigue.

The paradoxical nature of marriage has intrigued and perplexed scholars and laymen alike for centuries. Psychologists such as John B. Watson in 1927 prophesized that marriage would not survive by 1977. About the same time, sociologists like Pitirim Sorokin and Carl Zimmerman also predicted its demise. (Bernard, 1970)

A rather common statement one hears nowadays is that "The last fifty years have apparently changed the marriage relation from a permanent and lifelong state to a union existing for the pleasure of the parties. The change thus swiftly wrought is so revolutionary, involving the very foundations of human society, that we must believe it to be the result not of any temporary conditions." (Thwing and Thwing in Reiss, 1971, 317) The only surprising thing about this statement is that it was made in 1887.

In spite of all the predictions regarding the collapse of the institution of marriage, it continues to survive. In fact, marriage still continues to be the most popular voluntary institution in our society with only 3 to 4 percent of the population never marrying at least once. And national statistics on marriage indicate that an increasing number of eligible individuals are getting married, rather than remaining single. (Vital Statistics,

David H. Olson, "Marriage of the Future: Revolutionary or Evolutionary Change?" from *The Family Coordinator*, October, 1972, pp. 383–393. Reprinted with permission.
* The author wishes to thank Robert G. Ryder, Roger Libby, and Robert Whitehurst for their helpful comments regarding this paper.

1970) For the third consecutive year, in 1970, there were over two million marriages in the country. The rate of marriage has also continued to increase so that the 1970 rate of 10.7 marriages per 1000 individuals was the highest annual rate since 1950. There has also been very little change in the median age of first marriage between 1950 and 1970, 22.8 to 23.2 years for males, and 20.3 to 20.8 years for females, respectively. (Population Census, 1971)

While getting married has increased in popularity, so has the number of individuals who have chosen to terminate their marriage contract. In 1970, there were 715,000 divorces and annulments in the United States, which is almost double the number in 1950 (385,000). Since 1967, the divorce rate has increased by 30 percent. (Vital Statistics, Vol. 19, 1971) The rate has progressively moved toward a cumulative rate, one divorce for every four marriages. The rate of divorce among those married under 18 is close to 50 percent. The ratio of divorced individuals compared to those married has increased in the last ten years. In 1960, there were 28 divorced men for every 1000 men married, and 35 in 1970. Comparable figures for females were 42 in 1960, and 60 in 1970. (Population Census, 1971) The number of divorces for married women over 15 years of age changed from 9.3 per 1000 in 1959 to 13.4 in 1969. (Vital Statistics, Vol. 20, 1971) Also, the average length of marriage has declined to an average of 7.1 years.

THE DATING-MATING GAME

In spite of the fact that quantitatively marriage continues to be very popular, the quality of the husband-wife relationship is often far less advantageous than individuals either expect or desire. One of the reasons that the marriage institution does not live up to its expectations is because of the many myths and unrealistic expectations that individuals bring to marriage. Another major factor that contributes to problems in marriage is the lack of preparation that society provides for this major decision in life. Whereas one expects that individuals will take years of schooling to adequately prepare for their occupation choice, it is assumed that individuals need no guidance in making what is probably the most significant decision in their life. For unlike a job, or even an occupation, which is relatively easy to change, it still is legally and emotionally much more difficult to change, or at least dissolve, a marital relationship. Individuals are given few useful guidelines to follow and then wonder why marriages are not as fulfilling as expected or desired.

From the vantage point of society, the present dating system which has evolved in this country is successful in that it effectively places most people into marriage at least once. But one of its major limitations is that it is too effective in that it pushes many into marriage who would not, and perhaps should not, get married. In other words, there are rather strong implicit sanctions against anyone who would prefer to remain single. Society does this by labeling individuals as deviant and maladjusted if they do not conform to societal expectations in this regard. The continuous push by parents and friends alike is rather persuasive and very effective. A more complete discussion of the third parties' influence on marriage is described in greater detail in a recent paper. (Ryder, Kafka and Olson, 1970)

This encouragement of heterosexual involvement begins so early that it is becoming more realistic to talk about dating beginning as early as elementary school. Broderick (1968) has documented a rather advanced level of heterosexual development and activity in fifth and sixth grades. Many children (84 percent of the females and 62 percent of the males) at this stage were already accepting the idea that they would eventually be married. Also, a high percentage (74 percent) of those wanting to eventually marry already had a girlfriend or boyfriend, and of those already having a friend, 66 percent reported having been in love.

What has developed, therefore, in this society is a *laissez faire* approach to the mate-selection process and this has helped to turn the process into a dating-mating game. The goal or major objective in this game is finding a suitable marital partner. The rules of the game are usually implicit rather than explicit and this results in a friendly confrontation, with increasing sexual intimacy (which is used as one of the most lethal weapons). The participants use strategies and counter-strategies within the limits of the unwritten rules in order to attain their goal, i.e., a suitable marital partner. While dating has turned out to be fun for some, it is often a hurtful and destructive game for many.

Although dating has been successful from a functional point of view, of facilitating the mate selection process and placing individuals into marriage, it has failed in a most essential way. It has failed because it does not assist couples in learning how to develop and maintain vital and meaningful relationships. Only recently have more of the youth become aware of the time inadequacies of the current dating system which has evolved in this country. They have become aware of the superficiality of dating and the over-emphasis and misuse of the purely sexual aspects of these relationships. As a result, there are increasing numbers who are trying to break away from the traditional dating-mating game by living together, either as couples or in groups. But simply living together is not *alone* going to prepare them to learn how to relate meaningfully, to adequately cope with differences and conflict, or to deal with long-term commitment. However, it is becoming increasingly clear that alternative models of mate selection are needed to prepare couples for lifelong commitment.

Fortunately, there are a few innovative programs that are just beginning to be used to train couples in more functional communication skills. (Miller and Nunnally, 1970) In some ways, however, this is really like giving birth control pills to a woman who just became pregnant—it is too little, too late. Dramatic changes are needed in the education and emotional preparation provided and changes in the social climate that continues to pressure individuals into marriage so early, so unaware, and so unprepared.

DEMYTHOLOGIZING THE MYTHS ABOUT MARRIAGE

One of the reasons that the marriage institution does not live up to its expectations is because of the many myths and unrealistic expectations that individuals bring to marriage. One of the most prevalent myths about marriage is the belief that "if an intimate relationship is *not* good, it will *spontaneously* improve with time." This myth not only leads couples into marriage but may keep many couples together in anticipation of change in their relationship. Initially, dating couples begin by saying, "If only we go steady, things will improve and he (or she) won't act this way." At a later stage they say, "If my steady and I were having difficulties, engagement might help resolve some of our problems." The same theme continues during engagement with the assumption that "marriage will help change or reform my fiancé." However, most newlyweds soon find greater difficulty in marriage than they anticipated, for not only do their past problems continue to exist, usually in greater intensity than before, but they also encounter new areas of conflict which result from living together. And many couples then feel that: "Our relationship isn't very fulfilling now that we are married, but if we only had a child, that would bring us closer and resolve many of our difficulties." I have even heard couples optimistically carry this theme further and admit that: "This one child has *not* helped our marriage, but if we had another child, our relationship would really improve." In general, all these myths are examples of the general theme that a relationship will spontaneously improve with increasing commitment and time.

Several other common myths have been described by Lederer and Jackson (1968) in their book on the *Mirages of Marriage*. Myths abound regarding the relationship between love and marriage such as: "People marry because they are in love," "Most married people love each other," "Love is necessary for a satisfactory marriage," and "All problems can be solved if you're really in love."

In search of a fulfilling life, many individuals falsely assume that "marriage is easy, the difficulty is finding the right person." Further, "who they marry is more important then when they marry," and therefore, "there is one best person for them to marry." They also assume that "the only way to be truly happy is to marry." They wishfully assume that "marriage will alleviate their loneliness." What they do not realize is that marriage often intensifies rather than eases loneliness. It is important to realize that if individuals cannot live with themselves, they will probably have considerable difficulty trying to live with someone else. (Ryder, 1970) Couples also assume that "their partner will be able to satisfy all their needs" and, therefore, "the more time and activities that are spent together, the better the marriage relationship."

Once couples begin having difficulty in marriage they falsely assume "that patterns of behavior and interaction they develop are easy to change" and "that a quarrel or disagreement can only be detrimental to their relationship." Many further maintain that "it is best *not* to express negative feelings about one's spouse." Couples assume that "if their spouse loves them, they will know what they are feeling or what they want." When marital problems become more extreme, many believe that "for the sake of the children, keeping a conflicted family together is preferable to divorce."

In regard to their sexual relationship, many couples falsely assume that "a good sexual relationship is easy to develop" and that "if there is a good sexual relationship, other problems will take care of themselves" and "sexual adjustment in marriage will result more from proper techniques than from proper attitudes." Couples also overemphasize the value and significance of sex in marriage and believe "sex will be one of the most fulfilling aspects of their marriage."

Unfortunately, too many individuals accept many of these myths about marriage and little is currently being done to demythologize these ideas. As a result, many couples enter marriage with idealistic and unrealistic expectations about what marriage can and will provide. It is usually not until after they have become disappointed and frustrated with their partner that they begin to face the realities of the marital relationship.

For further details about the prevalence of these and related myths, a Premarital Attitude Scale (PMAS) was developed and used to assess the attitudes of family specialists and college students on many of these issues. (Olson, 1967; Olson and Gravatt, 1968)

A SEXUAL REVOLUTION OR EVOLUTION?

In 1938, Terman predicted that: "The trend toward premarital sexual experience is proceeding with extraordinary rapidity . . . . In the case of husbands the incidence of virginity at marriage is 50.6 percent in the oldest group and only 32.6 percent in the youngest. The corresponding drop for wives is from 86.5 percent to 51.2 percent. If the drop should continue at the average rate shown for those born since 1890, virginity at marriage will be close to the vanishing point for males born after 1930 and for females born after 1940." (321–22)

Kinsey's data on females (1953) indicates the rate of premarital sex (PMS) was about 49 percent. Comparable data from the Burgess and Wallin research (1953) found about 68 percent of the males and 47 percent of the females had premarital sex. A recent study by Kaats and Davis (1970) has indicated similar results of PMS, 60 percent for males and 41 percent for females. Another recent study (Bell and Chaskes, 1970) of female premarital sex patterns in 1958 and 1968 found only a small increase in rate for females from 31 to 39 percent, respectively. One of the best designed studies of sexual attitudes and behaviors of young people in three cultures was conducted in 1958 and replicated in 1968 by Christensen and Gregg. (1970) They found in their midwest sample a rather prominent increase in PMS in females between 1958 and 1968, 21 to 34 percent respectively, but no change in the rate for males, 51 to 50 respectively. All of these recent studies actually are underestimates of the actual rate of PMS because the individuals studied were middle class college students who were not yet married. These studies are not representative because it is known that lower class individuals have higher rates of PMS than college students. Further, the actual rates of PMS cannot accurately be assessed until the individuals are actually married. This latter fact is particularly important since PMS still occurs most frequently with one's potential spouse. (Bell and Chaskes, 1970)

On the basis of these studies, it is clear that Terman's prediction that virgin marriages would be only a historical fact has not been realized. However, there have been noticeable changes in female attitudes and behavior. The most dramatic change, which might even be called a female revolution, is the increasing PMS rates for females, which Christensen and Gregg (1970) found changed in the last decade from 21 to 34 percent. This has resulted in a growing convergence in the rates of PMS between the sexes (50 and 34 percent for males and females respectively). This study also showed considerable liberalizations in the attitudes toward PMS in the last decade, again most dramatically in females. This has resulted in fewer differences between PMS attitudes and behavior, so that fewer people are violating their own values and, therefore, there is less guilt associated with PMS. Although the rate of PMS increased, there was an increasing tendency to limit their sexual activity to one partner.

Another trend found in the study by Bell and Chaskes (1970) was that PMS was less dependent on the commitment of engagement than it was a decade ago. While more PMS occurred during engagement, from 31 percent in 1958 to 39 percent in 1968, the PMS rates increased more drastically in dating, from ten to 23 percent, and going steady, from fifteen to 28 percent, stages.

MARITAL SEX

While there is considerable data on premarital sexual behavior, there is a dearth of empirical data on the sexual relationship in marriage. In fact, little has been done since Kinsey's initial data on the male (1948) and female (1953). Cuber and Harroff (1965) have described the sexual relationships of *Significant Americans* within the context of a relationship typology. However, they did not provide specific normative data about these couples' sexual relationships. Perhaps the largest sample of data on early marriage and sexual behavior is contained in a longitudinal study of 2000 couples conducted by Robert Ryder and the author. Unfortunately, the data on marital sexual behavior has not yet been analyzed. The major source of information, therefore, comes from therapists who find sexual problems to be both a *cause* and a *symptom* of most marital difficulties. We can only hope that the next decade will provide more substantive normative data on this significant aspect of marital behavior.

EXTRA-MARITAL AND GROUP SEX

Unlike the lack of research on sex in marriage, there have been several recent investigations into the *extra* in extra-marital sex (EMS). Kinsey (1948) provided the first extensive data on EMS and reported that by the age of 40 about one-quarter (26 percent) of the females and one-half (50 percent) of the males had at least one such affair. A more recent study by Whitehurst (1969) was done on 112 upper middle class business and professional men. He found that 67 percent had no EMS, 9 percent played around but had no serious sexual involvement, 16 percent had limited affairs, and only about 3 percent had rather lengthy affairs. He found that those with the highest levels of EMS more often were alienated, especially showing high levels of social isolation and powerlessness.

Another recent study of EMS was conducted by Johnson (1969) in which 100 middle class couples were investigated. He found 28 percent of the marriages were involved in at least one affair. The marital adjustment of the couple was not related to EMS, for an equal number of couples with high marital adjustment had affairs or passed up the opportunity. However, it was found that husbands, but not wives, who had lower levels of sexual satisfaction were more likely to become involved in affairs. An important finding was the significance of a "perceived opportunity" for having EMS. About 40 percent of those who "perceived" an opportunity took advantage of the situation.

A more expanded discussion on extramarital sex is contained in a recent book, *Extra-Marital Relations*, edited by Neubeck. (1969) Neubeck offered a useful perspective on EMS when he discussed the unrealistic expectation that marriage will meet all the needs of both spouses at all times. While spouses permit each other some freedom to relate to others, "faithfulness is ordinarily seen as faithfulness in the flesh." (22) The unreality of such expectations is demonstrated by the number of involvements, sexual and emotional, that violate these ideals.

While married individuals typically have had unilateral affairs, recent evidence has indicated that more couples have jointly sought out another couple(s) for group sexual experiences. In a recent book by Bartell (1971) he describes a study of 280 swinging couples. He estimates that perhaps as many as one million couples are presently experimenting within this general context. Many are "respectable" suburbanites who use this experience to relieve boredom. Contacts are made purely for sexual reasons and are usually not maintained for more than a few meetings. It appears, however, that this style of life is seldom maintained permanently because of the large amount of time and energy which is needed to simply locate new partners. Also, many come to realize that the experience does not provide the degree of satisfaction they expected.

In conclusion, it appears that while new patterns of relating sexually are evolving, there is not a significant change in the sexual behavior of individuals or couples to label any changes as revolutionary. However, it does appear that there are several trends that have implications for sexual behavior in the future. First of all, there appear to be noticeable changes in both attitudes and behaviors of females which will lead to a greater convergence with the male in society. This could lead to a further decline in the traditional double standard of sexual behavior. Secondly, the openness and frequency with which sexual matters are discussed is increasing, not only in the mass media but also interpersonally. As a result, the discrepancy between attitudes and behaviors in both sexes shows signs of diminishing and as this continues there will be fewer guilt feelings associated with sexual behavior. Thirdly, there is a trend away from restricting the sexual experience only to a relationship where there is some type of mutual commitment, i.e., engagement or marriage. While a good sexual relationship might still be confined to a love relationship, love has also become more broadly defined to include more than just a marriage relationship. While these are only trends and do, in fact, reflect evolutionary changes in both sexual attitudes and behaviors of individuals in society, they do not indicate any type of sexual revolution that would dramatically affect the institutions of marriage and the family.

ALTERNATIVE STYLES OF LIVING

In an attempt to change the qualitative aspects of marriage, there is a growing interest in re-structuring the mate selection process and the traditional monogamous conjugal marriage where husband and wife live alone in their own apartment or home. Discussion of alternative living styles has lately become rather prominent in the mass media. (*Futurist*, April, 1970)

One trend is the increasing numbers of college students and other young people living in arrangements other than segregated male-female dormitories or sorority or fraternity houses. Some are collectively renting large houses and forming communal arrangements. While the housing arrangement is communal, there is a great deal of diversity in the interpersonal life styles these individual residents adopt. Some legitimately qualify as communal arrangements where expenses, tasks, and experiences are shared. But many communes often revert to being more like traditional boarding houses where there is little cooperative interest or emotional commitment to others in the house.

Likewise, heterosexual cohabitation takes a variety of forms, from simply sharing a room with one or more individuals, to sharing a bed and a room as a couple, either alone or with other individuals. Macklin (1971) found in a survey of 150 under-classmen at Cornell University that 28 percent had recently lived under some form of cohabitation. Some of the reasons for cohabitating given in the Macklin study included: a search for more meaningful relating, avoidance of the dating game, avoiding the loneliness of a large university, and the testing of the relationship. In most of the relationships there was a strong affection but marriage was not seen as an immediate possibility. Macklin indicated that about three-quarters of the relationships involved a girl moving in to share a boy's room in an apartment or house he shared with other males. Usually these arrangements were not planned but simply conveniently available at the time they made the decision. Students in the Macklin survey (1971) had mixed feelings about the success of the experience, but over half felt the advantages outweighed the numerous problems they encountered. Of the problems, a variety of sexual problems was the most pervasive issue. Parental disapproval also was frequently encountered, as was interpersonal issues relating to commitment, communication of feelings, and lack of privacy.

It appears that colleges and universities are becoming more responsive to these changes in student attitudes and behaviors. Universities are now becoming more lax in enforcing their regulations regarding *locus parentis*. There are also increasing numbers of coeducational dormitories that permit a variety of living arrangements.

In addition to new styles of living among unmarried individuals, there are others who are forming multilateral marriages in which usually three or more individuals form a group marriage arrangement. An active proponent of group marriage is Robert Rimmer, author of *The Harrad Experiment* and *Proposition 31*, who feels that new experimentation in sex and marriage is needed to break away from the problems with monogamous marriage. Larry and Joan Constantine (1970; 1971) have attempted to study most of these marriages they could locate, which to date numbers approximately 35 to 40. On the average, these arrangements have not lasted more than a year. The Constantines stated that "We must conclude . . . that multilateral marriage, though a promising growth-oriented form of marriage, is itself a structure limited to a relative few." (1970, 45)

Recently more research has also been done on a small sample of approximately 20 to 30 unconventional marriages that were found in the total sample of 2000 couples who were part of the longitudinal study of early marriage conducted at the National Institute of Mental Health by Robert Ryder and the author. Details of this clinical investigation are contained in a paper entitled Notes on Marriage in the Orbit of the Counterculture. (Kafka and Ryder, 1972) There are several characteristics which define the ethos espoused by these unconventional couples. There is an intended dominance of feelings over cognition, a present versus future orientation, avoidance of conventional role expectations and traditional patterns of marriage, a high evaluation in "working things out," an intense concern with increasing and maintaining openness and heightened intimacy, disavowal of materialistic goals, and high evaluation of play and travel. In spite of their attempts to build this ethos into their daily lives, they were not able to maintain these ideals without, at times, unwittingly slipping back to many of the traditional problems they wished to avoid. For example, their attempts at role reversal were often difficult to maintain and proved to be at times more than either could cope with and consequently there was a "return to the conventional." Although sexual possessiveness was devalued they found that "hang-ups" often interfered; for example, the jealousy they experienced when their partner had an affair with a friend. These couples generally exhibited a more meaningful vital and working relationship than the majority of conventional couples sampled in this study. Both their satisfactions and frustrations were experienced with greater intensity and both extremes occur with greater frequency than in conventional marriage.

These couples seldom achieved what they desired and they often found themselves "reverting to the conventional style." These marriages also had a higher rate of divorce than the more conventional sample. Paradoxically, one might conclude that the most vital relationships are the ones that do not last.

In conclusion, although increasing numbers of young people are experimenting with alternative styles of relating as a substitute for the traditional dating game, there is little evidence that this is more than a newly emerging developmental stage in the mate selection process. This newly emerging stage would perhaps come as an extension of the engagement period and might appropriately be called experimental marriage. While this experimentation might delay marriage temporarily for some of them, the vast majority will still adopt a more or less conventional conjugal marriage. While this experience might not result in radically different types of marriage, it might contribute to assisting couples in developing a qualitatively different type of marriage relationship or, at least, more adequately prepare them for the types of problems they will encounter in marriage. According to present evidence, there is only a small percentage of couples who actually attempt to develop and permanently maintain a more unconventional marriage from the traditional monogamous conjugal type.

If any single aspect of marriage is in the greatest state of change, it is the expectations regarding the appropriate role relationship between a husband and wife. And as was true in the area of changing premarital sexual behavior, it is primarily a female revolution. Women, spurred on by women's liberation groups, are increasingly demonstrating against their second class status in marriage in this society. It is true that our society has prescribed roles for husbands and wives that are based not on interest or ability, but on tradition. Tradition has also helped maintain the double standard in sexual and nonsexual areas.

However legitimate the criticisms regarding the woman's role in marriage, changing expectations do not necessarily result in changing actual role relationships that couples adopt. What is happening as a result of these changing expectations is that couples are increasingly being forced into a situation, primarily by the wife, where they must negotiate or renegotiate the way they will structure their role relationships rather than simply accept the traditional definitions. Although this is creating a crisis situation for some, it is providing the opportunity for others to create a new and, hopefully, more vital relationship for both individuals. If these expectations are not realized, it will cause increasing role conflict and growing dissatisfaction with marriage, especially for women, who have traditionally been the defenders of the marriage institution. This is the revolution in marriage. And to paraphrase Otto (1970), what will destroy marriage is not change but the inability of individuals within it to change.

REDEFINING A SUCCESSFUL MARRIAGE

While a successful marriage has often been determined by its longevity (i.e., those having twenty-fifth anniversaries) or by how well it fulfills the traditional roles prescribed by society (husband being a good provider and wife being a good housekeeper and mother), there is an increasing awareness that these criteria are not necessarily associated with a successful marriage. Youth has begun to seriously question these criteria and they have become somewhat cynical about marriage because of the alienated, conflicted, and devitalized marriages they see their parents and other adults tolerate. Perceptive as they are, they increasingly see marriage as a relationship that is less often cherished than simply tolerated and endured.

In recent years, there seems to be some change in the criteria used to evaluate the success of a marital relationship. Increasingly, individuals are seeking a relationship that will provide growth for them as individuals and as a couple. More than a companionship marriage as defined by Burgess, there is a search for an authentic and mutually actualizing relationship. Ideally, the successful marriage is seen as a relationship context in which growth and development of both partners is facilitated to a greater extent than it could be for either of these individuals outside the relationship. While this has been one function of marriage that has been implicitly assumed, it has not been explicitly demanded until recently.

Ironically, although more individuals are beginning to evaluate marriage in respect to this criterion, most couples have been unable to achieve this idealized type of relationship. One of the main reasons for this is that society has not adequately prepared individuals to relate in a meaningful way that will facilitate mutual growth within a relationship. As a result, if growth occurs, more commonly it occurs in only one of the individuals. And paradoxically, the greater the growth in one partner in a relationship, the greater the chance the couple will grow further apart rather than closer together. This is often true when both individuals grow also, because they usually do not share the same growth experience and do not use the experience to further develop their relationship. As a result, many couples today are becoming increasingly frustrated because they have rejected the more traditional definition of a successful marriage and yet are having difficulty achieving the type of mutually actualizing relationship that they are striving to achieve. It, therefore, appears that a successful marriage continues to be a difficult and elusive objective to achieve.

NEEDED: A NEW LEXICON ABOUT MARRIAGE

If nothing else productive comes from considering the alternative styles of marriage, it has certainly demonstrated the inadequacy of our present language for describing and classifying marriage and non-marriage relationships. Even the language used by anthropologists is insufficient to describe the varieties of heterosexual or homosexual relationships and the range of new life styles and communal arrangements on the contemporary scene. This might be a primary reason that family professionals have been unable to develop an adequate typology of marital relationships and another reason why there has been so little substantive research in this area.

Marriage research has, unfortunately, been too concerned with describing marriage along the elusive dimensions of "marital happiness" or "marital satisfaction" or "marital adjustment." The numerous problems with conceptualizing and operationalizing concepts have been reviewed elsewhere (Hicks and Platt, 1970), but their inadequacy becomes even more apparent when describing and classifying unconventional life styles. Family researchers and theorists alike have also limited themselves to simplistic concepts such as "family decision making" and "family power structures." Recent evidence suggests that not only is family power a difficult concept to define and operationalize, but that the various measures used have almost no relationship to each other (Turk and Bell, 1972), and that these measures also lack validity. (Olson and Rabunsky, 1972)

General dimensions that have emerged from this renewed focus on marriage indicate a need for concern with commitment to a relationship rather than primary attention being given to simply whether the couple remains married, i.e., permanence. Attention also needs to be given to a typology of relationships rather than simply classifying a couple as happy. Some preliminary work in this regard was done by Cuber and Harroff (1965) when they classified marriages according to five relationship categories of vital, total, conflict-habitual, passive-congenial, or devitalized. One also needs to know more about the actual interpersonal dynamics in marriage. Newly emerging system concepts such as circular causality, homeostasis, and transaction may aid in this regard.

What is meant by the concepts of marriage and family must also be clearly defined. Are these relationships best defined as legal contracts, verbal commitments, or a definition based on the structure and functions these relationships develop? There need to be new distinctions, such as between emotional monogamy and sexual monogamy. Also, the adaptability (Vincent, 1966) of individuals and relationships needs to be better understood. Attention should also be given to the effects of insitutionalizing affection and commitment. Rather than focusing so exclusively on the type and degree of maladjustment that exists in marriage, more attention also needs to be given to marital health (Vincent, 1967) and ways in which individuals and relationships can be helped to become more self-actualizing.

RECOMMENDATIONS REGARDING MARRIAGE

After surveying marriage from a variety of perspectives, it is readily apparent that this institution, like many in this society, has not been the panacea that many have envisioned. Rarely is marriage found to be a vital and fulfilling relationship for both spouses. In part, this might be caused by the way we have institutionalized this affectionate relationship. But it also is a reflection of the inability of individuals to relate in meaningful ways and the unrealistic expectations individuals bring to marriage. The following proposals are offered as guidelines and recommendations that might help make marriage a more meaningful and vital relationship.

1. Individuals should not be encouraged to marry at an early age but should wait until they have matured emotionally and have established themselves in their chosen profession.

2. All individuals should not be encouraged or pressured into marriage.

3. Individuals and couples should be encouraged to experiment with a variety of life styles in order to choose the style which is most appropriate for them.

4. Couples should be encouraged to openly and honestly relate rather than play the traditional dating-mating game.

5. Couples should not get married until they have established a meaningful relationship and resolved their major difficulties; for marriage will only create, rather than eliminate, problems.

6. The decision of parenthood should be a joint decision which should follow, rather than precede (as it does in about one-third of the cases), marriage.

7. Couples should not have children until they have established a strong and viable marriage relationship.

8. Couples should be creative and flexible in how they work out their changing roles and mutual responsibilities, not only during their initial phases of marriage, but throughout their marriage relationship.

Individuals would have greater freedom to develop in these ways if they were given societal support rather than implicit and explicit restrictions and constraints. There are a few specific ways in which legal and legislative reform would facilitate these opportunities.

1. Marriage laws should be made more stringent in order to encourage individuals to take this major decision more seriously. Presently it is easier in most states to obtain a marriage license than a license to drive a car.

2. No fault divorce laws should be developed while still providing for adequate support for children. California and Florida have already taken constructive steps in this direction.

3. Premarital, marital, and divorce counseling should be offered to all individuals regardless of their ability to pay.

4. Tax laws should be changed so as not to unduly discriminate against any particular life style.

5. Sex laws which prohibit any form of sexual behavior between consenting individuals should be changed to allow for individual freedom and development.

FUTURE EVOLUTION OF MARRIAGE

Historically, the types and variety of ways in which couples arrange their marriages have always been changing and evolving. These emerging styles have been both responsive to societal change and a cause of change. In fact, in some ways the marriage institution is an emotional thermometer of contemporary society and also an indicator of future trends. The fact that there are beginnings of a female revolution is already, and will continue to be, reflected both in marriage and society. There are also indications that youth are increasingly questioning many of the institutions in our society, including the marriage institution. Both these groups are challenging marriage as it has been traditionally defined and they have been actively experimenting with alternative ways of arranging their lives and marriages. This might lead to a greater variety of ways in which couples define their relationship, arrange their living styles, and carry out the traditional functions of marriage.

While some may feel that these attempts at change are the cause of society's problems, these behaviors might more appropriately be seen as a solution to problems in marriage and also in society. Some unrealistically fear that the institution of marriage might be radically changed. There is, however, little need to be concerned because institutionalized forms of behavior are difficult to dramatically change. In addition, highly industrialized society offers strong support for the style of marriage that has evolved. Lastly, emotional development will tend to minimize any excessive change. As Reiss (1970) stated:

> Our emotions will continue to close off many avenues of change and our habits will further reinforce this. Thinking is a time-consuming activity that often leads to painful revelations. Habit and emotional responses are our way of easing that pain. (397)

But one must not be afraid of change or afraid to challenge ideas and traditions, no matter how sacred. A great concern is with facilitating the growth and development of individuals in and out of marriage, as Otto (1970) appropriately stated:

> What will destroy us is not change, but our inability to change— both as individuals and as a social system. It is only by welcoming innovation, experiment, and change that a society based on man's capacity to love man can come into being. (9)

REFERENCES

Bartell, Gilbert D. *Group Sex.* New York: Peter H. Wyden, 1971.

Bell, Robert R. and Jay B. Chaskes. Premarital Sexual Experience among Coeds, 1958 to 1968. *Journal of Marriage and the Family*, 1970, 32, 81–84.

Bernard, Jessie. Woman, Marriage, and the Future. *Futurist*, 1970, 4, 41–43.

Broderick, Carlfred B. and George P. Rowe. A Scale of Preadolescent Heterosexual Development. *Journal of Marriage and the Family*, 1968, 30, 97–101.

Christensen, Harold T. and Christina F. Gregg. Changing Sex Norms in America and Scandinavia. *Journal of Marriage and the Family*, 1970, 32, 616–627.

Constantine, Larry L. and Joan M. Constantine. Where Is Marriage Going? *Futurist*, 1970, 4, 44–46.

Constantine, Larry L. and Joan M. Constantine. Group and Multilateral Marriage: Definitional Notes, Glossary and Annotated Bibliography. *Family Process*, 1971, 10, 157–176.

Cuber, John F. and Peggy B. Harroff. *The Significant Americans.* New York: Appleton-Century, 1965.

Hicks, Mary W. and Marilyn Platt. Marital Happiness and Stability: A Review of the Research in the Sixties. *Journal of Marriage and the Family*, 1970, 32, 553–574.

Hill, Reuben. The American Family of the Future. *Journal of Marriage and the Family*, 1964, 26, 20–28.

Johnson, Ralph E. Some Correlates of Extramarital Coitus. *Journal of Marriage and the Family*, 1970, 32, 449–456.

Kaats, Gilbert R. and Keith E. Davis. The Dynamics of Sexual Behavior of College Students. *Journal of Marriage and the Family*, 1970, 32, 390–399.

Kafka, John S. and Robert G. Ryder. Notes on Marriage in the Orbit of the Counter-Culture, Unpublished manuscript, 1972.

Kinsey, Alfred C., Wardell B. Pomeroy, Clyde E. Martin, and Paul Gibbard. *Sexual Behavior in the Human Female*. New York: Sanders, 1953.

Kinsey, Alfred C., Wardell B. Pomeroy, Clyde E. Martin, and Paul Gibbard. *Sexual Behavior in the Human Male*. New York: Sanders, 1948.

Lederer, William J. and Donald D. Jackson. *The Mirages of Marriage*. New York: W. W. Norton, 1968.

Maslow, A. H. A Theory of Human Motivation. *Psychological Review*, 1943, 50, 370–396.

Maslow, A. H. *Motivation and Personality*. New York: Harper and Row, 1954.

Miller, Sherod and Elam Nunnally. A Family Developmental Program of Communication Training for Engaged Couples. Monograph Family Study Center, University of Minnesota, 1970.

Neubeck, Gerhard (Ed.) *Extramarital Relations*. Englewood Cliffs, New Jersey: Prentice-Hall, 1969.

Olson, David H. Student Attitudes Toward Marriage. *College Student Survey*, 1967, 1, 71–78.

Olson, David H. and Arthur G. Gravatt. Attitude Change in a Functional Marriage Course. *The Family Coordinator*, 1968, 17, 99–104.

Olson, David H. and Carolyn Rabunsky. Validity of Four Measures of Family Power. *Journal of Marriage and the Family*, 1972, 34, 224–234.

Otto, Herbert A. (Ed.). *The Family in Search of a Future*. New York: Appleton, Century and Crofts, 1970.

Reiss, Ira L. *The Family Systems in America*. New York: Holt, Rinehart, and Winston, 1971.

Ryder, Robert G., John S. Kafka, and David H. Olson. Separating and Joining Influences in Courtship and Early Marriage. *American Journal of Orthopsychiatry*, 1971, 41, 450–464.

Ryder, Robert G. An Opinion on Marriage. *Mademoiselle*, (January) 1971.

Satir, Virginia. Marriage as a Human-Actualizing Contract. In Herbert A. Otto (Ed.) *The Family in Search of a Future*. New York: Appleton, Century and Crofts, 1970.

Sussman, Marvin B. and Lee Burchinal. Kin Family Network: Unheralded Structure in Current Conceptualizations of Family Functioning. *Marriage and Family Living*, 1962, 24, 231–240.

Sussman, Marvin B. Relationships of Adult Children with their Parents in the United States. In Ethal Shanas and Gordon F. Streib (Eds.). *Social Structure and the Family: Generational Relations.* Englewood Cliffs, New Jersey: Prentice-Hall, 1965.

Terman, Lewis M. *Psychological Factors in Marital Happiness.* New York: McGraw Hill, 1938.

Turk, James L. and Norman W. Bell. Measuring Power in Families. *Journal of Marriage and the Family*, 1972, 34, 215-223.

Vincent, Clark E. Familia Spongia: The Adaptive Function. *Journal of Marriage and the Family*, 1966, 28, 29–36.

Vincent, Clark E. Mental Health and the Family. *Journal of Marriage and the Family*, 1967, 29, 18–39.

Whitehurst, Robert N. Extra-Marital Sex: Alienation of Extension of Normal Behavior. In Gerhard Neubeck (Ed.) *Extra-Marital Relations.* New York: Prentice-Hall, 1969.

Issues of Dating

One modern problem is the question of the age when dating should start. Some families are still trying to set the age of 16 years as the time to allow dating, but parents in this situation get a great deal of pressure from their teenage children, especially if their friends have no such regulations.

Dating is part of the socialization process in our culture, a way in which young people learn male-female roles. As Jerome Kagan points out in the first selection in Part 2, certain inclinations and behavior have long been associated with masculinity, while other traits are linked with femininity. Although young people today question some of these sex distinctions, in almost every classroom poll the majority prefer to keep things as they are for the first date and during the early stages of dating: the man asks for the date, pays the cost of it, and escorts the woman. When more equality develops between the sexes, the woman will also ask for dates, provide the car, pay the bills, and have all the rights and responsibilities a man has under the present system.

J. R. DeLora indicates that early stages of dating are male-dominated but later stages move in a more egalitarian direction. When a couple is going steady or is "engaged to be engaged," the girl is free to call the boy for a date and to share expenses. Should this kind of egalitarianism come earlier in dating?[1]

Not all dates succeed. Some people hesitate to date a variety of individuals because they fear failure. Failure, like success, is interpreted personally: Something is wrong with me. This may not be true at all. In a study of dating failure, students reported more traumatic dates in the pre-college years than in college. Apparently, individuals who can recognize failure and the causes for it can meet later social catastrophes with greater ease and less ego threat. Some failures can be avoided, but

[1] Jack R. DeLora, "Social Systems of Dating on a College Campus," *Marriage and Family Living*, Vol. 25, No. 1 (February 1963), pp. 81–84.

a teenager is likely to have only limited coping mechanisms. To help make a social situation easier, for example, the person who arranges a blind date should be honest, should select carefully, and not "oversell" the other person. And a young person should not be discouraged; if one date falls flat, the next one may succeed.[2]

Dating is a social system and in its early stages is influenced a great deal by group pressures. Friends at work or at school help each other select their dates; indeed, peers may have much more influence than do parents in the modern system. This influence is usually informal at first, but it may be formalized in such organized groups as clubs, fraternities, and sororities. As a study by Richard F. Larson and Gerald R. Leslie shows,[3] sororities and fraternities, whose members are very apt to date each other, help foster dating homogamy. These organizations have places to entertain, see to it that members meet each other, and provide enough variety in social gatherings to suit the needs or interests of nearly everyone in the group. This helps put the members at ease and leads to friendships, work sharing, casual dating, serious dating, and finally to marriages.

It is difficult for some people to get dates; there may not be enough men or enough women to go around—hence the dating bureau, lonely hearts club, and computer dating system. College students are generally reluctant to get involved with "computer dating." They may be rebelling against the machine, or it may be a matter of personal pride—the feeling that one's own personality and social skills should be enough to attract the opposite sex without help of a gadget. Studies of computer dating, which have been either piecemeal or highly technical, are not included in this book.

Computer dating may help men and women meet each other, but it cannot overcome two problems: a socially acceptable place to go on a date and increasing cost. There are not many things couples can do on a date which are free. College students can attend many free functions, but non-students do not have this privilege. The price of movies, bowling, and food is high enough that young people need a good income or allowance to date frequently. Have you made a study of places to go and things to do on a date in your community? How does the cost relate to the frequency of dating, or to the variety of dating situations?

Sweden, well known for its experimentation with interpersonal freedom, has attempted new role relationships, giving men and women equal rights and responsibilities as far as possible. But even Sweden has no com-

[2] Ruth Albrecht, "A Study of Dates That Failed." Paper presented at the annual meeting of the Southern Sociological Society, New Orleans, 1969.
[3] Richard F. Larson and Gerald R. Leslie, "Prestige Influence in Serious Dating Relationships of University Students," Social Forces, Vol. 47, No. 2 (December 1968), pp. 195–202.

pletely satisfactory solution to the problem of premarital or extramarital sex. Inger Becker, in her article, "Men, Beware Women," describes the background for the changes in Sweden and pictures the problems that have emerged. Her statements, which may seem rather strong, convey one part of the picture: what freedom has done to women. She does not state what this lifting of responsibility has done to men.

Young people today claim, or have been told, that things have changed a great deal since their parents were young. Are generational differences so large? John W. Hudson and Lura F. Henze replicated research originally done in 1939 and 1956, and found the generations had very similar criteria for mate selection. What characteristics do you want in a marriage partner? Rank the traits as you would like them in your ideal mate, and see if you agree with the ones in this study.

Greater freedom today includes a larger number of alternative types of relationships between the sexes. Many couples, for example, have the freedom and opportunity to decide about living together before marriage or instead of getting married. Eleanor D. Macklin suggests that cohabitation is becoming more common, at least among college students. She points out, however, that there are differing opinions of what living together means, and suggests that students need help in defining and adjusting to this new type of relationship.

Margaret Mead made headlines by describing a "new" kind of marriage. Miriam E. Berger in her article, "Trial Marriage: Harnessing the Trend Constructively," tells how trial marriages have been managed in other cultures and in other periods in history. Our own country has had examples of trial marriages and of "bundling"—or sharing a bed—which might be considered a form of trial marriage or just a courtship pattern. The author summarizes Dr. Mead's suggestions for a two-step marriage and presents some reactions to it. The article includes positive ideas about trial marriages and offers questions that need to be answered by any person considering a trial marriage or who is now involved in one.

3 *Jerome Kagan*

Check One:
☐ Male ☐ Female

Every person wants to know how good, how talented, and how masculine or feminine he or she is. Of the many attributes that go into the concept of self, sex-role identity is one of the most important.

It may seem odd that anyone should be unsure of his sex-role identity. A five-foot, 11-inch, 18-year-old human with X and Y chromosomes, testes, penis, and body hair is, by definition, a male. It would seem that all such men should regard themselves as equally masculine. But the human mind, in its perversity, does not completely trust anatomical characteristics and insists upon including psychological factors in the final judgment. Man is as foolish as the cowardly lion who had to be reassured of his courage by the Wizard of Oz.

A sex-role identity is a person's belief about how well his biological and psychological characteristics correspond to his or her concept of the ideal male or female. The definition of the ideal—the sex-role standard—is influenced by the values of his particular culture. A Kyoto girl is taught that gentleness is the most important feminine quality; a Los Angeles girl learns that physical beauty is an essential quality.

A person is said to have a strong or firm sex-role identity when his subjective judgment of himself comes up to the standards of the ideal. If there are major discrepancies between the ideal and a person's view of himself, he has a weak or fragile sex-role identity.

To get at the dynamic significance of a person's sex-role identity, we must confront four questions: (1) How does a person initially learn sex-role standards? (2) Just what is the content of the standards? (3) Are some sex-role standards generalized across cultures? (4) What are the implications of a firm sex-role identity and a fragile one?

A child learns sex-role standards the way he learns many other con-

Jerome Kagan, "Check One: Male/Female." Reprinted from *Psychology Today* Magazine July, 1969. Copyright © Communications/Research/Machines/Inc.

cepts. He learns that an object that is round, made of rubber, and bounces is called a ball. He learns more about the definition of a ball by watching how it is used, by listening to people talk about it, and by playing with one himself. By the age of two he has learned that certain objects are called boys and men; others, girls and women. He learns the definition by noting what they do, how they look, and what they wear, and by listening and watching as others discuss the sexes. The categorization of human beings into the two sexes, usually in place by two and a half years, is one of the earliest conceptual classifications a child makes.

Sex roles are defined not only by physical attributes and behavior, but also by opinions, feelings, and motives. Most American girls regard an attractive face, a hairless body, a small frame and moderate-sized breasts as ideal physical characteristics. American boys regard height, large muscles, and facial and body hair as ideal.

Some psychological traits that differentiate males from females are changing in American life. Aggression is one of the primary sex-typed behaviors. The traditional sex-role standard inhibits aggression in females, but licenses and encourages it in boys and men. It is difficult to find a psychological study of Americans that fails to note more aggressive behavior among males than among females.

Young children agree that males are more dangerous and punishing than females. This view also persists at a symbolic level: Six-year-olds believe that a tiger is a masculine animal, and that a rabbit is feminine. In one experiment, pairs of pictures were shown to young children. On the first run the child selected from each pair the picture that was most like his father. The second time, the child selected the picture that was more like his mother. In the third run, he picked the one more like himself. Boys and girls alike classified the father as darker, larger, more dangerous, and more angular than the mother. The boys classified themselves as darker, larger, more dangerous, and more angular than the girls.

These perceptions are not limited to our culture. Charles Osgood of the University of Illinois showed similar pairs of abstract designs or pictures to adults from four different language groups: American, Japanese, Navajo, and Mexican-Spanish. He asked each adult to indicate which picture of the pair best fitted the concept of man and which fitted the concept of woman. As the children had done, the adults from all four cultures classified men as large, angular, and dark and women as small, round, and light.

Dependency, passivity, and conformity are also part of the traditional sex-role standard. Females in America and in most European countries are permitted these qualities; boys and men are pressured to *inhibit* them. Thus men experience greater conflict over being passive; females experience greater conflict over being aggressive.

These differences over aggressive and dependent behavior are reflected in a person's action, and in a reluctance to perceive these qualities in others. As part of an extensive personality assessment, 71 typical, middle-class American adults watched while some pictures depicting aggression and some depicting dependency were flashed onto a screen at great speed. Each person was asked to describe each picture after it was flashed seven times. The women had greater difficulty than the men in recognizing the aggressive scenes; the men had greater difficulty in recognizing the dependency scenes.

Sex-role standards dictate that the female must feel needed and desired by a man. She must believe that she can arouse a male sexually, experience deep emotion, and heal the psychological wounds of those she loves. The standards for males also stress the ability to arouse and to gratify a love object, but they also include a desire to be independent in action and to dominate others and to be able to control the expression of strong emotions, especially fear and helplessness.

The American male traditionally has been driven to prove that he was strong and powerful; the female to prove that she was capable of forming a deeply emotional relationship that brought satisfaction and growth to the partner—sweetheart or child.

These values are reflected in the behavior of young children from diverse cultures. John and Beatrice Whiting of Harvard University observed children from six cultures and found that the boys were more aggressive and dominant than the girls. The girls were more likely than boys to offer help and support to other children.

In one study, my colleagues and I observed two-year-old boys and girls in a large living room. The girls were more likely than boys to stay in close physical contact with their mothers during the first five minutes. Then a set of toys was brought into the room and the children were allowed to play for a half hour. Most children left their mothers immediately and began to play. However, after 15 or 20 minutes many became bored and restless. The girls tended to drift back to their mothers, while the boys preferred to wander around the room. Michael Lewis of Educational Testing Services has reported similar differences in children only one year old. Linda Shapiro of Harvard has studied pairs of two-year-olds (two boys and two girls) in a natural setting and found the girls more trusting, more cooperative, more nurturing, and less fearful of each other than the boys.

It is interesting to note that the rhesus monkey and the baboon, who are not taught sex-role standards, display behavioral differences that resemble those observed in young children. Harry Harlow and his colleagues at the University of Wisconsin have found that threatening gestures and rough-and-tumble contact play are more frequent among young male than among young female monkeys, whereas passivity in stress is more frequent among the females.

Some of the differences between males and females seem to stretch across cultures and species, suggesting that sex-role standards are neither arbitrary nor completely determined by the social groups. Each culture, in its wisdom, seems to promote those behaviors and values that are biologically easiest to establish in each of the two sexes.

The individual's sex-role identity, as noted, is his opinion of his maleness or femaleness, not a summary of his physical attributes. In one study, Edward Bennett and Larry Cohen of Tufts University asked American adults to select from a list of adjectives those that best described their personalities. The women described themselves as weak, fearful, capable of warmth, and desirous of friendly and harmonious relationships with others. The men described themselves as competent, intelligent, and motivated by power and personal accomplishment.

Sex-role identity differences among children arise from three sources:

First, a family-reared child is predisposed to assume that he or she is more like his or her parent of the same sex than like any other adult, and is inclined to imitate that parent. If a father is bold and athletic, his son is more likely to believe he possesses these masculine attributes than is a boy whose father is not athletic.

Second, the child is vulnerable to the special definition of sex roles shared by his peer group. A boy who is clumsy on the playing field is more likely to question his sex-role identity if he lives in a neighborhood devoted to athletics than he is if he lives in a community that values intellectual prowess.

Third, sex-role identity depends heavily on the quality of sexual interaction in adolescence. The sex-role identity has two important six-year periods of growth: one prior to puberty when acquisition of peer valued sex-role characteristics is primary, and one during adolescence, when success in heterosexual encounters is crucial. If the adolescent is unable to establish successful heterosexual relationships, he will begin to question his sex-role identity. To the adult, the potential for attracting the affection of another and entering into a satisfactory sexual union is the essence of the sex-role standard.

Let us consider the implications of a firm sex-role identity and a fragile one. Each of us tries all the time to match his traits to his notion of the ideal sex role. This is but one facet of the human desire to gain as much information about the self as possible. When one feels close to his ideal standard, his spirits are buoyed. He is confident he can come even closer, and he makes the attempt. If he feels he is far from his standard, he may turn away from it and accept the role of a feminine man (or a masculine woman). Acceptance of a culturally inappropriate role reduces the terrible anxiety that comes from recognizing in one's self a serious deviation from an ideal that cannot be obtained. The only possible defense is to redefine the ideal in attainable terms.

The continuing attempt to match one's attributes to the sex-role ideal allows men to display a more intense involvement than women in difficult intellectual problems. Males are supposed to be more competent in science and mathematics; as academic excellence is necessary for vocational success, it, therefore, is an essential component of a man's sex-role identity.

Adolescent girls view intellectual striving as a form of aggressive behavior because it involves competition with a peer. Since many females believe they should not be overly competitive, they inhibit intense intellectual striving. A visit to college dining halls often reveals males arguing so intensely that the air crackles with hostility. Intense debate in the female dining hall is less frequent because it threatens the girl's sex-role identity. Men seem to be better able to argue about an issue because they do not always take an attack on an opinion as an attack on the person.

Although intense intellectual striving is more characteristic of adult men than it is of women, this is not the case among young children. In the primary grades, girls outperform boys in all areas. The ratio of boys to girls with reading problems ranges as high as six to one. One reason for this difference is that the average American six- or seven-year-old boy sees school as a feminine place. On entering school he meets female teachers who monitor painting, coloring, and singing, and put a premium on obedience, suppression of aggression and restlessness. These values are clearly more appropriate for girls than for boys. Studies of children affirm that they see school as feminine and seven-year-old boys naturally resist the complete submission it demands. If this is true, a community with a large proportion of male teachers should have a smaller proportion of boys with serious reading retardation. Some American communities, such as Akron, Ohio, are testing the hypothesis.

Depression and anxiety affect the sexes differently. Women are likely to suffer psychological stress when it is suggested that they are not attractive, loving, or emotional. Some women experience serious depression after giving birth because they do not feel strong love for the infant and they question their femininity. Men become anxious at suggestions that they are impotent or not competent, successful or dominant. Depression is likely to follow a man's career failure.

The sex-role standards of a society are not static, and changes in the standards that surround sexuality and dependence are just becoming evident. The American woman has begun to assume a more active role in sexual behavior; her mother and grandmother assumed passive postures. This reach for independence has extensive social implications. Some college-educated women feel that dependence, especially on men, is an undesirable feminine trait. They want to prove that they can function as competently and autonomously as men and this pushes them to develop academic and career skills.

Why? The intense effort spent on getting into and staying in college has persuaded the young woman that she should use her hard-won intellectual skills in a job. And technology has made it less necessary for a woman to do routine housework and forced her to look outside the home for proof of her usefulness.

Most human beings seek the joy of accomplishment. A man tries to gratify this need in his job and he has something concrete with which to prove his effectiveness—an invention, a manuscript, a salary check. Woman once met her need to be useful by believing that her sweetheart, husband, or children required her wisdom, skill, and personal affection. Instant dinners, permissive sexual mores, and freedom for children have undermined this role. It is too early to predict the effect of this female unrest. It should lead to a more egalitarian relation between the sexes. It could make each partner so reluctant to submerge his individual autonomy and admit his need for the other, that each walks a lonely, and emotionally insulated path. Let us hope it does not.

4 *Inger Becker*

Men, Beware Women

Throughout the western world the trend seems to be towards greater sexual freedom. As sexual relations among unmarried persons have always been fairly common in Scandinavia, and are now generally accepted for both men and women, some of the problems which are being discussed in Scandinavia today may in a few years have to be faced in country after country—and should in certain countries be faced now. In this article I shall talk especially about Sweden which has the largest population of the Scandinavian countries.

So-called free love in Sweden refers, in general, to the young and the unmarried. Nothing indicates that married people allow themselves —and each other—more "freedom" than married people elsewhere. Conjugal infidelity, though usually not regarded in terms of sin, is considered as a personal insult to the spouse or a betrayal.

Sexual freedom for both men and women and the gradual disappearance of the "double standard" are an aspect of the emancipation of women, closely connected with women's increasing financial independence. Obviously a woman who earns her own living and takes responsibility for herself cannot be told what to do and what not to do on the grounds that men prefer it that way. And so men, at least in Sweden, have stopped preferring virgins. Hardly anyone expects a woman to be virgin when she marries—even if she marries young—or even to marry any of the first men she has had sexual relations with. Girls do not get a bad reputation because they have sexual intercourse; and a baby, though unfortunate for a number of reasons, is not a disgrace. In the family column of Swedish newspapers you find unmarried mothers announcing births. The equality

Inger Becker, "Men, Beware Women." This article first appeared in *New Society*, the weekly review of the social sciences, 128 Long Acre, London, WC2 England. Reprinted by permission.

is not complete, however. There are some subtle differences. There are also some shortcomings about equality.

When people in Scandinavia discuss the equality of men and women, they often point out that women have been suppressed for thousands of years. Somehow this fact is supposed to excuse anything any woman does—or fails to do—today.

In Sweden women got the right to vote and be elected in 1921. This means that women who are now under 45 years old were born into a country where women and men had equal political rights, at least formally. The women who are under 66 years old reached their majority just in time to practise their rights from the start. Of course, many other injustices remained to be corrected during the following decades; but most Swedish women alive today were never suppressed—nor did most of the men who live today suppress us. It should also be kept in mind that men gave women the vote as well as all other initial legal rights enabling them to act for themselves.

I say this because the emancipation of women has failed to turn men and women into *fellow human beings*. To most women, men are still adversaries: adversaries to flatter and please and cajole into treating them well, or adversaries to fight. The ultimate aim of equal rights for men and women must be to make us all primarily human beings, secondarily men and women. It is often objected that this would kill all excitement and romantic thrill. But I don't see why it should be more romantic for a girl to go out with a man when all the time a little computer works somewhere in her brain, figuring out how much her standard of living would improve if he were to marry her, rather than if she goes out with him simply because she likes him as a person and is attracted to him as a man.

Unfortunately it takes less time and effort to marry a doctor than to become a doctor oneself—and it gives exactly the same social and financial status. Under such conditions, a man cannot know whether a woman is in love with *him* or with all the things he has to offer her socially and materially. She may not even know it herself.

An intense public discussion has been going on in Sweden during the last decade which is usually referred to as the "sex role debate." We no longer speak of feminists—we speak of people who are more or less radical on sex role matters. The word "radical" in this connection has no political connotation. All the political parties, including the Conservative Party, have their sex role radicals. Any Swedish woman who wants to has a very great choice as to what she could do with her life. She has the same political and legal rights as a man, the same rights to education and a career, and the same rights to financial aid for study and vocational training (schools and universities are free in Sweden, the financial aid refers to living expenses during the years of study or training). The principle of equal pay for equal work was laid down a few years ago. Moreover, the authorities as well as the various sectors of the economy are actively encouraging her to be unconventional in her vocational choice: she should choose a profession or an occupation which suits her interests and abilities and not worry about whether, traditionally, her choice would be considered a "masculine" or a "feminine" one. In a country with a shortage of labour it is a waste to have half the adult population doing a limited number of jobs while the other half is engaged in thousands of different kinds of work.

So far the sex role debate has mostly been devoted to demanding better possibilities and more rights for women—while paradoxically letting them keep the privileges obtained in a quite different society. And yet the most radical change in the situation of woman would be if she were to realise the importance of taking more responsibility, and of developing into an independent human being. If they want to be men's equals, women should accept the same responsibility.

Women have it too easy. In a highly competitive society, where men are driven to ulcers and heart attacks by the fear of professional failure, it is indeed a great privilege to be able to set out on a career knowing, as women do, that if they do not succeed they lose face neither as human beings nor as women. People may not even know if a woman fails: she may get married and pretend she "sacrificed her career" in order to make a good home.

Woman's body has always been her foremost means of subsistence. It still is. Even married women with a career usually have a higher standard of living than their own income would give them. They are usually married to men who make more money than they do themselves. To a great extent this is due to earlier injustices, but it is also due to the fact that women do not take their career as seriously as men do. They do not see work and professional achievement as a necessary part of human existence, but rather as something they should have the right to devote themselves to *if they feel like it*. Although in Sweden as many girls as boys pass matriculation, boys then proceed to choose occupations or professions requiring longer training than the girls do—and leading to better paid positions. The girls are all the time aware of the "free choice" to work or be supported. They know that it is sufficient for them to take any kind of short training course enabling them to take jobs to earn money for clothes and cosmetics, but that their final standard of living will be provided by a man.

Obviously the less one puts into a job, the less one gets out of it. Work requiring little training is frequently tedious routine work, whereas years of serious study lead to interesting and well paid positions. But when a woman gets too bored by her routine job she can always hope for a man to come along and save her from job, boredom and responsibility. It is incredibly easy for a woman who is bored by her work to fall in love. And incredibly easy to become pregnant if the man does not seem to make up his mind quickly enough.

In a country like Sweden, where family planning and contraceptive techniques are taught at school, where advertisements for contraceptives are seen everywhere, where no one, not even the church, objects to the use of contraceptives, and where any woman can have a diaphragm or a loop fitted or contraceptive pills prescribed without being questioned as to marital status, unplanned pregnancies ought to be the exception rather than the rule. But some preliminary research figures seem to indicate that about 50 percent of the children born in Sweden are, if not unwanted, at least unplanned. And in one third of all marriages children are born before or during the first seven months of marriage.

Psychologists should investigate the possible connection between getting pregnant and being fed up with school or job. If women bring children into the world for escapistic reasons, perhaps this should be made less tempting and the men protected by appropriate legislation.

Previously it was always the woman who had the most difficult and risky position in a sexual relationship. It was therefore necessary to protect by legislation not only the child born out of wedlock but also the unmarried mother. The father usually "managed anyway." He had, of course, to pay the contributions towards the support of the child (Swedish law is very rigid in this respect and rigidly enforced) and a man in modest circumstances might find it hard to pay. But the consequences for the mother were still much more severe. She had to bring up the child and bear both the heavier financial burden and (until recently) the social stigma.

The social stigma persists to limited extent in some circles, but in others it has been replaced by something at least as harmful: a romantification of the unmarried mother, especially if she happens to be a young girl. If she is a schoolgirl, she often becomes the heroine of the class. Her classmates help her knit baby clothes. The mother of a 17-year-old daughter reported that when she brought up the subject of contraceptives with her daughter, the girl answered: "But mother, wouldn't it be fun for me to have a cute little baby?"

Under present Swedish law, if a child is born out of wedlock, the mother has complete custody of the child. The father has no rights whatsoever. He cannot influence the bringing-up of the child, he cannot even see the child unless the child's mother agrees. But he must pay. There is no way of escaping, except giving up his career altogether and becoming a social-welfare case. As long as he has an income the authorities will

see to it that he pays or that his employer deducts from his salary or wages
the amount fixed by the court.

"He should have thought of this before." Comments like these were
relevant in earlier times, when women had no means of protecting themselves against pregnancies. However, in Sweden today the situation is
reversed: not the woman, but the man, has the most risky position. A
man is almost at the mercy of the woman he happens to have sexual
relations with.

Contraceptive pills and the loop give women a definite advantage over
men. A woman can protect herself and know that she is protected. She
can also fail to protect herself, and the man has no way of knowing.
If a woman wants a child—whether for romantic reasons or because she
counts on the man to marry her if she becomes pregnant—she may use
the man as a breeding bull: "You do not have to be careful. I am taking
contraceptive pills." If a man wants to be absolutely sure of not risking to
become a father he must thus always use a rubber contraceptive. A woman
who knows that she takes her pills conscientiously becomes indignant if
the man insists on using contraceptives. So does a woman who planned
to get pregnant. But how is a man to distinguish between indignation
and indignation?

Thus it has reached a point in Sweden where legislation should no
longer protect the mother and the child, but the father and the child. The
woman can today protect herself *if she wishes* and legislation should
rather induce her to do so than encourage her to be irresponsible. For
instance, if the law no longer forced a man to contribute towards the
support of a child which he did not want to be born, women might then
become less apt to be careless about contraceptives, less apt to bring
children into the world because they want a doll to play with and less apt
to trap a man into marrying them.

Women want it both ways: they want freedom and independence, as
far as it is fun. But they also want to retain their right to be weak and
helpless and to be protected by a man. They want to vote, equal pay,
sexual freedom and a husband who washes dishes, and yet at the same
time they want to be courted and pampered in the traditional way. Indeed,
having a husband who washes dishes or does other traditionally feminine
work seems to be one of the important symbols of emancipation and
prestige. It is not counted at all if a husband washes the car, changes a
fuse, does repairs in the flat or lots of things that husbands usually do. No,
unless he washes dishes or vacuum-cleans the flat he is not considered to
be helping his wife. The man is expected both to wash dishes and bring
her flowers.

5 *John W. Hudson & Lura F. Henze*

Campus Values in Mate Selection: A Replication

Past research indicates the influence of social class and family in the mate selection process which, in large part, accounts for the endogamous quality of mate selection.[1]

It has long been recognized that the family is the major agency of socialization. While the process of socialization never ends, it does decelerate with most learning taking place when the person is young.[2] The choice of a mate is limited by the individual's formation of generalized-value systems before maturation.[3] Values learned early in life tend to persist.

In the mass media, college students are often depicted as having departed from the traditional values of the society.[4] Thus, the youth of today are frequently charged with being less serious in mate selection than were young people a generation ago. Is this mass media image valid?

Since societal values regarding the family tend to change slowly, it is to be expected that values expressed in mate selection would vary little from one generation to the next. Parents play highly significant roles in the courtship of their children in that they have much to do with the kind of person the child will choose as a mate.[5] Whether consciously or unconsciously, the person's value system serves as criteria for mate selection.

The thesis of this paper is that the value system of the current college

John W. Hudson and Lura F. Henze, "Campus Values in Mate Selection: A Replication." *Journal of Marriage and the Family*, Vol. 32, No. 4 (November 1969), pp. 772–775. Reprinted by permission.

This is a slightly revised version of a paper prepared for presentation to the annual meetings of the Rocky Mountain Social Science Association, Denver, Colorado, May 3–4, 1968. This research was supported by a grant from Arizona State University. We are indebted to John A. Ballweg, James R. Hudson, George Kupfer, and the registrar at Arizona State University for their part in drawing the random samples at their universities.

49

population regarding mate selection is not as different from the college population of a generation ago as thought by parents and portrayed by the mass media.

To compare values in mate selection held by college students today with those of earlier years, the literature was reviewed for relevant research. This review indicated that among the studies cited most often were the "Campus Values in Mate Selection" done by Hill and McGinnis.[6] These studies were selected for replication as they focused on personal characteristics related to mate selection and because the students who were the respondents in 1939 are the parental generation of today.

The earlier studies of "Campus Values in Mate Selection" were done at the University of Wisconsin in 1939 by Reuben Hill and in 1956 by Robert McGinnis. In the initial study by Hill, participants were enrolled in a noncredit marriage course. In the 1956 study McGinnis drew a one-percent systematic sample from the university student directory.

PROCEDURES

To broaden the base of this study, an investigation was conducted on four campuses located in widely separated geographic regions—three in the United States and one in Canada. The American colleges selected were Arizona State University, the University of Nebraska at Omaha, and the State University of New York at Stony Brook. The Canadian college chosen was the University of Alberta at Edmonton.

A copy of the "Campus Values" questionnaire, together with a cover letter explaining the nature of the study and a postage-paid return envelope, was mailed to each student in the sample. The original questionnaire had been prepared by Reuben Hill and Harold T. Christensen.

DESCRIPTION OF THE QUESTIONNAIRE

Included in the questionnaire were the usual background items of age, sex, marital status, education, and family data. The evaluative section included preferences on age at time of marriage, age difference between husband and wife, number of children, and personal characteristics. The personal characteristics were 18 traits to be evaluated according to their degree of importance in choosing a mate. Provision was made for the respondent to add any further personal characteristics which he felt should be included.

Students were asked to assign a numerical weight of "three" to characteristics which they believed were indispensable, "two" to traits important but not indispensable, "one" to those desirable but not important, and "zero" to factors irrelevant in mate selection. Thus, respondents evaluated each trait and assigned an appropriate numerical weight to each; the investigators then ranked the traits on the basis of mean values computed from the numerical weights. For the purposes of this paper, the terms "ranked" and "evaluated" are used synonymously.

DESCRIPTION OF THE SAMPLE

A one-percent random sample of full-time students at each of the four universities was drawn by the registrars' offices. Questionnaires were mailed to a total of 826 students; 566 (68.5 percent) were returned and usable.

The sample included 337 males and 229 females. The median age was 21.6 years for men and 20.4 years for women. Seventy-six percent of the men and 82 percent of the women were single.

FINDINGS

AGE FACTORS IN MATE SELECTION

College men and women in the 1967 sample indicated a preference for marriage at an earlier age than had been indicated in the previous studies. (See Table 1.) The median preferred age at marriage for men in 1939 was 25.1 years and was 24.9 years for the 1956 sample. The age preference dropped to 24.5 years in 1967. The median age preference for women in 1939 was 24.0 years, and in 1956 and 1967, it declined to 22.9 and 22.5 years, respectively.

In all three studies, males and females agreed that the husband should be older than the wife but did not agree on the preferred age difference. Women preferred a greater age gap between spouses than did men.

TABLE 1 Median preferences (by sex and year) regarding age at marriage, difference in age between husband and wife, and number of children.

Year	Preferred age at marriage		Preferred age difference between husband and wife		Preferred number of children	
	M	F	M	F	M	F
1939	25.1	24.0	2.3	3.4	3.3	3.5
1956	24.9	22.9	1.2	2.1	3.6	3.9
1967	24.5	22.5	1.5	2.0	2.9	3.3

NUMBER OF CHILDREN PREFERRED

In all three time periods investigated, women preferred more children than did men. The trend was toward more children wanted by men and women in 1956 (3.6 and 3.9) than in 1939 (3.3 and 3.5), and fewer children in 1967 (2.9 and 3.3) than in either of the earlier periods.

PERSONAL FACTORS IN MATE SELECTION

The data indicate that from one time period to the next, three of the 18 items, as evaluated by men, maintained the same rank and 11 did not vary by more than one place. (See Table 2.) Males, in all three studies, evaluated dependable character as the most indispensable personal characteristic in a mate. Sociability and favorable social status consistently held their rank of twelfth and sixteenth place, respectively, in 1939, 1956, and 1967.

Chastity, as evaluated by men, declined to a greater degree than did any other characteristic. This was indicated by mean scores as well as by rank. In 1939 the mean score for chastity was 2.06, and in 1967 it was 1.28. In rank, the decline was from tenth place to fifteenth.

Greater emphasis was placed on good looks by males in 1967 than

TABLE 2   Rank of 18 personal characteristics in mate selection based on mean value, by year and sex.

	Male			Female		
	1939	1956	1967	1939	1956	1967
1. Dependable character	1	1	1	2	1	2
2. Emotional stability	2	2	3	1	2	1
3. Pleasing disposition	3	4	4	4	5	4
4. Mutual attraction	4	3	2	5	6	3
5. Good health	5	6	9	6	9	10
6. Desire for home-children	6	5	5	7	3	5
7. Refinement	7	8	7	8	7	8
8. Good cook-housekeeper	8	7	6	16	16	16
9. Ambition-industriousness	9	9	8	3	4	6
10. Chastity	10	13	15	10	15	15
11. Education-intelligence	11	11	10	9	14	7
12. Sociability	12	12	12	11	11	13
13. Similar religious background	13	10	14	14	10	11
14. Good looks	14	15	11	17	18	17
15. Similar educational background	15	14	13	12	8	9
16. Favorable social status	16	16	16	15	13	14
17. Good financial prospect	17	17	18	13	12	12
18. Similar political background	18	18	17	18	17	18

in either of the earlier studies. During the time period under study, health declined in importance from fifth to ninth place. The traits which moved consistently upward from 1939 to 1967 were mutual attraction, good cook-housekeeper, and similar educational background—each moved up two positions. The characteristic which fluctuated the most was similar religious background, which changed from thirteenth place in 1939 to tenth in 1956 and declined to fourteenth in 1967.

In the responses by women, no trait was consistently evaluated as more important in 1956 and 1967 than it had been in 1939. One of the eighteen traits—good cook-housekeeper—ranked sixteenth in all three studies; the rank of eight other traits did not vary by more than one place. Emotional stability and dependable character ranked first or second in each time period studied. Women gave the least weight to good looks and similar political background.

For women, the evaluation of chastity declined to a greater extent than for any other characteristic. This was indicated by mean scores and by rank. The mean score for chastity was 2.0 in 1939 and .93 in 1967, while the rank in 1939 was tenth and in 1956 and 1967 it was fifteenth. Ambition, good health, and sociability moved downward with consistency. Fluctuation was greatest for education-intelligence which ranked ninth in 1939, fourteenth in 1956, and seventh in 1967.

Male and female responses to the additional question asking for further characteristics felt to be important in mate selection were insufficient to warrant analysis.

Preliminary analysis of data from the four colleges indicates no significant differences in student responses from one campus to the others. Analysis of data from each of the campuses will be reported in a subsequent paper.

CONCLUSIONS

PREFERENCE IN AGE FACTORS

This study has indicated that the preferred age at first marriage has continued to show a decline since the 1939 study. A sidelight of the younger age at first marriage in the United States has been an increase in the proportion of college students who marry and remain in school.[7] It has been noted by other writers that, while student marriage was not unknown during the 1930s, it was not widespread.[8] Prior to World War II married students were rare and frequently prohibited from enrollment. Today they are an accepted fact.

From discussions with college students, the investigators have concluded that there has been increased emphasis on dating at the pre-teen level and that this pattern has been initiated largely by parents and school systems. According to students, a further parental influence in the early stages of dating has been the insistence that dating partners be drawn from the same age and social group. This early requirement of dating a person from the same age group structures the subsequent dating pattern. Since mate selection is a function of whom one dates, the age gap between husband and wife has narrowed in terms of preferences stated by college students and according to Parke and Glick.[9]

The overall decline in preferred age at first marriage is probably a reflection of both economic conditions and the current high value placed on marriage. The convergence in agreement on age differential is probably the result, in part, of changes in dating and mate selection patterns as well as changes in female status.

PREFERENCE IN NUMBER OF CHILDREN

The findings do not constitute an adequate basis for predictions of future birth rates. Birth rates and desired number of children are very sensitive to social and cultural conditions. Thus, little significance can be attached to changes in the number of children wanted by students in 1939, 1956, and 1967 since factors which influence preferences are closely linked to cycles and fashions of the time.

PERSONAL CHARACTERISTICS

When the eighteen characteristics were ranked and a comparison was made between the findings of the three studies, it became apparent that over the years there has been a striking consistency in student evaluation of desired traits in a mate. For example, college students today assign the same importance to dependable character as did college students a generation ago.

Good health, as evaluated by both men and women, has become less important in mate selection. This is probably a reflection of the general improvement in overall health which has, in part, resulted from the increased availability of comprehensive medical services and health insurance.

The personal characteristic which evidenced the greatest decline in rank was chastity. Although chastity ranked in fifteenth place for both sexes in 1967, this does not indicate that the same importance is placed on this factor by men and by women. When the mean values are examined, it is evident that the double standard is still operating. Men continue to evaluate virginity as a more important characteristic for a wife than women do for a husband, as evidenced by the mean scores. It should be noted that the lowered evaluation of chastity may not indicate that it is less important; the change in rank may simply indicate that other attributes have become more meaningful since the time of the Hill study.

SUMMARY

While this study does not clearly and precisely add to theory construction, it does add substantive material which suggests generational stability in criteria used in mate selection. For although a child may rebel against domination, he cannot escape the ideas conditioned in him from his childhood.[10]

In 1967, compared to 1939, there have been changes in the behavior patterns of the college populations studied in terms of age factors in mate selection and in marrying while in college. However, this change is compatible with the high value placed on marriage by the parental generation —who were the college students of 1939—and the younger generation who are the students today.

The charge that young people have departed from traditional values and are less serious about mate selection is not given support by the present study. Indeed, the findings suggest that youth's values regarding the importance of personal characteristics in mate selection are much the same today as they were a generation ago.

It might be said in conclusion that social change in the area of mate selection has not been as great as indicated by the press, feared by the parent, and perhaps hoped by the youth.

ENDNOTES

1. Ira L. Reiss, "Social Class and Campus Dating," *Social Problems*, 13:2 (Fall, 1965), p. 195. August B. Hollingshead, "Cultural Factors in the Selection of Marriage Mates," *American Sociological Review*, 15 (October, 1960), p. 627.
2. Kingsley Davis, "The Sociology of Parent–Youth Conflict," *American Sociological Review*, 5 (August, 1940), p. 524.
3. Marvin B. Sussman, *Sourcebook in Marriage and the Family*, Boston: Houghton Mifflin Company, 2nd ed., 1963, p. 63.
4. Stephen Birmingham, "American Youth: A Generation Under the Gun," *Holiday*, 37 (March 1, 1965), p. 44.
5. Alan Bates, "Parental Roles in Courtship," *Social Forces*, 20 (May, 1942), p. 483.

6. Reuben Hill, "Campus Values in Mate Selection," *Journal of Home Economics*, 37 (November, 1945). Robert McGinnis, "Campus Values in Mate Selection: A Repeat Study," *Social Forces*, 36 (May, 1959).

7. Paul C. Glick, *American Families*, New York: John Wiley and Sons, Inc., 1957, p. 57.

8. Jesse Bernard, *Dating, Mating and Marriage*, Cleveland: Howard Allen, Inc., 1958, pp. 217–218. Victor A. Christopherson and Joseph S. Vandiver, "The Married College Student, 1959," *Marriage and Family Living*, 22 (May, 1960), p. 122. Ernest Haveman, "To Love, Honor, Obey and Study," *Life*, 38:21 (May 23, 1955), p. 152.

9. Robert Parke, Jr. and Paul C. Glick, "Prospective Changes in Marriage and the Family," *Journal of Marriage and the Family*, 29:2 (May, 1967), p. 249.

10 Robert H. Coombs, "Reinforcement of Values in the Parental Home as a Factor in Mate Selection," *Marriage and Family Living*, 24 (May, 1962), p. 155.

6 Eleanor D. Macklin

Heterosexual Cohabitation Among Unmarried College Students*

This article is an initial exploration of unmarried cohabitation as experienced by female students at Cornell University, and includes a description of the nature of the relationship, the reasons for involvement, and attendant problems and benefits. Discussion is based on intensive interviews with fifteen junior and senior women, and questionnaire responses from twenty-nine junior and senior women, all of whom had experienced cohabitation. The author suggests that living together unmarried is becoming an increasingly common aspect of campus courtship and is frequently associated with the "going steady" phase of the dating relationship. Implications for research and education are indicated.

During the past five or six years there have been periodic allusions in the popular press to a developing pattern of cohabitation among unmarried youth (*Newsweek*, 1966; *Esquire*, 1967; Grant, 1968; McWhirter, 1968; Schrag, 1968; *Time*, 1968; Bloch, 1969; Karlen, 1969; Rollin, 1969; Sheehy, 1969; *Life*, 1970; Coffin, 1971), but little attempt has been made to explore this phenomenon in the professional literature. The majority of research has continued to dwell on questions regarding the sexual values and attitudes of college students, documenting their increased willingness to engage in and to approve of premarital sexual relations (Bell and Chaskes, 1970; Cannon and Long, 1971; and Christensen and Gregg, 1970;

Eleanor D. Macklin, "Heterosexual Cohabitation Among Unmarried College Students," from *The Family Coordinator*, October, 1972, pp. 463–472. Reprinted with permission.

* This article is based on a working paper prepared for presentation at the 1971 Groves Conference on Marriage and the Family. The author is indebted to Frank H. Sadowski who helped to conduct interviews and summarize the data, and to Bonni Schulman and Marianne Stein who assisted in the development and pretesting of the questionnaire.

Herr, 1970; Kaats and Davis, 1970; Mosher and Cross, 1971; Luckey and Nass, 1972), but providing little information about the changes in living patterns which are simultaneously occurring. Exceptions include a series of published interviews with cohabiting college couples (Ald, 1969), an unpublished master's thesis based on interviews with twenty-eight cohabiting student couples at the University of Iowa (Johnson, 1968), the unpublished work on "unmarried college liaisons" ("unmalias") by sociologist Robert N. Whitehurst (1969), a study of student and parental attitudes with respect to the university's responsibility in the area of off-campus cohabitation at Michigan State University (Smith and Kimmel, 1970), and a call for further research and counseling facilities by emotional health consultant Miriam Berger. (1971)

It was because so little was known about the current patterns of cohabitation among college youth that the present study was undertaken. This report summarizes the initial pilot phase of this research. In order to obtain a more complete picture of the various forms which living together might assume, a fairly inclusive definition of cohabitation was adopted: To share a bedroom for at least four nights per week for at least three consecutive months with someone of the opposite sex. Throughout this paper, this definition of cohabitation will be used.

The objectives of this phase of the research were to gain an estimate of the prevalence of this experience, and an understanding of the nature of the relationship, the reasons for involvement, and the problems and benefits experienced. A series of four-hour semistructured interviews was conducted in April, 1971, with fifteen junior and senior female students at Cornell University, Ithaca, N.Y., who had experienced heterosexual cohabitation. In September, 1971, a questionnaire based on the interview schedule was given to 104 junior and senior women in a course on adolescent development at Cornell. Of the eighty-six who responded, twenty-nine had experienced cohabitation. The fifteen interviewees had been involved in a total of twenty such relationships (eleven had experienced one such relationship, three had had two, and one, three). The twenty-nine questionnaire respondents had experienced a total of thirty-five cohabitation relationships (twenty-four had had one, four had had two, and one had had three).

The following discussion will be based on the informatioin obtained from the combined group of forty-four cohabitants. Questionnaire data will serve as the basis for all quantitative reporting, but it should be understood that interview data were generally corroborative.

PREVALENCE

From the present data one can only surmise the frequency with which cohabitation currently occurs at Cornell. Of the eighty-six junior and senior women who completed the questionnaire,[1] 34 percent had already had such an experience by the beginning of the 1971 fall term. When these eighty-six students were asked to predict what percentage of Cornell undergraduates probably experience cohabitation prior to graduation, almost three-quarters predicted that 40 percent or more would do so. When asked how many of their close friends had experienced or were experiencing cohabitation, only 7 percent said "none," and over 40 percent said "many" or "most."

Of the fifty-seven respondents who had not experienced cohabitation as defined, almost two-thirds checked that they had stayed with someone but not for as long as indicated in the definition. When asked why they had not cohabited, the large majority indicated that it was because they had not yet found an appropriate person. A few checked that it would be unwise for them at present due to the stage of their relationship, their immaturity, the possibility of discovery, or physical impracticality. Only one person said she had not because it would be wrong to do so outside of marriage.

Further clues to the frequency of cohabitation come from the questionnaire pretest which was given to two undergraduate classes in April 1971. Of 150 underclassmen responding, 28 percent indicated having experienced cohabitation. From an upper-class seminar on delinquency taught by the author, twelve of the twenty students volunteered to be interviewed regarding their cohabitation experience. One is led to conclude from all available evidence that cohabitation is a common experience for students on this particular campus and is accepted by many as a "to-be-expected" occurrence.

DESCRIPTION OF THE COHABITATION EXPERIENCE

A wide variety of types of cohabitation experiences were revealed: among them, living with a male roommate in a co-op (with no sexual involvement and with both roommates having other romantic attachments), living in a tent while traveling in Europe, sharing a dormitory or a fraternity room, or sharing a room with another cohabiting couple. However, the most common pattern was for the girl to move into the boy's room (or vice versa) in an apartment or house which he was sharing with several other males (one of whom might also have a girl living in). Graduate student pairs are more likely to live alone in an apartment or a house; freshman couples are more likely to share a dormitory room. Very few couples shared their bedroom with a third person.

In the majority of cases, living quarters had not been obtained initially with living together in mind (although many men arrange to have a single room in order to allow privacy for any potential entertaining). Living arrangements were not usually jointly arranged until the second year of a relationship. However, even then, couples were hesitant to arrange for a single joint living situation, and planning simply involved ensuring that the potential apartment-mates were willing to have a girl share the premises. Practically all girls also maintained a room in the dormitory or sorority or in an apartment with other girls. Most went back once a day for a few hours to visit, get messages or mail, exchange clothes, shower, or study. Maintaining a separate residence precludes having to explain to parents, ensures a place to live if the relationship is not working well, helps maintain contact with female friends, serves as a convenient place to study, and provides often necessary storage space (the boy's room being too small to hold both sets of belongings).

In about half of the relationships, the couple spent seven nights a week together. In the remaining half, the girl returned to her own room one or two nights a week in order to see her friends and to allow him time with his friends. It should be noted at this point that spending the night together, even in the same bed, need not imply a full sexual relationship. Aside from the instance of the non-emotionally involved coed roommates, there were couples who had lived together for more than three months without intercourse because they did not yet feel ready for this experience (these were usually virgin women). The irony of this is the frequency with which the older generation refuses to accept that this could be true, or if it is, insists that the male must be a "queer."

There was a wide range in amount of time spent together. The majority reported being together about 16–17 hours a day on weekdays (5 p.m. to 8 a.m. plus lunch). Most couples shared at least two meals a day, although occasionally dinner was eaten separately because of the inconvenience involved in having an extra person at dinner or because her parents had already paid for her meals on campus and funds were tight. There was practically no instance of total pooling of finances in these relationships, although the couple normally shared food and entertainment expenses. Usually the girl paid her way and maintained her own separate finances, either because the couple could not afford otherwise or as a matter of principle. When there were chores involved, the couple generally did them together (e.g., shopping or laundry), although there was a tendency for the girl to assume responsibility for cooking and cleaning. There was a wide range in the degree to which they shared activities (e.g., classes, study, or hobbies) or spent time with others. The tendency was to share the majority of activities, to have many mutual friends, and to spend much of their time with others as opposed to time only with one another.

WHY STUDENTS LIVE TOGETHER

There are three aspects to the question of why students are now living together: the circumstances existing at the particular institution, the broader societal reasons, and the personal motivations of the specific students.

Changes in dormitory regulations and the slow demise of *in loco parentis* have greatly facilitated the development of the new pattern. If one goes back to earlier issues of the campus newspaper (*Cornell Daily Sun*, 1962, 1963, 1964), one notes that in 1962, a graduate student was indefinitely suspended from the University for living with a woman in his apartment, and in 1964, a male student was reprimanded for staying overnight at a local hotel with a non-University female. Sexual morality was considered a legitimate concern of the University faculty and "overnight unchaperoned mixed company" was considered by the Faculty Council on Student Conduct to be a violation of sexual morality. (*Cornell Daily Sun*, 1962, 2)

Today, Cornell students are free to live in much the same way that nonstudents who are living and working in the outside world are free to live: they are likely to be residing in a structure which also houses persons of the opposite sex (many of the dorms are now coed, with men and women segregated by floors, wings or suites, although there is experimentation with men and women living on the same corridor); if they are sophomores or beyond, they are free to elect to live off campus; and they may entertain someone of the opposite sex in their room at any time during the 24-hour day. Official policy still prohibits "continuous residence" with someone of the opposite sex in the dormitory setting, but this is difficult to police.

These changes in curfew and dormitory policy must be seen as a reflection of broader social changes: a change in the status of women which makes it difficult to justify different regulations for men and for women, youth's increasing demand that they no longer be treated as children, a questioning of the rigid sexual mores which have traditionally governed people's lives, a greater willingness to grant individuals the right to select their own life style, and the increasing availability of contraception and abortion services.

When students are asked to hypothesize why cohabitation has become more common and more open, they mention youth's search for meaningful relations with others and the consequent rejection of the superficial "dating game"; the loneliness of a large university and the emotional satisfaction that comes from having someone to sleep with who cares about you; the widespread questioning of the institution of marriage and the desire to try out a relationship before there is any, if ever, consideration of permanency; the desire on the part of many to postpone commitment until there is some certainty that individual growth will be compatible with growth of the relationship; the fact that young people mature earlier and yet must wait so long until marriage is feasible; and the fact that the university community provides both sanction and feasibility for such a relationship to develop. Given peer group support, ample opportunity, a human need to love and be loved, and a disposition to question the traditional way, it seems only natural that couples should wish to live together if they enjoy being together. One might almost better ask: Why do students choose *not* to live together?

When one asks students why they personally become involved in a cohabitation relationship, one finds a mixture of enjoying being together and expediency (e.g., too far to drive her home at night, easier to stay than to get up and go back at midnight, less expensive, someone else living with one's roommate, or partner was sick and needed someone to care for him). On occasion, curiosity about what it would be like to live with the opposite sex was involved, and sometimes "to test out the relationship" was mentioned, but it was rarely such a purposeful act.

In fact, living together was seldom the result of a considered decision, at least initially. (Cf., Ryder, Kafka and Olson's concept of "unquestioned beginnings" which they suggest characterize much of courtship in our society.) Most relationships involved a gradual (and sometimes not so gradual) drifting into staying together. The general pattern was to stay over one night; in several weeks, if all was well, to stay for the weekend; in another few weeks to add a week night; in another few weeks, a second week night, and so forth. In half the relationships the couple had begun staying together four or more nights a week by the end of four months of dating.

If and when a decision with conscious deliberation was made, it was usually precipitated by some external force (e.g., need to make plans for the summer or next fall, graduation, unexpected pregnancy, or necessary housing or room change). Until this time, there was only a mutual, often unspoken, recognition of the desire to be together—a natural progression of the relationship.

NATURE OF THE RELATIONSHIP

When asked to indicate the nature of the relationship at the time they began living together four or more nights per week, about half checked that they "had a strong, affectionate relationship, not dating others" (i.e., "going steady"—although they resisted this term). Another large group indicated that they "had a strong affectionate relationship but were also open to other relationships." Only a few indicated tentative engagement; even fewer stated that they were just "friends." See Table 1.

TABLE 1 Nature of relationship when couple first started living together for at least four nights per week, as reported by 29 upperclass female students for 35 cohabitation relationships.

Nature of relationship	Number of relationships
1. Formally engaged	1
2. Tentatively engaged (contemplating marriage)	3
3. Strong, affectionate relationship; not dating others ("going steady")	17
4. Strong, affectionate relationship; open to other dating relationships	12
5. Friends	1
6. Other ("met and immediately started living together")	1
Total	35

It is interesting to note that the above is very similar to answers given by all 86 questionnaire respondents when asked what kind of relationship they felt should exist before college-aged students cohabit. (see Table 2) One is impressed by the fact that cohabitation is more frequently associated with the "going steady" stage of a relationship than with engagement, even tentative engagement.

The initial commitment to the relationship varied greatly. Some saw it strictly as temporary (e.g., "while traveling," "he was planning to leave Ithaca," or "he was already committed to someone else") and a few, at the other extreme, definitely planned "marriage in the future when it was more convenient." But the vast majority entered it either with a "let's see" attitude (i.e., to test the relationship—to stay together as long as it was mutually satisfying), or—a somewhat more definite commitment—planned to do all they "could to develop a lasting relationship, but future marriage was not definite."

This raises some question about the label "unmarried marrieds" which has often been applied in the popular literature to unmarried cohabitation. Most of the undergraduate couples did not consider themselves married in any sense of the word. Not only did they not consider themselves married, they rarely considered marriage as a viable alternative to their present cohabitation. When asked, "Did you consider the possibility of getting married instead?", a frequent response was "Heavens no!" Marriage might be seen as a possibility for the future, but the distant future. The future seemed too indefinite to plan that far ahead, they needed more time

TABLE 2 Responses of 86 upperclass female students to "what kind of relationship do you feel *should* prevail before college-aged students cohabit?"

Nature of Relationship	Percent of Respondents
1. Married	4
2. Formally engaged	—
3. Tentatively engaged (contemplating marriage)	8
4. Strong, affectionate relationship; not dating others ("going steady")	60
5. Strong, affectionate relationship; open to other dating relationships	15
6. Friends	8
7. Other (e.g., "anything acceptable to both parties")	5
Total	100%

to grow and develop before considering marriage, and it was financially impractical. Moreover, marriage appeared to have some negative connotations for many of these students—it was seen as limiting their freedom and their growth (cf., the period of youth as discussed by Keniston in *Young Radicals*), and they feared falling into the traditional roles they associated with being wives, even though over two-thirds of those interviewed said their parents would consider their own marriage "very successful."

PROBLEMS ENCOUNTERED

As with any real relationship, these were not always blissful. It was encouraging that those interviewed seemed very aware of the problem areas and were able to verbalize about them easily.

Problems could be divided into four major categories: emotional problems, sexual problems, problems with parents, and problems related to the living situation. (In the interviews, no one had experienced problems with the community; thus the question was not included in the questionnaire.)

The major emotional problem (see Table 3) was the tendency to become overinvolved and to feel a subsequent loss of identity, lack of opportunity to participate in other activities or be with friends, and an overdependency on the relationship. On the basis of the available data, one is tempted to hypothesize that how this issue is dealt with and the success with which it is handled are major determinants of the outcome of the relationship. The problem of how to achieve security without giving up the freedom to be oneself, and how to grow together and yet leave enough space so the individuals can grow also, appears central.

Other problems in this category were feelings of being trapped (should

TABLE 3 Extent to which emotional, sexual, and living situation problems were experienced in 35 cohabitation relationships as reported by 29 upperclass female students (categories are ordered by number of persons reporting the problem).

Problem area	Number indicating No problem	Some problem	Average rating given by those indicating some problem*
Emotional Problems			
1. Overinvolvement (loss of identity, lack of opportunity to participate in other activities or with friends, overdependency)	14	21	2.7
2. Jealousy of partner's involvement in other activities or relationships	14	15	3.1
3. Feeling of being trapped	18	15	2.9
4. Feeling of being used	19	13	2.6
5. Guilt			
—at beginning of relationship	20	9	3.7
—during relationship	25	5	3.8
—at end of relationship	15	2	4.0
6. Lack of feeling of "belonging" or of being "at home"	22	9	3.4
7. Other "will have to separate for a while after his graduation"	—	1	3.0
Sexual Problems			
1. Differing degrees or periods of sexual interest	10	23	3.4
2. Lack of orgasm	11	21	3.6
3. Fear of pregnancy	15	15	3.1
4. Vaginal irritation or discharge after intercourse	17	15	3.4
5. Discomfort of partner during intercourse	18	10	3.7
6. Impotence of partner	23	6	3.0
Problems Related to Living Situation			
1. Lack of privacy	15	17	3.4
2. Lack of adequate space	19	13	3.0
3. Did not get along with apartment or housemates	20	6	2.2
4. Lack of sufficient money	26	6	3.3
5. Disagreement over use of money, sharing of money, etc.	27	4	3.5

* Respondents were asked to rate each problem from 1 to 5, with 1: great deal of problem, 5: no problem (no other points defined). The last category (5: no problem) has been separated because it may be qualitatively different from the other rating categories. Average ratings are therefore based on ratings from 1 to 4; thus, the lower the average rating the greater the problem for those experiencing it.

break up but afraid to do so), feelings of being used, jealousy of partner's involvement in other activities or relationships, and lack of feeling of belonging (e.g., "When I expect that he will share his money with me now that my parents have cut me off, he reminds me that we are not married").

It should be recognized, however, that although there were a few who indicated that these problems caused them a great deal of trouble, the majority indicated little or no problem. It is also important to note that more than two-thirds indicated no feelings of guilt, and the remainder indicated only a minimal amount. In the interviews, when guilt was stated to be present, it was usually related to having to conceal the relationship from parents or it occurred in those instances where they knew that the relationship could not last.

Sexual problems were common. (see Table 3) Only a few indicated "no problem" in this area. Differing degrees or periods of sexual interest, lack of orgasm, fear of pregnancy, vaginal irritations, feelings of sexual inhibition, and less satisfaction with sex as the relationship deteriorated were the more frequently mentioned problems. However, in spite of problems, over three-fourths of the respondents rated the relationship as sexually satisfying. Practically all used contraception (over 80 percent used either the pill or the diaphragm), with about two-thirds of these having started contraception before or at the time of the first intercourse in the cohabitation relationship.

A major problem area was parents. More than one-fourth indicated that parents had caused "some" or "many" problems: parental disapproval of the boy, fear of discovery, guilt because they were deceiving or hurting their parents, rejection by or ultimatums from parents, and most frequently, sadness at not being able to share this important part of their lives with their parents. Because of fear of disapproval or unpleasant repercussions, more than two-thirds had tried to conceal the relationship from their parents—by not telling them the whole story, by distorting the truth, and by developing often elaborate schemes to prevent discovery. Almost half of the respondents believed their parents to be unaware of their cohabitation, with the remainder divided equally between those who felt they definitely knew, those who thought they probably knew, and those who were unsure. The boy's parents were much more likely to be aware.

Problems related to the living situation were considered minimal. Lack of privacy, lack of adequate space, lack of sufficient funds or disagreement over money, and friction with apartment mates were all mentioned, with lack of space or privacy and tension with others in the living situation the most common. It should be noted that there was practically no problem experienced as a result of the external community, i.e., landlords, local employers, school administration, neighbors, or contemporaries. In fact, the great majority felt their friends strongly approved of and supported their relationship. In cases where this was not true, it was because friends considered the particular relationship rather than the cohabitation *per se* undesirable.

BENEFITS

It is important that the problems not be seen as outweighing the values of such relationships. More than half rated their relationship as "very successful," and more than 80 percent checked that it was "both maturing and pleasant." Even in those few cases where the relationship was said to be "painful," they emphasized the personal growth which had occurred, e.g., "I question whether I'd understand myself as well without the hard times." In no case was the experience rated "very unpleasant" or "not at all maturing," and in no case was it considered primarily detrimental to the person involved. In more than 60 percent of the cases, they would do it over again with the same person, even in those relationships which had broken up at the time of the report.

The benefits seen by the participants included a deeper understanding of themselves and of their needs, expectations, and inadequacies; increased knowledge of what is involved in a relationship and of the complexities of living with someone else; clarification of what they wanted in a marriage; increase in emotional maturity and in self-confidence, e.g., "learned not to commit myself too soon," "learned through breaking up how much strength I have," increased ability to understand and relate to others; emotional security and companionship; and confidence in the possibility for success of the particular relationship, e.g., "because we have coped with problems and come out top side, I have more faith that we will be able to do so again." The main undercurrent in the data was the many ways in which the experience had fostered growth and maturity. All persons interviewed indicated that they would not consider marriage without having lived with the person first, and all—while hesitant to say what others should do—felt the move toward cohabitation could only be seen as a healthy trend.

OUTCOME OF THE RELATIONSHIP

At the time of the questionnaire, one-third of the relationships had dissolved (having lasted an average of four and one-half months from the time they began staying together four or more nights a week), one-third were married or planning to be married, and another third were still in the process of defining the relationship (either were still living together but not yet contemplating marriage, or were still "going together" but not living together—either because the partner was away or they sought more freedom than they had when living together). A somewhat larger portion of those interviewed had broken their relationship, but this may be due to the fact that the interview was later in the academic year. The 23 relationships which were still in process had existed an average of 13 months, with five having continued for two or two and one-half years.

IMPLICATIONS

1. It appears that cohabitation has become an increasingly common aspect of courtship on the campus studied and one could predict that the trend will proliferate.

Although the phenomenon of unmarried persons living together is obviously not a new one, either in this society or others (Berger, 1971), it has certainly not been a common phenomenon among unmarried middle class youth in the United States until quite recently. Some pass it off by saying it is merely a more open expression of what students have been doing sexually on the sly for years, but this suggests a very narrow interpretation of the present situation. The pattern which is currently evolving appears to be primarily concerned with total relationships and only incidentally with the sexual aspects. It is this concern with getting to know another as a whole person and the emphasis on sharing as openly and as completely as possible with that person, which is probably the major new dimension being added to old courtship patterns.

2. There is some question whether cohabitation as now practiced on the college campus fits the concepts of trial marriage, premarital marriage, companionate marriage, or two-stage marriage which some have sought to apply to it. (Berger, 1971; Grant, 1968; Karlen, 1969; LeShan, 1971; Mead, 1966) Trial marriage, for instance, tends to imply a level of commitment usually associated with the engagement portion of the courtship continuum which is not characteristic of the campus relationships studied. These students do not in general see themselves as consciously testing or even contemplating a potential marriage, at least not initially. Instead, in most cases, living together seems to be a natural component of a strong, affectionate "dating" relationship—a living out of "going steady"—which may grow in time to be something more, but which in the meantime is to be enjoyed and experienced because it is pleasurable in and of itself.

3. In addition to the question of whether it does in fact lead to healthier marriages or more "fully functioning" persons, there are other intriguing issues. For instance, what is the relationship between commitment to a relationship and identity formation? To what extent must one have developed a strong identity before one can achieve a strong intimate relationship (in Erikson's sense)? What chance is there for a mature, mutual relationship when the individual is still so necessarily focused on his own development? How much commitment to a relationship is necessary for

it to have a strong chance of success? Alternately, does early commitment to a relationship hinder identity development? When a person should be at a point of maximum identity development, is it healthy for him to be devoting so much of his energy to the development of a relationship or will this simply accelerate the process? These become very real problems as cohabitation inevitably occurs earlier and becomes increasingly common as a freshman experience.

4. There is a great need to help society adjust to the evolving courtship patterns. Parents in particular tend to see cohabitation as antithetical to all that they consider healthy or moral. They need help if they are to understand and to react without alarm, recrimination, and rejection. Consideration will have to be given to legal implications of the new patterns—some present laws conflict and maybe should be changed, and some new protections for the rights of unmarried participants may be necessary. The professions touched by the new trends are myriad. Bankers, for instance, as they seek to help parents write wills and set up trust funds, and as they themselves seek to administer these trusts, find themselves confronted with having to understand and interpret the new patterns. Students in particular need more realistic preparation, both at home and in school, and more opportunity for relationship and sex counseling, if they are to cope as responsibly and effectively as possible with the increased freedom and the new pressures. The first step, which most of the adult population has not yet taken, is to acknowledge that the changes are actually occurring and to be willing to entertain the hypothesis that they may indeed be an improvement on the traditional patterns.

ENDNOTE

1. Of the 104 junior and senior women in the class, eighty-six completed the questionnaire. Of these, fifty-eight handed it in on the due date and twenty-eight after a follow-up request. Since the percentage of cohabitants was the same for the initial and the follow-up respondents, it is assumed that the percentage would be similar for the eighteen non-returnees.

REFERENCES

Ald, Roy. *Sex Off Campus*. New York: Grosset and Dunlap, 1969.

Bauman, Karl E. Selected Aspects of the Contraceptive Practices of Unmarried University Students. *Medical Aspects of Human Sexuality*, August 1971, 5, 76–89.

Bell, Robert R. and Jay B. Chaskes. Premarital Sexual Experience among Coeds, 1958 and 1968. *Journal of Marriage and the Family*, 1970, 32, 81–84.

Berger, Miriam E. Trial Marriage: Harnessing the Trend Constructively. *The Family Coordinator*, 1971, 20, 38–43.

Bloch, Donald. Unwed Couples: Do They Live Happily Ever After? *Redbook*, April 1969, 90+.

Cannon, Kenneth L. and Richard Long. Premarital Sexual Behavior in the Sixties. *Journal of Marriage and the Family*, 1971, 33, 36–49.

Christensen, Harold T. and Christina F. Gregg. Changing Sex Norms in America and Scandinavia. *Journal of Marriage and the Family*, 1970, 32, 616–627.

Coffin, Patricia. Young Unmarrieds: Theresa Pommett and Charles Walsh, College Grads Living Together. *Look*, January 26, 1971, 634+.

College and University Business. Parents OK Strict Rules. December, 1968, 16.

Cornell Daily Sun, October 9, 1962; October 8, 1963; March 6, 1964.

Crist, Takey. *The Coed as a Gynecological Patient.* University of North Carolina, Chapel Hill, North Carolina, 1970. (mimeo)

Davids, Leo. North American Marriage: 1990. *The Futurist*, October 1971, 190–194.

Esquire. Room-Mates. September 1967, 94–98.

Fell, Joseph P. A Psychosocial Analysis of Sex-Policing on Campus, *School and Society*, 1970, 98, 351–354.

Fleming, Thomas and Alice Fleming. What Kids Still Don't Know About Sex. *Look*, July 28, 1970, 59+.

Grant, A. No Rings Attached: A Look at Premarital Marriage on Campus. *Mademoiselle*, April 1968, 66, 208+.

Hall, Elizabeth and Robert A. Poteete. A Conversation with Robert H. Rimmer about Harrad, Group Marriage, and Other Loving Arrangements. *Psychology Today*, 1972, 5, 57–82.

Herr, Sylvia. Research Study on Behavioral Patterns in Sex and Drug Use on College Campus. *Adolescence*, Spring 1970, 5, 1–16.

Hunt, Morton. The Future of Marriage. *Playboy*, August 1971, 117+.

Johnson, Michael P. *Courtship and Commitment: A Study of Cohabitation on a University Campus.* Master's thesis. University of Iowa, Iowa City, 1969.

Kaats, Gilbert R. and Keith E. Davis. The Dynamics of Sexual Behavior of College Students. *Journal of Marriage and the Family*, 1970, 32, 390–399.

Karlen, Arno. The Unmarried Marrieds on Campus. *New York Times Magazine*, January 26, 1969, 29+.

Keniston, Kenneth. *Young Radicals.* New York: Harcourt, Brace, and World, 1968.

LeShan, Eda J. *Mates and Roommates: New Styles in Young Marriages.* Public Affairs Pamphlets, No. 468, 1971. Public Affairs Pamphlets, 381 Park Ave. So., New York 10016.

Lever, Janet and Pepper Schwartz. Men and Women at Yale. *Sexual Behavior*, October 1971.

Life. Coed Dorms: An Intimate Campus Revolution. November 20, 1970, 32+.

Luckey, Eleanore B. and Gilbert D. Nass. Comparison of Sexual Attitudes in an International Sample of College Students. *Medical Aspects of Human Sexuality*, 1972, 6, 66–107.

Malcolm, Andrew H. Sex Goes to College. *Today's Health*, April 1971, 27–29.

McWhirter, William A. The Arrangement at College. *Life*, May 31, 1968, 56+.

Mead, Margaret. A Continuing Dialogue on Marriage: Why Just Living Together Won't Work. *Redbook*, April 1968, 130, 44+.

Mead, Margaret. Marriage in Two Steps. *Redbook*, July 1966, 127, 48+.

Mosher, Donald L. and Herbert F. Cross. Sex-Guilt and Premarital Sexual Experiences of College Students. *Journal of Consulting and Clinical Psychology*, February 1971, 36, 27+.

Moss, J. Joel, Frank Apolonio, and Margaret Jensen. The Premarital Dyad During the Sixties. *Journal of Marriage and the Family*, 1971, 33, 50–69.

Newsweek. Unstructured Relationships: Students Living Together. July 4, 1966, 68, 78.

Packard, Vance. *The Sexual Wilderness.* New York: David McKay, 1968.

Peters, Muriel and William Peters. How College Students Feel About Love, Sex, and Marriage. *Good Housekeeping Magazine*, June 1970, 85+.

Reiss, Ira L. The Sexual Renaissance in America: Summary and Analysis. *Journal of Social Issues*, April 1966, 22, 123–137.

Rimmer, Robert H. *The Harrad Experiment.* Los Angeles: Sherbourne Press, 1966.

Rockefeller, John D. III. Youth, Love and Sex: The New Chivalry. *Look*, October 7, 1969, 32+.

Rollin, Betty. New Hang-up for Parents: Coed Living. *Look*, September 23, 1969, 22+.

Ryder, Robert G., John S. Kafka, and David H. Olson. Separating and

Joining Influences in Courtship and Early Marriage. *American Journal of Orthopsychiatry*, April 1971, 41, 450–464.

Sarrel, Philip M. and Lorna J. Sarrel. How We Counsel Students on Sex Problems at Yale. *The Osteopathic Physician*, June 1971.

Schrag, Peter. Posse at Generation Gap: Implications of the Linda LeClair Affair. *Saturday Review*, May 18, 1968, 51, 81.

Sheehy, Gail. Living Together: The Stories of Four Young Couples Who Risk the Strains of Nonmarriage and Why. *Glamour*, February 1, 1969, 136+.

Smith, Patrick B. and Ko Kimmel. Student-Parent Reactions to Off-Campus Cohabitation. *Journal of College Student Personnel*, May 1970, 188–193.

Time. Linda, the Light Housekeeper. April 26, 1968, 51.

Whitehurst, Robert. The Unmalias on Campus. Presented at NCFR Annual Meeting, 1969. Copy available from author, University of Windsor, Windsor, Ontario, Canada.

Whitehurst, Robert. The Double Standard and Male Dominance in Non-Marital Living Arrangements: A Preliminary Statement. Paper presented at the American Orthopsychiatric Association Meeting, New York, 1969. Copy available from author, University of Windsor, Windsor, Ontario, Canada.

7 *Miriam E. Berger*

Trial Marriage: Harnessing the Trend Constructively

ANTHROPOLOGICAL AND HISTORICAL SURVEY

Trial marriage has been practiced among the Peruvian Indians of Vicos in the Andes for more than four centuries (Price, 1965; MacLean, 1941). Arranged by the parents in the earlier form, the purpose was to test the girl's work abilities and the couple's general compatibility. In modern Vicos there is a free choice of marriage partners with romantic love playing an important role, but men still seek responsible, hardworking girls who have mastered household skills and can help in the fields. Study of couples who entered a trial marriage for the first time indicated that the average duration of such trials was less than fifteen months and that 83 percent of the relationships were finalized with marriage. There was no stigma if the couple had children, but did not marry. Permanent separations after marriage were rare, occurring in two to three percent of the cases. One of the advantages of these trial marriages noted by Price was the ease of transition from adolescence to adulthood. The couple acquired certain social and sexual advantages of adulthood without assuming full responsibility.

The Trobrianders had a "bachelor's house" in which courting couples slept together and had exclusive sex prior to marriage. In contrast to Western civilization, before marriage Trobriand couples were not permitted to eat together or share any interests, except sex (Malinowski, 1929).

In the eighteenth century, Maurice of Saxony, illegitimate son of the Elector Augustus the Strong and Countess Aurora of Konigsmark, sought a solution to the marriage problem. He recommended temporary marriages,

Miriam E. Berger, "Trial Marriage: Harnessing the Trend Constructively." *The Family Coordinator*, Vol. 20, No. 1 (January 1971), pp. 38–43. Reprinted by permission.

contracted for a limited time. If the partners agreed, the contract could be prolonged, but marriage for life was a "betrayal of the self, an unnatural compulsion" (Lewinsohn, 1956).

"Bundling" originated in Europe and was brought to the New World in the eighteenth century. In New England, where it was too cold to sit up late, courting couples were permitted, with parental approval, to get into bed with their clothes on. Some bundling experiences were probably innocent, especially when they included a center-board for the bed (Marriage Museum), but "certainly many got sexually involved and married when conception occurred" (Scott, 1960; Fielding, 1961).

"Trial nights," an old Teutonic custom (Marriage Museum), is still practiced today in Staphorst, Holland, an insular, inbred town whose customs have for centuries sealed them off from contemporary life. The swain spends three nights a week with his girl friend, with the knowledge of her parents who hope she will prove fertile. Until she becomes pregnant, there can be no marriage. If she is barren, the community regards her with primitive suspicion and contempt. Once she is pregnant, however, the marriage must take place (Gibney, 1948).

TWENTIETH CENTURY AMERICA

The first American to propose trial marriage as a concept was Judge Ben B. Lindsay (1927). Bertrand Russell, who was then teaching in New York, approved of Lindsay's Companionate Marriage, but felt it did not go far enough. Russell favored trial marriage for university students and believed that work and sex were more easily combined "in a quasi-permanent relationship, than in the scramble and excitement of parties and drunken orgies" that were prevalent during the Prohibition Era. Russell felt that if a man and woman chose to live together without having children, it was no one's business but their own. He believed it undesirable for a couple to marry for the purpose of raising a family without first having had sexual experience (Russell, 1929).

Lindsay and Russell were ostracized, and the concept of trial marriage lay dormant until an evolving sexual morality led anthropologist Margaret Mead to revive it (Mead, 1966). Building on Lindsay's Companionate Marriage, she recommended a two-step marriage: *individual*, in which there would be a simple ceremony, limited economic responsibilities, easy divorce, if desired, and no children; and *parental marriage*, which would be entered into as a second step by couples who were ready to undertake the lifetime obligations of parenthood, would be more difficult to enter into and break off, and would entail mutual continuing responsibility for any children. Her rationale was that sex, now considered a normal need in

youth, often drove them into premature and early marriage, frequently leading to unhappiness and divorce. She made the plea that divorce be granted
before children are conceived, so that only wanted children of stable marriages are brought into the world. Responses to Dr. Mead's proposal
(Mead, 1968), ranged from disapproval for tampering with tradition
(instead of helping couples adjust to traditional marriage) to complaints
from students for setting up too much structure. A typical student response
was: "Why get married? Why can't we live together, with a full sex life,
with no pregnancy, until we're ready to get married and have children?"

Margaret Mead's two-step marriage was elaborated on by Michael
Scriven, a philosophy professor, who proposed a three-step plan:

> We try to make one institution achieve three aims, which all
> too often lie in perpendicular dimensions. The aims are sexual
> satisfaction, social security and sensible spawning. The solution
> would be to create three types of marriage arranged so that any
> combination is possible: preliminary, personal and parental mar-
> riage. The first would simply be legitimized cohabitation, contrac-
> tually insulated against escalation into "de facto" commitment.
> It would be a prerequisite for other kinds and would impose a
> period of a year's trial relationship before the possibility of con-
> version to personal marriage. . . (Scriven, 1967)

In *The Sexual Wilderness,* Vance Packard (1968) concluded that the
first two years of marriage are the most difficult. He recommended a
two-year confirmation period, after which the marriage would become
final or would be dissolved. Packard felt that this proposal differed from
trial marriage because the couple would marry in earnest and with the
hope that the marriage would be permanent. He saw trial marriage as
highly tentative and little more than unstructured cohabitation. Packard's
concept is based on his conviction that the expectation of permanency
contributes to success in that it motivates a couple to work hard to adapt-
ing, and is, in fact, a strong stabilizing and reinforcing factor.

In "Marriage as a Statutory Five Year Renewable Contract," Virginia
Satir, family therapist, said:

> Maybe there needs to be something like an apprentice period . . .
> in which potential partners have a chance to explore deeply and
> experiment with their relationship, experience the other and find
> out whether his fantasy matched the reality. Was it really possible
> through daily living to have a process in which each was able to
> enhance the growth of the other, while at the same time enhancing
> his own? What is it like to have to undertake joint ventures and
> to be with each other every day? It would seem that in this socially

approved context, the chances of greater realness and authenticity continuing would be increased, and the relationship would deepen, since it started on a reality base. (1967)

Another variation of the renewable contract concept was proposed by Mervyn Cadwallader, a sociology professor, in "Marriage as a Wretched Institution":

Marriage was not designed to bear the burdens now being asked of it by the urban American middle class. It was an institution that evolved over centuries to meet some very specific needs of a non-industrial society . . . Marriage was not designed as a mechanism for providing friendship, erotic experience, romantic love, personal fulfillment, continuous lay psychotherapy, or recreation. Its purposes . . . have changed radically, yet we cling desperately to the outmoded structures of the past . . . The basic structure of Western marriage is never questioned, alternatives are not proposed or discussed . . . Why not permit a flexible contract, for one or more years, with periodic options to renew? If a couple grew disenchanted with their life together, they would not feel trapped for life . . . They would not have to go through the destructive agonies of divorce, and carry about the stigma of marital failure, like the mark of Cain on their foreheads. Instead of a declaration of war, they could simply let their contracts lapse and while still friendly, be free to continue their romantic quest . . . What of the children in a society that is moving inexorably toward consecutive, plural marriages? . . . If the bitter and poisonous denouement of divorce could be avoided by a frank acceptance of short-term marriages, both adults and children would benefit. Any time spouses treat each other decently, generously, and respectfully, their children will benefit. (Cadwallader, 1966)

Today many young people have carried the concept of trial marriage a step further, as Bertrand Russell advocated, by living with a roommate of the opposite sex. Sociologist Robert N. Whitehurst coined a word to describe them, "unmalias," a condensation of unmarried liaisons (1969). Whitehurst mentions some of the problems encountered by students who have an "experimental semester of living together, such as when a male senior must leave the campus for graduate school, job, or military service (1969).

The Harrad Experiment (Rimmer, 1966) incorporated some of the above mentioned ideas on trial marriage and added some new dimensions. In Rimmer's novel, college students lived with computer-selected roommates of the opposite sex. Unlike the informal arrangements now made by college students on their own (Karlen, 1969; Life, 1968), the Harrad

Experiment was controlled and guided by the Tenhausens, a husband-and-wife team of sociologist and marriage counselor. The novel focused on several couples who married after four years of living together. The students attended various neighboring colleges, but roomed at Harrad during the four years, and were required to take a course in human values at Harrad taught by the Tenhausens and to do required reading in the subjects of marriage, love, sex, contraception, moral values, philosophy, etc. Whenever the students were troubled about their relationships, the Tenhausens were available for consultation. There was also considerable peer support through endless discussions of common problems. Rimmer favored a structured, socially approved form of pre-marital experimentation that would give the male and female an opportunity to realize themselves fully, without guilt, and to adjust to their new marital roles without legal entanglement, recognizing marriage as the commitment a couple makes to society when they decide to have children (1969). Accused of trying to undermine America's family structure Rimmer asserted that, on the contrary, he believed a strong family to be a *sine qua non* of social existence and that his proposals would strengthen and preserve that structure.

In an article in *The Humanist* (1970) Rustum and Della Roy discussed alternatives to traditional marriage in view of the increasing divorce rate:

> By one simple swish of tradition, we can incorporate all the recent suggestions for trial marriage . . . and cover them all under the decent rug of the "engagement"—engagements with minor differences—that in today's society, they entitle a couple to live together, but not to have children . . . By no means need this become the universal norm.

NCFR WORKSHOP

A workshop led by the author was conducted at the annual meeting of the National Council on Family Relations in 1969. The participants were primarily college instructors of marriage and family courses, but included a social worker, a clergyman, a sociologist, and a college counselor of students. The following is a summary of the highlights of the workshop:

It was agreed that there ought to be alternative methods of courtship, approved by society, that would serve as a better preparation for marriage than dating. Those opposed to trial marriage as one such alternative felt it was not the same as a real marriage and therefore not a valid preparation for marriage. It was also subject to exploitation and abuse, as was any method of courtship, and was more to the interest of the male than the female, who is likely to be more concerned about security. Opponents also pointed out that it takes a great deal of maturity to make a relationship work, and if a couple are not mature enough to marry, they may not be mature enough to end a relationship when indicated, nor to cope with the attendant rejection, not to mention accidental pregnancy, or a partner who flits from one relationship to another.

Those who favored trial marriage felt it should be morally sanctioned by society as an optional alternative.

CLERICAL ATTITUDES

Although many clergymen disapprove of trial marriage, there have been some notable exceptions. Typical of the negative opinion is that of Dean John Coburn of the Episcopal Theological School, Massachusetts:

> How can two people trust one another on a temporary basis? Marriage is a total commitment, and trial marriage is a contradiction in terms. (Eddy, 1968)

On the other hand, a Unitarian minister, Robert M. Eddy (1968), regarding the casual promiscuity and resulting unwanted children as tragic developments of the "new morality," offered the following alternatives:

1. that parents continue the financial support of their college-attending children who are having companionate marriages
2. that it be illegal for youngsters under the age of seventeen to conceive; that seventeen to nineteen year olds, after obtaining parental consent, might live together with the privileges and responsibilities of the relationship defined by a contract as detailed or loose as the parents would desire. Such a relationship could be solemnized by a rite similar to the wedding ceremony and could be ended by mutual consent, as long as the couple did not have children. The next type of cohabitation agreement essentially would be identical to the present marriage relationship, but under the new system, would be limited to adults and would be, in effect, a license to raise children.

HARNESSING THE TREND CONSTRUCTIVELY

Whether one's professional or religious beliefs lead to a view of trial marriage as conservative or radical, acceptable or sinful, a valid or non-valid preparation for marriage, there may be a need to recognize that trial marriage and its variations are being practiced by some young people (Eddy, 1968; Karlen, 1969; Life, 1969; Whitehurst, 1969). As a marriage counselor and emotional health consultant, the author proposes a service that would guide and serve young people who do venture into trial marriage, legal or otherwise, so that they learn from their experiences, rather than stumble blindly from one relationship to another. It is recommended that they assess the experience with a consultant, exploring, individually or in a group, some of the following:

What did I learn about myself from this experience? How did I adjust to living with a peer, as distinguished from living with parents and siblings, or alone? What have the problems of adjustment been? Would I have the same problems with another roommate or spouse? How much did I contribute to these problems and how much was the responsibility of the partner? What neurotic games did we play? What hangups did I bring to the relationship that were reinforced by our interaction? What kind of person do I need to live with, dominant, submissive, detached, involved, affectionate, etc.? What was our style of communication, constructive (Gordon, 1968), silent treatment, hitting below the belt? (Bach, 1968). How effectively do I communicate my needs and feelings? How did our communication problems affect our sexual adjustment? On the assumption that personal happiness is achieved through satisfying closeness to another human being, what problems did I have in achieving and maintaining that closeness?

The author would like to see colleges take the leadership by providing emotional health consultants for the preventive service described above, in addition to the usual counseling services. To encourage college students to avail themselves of the service, its use is recommended as a preventive mental health measure, e.g., at the end of each year when living arrangements are likely to be changed, when students finish the first year in a dormitory, whether single-sex or co-ed dorm, the second and third years with a roommate of the same sex, and whatever the arrangement is for the fourth year. Once accustomed to using the service and finding the consultant understanding, nonjudgmental, and helpful in developing insight, the student is more likely to use the service to discuss any relationships with the opposite sex. Periodic checkups would give the consultant a chance to know a student and to provide direction and guidance. When a student is ready to marry his current partner or someone else, his selection of a mate will have greater sophistication and insight, or he may be motivated if he had repeated adjustment problems with successive roommates, to obtain counseling (Kardiner, 1970). If colleges initiated such a preventive service, it would, in time, become acceptable for non-collegians, In urban centers where many young people live away from their families, the service is available through the facilities of "Check-Up" for Emotional Health; it could also be available in community settings, such as family agencies, premarital counseling services, Ys, community mental health centers, and religious organizations.

RESEARCH INDICATIONS

One critical issue is whether trial marriage is a valid test and preparation for marriage. Some probably know of couples for whom trial marriage culminated in a satisfactory legal marriage. Nevertheless, the following case studies raise questions about the validity of trial marriage as a test:

Sue, age 24, was referred for psychotherapy because of severe anxiety symptoms that had their onset immediately after marriage. She had lived with her husband six months prior to marriage, during which phase she had been relaxed, her real self, and not unduly concerned over the success of the relationship. Exploration revealed that Sue was so anxious for the marriage to succeed that she was repressing all negative feelings, and denying her identity in an effort to fulfill her image of a good wife. Now she was afraid of becoming as aggressive, argumentative, and opinionated as she had been as a teenager.

Ada, age 22, came for psychotherapy because of severe obsessional symptoms. Since her marriage two years earlier, she had been frigid. She had lived with her husband weekends for one year prior to marriage, during which phase she had experienced orgasm. The source of conflict revealed in the exploration was that after marriage she felt her husband was too demanding sexually, that he valued her only for sex, which made it demeaning to her, and that she found it difficult to limit him. She had transferred her excessive need to have her parents' approval to having her husband's approval, resolving the conflict by denying her resentment and thereby becoming frigid and obsessional.

Sue's and Ada's trial marriages were not deliberate tests; both had drifted into their living-together experiences. Perhaps, when the trial marriage is deliberate, similar anxieties would occur before, rather than after the permanent marriage. Was it just that trial marriage was not a valid test for these women with neurotic personalities? It is only the troubled who come to the attention of the professional. Study of the marriages of a large sample of couples who first had trial marriages might provide more reliable information upon which to base a conclusion. In planning the research design, it would be necessary: (1) to distinguish between deliberate trials and unstructured cohabitation that happened to result in permanency; and (2) to explore whether motivation to adapt (Packard, 1968; Lederer and Jackson, 1968) differed during the trial and in permanency.

REFERENCES

Bach, George and Peter Wyden. *Intimate Enemy*. New York: W. Morrow and Company, 1968.

Cadwallader, Mervyn. "Marriage as a Wretched Institution," *Atlantic Monthly*, 1966, 218 (5), 62–66.

Eddy, Robert M. "Should We Change Our Sex Laws?," *The Register-Leader*, March 1966, Detroit, Michigan.

Eddy, Robert M. "Why We Must Allow Sexual Freedom for Teens," *Pageant*, September, 1968, 118–129.

Fielding, Wm. J. *Strange Customs of Courtship and Marriage*, London: Souvenir Press, 1961.

Gibney, Frank. "The Strange Ways of Staphorst," *Life*, September 27, 1948, 2–8.

Gordon, Thomas. *Parent Effectiveness Training*. 110 South Euclid Avenue, Pasadena, California.

Kardiner, Sheldon H. "Convergent Internal Security Systems—A Rationale for Marital Therapy," *Family Process*, 1970, 9(1), 83–91.

Karlen, Arno. "The Unmarried Marrieds on Campus," *New York Times Magazine*, January 26, 1969, 29–30.

Lederer, Wm. J. and Don D. Jackson. *The Mirages of Marriage*. New York: W. W. Norton and Company, 1968, Ch. 21–23.

Lewinsohn, Richard. *The History of Sexual Customs*, New York: Harper Brothers, 1958. Original edition in German, 1956, translated by Alexander Mayce.

Lindsey, Ben B. "The Companionate Marriage," *Redbook*, October 1926; March 1927.

MacLean, R. "Trial Marriage Among the Peruvian Aborigines," *Mexican Sociology*, 1941, 1, 25–33, in Spanish.

Malinowski, Bronislaw. *The Sexual Life of Savages*. London: Geo. Routledge and Sons, 1929.

Marriage Museum, formerly located at 1991 Broadway, New York, N.Y.

Mead, Margaret. "Marriage in Two Steps." *Redbook*, 1966, 127, 48–49.

Mead, Margaret. "A Continuing Dialogue on Marriage," *Redbook*, 1968, 130, 44.

Packard, Vance. *The Sexual Wilderness.* New York: David McKay Company, 1968, 466–468.

Price, Richard. "Trial Marriage in the Andes," *Ethnology,* 1965, 4, 310–322.

Rimmer, Robert H. *The Harrad Experiment.* Los Angeles: Sherbourne Press, 1966.

Rimmer, Robert H. *The Harrad Letters.* New York: New American Library, Signet Book No. 4037.

Russell, Bertrand. *Marriage and Morals.* New York: Liveright Publishing Company, 1929.

Rustum, Roy and Della Rustum. "Is Monogamy Outdated?" *The Humanist,* 1970, 30 (2), 24.

Satir, Virginia. "Marriage as a Statutory Five Year Renewable Contract." Paper presented at the American Psychological Association 75th Annual Convention, Washington, D.C., September 1, 1967. Copy available from author, P.O. Box 15248, San Francisco, Calif. 94115.

Scott, George Ryley. *Marriage—An Inquiry Relating to all Races and Nations from Antiquity to Present Day.* New York: Key Publishing Company, 1960.

Scriven, Michael. "Putting the Sex Back into Sex Education," *Phi Delta,* 1968, 49 (9), based on a paper given at a Notre Dame University Conference on "The Role of Women," Fall, 1967.

Whitehurst, Robert. "The Unmalias on Campus," presented at NCFR Annual Meeting, 1969. Copy available from author, University of Windsor, Windsor, Ontario, Canada.

Whitehurst, Robert. "The Double Standard and Male Dominance in Non-Marital Living Arrangements: A Preliminary Statement," paper presented at the American Orthopsychiatric Association Meeting, New York, 1969. Copy available from author, University of Windsor, Windsor, Ontario, Canada.

WHAT DO YOU THINK?

Two young people were walking along the street side by side, but not touching each other. Both had brown, shoulder-length hair, and were wearing dark slacks, long plaid shirts, and sandals. Their conversation seemed alive, animated, and interesting. As they moved along they kept the same stride, and there was no way of telling their sex. They turned at the entrance of an apartment house and solved part of the sex puzzle— one was wearing a mustache, the other wore makeup and lipstick.

Refer to the Kagan article and indicate to what degree young people are extending sex role identity.

What is the value of maintaining sex differences socially and in appearance? What would you recommend?

Which male and female characteristics do you think should be maintained? Include clothes, appearance, manners or ways of acting, and other triats.

Six girls and six boys have formed a group. They get together in the home of one member, meet for coffee in a favorite spot, go on picnics, or play tennis or other sports. There is little social pairing, and the boys may or may not call for the girls or take them home. They talk, exchange ideas, get into arguments, and settle their differences without rancor. They seem to like this sort of arrangement and feel it is superior to dating just one person. The members still have years of schooling ahead of them and do not wish to get serious about one person at this time.

What are the social and developmental benefits of such a group?

In what ways is this a satisfactory or unsatisfactory means of getting to know people of the opposite sex before marriage? How does it meet the need for personal attention?

For what sort of marriage relationship might this experience prepare a person?

Anna belongs to a sorority, but Arnold is working his way through college and can not afford a fraternity. They had been dating before they came to college and continue to do so. Anna's sorority sisters keep introducing her to various fraternity men and encourage her to double date with them. Arnold does not wish to stand in her way and wants her to enjoy herself. He loves Anna and hopes to marry her some day. They are not engaged, but Anna loves Arnold and hopes to marry him after she finishes college. She does not want to lose him but also does not want to be at odds with her sorority sisters.

Is that the proper attitude for Arnold to take if he really loves Anna? What should Anna do?

What are the dating problems for two people who have three or four years of study ahead of them and then have to get started in a career?

Jim's wife divorced him and he lived alone for a while but did not like it. He was a forty-four-year-old college professor who found the female students too young to catch his interest so he registered with a computer dating service. One match was with June, a thirty-eight-year-old librarian who had never married. Both of them met other possible dates in their work or through friends but the computer service was more convenient. This way, they knew before they met that both of them liked to dance, go to parties, play tennis, go to concerts, and to read. Like most of the computer registrants in this age bracket, they wanted to get married.

Is it respectable to use the computer to help you find a mate?

How is using a dating service different for older people than for people around twenty years old?

Is it better to let a machine do your selecting or to trust to nature and luck?

Issues of Premarital Sex

The topic of premarital sex is packed with issues. One of these is the variety of codes for sexual behavior outside of marriage. Most studies have been concerned with the number of people who participate in premarital sex activities, but so far, few researchers are studying the meaning of this—the feelings, emotions, and reactions of participants. The articles in Part 3 present a variety of opinions and point up important issues.

One view is expressed by Robert R. Bell and Jay B. Chaskes, who duplicated a 1958 study to find out what changes had since taken place in the behavior and attitudes of college coeds. Most of the girls studied lived at home rather than in a dormitory, so their activities may reflect the behavior patterns and value systems of their communities rather than those of the college peer group. One issue is raised here in that many of the girls had sex relations in the early stages of dating, perhaps before love was present. The study suggests that attitudes toward sex relationships have changed. The coeds engaging in premarital coitus do not consider it necessary to have a definite engagement before they do so, and they are less likely to feel they "went too far." Even without a promise to marry, they are less likely to have guilt feelings about their sexual behavior.

Jessie Bernard, in "The Fourth Revolution," covers the recent fundamental changes in sexuality, procreative and nonprocreative, and presents some current issues, especially those which emerged with the Pill. Her stimulating ideas should interest men and women regardless of their attitudes about women's liberation.

Dana L. Farnsworth, a physician with the student health services at Harvard University, points out issues that concern the student, his family, and the college or university, in "Sexual Morality and the Dilemma of the Colleges." He includes a good outline of the important principles of traditional morality and of the new morality. Students want freedom to make their own decisions and may resent advice or regulations stemming from parents or university administrators. At the same time, however, students may end up with less control over their own behavior because peer pressure may become so powerful that it will deprive them of the very freedom they seek.

Illegitimacy is a consequence of sexual behavior, but is also related to a variety of other social factors. Professor Phillips Cutright studied the trend of illegitimate births in other countries and found that, in Europe, the rate was high in 1880 and then dropped, but so did the marital fertility rate. The two rates seem to move together and the reduction is due mainly to the increase in the use of birth control. Cutright studied the effects of various governmental subsidies for the care of children and found that the illegitimacy rate was lower in the states paying high benefits than in those with low payments. The social stigma theory is discussed, and the author also analyzes teenage sexual behavior and the possible results of the so-called sexual revolution. He lists the characteristics of women most apt to become unwed mothers and evaluates the educational programs that encourage the use of contraception.

Much has been written and said about abortion and its immediate consequences, but not much research has concerned its long-term consequences. Elizabeth M. Smith studied people one to two years after they requested an abortion and found that the majority did not suffer emotional upsets due to the experience. She presents tabular material to show a variety of social traits found among the women at the time the abortion was requested, and also records their behavior after the abortion.

So far, we have little data on the unmarried father but suggest that readers keep up with developments in this area. A few men admit to unwed fatherhood, want more control over what happens to the child, and ask for the rights of parenthood to take the child or have it adopted within their own kinship group. Recent court cases favor such petitions and men may bring additional suits in the future.

8

Robert R. Bell & Jay B. Chaskes

Premarital Sexual Experience Among Coeds, 1958 and 1968

Over the past twenty-five years it has been generally assumed in the mass media that the premarital sexual experiences of American girls have been steadily increasing. Furthermore, it is frequently assumed that the college girl has been at the forefront in attaining greater sexual experience. However, in the past the assumption as to increasing sexual experience among college girls has not been supported by research findings. In general, the studies have shown that the significant increase in premarital coital experience for unmarried girls occurred in the 1920s and since that time there have been no striking changes in their probabilities of having premarital coitus (Bell, 1966). One of the authors, after an extensive look at past studies, came to the conclusion that "there is no evidence to suggest that when women born after 1900 are compared by decades of birth, there are any significant differences in their rates of premarital coitus (Bell, 1966:58).

The writers believed that a change *has* been occurring in the sexual experiences of college girls since the mid 1960s. In recent years, even more so than ever, the group primarily responsible for rebellion among the young has been the college student. While there has always been rebellion by the younger generation toward their elders, it probably never has been as great in the United States as it has been since the mid 1960s. In recent years youths have not only rebelled, but have also rejected many aspects of the major institutions in American society. The mid 1960s have produced an action generation and their *modus vivendi* has been to experience, to confront, to participate, and sometimes to destroy. Since the mid 1960s a small but highly influential proportion of college students has been deeply

Robert R. Bell and Jay B. Chaskes, "Premarital Sexual Experience Among Coeds, 1958 and 1968." *Journal of Marriage and the Family*, Vol. 32, No. 1 (February 1970), pp. 81–84. Reprinted by permission.

involved in the civil rights movement and then in the protest over the Vietnam War. What may be most important about this generation of college students is that many are not just alienated as others have been in the past, but are *actively* alienated.

Many college students now believe that a number of the norms of adult institutions are not only wrong but also immoral. This is the view held by many college students toward the treatment of the Black, toward the war in Vietnam, toward American political procedures, and so forth. It therefore seems logical that if many of the norms of these institutions are viewed as wrong and immoral by large numbers of the younger generation, they are also going to be suspicious and critical about other norms in other adult controlled institutions. Certainly a social institution that one would expect the younger generation to view with skepticism would be that concerned with marriage and sexual behavior. This increasingly negative view of adult institutions plus other factors led to the hypothesis that significant changes have been occurring in the premarital sexual experiences of college students since the mid 1960s. Before examining some research data as to whether or not there have been changes in sexual experience, we may briefly examine some other social factors that might be related to change in premarital sexual experiences.

One important factor of the 1960s has been the development, distribution and general acceptance of the birth control pill. On most large university campuses the pill is available to the coed, or it is easy for her to find out where to get it in the local community. While studies have shown that fear of pregnancy has not been a very important deterrent to premarital coitus for a number of years, it now seems to have been largely removed for most college girls.

A second influence since the mid 1960s has been the legitimization of sexual candor. In part the new sexual candor has been legitimized by one of the most venerable of American institutions—the Supreme Court. In recent years the young person has had access to a level of sexual expression far greater than just ten years ago. In the past year, even the most conservative of the mass media, that of television, has begun to show it. This new sexual candor, whatever its original cause, is often seen by the rebelling younger generation as "theirs" in that it, too, critically subverts the traditional institutions. As a result the sexual candor of the late 1960s is often both a manifesto and a guidebook for many in the younger generation.

Finally, it must also be recognized that the rebellion of the younger generation has been given both implicit and explicit approval by many in the older generation. Many adults want to think of themselves as part of the younger generation and its youth culture. For example, this is seen in the music and fashion of the youth culture which has had a tremendous impact on adults. It would seem that if many adults take on the values of the youth culture, this would raise questions as to the significance of many of their adult values for the youth world. In other words, the very identification of many adults with youth culture contributes to adult values having less impact on college youths.

In brief, it was assumed that the social forces developing in the mid 1960s led to a rapid increase in the rejection of many adult values, and the development of increasingly important patterns of behavior common to a general youth culture. For the reasons already suggested, one change would be an increased rate of premarital coitus among college girls along with less feelings of guilt about these experiences.

METHOD

In 1958, the senior author did a study of premarital sexual behavior and attitudes among a sample of coeds in a large urban university (Bell and Blumberg, 1959, 1960). In 1968 it was decided to use the same questionnaire with a sample of coeds in the same university. A careful effort was made to match the 1968 population with that of 1958 according to a number of variables. It was possible to match the two samples by age and by the class standings of the coeds. The two time groups were alike in social class background as measured by the education and occupations of their fathers. The distribution of the two samples by religious backgrounds was also the same. The 1958 sample included 250 coeds and that of 1968 included 205 coeds.

There had been no change in the ten-year period as to the mean age of first date for the two samples; in 1958 it was 13.3 and in 1968 it was 13.2 years of age. There was a significant difference in the number of different individuals ever dated by the coeds in the two time samples. In 1958 the mean number of different individuals dated was 53, while in 1968 it was only 25. In 1968 the coeds went out on dates just as often but went out more often with the same individuals in a dating relationship than did the coeds in 1958.

There was no significant difference in the two time samples as to whether the coeds had ever gone steady. In 1958, 68 percent of the coeds had gone steady at least once, while in 1968 this had been the experience for 77 percent. Furthermore, there was no significant difference as to age at first going steady. In 1958 the mean age was 17.0 years and in 1968 it was 16.7 years of age. There were some slight differences as to engagement experience. Somewhat more girls in 1968 had ever been engaged; 37 percent as compared to 22 percent in 1958. However, coeds in 1968 were somewhat older when they first became engaged (20.5 years) than were the coeds in 1958 (19.1 years).

In the discussion that follows there will first be a presentation of some comparative data about the two coed populations of 1958 and 1968. Secondly there will be a discussion with further analysis of the 1968 population of coeds.

COMPARISONS OF 1958 AND 1968 COED POPULATIONS

The data to be discussed refers to the highest level of intimacy ever reached by the coed in a specific relationship of dating, going steady, and engagement. Table 1 shows the number of percent of girls in 1958 and 1968, by religion, who had intercourse while dating, going steady, or engaged. An examination of the totals indicates some significant changes from 1958 to 1968. The number of girls having premarital coitus while in a dating

TABLE 1   Females, number and percent having intercourse, by dating relationship and religion, 1958 and 1968.

| | Jew | | | | Protestant | | | |
| | 1958 | | 1968 | | 1958 | | 1968 | |
	%	No.	%	No.	%	No.	%	No.
Dating	11	(15)	20	(25)	10	(6)	35	(17)
Going Steady	14	(13)	26	(26)	20	(8)	41	(16)
Engaged	20	(7)	40	(19)	38	(6)	67	(8)

| | Catholic | | | | Totals | | | |
| | 1958 | | 1968 | | 1958 | | 1968 | |
	%	No.	%	No.	%	No.	%	No.
Dating	8	(4)	15	(6)	10	(25)	23	(48)
Going Steady	14	(4)	17	(4)	15	(25)	28	(46)
Engaged	56	(7)	18	(3)	31	(20)	39	(30)

relationship went from 10 percent in 1958 to 23 percent in 1968, and the coitus rates while going steady went from 15 percent in 1958 to 28 percent in 1968. While there was some increase in the rates of premarital coitus during engagement, from 31 percent in 1958 to 39 percent in 1968, the change was not as striking as for the dating and going steady stages. Further examination of the data suggests that in 1958, the relationship of engagement was very often the prerequisite to a girl having premarital sexual intercourse. Engagement often provided her with a high level of emotional and future commitment which she often felt justified having coitus. However, in 1968 it appeared that the need to be engaged and all it implied was much less a condition the coed thought necessary before sexual intercourse. Therefore, the data suggests that the decision to have intercourse in 1968 was much less dependent on the commitment of engagement and more a question of individual decision regardless of the level of the relationship. To put it another way, if, in 1958, the coed had premarital coitus, it most often occurred while she was engaged. But in 1968, girls were more apt to have their first sexual experience while dating or going steady.

Table 1 also shows the changes that have occurred in rates of premarital coitus at the three stages of dating involvement by religious background. Both the Protestant and Jewish girls show a consistent increase in rates of premarital coitus at dating, going steady, and engaged levels from 1958 to 1968. (The number of Catholic coeds is too small for analysis.) In general, the pattern by religious background in 1968 was the same as 1958. Protestant girls had the highest rates of premarital coitus, next came the Jewish coeds, and the lowest rates were for Catholic girls. It would appear that both the Protestant and Jewish girls have been susceptible to the patterns of change, although the rates are greater for Protestant coeds.

The respondents were also asked at each stage of the dating relationship if they had ever felt they had gone "too far" in their level of intimacy. Table 2 shows the percentage of coeds by dating relationship, who said they had at some time, felt they had gone "too far." Table 2 reveals that

TABLE 2 Females, percent having intercourse, by dating relationship who felt they "went too far," in 1958 and 1968.

	1958 Percent (N = 250)	1968 Percent (N = 205)
While dating	65	36
While going steady	61	30
While engaged	41	20

the percentage of coeds feeling guilty about coitus was reduced by approximately half at all three dating levels from 1958 to 1968. It may also be seen that there were significantly less feelings of guilt about coitus during engagement, while in 1968 variations in feelings of guilt were less differentiated at the three stages of dating involvement. In general, when the data of 1958 is compared with 1968 the indication is that in 1968 the coeds were more apt to have had intercourse at all levels of the dating relationship and at the same time felt less guilty than did their counterparts in 1958.

SOME FURTHER ANALYSIS
OF THE 1968 SAMPLE

Given the indication of change in the sexual behavior and attitudes of coeds from 1958 to 1968, it is useful to look a little more in detail at the 1968 sample. The sample was analyzed by a number of variables to see if there were any significant differences. No significant differences were found by father's occupation, father's education, marital status of parents, mother working, or number of siblings. One variable that did show statistically significant differences was that of religious attendance. Those coeds, regardless of religious background, who had the highest rates of religious attendance had the lowest rates of premarital coitus and the greatest feelings of guilt when they did have coitus.

In the 1968 population of coeds it was found that there was a relationship between age of first date and the probability of having premarital coitus. Coeds who had their first date at 14 years of age and younger (as compared to 15 years of age and older) had overall higher rates of coitus (31 percent vs. 12 percent). However, there were no significant differences as related to age at first going steady or first engagement. One explanation for the higher frequency of coitus among those who start dating younger is that they have been dating relatively longer and therefore have had more opportunity. It may also be that girls who start dating younger are more sexually mature, both physically and socially.

It was found that girls who dated more different boys (21 or more vs. 20 or less) had higher rates of premarital coitus (36 percent vs. 14 percent). This difference is in part a reflection of the fact that some girls who have few dates are extremely conservative in their sexual behavior. On the other hand the coeds who dated a large number of different boys often had a wide variety of experiences and a greater probability of sexual intimacy. There was also some indication of a relationship between the number of times a girl went steady and her probability of having premarital coitus. When coeds who had gone steady three or more times were compared with those who had gone steady one or two times, the intercourse rates were 46 percent vs. 22 percent. It may be that some girls who have intercourse are inclined to define that relationship as going steady whether in actual fact it may or may not have been.

As pointed out, studies in the past have consistently shown that for the coed who has premarital coitus, it has usually been limited to one partner and then during engagement. "The studies indicate that being nonvirgin at the time of marriage is not an indication of extensive premarital experiences with a variety of partners" (Bell, 1966:58). If the assumption earlier suggested is true, it would be expected that a number of the coeds in the 1968 sample would have had their first premarital sexual experiences while dating and going steady, rather than waiting until engagement.

When all girls in the 1968 sample who were ever engaged and who had ever had premarital coitus were analyzed, it was found that only 19 percent had limited their coital experience just to the period of engagement. Expressing it another way, of all girls who were ever engaged and ever had premarital coital experience, 75 percent had their first experience while dating, 6 percent while going steady and 19 percent during engagement. For all coeds with premarital coital experience at each stage, 60 percent had coitus while dating, going steady, and engagement.

These data suggest important changes in the premarital coital experience of coeds. No longer is the girl so apt to have her degree of sexual intimacy influenced by the level of the dating relationship. There is also some evidence that girls having premarital coitus are having this experience with more different individuals. For example, of all those girls who had premarital coitus while in a dating relationship, 56 percent had more than one partner—in fact, 22 percent had coitus in a dating relationship with five or more partners.

SUMMARY

If one were to construct a continuum of sexual experience and attitudes by which coeds in various colleges and universities in the United States might be measured, it seems that the sample studied would fall somewhere in the middle. In fact, there is some reason to argue that the sample may be somewhat conservative in that most of the coeds lived at home and a disproportionate number of them were Jewish. Yet, in dealing with the same general population over a ten year period the factor of change can be noted. The most important finding of this study appears to be that the commitment of engagement has become a less important condition for many coeds engaging in premarital coitus as well as whether or not they will have guilt feelings about that experience. If these findings are reasonably accurate, they could indicate the first significant change in premarital sexual behavior patterns since the 1920s. The findings indicate, furthermore, a widening slit between the conventional morality of the adult world and the real behavior common to many groups of young people. However, it should be kept in mind that this study was with small samples at one university and must be seen only as an indication of sexual behavior change and not as an argument that a national change has occurred. Further research with larger and better samples is needed before any broad generalizations may be made.

REFERENCES

Bell, Robert R. (1966) *Premarital Sex in a Changing Society*. Englewood Cliffs: Prentice-Hall, Inc.

Bell, Robert R. and Leonard Blumberg (1959) "Courtship intimacy and religious background," *Marriage and Family Living* XXXI (4) (November) : 356–360.

———— (1960) "Courtship stages and intimacy attitudes," *The Family Life Coordinator*, VIII (3) (March) : 61–63.

9 *Jessie Bernard*

The Fourth Revolution

THE NATURE OF CONSENSUS AND SOCIAL ISSUES

The consent given to any specific status quo—the consensus on which it rests—may vary all the way from enthusiastic acceptance to reluctant and grudging tolerance, accompanied even perhaps by nonconformity to it. People sometimes give their implicit consent to a norm but do not feel they must conform to it. During prohibition, many people voted dry but drank wet. People may even give more than grudging consent to norms they violate. They may be active and enthusiastic supporters of norms to which they do not personally conform. Consensus, that is, does not necessarily imply conformity. Institutional nonconformity to community norms is a common sociological phenomenon (1, Chapter 27).

But when a number of people withdraw their consent—the number is indeterminate, depending on their interest, drive, and insistence—issues arise. Even before issues can be raised, a de-tabooing process must take place with respect to the norms which are to be challenged. For the basic tenets of any status quo—especially those embedded in the mores—tend to have powerful, often mystical, sanctions; they are sacred; not discussable.[1]

Issues are alternative ways for dealing with specific problems. Social issues arise when an old consensus has broken down or when a new one

Jessie Bernard, "The Fourth Revolution." *The Journal of Social Issues,* Vol. 22, No. 2 (April 1966), pp. 76–87. Reprinted by permission.

There are sexual revolutions in process all over the world. The discussion here refers primarily to the West and especially to the United States. This revolution may be viewed as fourth not only in time but also as fourth in the so-called triple revolution of automation, population, and race. Or fourth in the series of revolutions noted by Ira Reiss: urban-industrial, romantic-love, and feminist (15, p. 218).

is in process of emerging. There are questions of policy—legislative or attitudinal—on which people have differing positions, none of which is consented to by all. The great fundamental social issues in the area of sex today have to do with the normative control of nonprocreative heterosexuality. Not that nonprocreative sexuality is a new phenomenon, for it is older than man himself, as we shall presently note. But because now it is possible "for the first time [in our history] to separate our reproductivity and our sexuality" (3, p. 501), that is, procreative and nonprocreative heterosexuality.

FOUR FUNDAMENTAL CHANGES IN SEXUALITY[2]

Once bisexual reproduction had evolved, the first great "sexual revolution" or evolutionary change may be said to have come when sex relations became social as well as merely biological in nature. The pollenization of plants was bisexual, but it was not social. The fish who deposited her eggs to be fertilized by a male was not in a social relationship with him. One might cavil about calling the sex life of insects social; but the relations between the sexes among many birds and mammals is undeniably social.[3]

A second major change in the relations between the sexes occurred when mating was no longer restricted to the female estrus. This was the first adumbration of the separation of reproduction and heterosexuality, or between procreative and nonprocreative heterosexuality.[4] Among animals which have a clear-cut mating season, the female's body shows readable signs of her condition when ovulation has taken place, and she either sends out unequivocal signals to the male that she is receptive or takes the initiative in seeking him out, presumably to ensure fertilization of the ready ovum. Ovulation, "the female sex act," is the important thing; the female is in control of sex relations. Coupling does not occur out of season.

Among the primates, however, where there is no such clear-cut mating season—unless one wishes to interpret the annual spring swarming of college youth on Florida or Bermuda beaches as symptomatic of a vestigial "mating season"—the relationships between the sexes become vastly complicated. Ovulation is no longer determinative of sex relations.[5] The female is no longer in control. The male may aggress or the female present herself to him even when she is not in estrus, when procreation is not likely. Reproduction is not, of course, divorced from heterosexuality; but heterosexuality is divorced from reproduction. The female monkey, for example, sometimes uses her sexuality in ways that have been whimsically labelled a form of prostitution; that is, she diverts a male with food by presenting herself to him and thus is able to appropriate the food for herself.

The third great revolution came with culture, which placed both pro-creative and nonprocreative sexuality under normative controls. These cultural constraints were by no means standardized throughout the world or over time; but, in some form or other, they were universal.

The fourth or current sexual revolution has to do with the confluence of two cultural subrevolutions, one normative and one technological. The normative deals with the resexualization of the female body; the technological, with the increasing feasibility of conception control, which further separates procreative and nonprocreative heterosexuality. Both revolutions began some time ago. The resexualization of the female body began at the turn of the century; it was furthered by a series of so-called marriage manuals in which sexual satisfaction for women was emphasized and the responsibility for producing it made a male concern. The technology of conception control has a long history. What is revolutionary about it in recent years is that it has now become feasible on a mass scale.

Either of the two revolutions alone would have had great impact on the relations of the sexes; in combination the impact was exponentially increased. That is, if the female body had been resexualized at a time when contraception was still uncertain or if feasible contraception on a mass scale had come in Victorian times, the impact of either would have been moderated. Occurring as they did together, they produced revolutionary changes, not so much with respect to procreative as with respect to non-procreative sexuality.

PROCREATIVE SEXUALITY[6]

It is not possible to make clear-cut distinctions between procreative and nonprocreative heterosexuality. The definition of procreative sexuality would certainly include all sex relations deliberately planned to produce conception and almost certainly all marital sex relations in which, whether conception was actively desired or not, no preventive measures were taken.

So far as procreative sexuality is concerned, the human female simply "deposits" her egg, as does the fish, and waits for the male to fertilize it. This is her contribution to reproduction; this is "the sex act" so far as she is concerned with it. The ejaculation of the sperm into the vagina is the male contribution; it is "the sex act" so far as he is concerned with reproduction. These *are* the processes of sexual reproduction; these *are* the sex acts involved in it. Once they have taken place, sex has no more to do with the matter.

Extrusion of the ovum has so little sensation, let alone pleasure, asso-ciated with it that most women never even know when it occurs.[7] Much self-research, in fact, is required to determine precisely when it does. The "male sex act," by way of contrast, is associated with great orgasmic pleasure. Orgasm can occur without ejaculation, even in infancy (18, p. 177), but not ejaculation without orgasm (18, 159). But in mature males they probably occur together most of the time. At least often enough that they become psychologically identified with one another (17). "The sex act," therefore, as a strictly reproductive process, has quite different meaning in the two sexes.[8]

Although "the sex act" in females—extrusion of the ovum—is never pleasurable, it is possible, but by no means necessary so far as reproduction is concerned, for "the male sex act" to be pleasurable to women as well as to men. The range of female reaction to "the male sex act" is wide, from painful suffering at one end, through complete indifference,[9] to orgasmic ecstasy at the other. The pleasure may be purely psychosocial, the female experiencing great pleasure as the source of the male's pleasure. At the other extreme, the physiological experience is identical to his. In any case, her suffering, pleasure, or boredom with "the male sex act" has nothing to do with conception, hence with procreation.

Female orgasm, or even pleasure, so far as reproduction is concerned, is extremely expendable. Cultures can "turn it off or on" without affecting their reproductive histories in the least. And, indeed, this is exactly what has been done in the West.

FEMALE SEXUALITY

Procreative sexuality demands nothing of women except ovulation; they can conceive in their sleep. If heterosexual relations—procreative or non-procreative—are to be pleasurable to women, the pleasure must be derived from "the male sex act." Here the impact of cultural constraints has been determinative. They have enormously influenced the responsiveness of the female body to "the male sex act."

Much of the normative structure for the control—often suppression—of sex has had to do with the behavior of women who were, in effect, assigned the task of supporting the existing norms. This was feasible because of the greater sexual plasticity of women. For one difference between the sexes, not often commented upon in the literature of sex differences, is the relatively greater cultural susceptibility of the female than of the male body to sexual constraints. This susceptibility is well documented in the history of the relations between the sexes in Western society (10). There have, for example, been centuries when the female body was not expected to be sexually responsive to the male sex act. In Victorian times women bragged of their frigidity; they were processed for it from childhood. Contrariwise, there have been centuries when female enjoyment of the male sex act has been permitted, if not necessarily actually cultivated; the female body was even viewed as especially lustful.[10]

The current sexual renaissance reflects an era which encourages—compels or coerces, some might say—women to equal if not outdo men in the enjoyment of the male sex act.

NORMATIVE CONTROL OF PROCREATIVE SEXUALITY

With the alleged exception of the Trobriand Islanders, who chose to ignore the relationship between sexual intercourse and conception, there has until recently tended to be practically universal acceptance of reproductive sexuality.[11] When large numbers of births were needed to replenish precarious populations, in the absence of specific knowledge of the processes of ovulation, reproductive sex played a large part in the normative thinking of the relations between the sexes. Because we relied so heavily on parents, or at least families to take care of children, we did what we could, with varying degrees of success, to restrict even reproductive sex relations to men and women who promised to cleave to one another till death did them part and who would be responsible for the care of all the children resulting from their union. Before or without such commitment, whether it occurred at the betrothal, as in Scandinavia, or at the marriage, sex relations were forbidden.

Since it was clear, even with the limited knowledge available, that the prevention of out-of-wedlock sex relations would absolutely prevent out-of-wedlock children, powerful sanctions were evolved to prevent such relations.[12] Especially for women there was almost no sin more heinous than non-marital sex relations.

In general, the normative structure with respect to procreative sex outside of marriage remains intact. Since we still rely heavily on parents for the rearing and socialization of children, we will probably continue to frown on out-of-wedlock births, however much we may attempt to mitigate the penalties of their status. But the issue will not necessarily be, as hitherto, the sex relations which produced the children; it may well be the irresponsibility of the partners in not preventing the conception. We will blame them for carelessness or irresponsibility rather than, as in the past, for sinfulness. There will, that is, continue to be consensus with respect to the wrongness of out-of-wedlock births, but the moral basis for the consensus will be disapproval of carelessness and irresponsibility rather than of extra-marital sex relations per se. In this respect, there is no revolution in progress or in sight. Some women may demand the right to have children without marriage; but no large movement in this direction is apparent.

If there is a revolution in the area of norms dealing with procreative sexuality, it will probably have to do with the limitation of family size. If concern about the population explosion grows, there may emerge norms which frown upon even marital procreative sexuality. The suburban matron who produces her sixth child for the community to find recreational and educational facilities for may provoke negative sanctions from her neighbors struggling under the weight of taxes for schools and other community facilities for children.

NONPROCREATIVE SEXUALITY

It was early recognized that there was more to sexuality than reproduction, that sexuality had many forms and widespread societal ramifications, that it served psychological and social functions quite unrelated to reproduction. Even the Catholic Church, which struggled with the problem of normative control of nonprocreative sexuality for centuries, insisting that sex relations were justified only for procreative purposes, finally, by permitting the rhythm method of contraception, conceded that sex relations between spouses may have other than only procreative functions within marriage.

If heterosexuality were only for reproduction, it would have the same place in our lives as in the lives of animals with a mating season. There would be incentive to engage in sexual activities only when the female was physiologically ready to conceive and offspring were wanted, or at least welcome. That situation does not even obtain among primates, certainly not among human beings.

But it is by no means easy to specify exactly the nature, let alone the function, of nonprocreative sexuality.[13] It is certainly not simple, unidimensional, or standardized. It is not even easy to define nonprocreative sexuality. Reproductive sexuality is, of necessity and even by definition, genital. The sperm must be deposited in the vagina. But nonprocreative sexuality, though it includes genital sex at one extreme, includes vastly more. Clearly self or mutual masturbation, homosexuality, bestialism, fellatio, cunnilingus, biting, petting, kissing, fetishism are sexual but not procreational. How about the pleasure derived from the sight of a beautiful nude body, in the flesh or in marble? Or the reactions to other kinds of stimuli which Kinsey reported? He defined them as sexual; they are not procreational. The pleasure congenial men and women derive from talking to one another—is this sexual? (The original definition of the term "to converse" included "to have sexual intercourse.")

Where, in brief, does one draw the line between the sexual and the non-sexual? Where does one leave off and the other begin? The indecisive discussions of Freud's all-encompassing definition of sexuality or libido show how difficult it is to define nonprocreative sexuality. No wonder Mary Calderone states that "society has not yet developed an open and honest answer to the questions 'What is sexuality for?'" and how "'can it be managed so as to be a constructive and creative force instead of a destructive and distortive one?'" (3, p. 502). One has only to ask what would a society be like if all forms of sexuality were forbidden (except heterosexual relations for the conception of children) to begin to sense the widely ramifying functions of nonprocreative sexuality and the confusing problems of normative control which it raises.

SOME CURRENT ISSUES

A variety of current issues exists in the area of sex per se (as distinguished from such *family*-related matters as divorce, abortion, illegitimacy, prostitution, and the like). What, for example, should be our attitudes, or what should be the law, with respect to homosexuality, sexual deviancy, perversions, pornography, obscenity?[14] At least with respect to homosexuality, a consensus appears to be in process of emerging, even among those who consider it wrong, which accepts private homosexual behavior between two consenting adults while at the same time restricting public demonstrations and protecting young men and boys from seduction. There appears to be a growing consensus that any manifestation of sex between adults which is acceptable and pleasurable to them in the privacy of their bedroom should be permitted without guilt or opprobrium. The courts seem to move in the direction of legitimizing fewer and fewer limitations on the written word (14).

A few years ago, there was an issue with respect to making contraceptive information freely available to married women at public expense; today that is no longer an issue. Many communities have incorporated the policy of using public funds for this purpose. It was recently an issue whether or not to supply such information to unmarried women; Brown University (19) and the University of New Hampshire (20) seem to have settled that one: college women may have such information at the discretion of the college physician. The issue will probably now take the form of whether to supply such information at the high school level and, if so, under what circumstances.

With respect to extra-marital relationships of married women, no revolution as yet appears to have occurred nor an issue to have been raised. There are reports from time to time of "wife-swapping clubs" or of "key clubs" and there is reported to be widespread tolerance of affairs for married women (2). But there does not appear to be any movement to establish normative sanctions for, or even reluctant consent to, such standards; and in the case of Negro women, there are still strong normative sanctions against them on the part, at least, of the white population.

The sex relations of mature unmarried women, especially if they are discreet, appear to be accepted in large cities although not, as yet, elsewhere. The private, personal life of mature adults appears less and less to be a matter of public concern.

Beginning in the 1920s, the premarital sex relations of young women was a major social issue. Since most young women are married by their early twenties, the issue had to do essentially with teenagers. The consensus which broke down and hence gave rise to issues was that premarital sex relations were always and unequivocally wrong under any circumstances. Ira Reiss has traced in detail the dissolution of that consensus and the issues which resulted. He has reported four major standards—abstinence, double standard, permissiveness without affection, and permissiveness with affection—which have successively replaced it (15).

At the other end of the age continuum has been an issue dealing with elderly widowed women who remarry. When it was discovered that some elderly recipients of social security benefits were "living in sin" rather than marrying and thus losing their benefits, provision was made to protect their social security payments even if they remarried.[15]

WHO'S IN CHARGE HERE?
THE ISSUE OF FEMALE AUTONOMY

When sex was purely reproductive in nature, ovulation was the central fact. Coupling occurred only when the female was in estrus. She might even make the sexual advances. In any case it was she who determined the relations between the sexes. In animals without a mating season, ovulation ceases to be the determinant in the coupling behavior of the sexes (5). It becomes incidental. More to the point, coupling ceased to be controlled by the female. She lost her sexual autonomy. She became subjectable to male aggression, even exploitation.

One of the tenets of the fourth revolution is sexual equality for women. It posits, implicitly if not always explicitly, identical sexuality in men and in women. The ideal would be one which eliminated the so-called double standard: "no more sexual exploitation."

The old exploitative pattern—requiring women to "submit" to their husbands—has certainly all but disappeared. Men today are not likely to take advantage of a resisting young woman (4, p. 89). But this does not mean that exploitation does not still exist. It may take the form of a subtler kind of coercion than a physical kind.

Girls and young women, for example, sometimes complain that if they do not acquiesce in men's urgings they are bludgeoned with the epithet "frigid" (8, 9). When the norms forbade all extramarital sex relations, a girl or woman could easily refuse male requests. When the norms are permissive, she has nothing to hide behind. If she does not wish to engage in sex relations—and most teenage girls probably do not[16]—she is left in an exploitable position. If in the past she had to say no to safeguard her self-respect, she must now say yes for the same reason—to avoid the dreaded epithet "frigid."

The old norms gave men the prerogative of initiating sex relations. This privilege, too, was part of the double standard which the fourth revolution opposes. The rationale for this aspect of the double standard, as Reiss has pointed out (15), has been, in part, that female sex drive and desire in the West was less powerful in women, so they had less need than men actively to seek genital sex relations. It may well be argued, however, that the double standard was a protection for men. It does appear to be true that women can tolerate abstinence better than men. But their orgasmic capacities—because of briefer refractory periods—are greater than men's. It is possible for them to make greater demands on men than men can fulfill. True, a woman cannot aggress against a man sexually; she must incite or excite or stimulate him so that he can "aggress" against her. If she fails, both lose. The reverse is not true. He can "aggress" against her in her sleep.

NO FINAL ANSWERS

The widespread possibility of nonprocreational heterosexuality by no means solves the problem of the relations of the sexes. It is certainly true, as Reiss says, that "for the first time in many millennia, Western society is evolving sexual standards which will tend to make men and women better able to understand and live with each other" (15, p. 264). But there is no final, absolute, and all-purpose pattern for the relations of the sexes equally well suited for all groups, all times, and all places, no solution to the problem of the "best" relations between them. There must, perhaps, always be the seeds of potential hostility between them, intrinsic to the relationship. We tend to hate those we are dependent on; for they have power over us; they can exploit our weaknesses. And no matter what we may say or do, the sexes are dependent on one another; they need one another. But they are different. Some normative patterns of relationships between the sexes favor men, some favor women. A pattern, for example, which puts the initiative in the hands of men means that women will sometimes be approached when they are not ready; a pattern which puts the initiative in the hands of women means that there will be times when men are denied or times when demands are made on them which they are not ready to meet. (Of the two, perhaps the first is the less costly to both sexes.)

It might be argued that different answers are required at different times. It might be argued, for example, that the Victorian consensus was a suitable one for an age that required a vast investment of human energy in the creation of capital. It gave men the prerogative of determining when and how often they would have sex relations; it put them in a dominant sexual position; it freed them from having to concern themselves about pleasing women. They could concentrate on the "really important" masculine things like work, making money, building factories, expanding markets, creating empires, and the like. It was, it could be argued, a good thing that women did not make sex demands on men, that sexuality in women was even viewed with horror. Their demands for attention, payable in sex, may well have been dysfunctional; it was a protection for men to have the sexuality of women soft-pedaled.

The Victorian sexual ethos, however, does not suit the twentieth century. A sex ethos for the twentieth century has to take the resexualization of women into account. It has to be one which reconciles the demands made on men by their work and the demands made on them by women. It has to be one also which reconciles the differences between the sexes in their respective life calendars. It has to be one, finally, which takes into account the separation of heterosexual relations and reproduction. If the achievement of nonprocreative sexuality has solved some issues, it has raised many more. Nor can we anticipate what they will be. For as yet we really do not know what the sexual renaissance ushered in by the fourth revolution implies for the future relations between the sexes.

ENDNOTES

1. The almost compulsive use of forbidden words and the elaborate preoccupation with coitus in modern writing, usually protected by court decisions, suggests that the de-tabooing process has not yet run its course. It is part of a vast effort to remove any vestige of taboo from the subject of sex. The professor of creative writing in a woman's college once threatened to go on strike if he received one more story recounting how the heroine lost her virginity. The difficulty many people still have talking about sex illustrates how powerful the taboo

has been. Some wonder how much longer the arts will have to concern themselves with the details of sex. When will writers once more take it for granted that the reader can supply the details of sexual intercourse, for example, without having them spelled out for him? When will it no longer be necessary to shout the forbidden words? Some people even question the value of entirely removing the taboo—and along with it the mystery from sex.

2. The first two changes here delineated should, strictly speaking, be viewed as evolutionary stages rather than as revolutions.

3. For an evocative and anthropomorphic exposition of this point see (5). The point is also made clear in the work of Harlow, who has shown so unequivocally that young monkeys have to be socialized into adequate adult sexuality; without such socialization they are sexually defective as adults (7).

4. Frank H. Hankins is credited with the quip that sex was now recreative as well as procreative. The quip is amusing, but the term recreative is not apt. It is too trivial, too superficial in its implications to characterize the phenomena of nonprocreative sexuality in all their variety and complexity. Nonprocreative sexuality may, indeed, be simply recreative—"fun and games"—but it may also be far more.

5. Actually, among human beings there may even be a reverse rather than a direct relationship between sexual desire and ovulation.

6. Procreative sexuality is the only kind usually recognized in so-called sex education courses among school children. Until recently it has been the only kind even medical students were exposed to. The fact that there was so much more to sex than procreation has made such limitations very clear. Lester A. Kirkendall (13) has been especially active in helping educators re-think the problem.

7. William James was once quoted as commenting on the tremendous pleasure a certain insect must experience when she came upon the leaf in a thousand that could stimulate her to release her eggs. This is a purely masculine point of view, seeing the depositing of eggs as analogous to the ejaculation of sperm.

8. It is interesting to speculate on what the reproductive history of mankind would have been if sperm-ejaculation were as lacking in pleasure as ovum extrusion. William Graham Sumner was once quoted as asking who would subject himself to the indignities of parenthood if the sex act were not pleasurable.

9. "From the most ancient to the most modern erotic art, the female has been portrayed on occasion as reading a book, eating, or engaging in other activities while she is in coitus; but no artist seems to have portrayed males engaged in such extraneous activities while in coitus" (12, p. 669).

10. Without historical research it is not possible to demonstrate the point, but a superficial glance suggests that the periods in which

women were most revered and honored were periods in which their bodies were desexualized and that the periods in which they were least revered were those in which they were lusty and sexually eager. The knight and his lady had a desexualized relationship, or rather a non-genital relationship, and the Victorian lady was in the same kind of relationship, on a pedestal. Conversely, the literary genre known as Satires against Women showed a low opinion of them as highly sexed creatures. Chaucer's *Wife of Bath* is a case in point.

11. Sometimes the acceptance was grudging, as with Paul, who accepted it only as better than burning. Some off-beat sects, such as the Oneida Community, which practiced Karezza, also rejected procreative sexuality.

12. The emphasis here on the prevention of out-of-wedlock sex relations to prevent out-of-wedlock birth does not mean that other factors were not also involved. The old consensus was also supported by those who invoked the Freudian hypothesis that civilization is, in effect, purchased at the price of sex (6). Bridges, sky-scrapers, atom bombs, and computers are purchased at the expense of libidinous energy. In simple and hence distorted form, if we want libido to be channeled into creative effort, we cannot channel it into sexual expression. The success of married students tended to discount this rationale among college students. The prevention of the spread of venereal diseases was also a rationale for the interdicting of non-marital sex relations. This argument was considerably attenuated with the discovery of antibiotic cures for syphilis. In 1965, it was predicted that syphilis would be eradicated by 1975 (21).

13. Orgasmic pleasure, to be sure, is one obvious end of nonprocreative sex. But if this were the only goal, the solution of the relations between the sexes would be vastly simplified; not simple, but less baffling than now. But more is usually demanded of nonprocreative sex. Says one male college student, "I think that it is the spiritual aspect of sex that makes it fun. Just plain 'raw' sex—I don't know how many people would be satisfied with that" (4, p. 89). Even after a couple has achieved the summum bonum of complete and synchronized orgasm, they still want more, they can still feel lonely if that is all they have.

14. Masturbation ceased to be an issue almost a generation ago; a new consensus which is permissive rather than punitive has emerged. A rear-guard action remains, but it is not salient. Bestialism is not an issue either; it is still consensually forbidden.

15. "If you could have qualified for benefits as a widow and remarried after reaching age 60, you will be eligible for whichever benefit is larger: either one-half the retirement benefit of your former husband, or a wife's benefit based on the earnings of your present husband" (17, p. 13).

16. Most young women in their teens, although suffused with sexuality,

are not driven by strong genital urges. If they had their way, most would not feel compelled to seek genital sex relations. Since most are married by their early twenties, premarital virginity is no hardship for them. They want caresses, tenderness, sexual appreciation; they want the interested attention of men; the relations they want are playful, meaningful, but biologically superficial. Advice-to-girls columns in newspapers, women columnists, etiquette books, teenage magazines all are approached by girls who want to know how to say no without alienating the boys.

REFERENCES

1. Bernard, Jessie. *American Community Behavior*, revised edition. New York: Holt, Rinehart, and Winston, 1962. Chapter 27.

2. Buck, Pearl. "The Sexual Revolution." *Ladies Home Journal*, 1964, September, 43–45, 102.

3. Calderone, Mary. "Sex and Social Responsibility." *Journal Home Economics*, 1965, 47, 499–505.

4. Calderwood, Deryck. "The Next Generation." *Humanist*, 1965, 25, Special Issue, 88–92.

5. Carrighar, Sally. *Wild Heritage*. Boston: Houghton Mifflin, 1965.

6. Freud, Sigmund. *Civilization and Its Discontents*. New York: Anchor, Doubleday, 1958.

7. Harlow, H. F. and Harlow, M. K. "Social Deprivation in Monkeys." *Scientific American*, 1962, 207, 34, 136–146.

8. Haworth, Mary. "She'd Rather Be Chaste Than Chased." *Washington Post*, August 12, 1965.

9. Hoffman, Betty Hannah. "How America Lives: Coeds in Rebellion." *Ladies Home Journal*, 1965, October, 82–84, 167–170.

10. Hunt, Morton M. *The Natural History of Love*. New York: Knopf, 1959.

11. Kinsey, Alfred C., Pomeroy, Wardell B., and Martin, Clyde E. *Sexual Behavior in the Human Male*. Phila.: Saunders, 1948.

12. Kinsey, Alfred C., Pomeroy, Wardell B., Martin, Clyde E., and Gebhard, Paul H. *Sexual Behavior in the Human Female*. Phila.: Saunders, 1953.

13. Kirkendall, Lester A. *Sex Education*. Discussion Guide No. 1, SIECUS, October, 1965.

14. Kling, S. G. *Sexual Behavior and the Law*. New York: Bernard Geis Associates, 1965.

15. Reiss, Ira L. *Premarital Sexual Standards in America.* New York: Free Press, 1960.

16. Schelling, T. C. *The Strategy of Conflict.* Cambridge: Harvard University Press, 1960.

17. Social Security Administration. *Social Security Amendments, 1965, A Brief Explanation.* Washington, D. C.: USDHEW, 1965.

18. Shuttleworth, Frank D. "A Biosocial and Developmental Theory of Male and Female Sexuality." *Marriage and Family Living,* 1959, 21, 163–170.

19. *Washington Post,* September 29, 1965.

20. *Washington Post,* October 13, 1965.

21. *Washington Post,* October 25, 1965.

10   *Dana L. Farnsworth*

Sexual Morality and the Dilemma of the Colleges

During the last few years much interest has been focused on sexual practices in the colleges, an interest stimulated in part by the demands of students for greater freedom in this area together with confusion on the part of parents and college officials as to what should be the proper standards of behavior. It is quite difficult for parents and children to talk together frankly about sexual matters because of the great gulf in experience between the two generations. The background of our present college generation is very different from that of their parents. Social change was quite rapid during the time the parents of today were maturing but is even more so at present.

Communication between older and younger members of the college communities also is hampered by many influences, including lack of a consensus as to what the central issues are, criticism of those who become interested in the subject and lack of persons competent to hold discussion groups.

The sexual behavior of college students may be changing in the direction of practices formerly attributed to members of lower socio-economic groups.[1] Reliable data on which to base such an opinion is not yet conclusive, but all general observations suggest this to be true. Not only is there thought to be a qualitative change in sexual practices but also an acceleration in such behavior. What was thought to be characteristic behavior at eighteen or twenty years of age may now be observed in persons sixteen to eighteen or even younger.

Dana L. Farnsworth, "Sexual Morality and the Dilemma of the Colleges." *American Journal of Orthopsychiatry*, Vol. 35, No. 4 (July 1965), pp. 676–681. Copyright ©, the American Orthopsychiatric Association, Inc. Reproduced by permission.

Presented at the 1965 annual meeting of the American Orthopsychiatric Association, New York, New York.

There appear to be three general points of view regarding sexual behavior which can be characterized as: (1) the traditional morality, (2) the new morality and (3) amorality. In the first of these, the traditional morality, the following principles are considered important:

Renunciation or control of instinctual gratification permits a reasonable degree of civilization (Freud).

Restraint tends to aid in developing a capacity for thoughtfulness concerning the welfare of others, particularly in a parental sense. Restraint also is thought to aid in the sublimation of sexual energies.

Marriage becomes one of life's most cherished institutions when sexual restraint is practiced.

The total moral fiber of a society is strengthened if sexual standards are maintained and weakened when sexual standards are ignored.

Young people need help in controlling their strong impulses during their formative years.

In the new morality:

Fidelity and consideration of others occupy a very high place.

Physical sex is supposed to occur only after the establishment of friendship and love.

Exploitation of the sexual partner is very much opposed.

A high ethical component is apparent in the thinking of those who adhere to this general view even though it may not be in accordance with views traditionally held, nor with the views of many religious groups.

In the third general viewpoint, which is in effect a somewhat amoral one, the central belief is that no restrictions are needed. If sexual impulses are allowed free rein, tension, anxiety and frustration will be lowered, and happiness, satisfaction in living and effectiveness increased. The main problem for those who hold this point of view is that of persuading other persons to accept this way of behaving.

Obviously, no one of these three viewpoints can be portrayed explicitly without some qualification. Any individual may move from one viewpoint to another, or he may adhere to one and act as if he upheld another. It is this discrepancy between outer appearance and private behavior that is confusing to many persons, young and old alike.

In the past, sexual behavior has been regulated in varying degrees by religious teachings and customs based on them and by fear of disaster if something goes wrong, such as detection, disease or pregnancy. These deterrents to free sexual behavior have become somewhat weakened, especially during the last few decades for reasons familiar to everyone. At the same time there does not appear to have been any major moral breakdown. This suggests that the present generation of young people is fully as moral as any in the past although for different reasons.

College officials are very much concerned about certain key issues with respect to sexual behavior. For example, pressures toward experience which the young person does not wish and for which he is not yet ready may be unduly effective. A certain "bandwagon" effect occurs when peer group pressures push young people into such behavior. Frequently these pressures become so strong that a young person subject to them may feel guilty for *not* indulging in behavior currently popular, just as he may feel guilty *for* doing so if his training has been conventional or idealistic.

Illegitimate pregnancies pose problems which are virtually insoluble in terms of the social, cultural and legal framework within which colleges must operate. It is probable that those persons who become pregnant are more disturbed emotionally than those who manage their lives without this complication. A recent study at a British university confirmed this thesis clearly.[2] The loss of any student because of the failure to manage sexual life successfully is always keenly felt by college officials as well as by the student's family.

Parental attitudes in general are not consistent enough for any guidelines or policy. Although opinions regarding sexual behavior are usually very firmly held, they are sometimes favorable and at other times unfavorable toward free sexual expression. Furthermore, when college administrators are called upon to take definite action in a given situation, there is a considerable tendency to blame such officials for their attempts at restoring order rather than looking at the original source of difficulty.

Freedom of choice is desired for all students, but when peer group pressures and the bandwagon effect become too strong, the individual may be deprived of this freedom.

I believe it is correct to assert that most college administrators do not wish to have a series of complicated and specific rules regarding behavior in this area; they realize that attempts at enforcement create many new problems. They do not wish to develop a spy system since the main purpose of the college experience is to enable students to develop the ability to make their own decisions—hopefully wise decisions. Most administrators are averse to impose on others their personal views, varying as these do from person to person, institution to institution and section to section in the country. Administrators also cannot and do not wish to ignore public sentiment in the communities surrounding the colleges.

The excessive emphasis on all aspects of sex and obscenity which is now prevalent in novels, plays and the mass media of communication may enable parents, teachers and others to become more honest about sexual education than has been possible up to now.

At the present time it seems to me that the following problems that are well nigh insoluble prevent the promotion of a satisfactory kind of sexual education. Religious views vary among sects as well as in different parts of the country. Contraception is not completely reliable no matter what assurances some people may give. For college students this reliability may be impaired by conscious maneuvering on the part of one partner to produce pregnancy. The strong views of parents either in the direction of freedom of sexual behavior or of control are not expressed in such a way as to be of much help. Those who have a vested interest in pornography are very ingenious in developing excellent arguments to prevent interference in their moneymaking activities. College administrators value freedom and dislike censorship. Drawing the line between these attitudes and the desire to be helpful in guiding the development of young people into channels which will not be destructive to their future is a very delicate matter. There is no consensus as to appropriate means of furthering sex education not only at the college level but at all stages of development. Variations in attitudes toward sexual education in different sections of the country make it almost impossible for any widespread program to be adopted. Not the least of the difficulties is that anyone working seriously for improved sexual adaptation almost invariably becomes the object of ridicule from his associates and others in the community.

Once a program is agreed upon, the question then arises as to who will carry it out. Should it be done by parents, physicians, members of the clergy, marital counselors, faculty members or some other group? If persons in any of these groups are willing to undertake this task, then how shall they be trained? How is it possible to separate the giving of factual information from moralizing?

College officials may be reticent about imposing their views on others, but they do wish to make it crystal clear that they uphold high standards of personal behavior just as they uphold intellectual integrity. They want to encourage as much thoughtfulness in this area of behavior as in any other. They wish to develop the kind of behavior which will not bring unnecessary unhappiness or disaster to young people as they fashion a way of life which will strengthen rather than weaken family life.

In my opinion, no particular viewpoint can be forced on young people, but there should be full and frank discussion in families, in groups, between couples and between older and younger colleagues in the colleges. If students are given answers without any real awareness of the issues, they will not be helped very much. If, however, a program is developed which will enable them to get a keen awareness of the issues that are involved, I believe that they will come up with better answers than our generation has been able to evolve.

After all, the problem is of more significance to young people than to those of the older generation. It is up to them to determine what kind of a world they want their children to live in. As they discuss sexual issues, it is desirable that they recall the nature of the training they experienced and the embarrassing situations they encountered in their childhood and to relate these experiences to their present problems. Finally, they should project their thoughts into the future in terms of developing attitudes toward sex which will be helpful as they begin to raise their own children. This three-dimensional approach to the problem helps bring some objectivity in place of the rather intense urgency with which most young adolescents and early adults view such problems.

Unfortunately, those who guide the policies of institutions get little help from parents, as I have already stated, because of the confusion and variety of their views, but I fear that they get even less help from the faculty. There is a tendency to leave all such matters to the dean's office and to give inadequate support to the idea that integrity confined to intellectual matters is quite insufficient and should be extended to all facets of behavior.

Even though the colleges are not *in loco parentis* to their students in the literal sense, they do have a responsibility to encourage them to adopt reasonable standards of behavior. There is no compelling reason for college administrators to be intimidated by the accusation that they are "upholding middle-class morals." The standards of morality and how they are determined and transmitted from one generation to another are proper and necessary subjects for continuing discussion between students and faculty members.

For parents, religious leaders, college officials and all others who have a responsibility for late adolescents and young adults in secondary schools and colleges, some standards or ideals of behavior are desirable. Let us first examine the principle, "All premarital sexual intercourse is undesirable." Deviations from that code of behavior have every imaginable variety, ranging from rape or the production of a child with illegitimate parents (at the most regrettable end of the spectrum of undesirable activities) to intercourse between engaged couples who expect to marry soon and who can marry at once if pregnancy occurs (at the least undesirable end). In each instance of departure from the ideal the individual knows of its undesirability and is aware of possible consequences. If unpleasant developments follow, he is in a position to learn from his experience; there is no one on whom he can reasonably project blame.

Let us assume another principle: "Premarital sexual relations are undesirable for those who are immature or cannot undertake the responsibility for a possible child, but for those who are mature and responsible, they are enriching and ennobling." Immediately a couple considering such relations must classify themselves, just at the time when it is only logical that they should be optimistic. It is easy to guess what the decision will be. If tragedy ensues, as it occasionally does, who can wonder that they are confused about society's inconsistent attitudes toward them.

Until we resolve our own confusions, we will not be in a favorable position to help our younger colleagues thread their way through the devious paths of development to sexual maturity. The experiences in our college psychiatric and counseling services lead us to believe that those who ignore the conventional standards are no more happy or effective than those who observe them. In fact, I believe that they have more depression, anxiety, agitation and other inhibiting emotional conflict than those who manage to adhere to their ideals.

A large proportion of the younger students who come from families with reasonable ideals feel more comfortable if limits are set, if some guidelines are evident, and if someone is present who cares enough about them to help them avoid disaster.

As college officials, we are more concerned with the quality of future marriages and the family life they make possible than with any particular physical act in which either partner may have been involved. Of course, this does not imply that the nature and extent of sexual activities before marriage is irrelevant to the success of that marriage.

If we are to progress in making sense out of this important area of personal development, we will need the sympathetic understanding and support of parents, faculty members and the students themselves. There should then follow innumerable personal discussions, seminars and other procedures for transmitting accurate information. At the same time the complex issues associated with choice of behavior should be explored. Opinions concerning sexual behavior should be expressed, but not put forth as scientific facts.

Sexual education and the formation of standards of sexual morality are not separable from other aspects of personal maturation, nor should they be unduly circumscribed as they are pursued in the colleges. The goal should be that of aiding each student develop a healthy personality in which sexuality plays a constructive and satisfying part rather than being considered undignified and regrettable.

ENDNOTES

1. Kinsey, A. C., W. B. Pomeroy, C. E. Martin and P. H. Gebhard. 1953. *Sexual Behavior in the Human Female*, W. B. Saunders Co., Philadelphia. pp. 293–296.
2. Kidd, C. B., R. Giel and J. B. Brown. 1964. *The Antecedent Mental Health of Pregnant Unmarried Women*. Proceedings of the British Student Health Association, Oxford, For Private Circulation. pp. 51–59.

11 *Phillips Cutright*

Historical and Contemporary Trends in Illegitimacy[1]

A review of historical trends in illegitimacy rates in European populations after 1750 finds a period of rising rates to around 1870 followed by one of declining rates to about 1940. The early rise in illegitimacy appears to have been related to increasing sexual activity, while the decline is ascribed to increasing use of birth control. Changes in illegitimacy rates since World War II are closely related to changing patterns of marital fertility control and timing of legitimate childbearing. Although illegitimacy may have a heavy impact on welfare programs, neither the AFDC program in the United States nor family allowance programs in other nations increase or decrease illegitimacy. The probability that an unmarried pregnant woman will marry prior to delivery is related to the level of out-of-wedlock pregnancies in various populations. The chances for legitimation are high when pregnancies are few. We reject the view that differences in social stigma explain the chances for legitimation. Changes in illegitimacy rates in the United States since 1940 were examined. The bulk of the increase in nonwhite rates is related to improved health conditions that have reduced involuntary fetal loss and have increased fecundity. The increase in sexual activity among unmarried women after 1940 appears to be quite small, particularly among teenage girls not about to marry. Many unwed mothers eventually marry, and their chances (some 20 years after the illegitimate birth) of heading a family without a husband seem little different from those of other ever-married women. However, the hardship of illegitimacy on the child and mother during early years and the social costs involved are sufficient to justify development of programs to reduce illegitimacy. The potential of various programs is considered.

Phillips Cutright, "Historical and Contemporary Trends in Illegitimacy," from *Archives of Sexual Behavior*, Vol. 2, No. 2, (1972) pp. 97–117. Reprinted with permission of the author and Plenum Publishing Corporation.

INTRODUCTION

This paper reviews trends in Western nations since 1750 and discusses some implications of these trends for various theories of illegitimacy. It then summarizes a study of trends in the United States from 1920 to 1968 and discusses the changes in the immediate causes of an illegitimacy rate that may account for the increase in illegitimacy in the United States. From this study is estimated the magnitude of the "sexual revolution" among unmarried women. Also measured is the likely impact of having a first illegitimate rather than a first legitimate birth on the status of unwed mothers some 20 years after the birth. The study concludes with an assessment of alternative means through which deliberate changes in social programs might cause a decline in illegitimacy.

TRENDS IN EUROPE: 1750 TO 1965

Trends in illegitimacy in European nations allow one to divide the years since 1750 into three periods. The first period extends from around 1750 to about 1870, the second from around 1880 to 1940, and the third includes the post World War II years.

The first explosion of illegitimacy in Western nations occurred after 1750. All across Europe, the rates drove upward, peaking between 1860 and 1880 in most nations (Shorter, 1971). Recent work (Shorter, 1972) attributes this long-run rise to social, demographic, and economic changes that resulted in the diffusion of modern ideas of self-expression and individualism to the lower classes, who, for the first time, had moved from a life situation that repressed nonmarital intercourse (and perhaps premarital sex with the future husband) to a situation in which family and community authorities were no longer able to exercise control. Thus rising sexual activity among couples who would not marry brought with it increasing illegitimacy rates.

After about 1880, illegitimacy rates all across Europe receded (Cutright, 1971a; Shorter et al., 1971). In nation after nation, the rates began a decline that continued through the 1930s. Was this period of declining illegitimacy rates accompanied by other changes that might support traditional explanations of illegitimacy? By "traditional explanations" I refer to common concepts of the deterrent effect of religious sanctions for transgression and the repressing effects of economic sanctions. A traditional theory popular with some social scientists is based on views of social disorganization—and the ill effects of urban life. According to this theory, urbanization, industrialization, wars, depressions, and other periods of social strife will "naturally" be accompanied by rising illegitimacy. These traditional views can be tested against the actual trends after 1880.

If there is a single sentence that can sum up the condition of most European nations from 1880 to 1945, it might be this: a period characterized by devastating and prolonged warfare, massive and repeated economic depression, unprecedented increases in urbanization and industrialization, and a massive secularization of populations which can be measured by the shift away from traditional church authority in matters of marriage, divorce, and birth control. All populations in Europe were affected, in varying degrees, by these enormous changes, which should, according to traditional views, increase illegitimacy. Yet, in all populations, illegitimacy rates began a decline that continued from one decade to the next. Secularization, urbanization, industrialization, and social disorders did not increase or even hold steady the high illegitimacy rates of the 1880s. What explains the decline of illegitimacy after 1880?

The decline in illegitimacy was accompanied by a common change in nearly all European nations—the decline of marital fertility rates. Declining marital fertility was not caused by a decline in coital activity; rather, the decline was due to increasing use of abortion and contraception —primarily *coitus interruptus* and condom. Increasing use of birth control by the married population during this period created a set of conditions that allowed birth control among the unmarried sexually active population to increase as well. It seems likely that illegitimacy declined in most nations because birth control increased. In some nations, a decline in common-law marriages whose issue were defined as illegitimate may also account for some part of the declining rate for older women. The decline in the rate was less pronounced among teenage girls, a fact that may be accounted for by a dramatic rise in fecundity among the young after 1880 (Tanner, 1968) as well as to improvements in other health conditions that decrease sterility and spontaneous fetal loss (Cutright, 1972a). Improvements in health conditions must have moderated the decline in illegitimacy after 1880, but no measures of this effect are available.

The third era in the history of illegitimacy began around 1940. Illegitimacy rates in Europe remained low during World War II; after the war, some nations experienced stable, others declining, and still others rising rates. We can statistically account for most of these different postwar patterns by examining differences among nations in the control of marital fertility and changes in the age at marriage and legitimate childbearing (Cutright, 1971a). We included in our analysis of change in post World War II rates the United States, Canada, Australia, and New Zealand, as well as Japan and 18 European nations that lack legal abortion-on-demand. The results of this study clearly show that illegitimacy rates will tend to rise when marital fertility rates indicate weak efforts to control legitimate childbearing; also, illegitimacy rates will tend to rise when the age at marriage is going down and when, therefore, the age at legitimate child-bearing is declining. The postwar rise in illegitimacy in the United States is not at all unusual. Other populations with similar behaviors (e.g., Canada, England and Wales, Scotland, New Zealand, and Australia) also experienced a similar rise in illegitimacy.

Nations with an early age at marriage (such as the United States) tend to have higher illegitimacy rates among young girls than do nations that have maintained a late age at marriage. Why should young girls have lower illegitimacy rates in nations in which young girls are not likely to marry? Consider the difference between Swiss and American girls. In Switzerland, women traditionally have not married until age 25 or later; younger girls are just that—girls—and may not be judged by most of the popula-tion as old enough to be eligible for sexual intercourse. This is not the case in the United States, where many girls marry and start legitimate childbearing by age 18. Legitimate childbearing at an early age may thus weaken normative controls over nonmarital sex at an early age, producing the observed higher levels of illegitimacy among young girls in populations where many young women marry.

If it were the case that early-age-at-marriage populations had weak control over fertility, while late-age-at-marriage nations had strong fertility control, one might argue that the observed difference in illegitimacy rates between the two types of populations was a function of higher use of effective birth control in the late-age-at-marriage nations. However, this is not true. Western nations with an early age at marriage moved from a late- to an early-age-at-marriage pattern because they were the first to practice effective control over family size. Nations that have maintained the late-age-at-marriage pattern tend to have weaker control over fertility. These populations tend to rely on delayed marriage rather than birth control to control completed family size.

Awareness of these historical trends and the changes that appear to explain them do not support traditional explanations of illegitimacy that rely totally on secularization or social disorganization views. Nor do the fluctuations over time give support to some psychological explanations of illegitimacy that view unwed mothers as typically "disturbed," "neurotic," "psychotic," or "acting out" various needs (Pauker, 1969). Also, analysis of illegitimacy rates among women with the same years of birth (Cutright, 1972b) indicates that the same cohort that had a very high illegitimacy rate at one age may have a low rate in later years; also, the same birth cohort of unmarried women may have a very low illegitimacy rate in their early years of childbearing but then have a high rate in the later years of childbearing. These findings, when considered along with the cyclical nature of illegitimacy rates, indicate that excessive reliance on psychological characteristics of unwed mothers to explain varying illegitimacy rates is no more useful than would be an effort to explain variation in unemployment rates with psychological variables.

ECONOMIC INCENTIVES AND ILLEGITIMACY

The revival of interest in economic sanctions as a means to control illegitimacy in the United States is, I believe, due to the expansion of the Aid to Families of Dependent Children (AFDC) program. In the "good old days," indigent unwed mothers and their children were—along with many indigent married mothers and their legitimate children—denied access to AFDC. This condition has changed, with the result that in spite of the enormous reduction of poverty in the United States after World War II, we find ourselves with rising welfare rolls. For illegitimate children, by way of example, I have calculated that in 1961 only 54% of white and 33% of nonwhite illegitimates were on AFDC; by 1969, these percentages had climbed to 87% of whites and 60% of nonwhites. Seventy-four percent of the rise in the number of illegitimates on AFDC between 1961 and 1969 was caused by increasing access or utilization of AFDC in the late 1960s. In 1969, about one in three AFDC children was illegitimate, and in 1971 the AFDC benefits to these children and their mothers ran about 2 billion dollars—or one third of AFDC expenditures (Cutright, 1972b).

Illegitimacy is one major cause of AFDC expenditures, but is AFDC a cause of illegitimacy? The answer to this question is no (Cutright, 1970). We have tested this view by comparing changes in illegitimacy rates and changes in benefits for whites and nonwhites since 1940. State illegitimacy rates change about equally, regardless of whether benefit levels increase, decrease, or remain stable. A second analysis relating the level of benefits and utilization of the program by poor women to the level of illegitimacy in 26 states for 1960 revealed that white and nonwhite illegitimate rates were lower in states paying higher benefits than in states paying low benefits (Cutright, 1972b).

A recent article (Cutright, 1971b) reviewed 1940 to 1965 trends in family or child allowance benefits and illegitimacy rates within a number of nations. The typical pattern within the same nation was stable or rising illegitimacy accompanied by a declining child benefit (caused by inflation). Comparisons of benefit levels and illegitimacy rates across nations in the same year found no association. As with AFDC, the child allowance type of income maintenance program is not a cause of illegitimacy.

Since neither family allowances nor AFDC benefits stimulate illegitimacy, the view that declining economic sanctions against the unwed mother and her child explain increases in illegitimacy can be rejected. The most plausible explanation of the lack of association between illegitimacy and economic "rewards" for children is that, unlike most legitimate children, illegitimate children are neither planned nor wanted (Cutright, 1971a). Unlike the legitimate child, the illegitimate child is the unintended result óf coital activity among persons whose characteristics limit effective use of contraception and abortion. These characteristics are discussed in a later section. The irrational nature of illegitimate childbearing is completely unlike the supposed rational childbearing behavior on which economic models of fertility are based (Robinson, 1971). Thus these economic models may account for high or low fertility in a population of married couples with perfect control over fertility (Bumpass and Westoff, 1970), but they are not useful in understanding illegitimate fertility.

STIGMA

The concept of social stigma as a control over illegitimacy first appeared in Europe and then made its way across the Atlantic. "Stigma" refers to norms concerning illegitimacy rather than to norms about nonmarital sex. Stigma is supposed to affect illegitimacy, not by deterring coitus, but by affecting the probability of marriage after an illicit pregnancy has occurred. Low-stigma populations do not hasten to the altar and legitimate the pregnancy before birth. In theory, they get married later. Therefore, illegitimacy rates of low-stigma populations are "high." High-stigma populations have many "forced" marriages, while low-stigma populations tend to marry after the illegitimate birth.

In low-stigma Sweden and Denmark, where this explanation of illegitimacy is popular, the higher risk of death to the illegitimate compared to the legitimate child is similar to the higher risk of death to illegitimate than to legitimate children in nations alleged to have high stigma. This should not be the case if it were true that the illegitimate child in Sweden or Denmark were really just a case of delayed marriage— if that were true, they should be protected by the kin group and have life chances equal to those of legitimate children. The higher risk of an illegitimate than legitimate death has been constant for 100 years in Sweden.

In the United States, comparison of whites and nonwhites reveals no evidence to support the theory so often used to explain white and nonwhite differences. In theory, low-stigma nonwhites are more likely to have illegitimate children than whites because the norm about legitimacy is weak, informal social sanctions on the nonwhite unwed mother are weak, and nonwhite women believe illegitimacy will not affect their chances for a normal family life. Therefore, marriage is more likely to occur for the nonwhite than the white unwed mother after the premaritally conceived birth. In fact, nonwhite unwed mothers appear no more or less likely than white unwed mothers to marry the alleged father after the birth (Bowerman et al., 1966; Sauber and Rubinstein, 1965). The effect of alleged low stigma on just delaying the marriage does not exist.

STIGMA AND THE TIMING OF "FORCED MARRIAGES"

Populations differ in the time between illicit conception and the date of marriage—among those women who marry in time to legitimate the pregnancy. Christensen (1960) notes that in low-stigma Denmark the modal legitimated child was conceived 5 months before the marriage, while in high-stigma Indiana pregnancy occurred just 1 to 3 months prior to marriage. A recent study of legitimated first births in Massachusetts (Whelan, 1972) compares the timing of pregnancy and marriage among whites and nonwhites. About 42% of white but only 17% of nonwhite legitimated first births resulted from pregnancies occurring within 84 days of marriage. Such data provide no proof that whites are more likely than nonwhites to be "forced" to marry, since the observed difference in the timing of pregnancy and marriage may simply be due to differences in the timing of premarital intercourse. Unmarried whites may be more likely than nonwhites to wait for a commitment to marry before becoming sexually active with the groom-to-be. If true, their out-of-wedlock conceptions will occur closer to the date of marriage than will be the case among nonwhites. In any case, the population of pregnant brides is only one segment of the sexually active unmarried population, and differences in characteristics of pregnant brides may be of little value in understanding the role of stigma in illegitimacy.

In the Bowerman study, a number of questions were asked which may give additional support to the view that social stigma has little to do with controlling illegitimacy. For example, about 30% of white and 10% of the nonwhite unwed mothers were pregnant by a man who could not possibly marry them—the man was already married (Bowerman et al., 1966). Further, only 14% of the white mothers said that both she and the alleged father were legally able to marry and actually "wanted" to get married at the time of the pregnancy; for nonwhites, the comparable figure is only 21% (Bowerman et al., 1966). (Some 18 months had gone by from birth to interview, and these women still were not married.) One concludes that these unwed mothers became unwed mothers, in large part, because they were copulating and became pregnant by a man they did not intend or want to marry and/or who they know neither wanted, intended, or was legally eligible to marry them. They copulated in spite of the knowledge that the pregnancy would not be legitimated.

Bowerman reports little difference between white and nonwhite unwed mothers on other measures that might relate to stigma—no difference in feeling of displeasure at the discovery that they were pregnant, no difference in change of residence due to social pressures relating to the illegitimate birth, no difference before and after the birth in residing with parents, no difference in aid by the kin group to the unwed mothers, no difference in their judgment that the illegitimate birth would not help their chances for later marriage, no difference in the perceived reaction of their girl friends, and no difference in offers of kin to adopt or care for the child.

If there is less difference than one might expect among white and non-white unwed mothers, this does not allow a conclusion that the respective populations of unmarried women have similar views about illegitimacy. All that appears clear at this point is that alleged differences in illegitimacy between these two populations are not related to stigma—at least as this hypothetical construct makes itself manifest in color differences in delayed marriage. Still, perhaps stigma is an important factor because it affects the probability that a pregnant unmarried woman will marry before the child is born.

STIGMA AS A CAUSE OF LEGITIMATION OF OUT-OF-WEDLOCK CONCEPTIONS

There is a large difference between white and nonwhite chances of marriage prior to the birth of a child conceived out of wedlock. For example, national data for 1964 to 1966 show that about 61% of all white but only 24% of all nonwhite out-of-wedlock conceptions carried to term were legitimated by marriage before birth (Cutright, 1972b). Is this difference evidence of higher stigma in the white than the nonwhite population? Is the white chance for legitimation high because social pressures force whites to marry and thus avoid the illegitimate birth?

By examining the chances for legitimation according to the characteristics of the pregnant unmarried woman, we can test this view. For example, the probability that an out-of-wedlock conception ending in a live birth will be legitimated is about the same for whites and nonwhites in the higher birth orders for women 20 and older. That is, a white with one or more children already born trying (presumably) to get married and legitimate her out-of-wedlock pregnancy has no better chances than does the similar nonwhite woman. The stigma theory thus fails to help a sizable portion of pregnant unmarried whites. Among girls under 20, marriage rates are higher for nonwhites than whites—so we cannot evoke a low nonwhite marriage rate to explain higher teenage illegitimacy among nonwhites. Rather, a nonwhite teenager is actually more likely than the white teenager to have a legitimated birth.

If it were true that the higher chances that a teenage white pregnancy will be legitimated by marriage were due to social pressures, we would expect that the economic status of teenage whites pregnant at marriage would be lower than the economic status of teenage white brides who were not "forced" to the altar. This expectation rests on the very great differences in out-of-wedlock pregnancy rates between low-income and nonpoor whites (Cutright, 1972b). Our research, however, found no income differences between the pregnant bride and the teenage bride who becomes pregnant shortly after her marriage. This lack of economic status differences between alleged forced and unforced marriages allows one to further question the view that the higher chance for legitimation among white than nonwhite teenagers is due to the greater likelihood of forced marriages in the white than the nonwhite population.

Finally, even if the white chances for legitimation were equal to those of nonwhites (24%), the white illegitimacy rate for 1964 to 1966 would have increased from the observed 11.3 to only 21.6. These figures may be compared to the nonwhite rate of 88.2 and thus allow one to conclude that although color differences in the chances of legitimation are large, they do not do a great deal to explain color differences in illegitimacy rates.

What does explain differences in the chances for legitimation between whites and nonwhites? First, we noted earlier that these differences are quite small for ever-pregnant women 20 and older, and are small for women 25 and older regardless of previous fertility. Since many more nonwhites than whites are in the higher birth orders, this is one factor to consider.

Secondly, within the same population over time, and among different populations measured at the same period, our cross national comparisons have found that the chances for legitimation are a function of the level and change in the level of the out-of-wedlock conceived birth rate (OW CBR) (Cutright, 1971a). Populations with high out-of-wedlock conceived birth rates will have low legitimation chances, while populations with lower levels of out-of-wedlock pregnancies will have higher chances for legitimation. For unmarried women 15 to 44, the out-of-wedlock conceived birth rate in 1964 to 1966 was 28 and 116 per 1000 for whites and nonwhites. When compared with other populations with different levels of OWCBR, the lower level of nonwhite than white chances for legitimation in the United States is to be expected.

The question, then, is not why the probability of legitimation is high or low—rather, the question is why the out-of-wedlock conceived birth rate is high or low—for it is the out-of-wedlock conceived birth rate that will determine not only the chances for legitimation but the illegitimacy rate as well. It has this effect because the OWCBR will be high when many unmarried women are copulating with men they will not or cannot marry; the OWCBR will be low when only couples planning marriage are sexually active—and these sexually active unmarried women will get married whether they become pregnant or not.

Since this review indicates that illegitimacy rates are not substantially affected by factors alleged to "force" couples to marry, and other evidence failed to support stigma explanations of illegitimacy, it may be time to discard the stigma theory.[2] In the meantime, it is possible to move from a theoretical debate to an examination of the immediate causes of fertility in order to understand how illegitimacy rates change. The following example is taken from an analysis of changes in U.S. illegitimacy rates over recent decades.

FACTORS THAT EXPLAIN CHANGES IN U.S. ILLEGITIMACY RATES

I have recomputed U.S. illegitimacy rates to take into account under-enumeration of unmarried women by Census and underregistration of births. Census undercount tends to inflate illegitimacy rates, especially among nonwhites, while underregistration of births in earlier years tended to deflate the count of illegitimate births and hence deflated the rate. With these corrected rates, we can look at trends since 1920 (Cutright, 1972*b*).

Between 1920 and 1940, the rate declined slightly among whites. Among nonwhites, it declined between 1920 and 1930 and then increased. By 1940, it was above the 1930 level, but still below the rate for 1920. After 1940, illegitimacy rates in both populations increased through 1965. Between 1965 and 1968, (the last year for which information is available) teenage illegitimacy continued to increase among whites and nonwhites; among whites 20 and older, the rates stabilized; among nonwhites 20 and older, the rates in the various age groups declined by 23 to 42% between 1965 and 1968! Now, what explains these trends?

Since I have eliminated chances for legitimation as an immediate cause of the illegitimacy rate, we have only the following factors to consider:

1. Changes in nonmarital sexual activity.
2. Changes in involuntary controls over conception—fecundity and sterility.

3. Changes in involuntary controls over gestation—spontaneous abortion.
4. Changes in voluntary control over conception by the sexually active—contraception.
5. Changes in voluntary control over gestation by the pregnant—induced abortion.

Comparison of 1930 and 1960 studies of contraceptive use by unwed mothers indicates that, if anything, some kind of effort to contracept was more likely in 1960 than in 1940 (Cutright, 1972b). This is certainly the case among nonwhites, since virtually any level of use in 1960 will be higher than it was in 1940, because effective contraception was not used by the nonwhite population in earlier years (Farley, 1970). Among whites, it is unlikely that the rise of illegitimacy was due to a decline in contraceptive use. When used, contraception to protect illicit coitus is wholly a male affair—the male will or will not use condom, or he will or will not withdraw (Bowerman et al., 1966). We have no reason to believe that white male use changed between 1940 and 1960, since the level of condom use by white married couples did not change in the white population over those years. Female methods only increased after the Pill—and this change may soon cause problems if young males begin to think that responsibility for contraception is wholly a female responsibility. In any case, one cannot say that illegitimacy increased between 1940 and 1968 because contraception declined.

I have estimated trends in induced abortion from trends in abortion death ratios—the ratio of maternal deaths from abortion to maternal death from nonabortion causes. Both the white and the nonwhite abortion death ratio declined from high levels in 1940 to low points in 1950, remained low during the early 1950s, and then started to rise again. These inferred trends in induced abortion follow the trends in white and nonwhite fertility, as well as other reports on induced abortion trends during the 1950s and 1960s (Cutright, 1972b).

By 1964, the abortion death ratios were about equal to the 1940 ratios. Thus a pregnancy was about as likely to be aborted in 1964 as in 1940. If so, the 1964 illegitimacy rate was not higher than the 1940 rate because abortion use had declined.

Although frequently ignored, involuntary controls over conception and gestation are crucial determinants of fertility rates for some populations during some periods of time. Such is the case for the nonwhite population from sometime before 1920 to around 1960. To a lesser extent, this is also true for whites.

Public health programs relating to the control of venereal and other diseases and to maternal and child health were fragmentary and ineffective prior to World War II. No mass treatment for venereal disease was available, and little effort to apply knowledge that existed was made for the poor population. Virtually the entire nonwhite population in those years was poor.

When we look at registered late fetal deaths among unmarried mothers over time (McCarthy, 1966), we can take this information, combine it with recent studies of spontaneous fetal loss at all gestations (Cutright, 1972b), and emerge with adjusted trends in spontaneous fetal loss for unmarried whites and nonwhites. We then add to this change the decline in sterility—the percent of ever-married women who remained childless after years of exposure during marriage. A final adjustment for increasing fecundity at very early years due to declining age at menarche allows us to compute the effect of changing health conditions on illegitimacy rates after 1940 (Cutright, 1972a). The technique simply is to ask what would the 1940 illegitimacy rate have been had women in 1940 been as healthy as women were in, say, 1960? When this is done, we find that 75% of the change in nonwhite illegitimacy to women 15 to 44 and 31% of the change in the white 15 to 44 rate are due to improved health conditions. That is, higher levels of fecundity and lower levels of sterility and spontaneous fetal loss (with the last factor being the most important) may explain 75% of the rise in nonwhite and 31% of the increase in white illegitimacy from 1940 to 1960. One effect of the public health program and improved diet was to increase the illegitimacy rate among women 15 to 44.

Given these levels of explained change in the rates with involuntary controls over gestation and conception, and the likelihood that changes in contraception and induced abortion can be ruled out, we can now ask how much sexual activity among unmarried women increased from, say, 1940 through 1968. The following analysis focuses on teenage girls because comment on "the sexual revolution" and the "problem of teenage pregnancy" is focused on this age group.

A TEENAGE SEXUAL REVOLUTION?

To estimate the change in sexual activity among unmarried girls after 1940, it is important to distinguish two types of young unmarried girls whose behavior may have changed. The first type is those girls who are involved with a male who will become their husband. These girls, if they have premarital sex, may become pregnant brides. The second group is those girls involved with a male who will not become their husband; these girls, if they have nonmarital sex, may become unwed mothers.

Using live birth data for unwed mothers and pregnant brides, we can estimate changes in sexual activity among each of these two types of unmarried women. The major assumption underlying this method is that voluntary controls over conception and gestation have changed very little over the time period. If, as we believe, this is true, then any difference in out-of-wedlock conceived births not explained by changes in health conditions must be due to increasing premarital or nonmarital sexual activity.

When the impact of improved health conditions is taken into account, the 1940 to 1968 change in the teenage nonwhite illegitimacy rate is 3.7 births per 1000; among whites, the comparable figure is 4.8 births per 1000. Thus, among those unmarried teenage girls who do not become brides, about 0.5% were more likely to give birth to an illegitimate child in 1968 as compared to 1940 because of increasing coital activity. To this initial estimate of rising sexual activity we must add a multiplier to account for the happy fact that some sexually active girls do not become pregnant. Elsewhere (Cutright, 1972b), we have estimated that between one in three to one in five girls sexually active at some time during a year will become pregnant and deliver an illegitimate child. Thus an estimate of rising sexual activity might conclude that between 2 and 3% more girls 15 to 19 who will not marry the sexual partner were sexually active in 1968 as compared to 1940. This indicates that the image of an abstinent past and a promiscuous present is exaggerated.

However, when we turn to changes in sexual activity among unmarried girls who will become brides (whether pregnant or not), we find much greater changes. Using Census reports (Gabrill and Davidson, 1969), we find that 26% of young (under 22 at age of marriage) white brides were pregnant in the 1960 to 1964 period compared to only 11% in the 1940 to 1944 period. Of this net gain of 15%, 11.5 cannot be explained by improved health among teenage whites. From a recent study of white Pennsylvania brides married in 1967 (Broderick, 1971), we find that perhaps one in every two sexually active teenage brides was pregnant at marriage. Therefore, we would multiply 11.5 times 2 and thus estimate a rise of 23% in premarital sex among young white brides. Among young nonwhites, bridal pregnancy increased by some 7%, but nearly 90% of change in teenage nonwhite fertility rates between 1940 and 1968 (compared to "only" 23% for whites) can be allocated to improved health (Cutright, 1972a). Therefore, little change in premarital sex among nonwhite teenage brides is possible.

With the exception of teenage white girls involved in a relationship that will end in marriage, our method of detecting changes in sexual behavior indicated only small changes among other types of young unmarried teenagers. We also note that during periods of stable bridal pregnancy (1920 to 1939) illegitimacy rates also were stable or changed only slightly. Periods of rising bridal pregnancy appear to be accompanied by rising illegitimacy in the United States. As premarital sex among couples committed to marriage increases, so does nonmarital sex among couples not planning marriage.

Finally, small increases in sexual activity among those not committed to marry can be seen to have "large" effects on illegitimacy rates. For example, among whites whose sexual activity results in illegitimate births, the 15 to 19 illegitimacy increased from 4 to 10 per 1000 between 1940 and 1968. About 5 points of this 6-point gain are independent of changes we would expect due to improved health. Some writers in looking at this change will note that the rates have doubled—which is true. But this doubling of the rate affected only about 0.5% of white teenagers and was apparently caused by a change in sexual activity among only 2 or 3%.

ECONOMIC CIRCUMSTANCES AND SOME CONSEQUENCES OF ILLEGITIMACY

Unwed mothers are disproportionally recruited from the ranks of the poor. From an investigation of state payments for medical care at delivery in California (Berkov, 1971) and estimates by Campbell (1968), we conclude that about 60% of white and 80% of nonwhite unwed mothers are poor—as defined by the Social Security Administration's low-income or near-poverty line (Orshansky, 1968). Further, there is little difference in poverty status with the age of the mother at delivery. When illegitimacy rates by poverty status are calculated, some interesting facts emerge. For example, among poor whites, the illegitimacy rate at age 15 to 19 for the years 1964 to 1966 was 33—among the nonpoor whites, the rate was less than 4. Among all age groups, the illegitimacy rate of poor whites was 42, and the rate for the nonpoor was 5. Among nonwhites 15 to 19, the illegitimacy rate for the poor was 102; the nonpoor rate was 34. For nonwhites of all ages, the illegitimacy rate for the poor was 129 and the rate for the nonpoor was 39.

Using the nonwhite rates by poverty status, we can estimate the immediate and direct effect of the higher risk of poverty among nonwhite than white women on the difference between white and nonwhite illegitimacy rates. When this is done, we find that about half of the higher nonwhite than white rate is explained by the larger proportion of nonwhites than whites who are poor.

Given the poverty status of unwed mothers, it is obvious that the health care of unwed mothers and their children will be inferior to that obtained by wed mothers. National data indicate that unwed white and nonwhite mothers have less frequent care prior to delivery than do wed mothers whose family income is under $3000 a year (Kovar, 1968). One consequence of this pattern of health care is that the illegitimate child is more likely than the legitimate child to be immature at birth. For this and other reasons, the infant mortality rate among illegitimate white births is 64% higher than it is among white legitimate births (National Center for Health Statistics, 1971). Among nonwhites, the difference is 13%— a finding that says more about the poor health of wed nonwhite mothers than it does about much else.

While these and other dismal short-run circumstances of illegitimacy have filled the pages of many Public Health reports, the long-run consequences of illegitimate childbearing have never been assessed. What effect, we ask, does having an illegitimate (rather than a legitimate) first birth have on the status of the women some 20 years after the birth?

From the national sample of women taken in the 1967 Survey of Economic Opportunity, we have collected information on fertility, marital status, female head status, and poverty status for both white and nonwhite women. All women were mothers, and they were age 59 or less at the time of the survey. About 42% of nonwhites and 50% of whites were aged 40 or older. We have over 6000 nonwhite and 10,000 white mothers. These women were classified according to the timing of their first birth relative to the date of marriage—if any. We have unwed mothers who never married, unwed mothers who married after the birth, pregnant brides, and women who conceived soon or in later intervals after their marriage. This is one way of representing the "fertility history" of a population of mothers. What difference does fertility history make?

First, some 92% of white and 82% of nonwhite unwed mothers had been married at the time of the survey. Since over 90% of both white and nonwhite women marry by age 30 to 34, it appears that nonwhite unwed mothers are somewhat less likely than other nonwhite women to marry. Among whites, there is no large effect on chances for eventual marriage.

Second, the effect of illegitimacy on the woman's risk of becoming a female head of family is moderate. For example, 11% of all white mothers in the sample were female heads—among the ever-married unwed mothers, the figure was just 13%. White pregnant brides were no more or less likely than nonpregnant brides to be a female head. On the other hand, 88% of white unwed mothers who did not marry were heads of a family— but only 8% of the white sample of unwed mothers were in this never-married group.

Among nonwhites, 33% of all mothers were heads of a family— among nonwhite unwed mothers who later married (82% of all unwed mothers), 27% were female heads—a risk which is less than that run by nonwhite mothers of legitimate first births. Among nonwhite unwed mothers who did not marry, 98% were heads of a family. For both whites and nonwhites, the critical step to becoming a female head is whether the unwed mother marries—not whether she does or does not have an illegitimate or legitimate first birth.

Since the status of female head rather than wife is such a critical predictor of a woman's poverty status, it comes as no surprise to find that fertility history is not a powerful or even useful predictor of later poverty status. Again, the important thing is whether the woman marries.

Fertility history is not an important determinant of the number of children ever born. In fact, unwed mothers who have never married, whether white or nonwhite, have lower fertility than ever-married women. Nonwhite unwed mothers who later marry have no more children than do nonwhites whose first child was legitimate.

While it appears true that later marriage by the unwed mother often erases much of the initial disadvantage of her illegitimate first birth, the short-run impact of illegitimacy on the mother and child and on public health and other public services is such that one may ask what social policy might do to reduce illegitimacy through direct public and private efforts. What is the prospect for deliberate change in illegitimacy rates?

DELIBERATE CHANGE IN U.S. ILLEGITIMACY RATES

Whatever one's theory of illegitimacy, the only policies that have program implications for deliberate change are those dealing with birth control. There is nothing government can do about sexual activity, and there is nothing government can or should do about legitimation of out-of-wedlock conceptions by forcing unwilling couples to marry. Of course, an increase in involuntary controls over conception or gestation through a decline in public health services is unthinkable. The only action left that we now seriously consider as possible public programs revolves around the provision of subsidized physician-prescribed contraception for indigent women, to be delivered as part of the so-called family planning program. What is the likely effect of this effort on illicit pregnancies and births?

I have written at length on the problem of increasing use of effective contraception by unmarried women (Cutright, 1971a). At the present time, the subsidized program in the U.S. is solely concerned with providing female contraception to indigent women. Such a program, however much it spreads to counties, cities, and hospitals that presently offer no aid, can have only a limited impact on illegitimacy. The reasons for this dismal assessment follow.

First, some intuitive reasons.

The characteristics of unmarried women who are most likely to become unmarried mothers that depress their potential use of effective physician-controlled female methods of contraception are these:

1. Low frequency of sexual intercourse. Sex is usually irregular and often unpredictable.
2. Youthful age. In 1968, nearly half of all unwed mothers were pregnant at age 18 or less and nearly 25%—one in four—were pregnant at age 16 or less.
3. Low parity. Seventy-three percent of white and 54% of non-white illegitimate births in 1968 were first births—63% of all illegitimate births were first births. None of these births can be prevented by post-partum contraception programs—the programs that most efficiently reach indigent married women.
4. Poverty status. As noted above, about 80% of nonwhite and 60% of white illegitimate births are to poor women. For a variety of reasons, poor people, even when married, are less likely than are the nonpoor to practice effective contraception.

To these four characteristics associated with ineffective contraception we must add a multiplier effect for marital status. That is, each of the above characteristics is less a deterrent to effective contraception for married than for unmarried couples. Perhaps the major reason sexually active women are not protected from the risk of pregnancy is because they are unmarried. Unlike the married woman, the unmarried woman who will become an unwed mother is wholly dependent on the male for protection—she herself does not contracept. (Unfortunately, we have few available means to make the male responsible.) Although the unmarried woman risking illegitimacy does not practice contraception while she is unmarried, she will, after marriage, contracept. Apparently, then, one must be married before female contraception can be defined as proper in the United States—especially among teenage girls.

Adding together sexual inexperience, low birth order, youthful age, irregular coital activity, poverty, and the status of being unmarried rather than married, one has a package of the "hard to reach" that is hard to beat. Still, intuition is often refuted by experience, and I now turn to evaluation of the actual impact of subsidized contraception programs on illegitimacy.

A recent study of trends in illegitimate births in various counties within the states of Georgia and Tennessee—some with large contraception programs and some with no programs at all—discovered no difference in illegitimate birth trends between counties with and counties without programs (Cutright, 1972b).

There are two reasons the programs do not work. First, many potential unwed mothers are excluded and, among those not excluded, many women are not in the program. But perhaps as important are the contraceptive failure rates to patients who are in the program. A recent study of three public and private programs, for example, reported that 27% of young Pill patients in these programs were pregnant within a year's time—in the same programs, 13% of young IUD patients were pregnant within 12 months (Tietze and Lewit, 1971). Still, that is a high IUD failure rate when contrasted with the much lower rates for older women. If we take an annual contraception failure rate to unmarried patients of only 10%, we can get a mathematical answer to this question: "What is the maximum effect a contraception program can have on reducing illicit pregnancies that end in live births?"

The size of this effect is dependent only on two factors—first, the percent of the sexually active population that is in the contraception program and, second, their failure rate before and after they become patients.

For the sexually active unmarried low-income population (the population that is the target group of subsidized programs), I estimate a contraceptive failure rate of 30% per year. This estimate, in turn, relies on estimates of the 1964 to 1966 pregnancy rates to unmarried low-income whites and nonwhites. These rates are about 145 per 1000 for whites and 208 per 1000 for nonwhites and include brides as well as unwed mothers. Applying a contraceptive failure rate that appears reasonable to these pregnancy rates gives us the number of 30 per 100 (Cutright, 1972b). These failure and pregnancy rates also suggest that about 48% and 69% of unmarried poverty-level whites and nonwhites aged 15 to 44 have intercourse at least once during that year. The mean number of coital acts is probably around 16—a number that may be compared to 80 (Westoff and Westoff, 1971) among married couples.

If the failure rate is 30 before the population enters a contraception program, the patient failure rate must be less than 30 if the program is to have any effect. The patient failure rate of 27% cited above is not much below 30. But assume the program gets the rate down to 10—a rate about equal to IUD failure rates among married couples in the 1960 to 1965 period (Cutright, 1971a). If as many as 40% of sexually active low-income women were in the program, illicit pregnancies would be reduced 27%. I doubt that more than 40% of unmarried women who are sexually active at any time during the year will ever be enrolled in a contraception program. Even if 70% get in the program, less than half of unwanted illicit pregnancies will be avoided—again assuming the low level of patient failure at 10%. Moreover, the 10% failure rate is just for 1 year—it has now been demonstrated that IUD and Pill dropout rates after 1 or 2 years in various public programs or patients under private care are often such that the majority of married women are left without either method after trying them for a while (Potter, 1971; Westoff and Westoff, 1971). If the married do not stay on IUD or Pill year after year, why would we expect the unmarried to do any better? The extended use effectiveness of all present contraceptive methods is exceedingly low— a fact that is recognized by only a few biomedical and demographic researchers.

So what safe and proven method do we have that will reduce illegitimacy or unwanted bridal pregnancy among the poor and the nonpoor, the young and the old, the never-pregnant and the ever-pregnant, the white and the nonwhite, the woman with and the woman without frequent sexual activity? We have very little in the contraception line. However, if the goal is extended to prevention of unwanted births, rather than the more limited task of preventing unwanted pregnancy, we can take a more hopeful view. Let's look at abortion.

WILL ABORTION WORK?

Under legal abortion in New York City, we now have a report (Pakter and Nelson, 1971) from the New York City Department of Health covering the first 9 months of the program. There were 448 legal abortions per 1000 live births to New York City residents in this period. For first births, the abortion ratio was higher—about 590 per 1000 first births; for women under 20, the ratio was 527 per 1000 live births—again higher than the total ratio; for nonwhites, the figure was 595—well above the 422 ratio for whites; in municipal hospitals which serve the poor, the ratio was 775 legal abortions per 1000 live births. These figures for residents of New York City indicate that the poor, the nonwhite, the young, and the never-pregnant are more likely to be aborted than are the other women. The reason for this is quite simple—these are the same women most likely to be pregnant but unmarried, or to be married but pregnant due to contraceptive failure. The very groups least likely to practice effective contraception are those most likely to use legal abortion when it is made available to them.

How much will abortion-on-demand reduce U.S. illegitimacy? The answer still awaits development of the New York program. However, illegitimate births during the third to ninth month following legal abortion ran 3% below the number in the same months of the preceding year. This small percentage decline should be seen in the perspective of an 11% annual rate of increase prior to the introduction of legal abortion. It is noteworthy that the 11% annual increase in the number of illegitimate births in New York City during the 1960s occurred during a period when the percent of the indigent population enrolled in a contraception program increased from about 0 to nearly 50%. Contraception did not work.

The experience of nations that have legalized abortion-on-demand all show that the impact of legal abortion on illegitimacy rates increases with time. After 6 to 8 years with legal abortion, the national illegitimacy rate in nations such as Hungary, Poland, Czechoslovakia, and Japan declined by 30% (Cutright, 1972b; Hartley, 1970). There is no evidence that any contraception program anywhere has ever done as much.

The American public is ready for legal abortion-on-demand. A 1971 poll in Massachusetts (Boston *Globe*, 1971), for example, showed that about 75% of Protestants, Jews, and non church members (55% of the population of the state) favored a change in the state law so that abortion would be a matter solely between the pregnant woman and her physician. Massachusetts Catholics were evenly split. In spite of the fact that Roman Catholics represent 45% of all Massachusetts adults—a figure nearly 20% higher than in the nation as a whole—62% of all adults in Massachusetts favored such a law. It seems safe to conclude that American adults now support laws that would allow abortion-on-demand. If we are to substantially reduce illegitimate births through programs in the near future, this will be done with legal abortion.

While the case for abortion-on-demand as a method of reducing unwanted illegitimate births seems to be rather well documented, and the case for contraception programs is not, I would like to add the following cautions—lest one become too enthusiastic for abortion, at the expense of contraception.

First, some unmarried women will use contraception if it is available, but will not abort if pregnant. Second, there seems little reason why failure rates in contraception programs need be as high as they are. Perhaps less reliance on the Pill and improved patient care will result in more effective programs. Third, improved contraceptive methods are on the way. In particular, new types of IUDs can be used by never-pregnant women. IUDs with much lower expulsion rates and greater effectiveness while in place than the present types should be available soon (Segal and Tietze, 1971). Fourth, the effect of marital status and poverty on effective contraception practice among older women appears to be lessening—witness the declines of 23 to 42% in illegitimacy rates between 1965 and 1968 among older nonwhite women. It would be premature to abandon the effort to increase the use of effective contraception by unmarried women simply because the task is difficult.

CONCLUSION

This review of trends in illegitimacy rates tested various traditional theories of illegitimacy. In general, popular explanations of illegitimacy which claim religious and economic sanctions as important sources of control were not supported by the evidence. Social scientific theories relying on vague notions of social stigma or social disorganization also failed to account for high or low rates in different populations or for changes in the rates over time.

We focused on the immediate causes of illegitimacy (sexual activity, voluntary and involuntary controls over conception and gestation) rather than on those factors more remote in a causal chain of events. It seems clear that an increase in nonmarital sex resulted in increasing illegitimacy rates in most European nations from around 1750 through 1880, but the question of why nonmarital sex increased may still be open to further study. We do not know why married and unmarried couples in Europe began a "demographic transition" from high to low fertility around 1880—we only know that the fertility rates declined because voluntary controls over conception and gestation increased. In the post World War II years, we do not know why marital fertility and the age at legitimate childbearing differed among nations—we only know that these changes in fertility behavior account for most of the national differences in changing post World War II illegitimacy rates.

Our analysis of illegitimacy trends in the United States distinguished between that portion of the increase in illegitimacy rates that could be ascribed to rising sexual activity and that which could be explained in physiological terms. Since unmarried women who are sexually active are divided between those who can and will marry the sexual partner and those who cannot or will not marry the partner, estimates of sexual activity among the "unmarried" should distinguish between these two types of women. When that was done, we found the larger increases in sex among the unmarried to be concentrated among white girls involved with a male who will become their husband. Although the changing level of nonmarital sex among the other types of unmarried girls involves only a small percent of the total population of unmarried women, these changes have effects on illegitimacy rates which tend to be exaggerated and used as evidence of a dramatic increase in nonmarital sex. The available evidence does not support the view that a change of revolutionary magnitude has occurred.

When the results of this research are applied to the problem of devising a program to reduce illegitimacy, we find that answers to traditional questions such as "Who is the unwed mother?" or "Why is she pregnant?" are unnecessary. A continuing effort over several decades to answer the question of what differentiates (in psychological terms) the pregnant from the nonpregnant unmarried woman has yet to deliver an answer (Pauker, 1969). Such questions are not asked of married women having unwanted legitimate children. Instead, the design of realistic programs to reduce unwanted legitimate births is based on improving the methods of controlling conception and gestation and reducing barriers that presently inhibit maximum use of the most effective methods available (Jaffe, 1971). The development of a program to reduce illegitimate births can proceed along similar lines.

ENDNOTES

1. This research was supported by Public Health Service Grant MH 15567 and by the Commission on Population Growth and the American Future. The views expressed here do not reflect those of either sponsor.

2. This paper cannot undertake a review of the role of attitudes in sorting out unmarried women who do or do not have illicit sex. Pauker's review (1969) of related research problems has noted that the lack of prospective research casts serious doubt on the validity of conclusions drawn from studies that compare unwed mothers with girls who are not unwed mothers. By the same token, girls who are sexually active may have different attitudes than inactive girls, but the cause-and-effect relationship between attitude and behavior can move from behavior to attitude as well as from attitude to behavior. Prospective studies of attitudes and behavior are required to settle the point. A permissive attitude need not result in permissive sexual behavior, and sexual behavior need not result in pregnancy or birth. It seems unlikely that changes in age-specific illegitimacy rates over extended periods of time can be explained by changes in norms or attitudes regarding premarital sex. For example, the illegitimacy rate for one age group may be going up while the rate for another age group in the same population is in rapid decline. The analysis (cited above) of change in illegitimacy rates between 1950 and 1960 was able to statistically account for national differences by measuring national differences in marital fertility control and timing. It seems unlikely that norms regarding nonmarital sex affect marital fertility behavior—thus providing a common cause to explain the change in marital and illegitimate fertility rates. Further, we note below a case of a large increase in illegitimacy caused by improved health, rather than by increased sexual activity. Also, the long-run decline in illegitimacy after 1880 appeared not to be caused by an increase in restrictive sexual norms but by an increase in effective birth control practices. Finally, large declines in illegitimacy among nations that have legalized abortion-on-demand (Hartley, 1970; Cutright, 1972b) occurred after World War II without a change in attitudes toward nonmarital sex.

REFERENCES

Berkov, B. (1971). Illegitimate fertility in California's population. Unpublished, pp. 1–15.

Boston *Globe* (1971). Massachusetts polls. March 24, p. 5.

Bowerman, C. E., Irish, D. P., and Pope, H. (1966). Unwed motherhood: Personal and social consequences. Institute for Research on Social Science, University of North Carolina, Chapel Hill (mimeo).

Broderick, C. (1971). Unpublished data tabulated by P. Cutright.

Bumpass, L., and Westoff, F. (1970). The "perfect contraception" population. *Science* 169:1177–1182.

Campbell, A. (1968). The role of family planning in the reduction of poverty. *J. Marriage Family* 30:236–245.

Christensen, H. T. (1960). Cultural relativism and premarital sex norms. *Am. Sociol. Rev.* 25:31–39.

Cutright, P. (1970). AFDC, family allowances and illegitimacy. *Family Planning Perspectives* 2(4):4–9.

Cutright, P. (1971a). Illegitimacy: Myths, causes and cures. *Family Planning Perspectives* 3(1):26–48.

Cutright, P. (1971b). Economic events and illegitimacy. *J. Comp. Family Stud.* 2:33–53.

Cutright, P. (1972a). The teenage sexual revolution and the myth of an abstinent past. *Family Planning Perspectives* 4(1):24–31.

Cutright, P. (1972b). Illegitimacy in the United States: 1920–1968. Final report to the Commission on Population Growth and the American Future. To appear in a volume, background papers printed by the Government Printing Office. (in press).

Farley, R. (1970). *The Growth of the Black Population*, Markham, Chicago.

Gabrill, H., and Davidson, M. (1969). Marriage, fertility and child-spacing: June 1965. U.S. Bureau of the Census, *Current Population Reports*, Series P–20, No. 186, Government Printing Office, Washington, D.C.

Hartley, S. F. (1970). The decline of illegitimacy in Japan. *Social Problems* 18:78–91.

Jaffe, F. (1971). Toward a reduction of unwanted pregnancy: An assessment of current public and private programs. *Science* 174:119–127.

Kovar, G. (1968). Visits for medical and dental care during the year preceding childbirth, United States—1963 births. National Center for Health Statistics, Government Printing Office, Washington, D.C.

McCarthy, A. (1966). Infant, fetal, and maternal mortality, United States—1963. National Center for Health Statistics, Government Printing Office, Washington, D.C.

National Center for Health Statistics (1971). Infant mortality rates by legitimacy status: United States 1964–66. *Monthly Vital Statistics Rep.* 20(5): Suppl., August 2.

12   *Elizabeth M. Smith*

A Follow-up Study of Women Who Request Abortion

*This paper reviews the literature on psychological effects of
induced abortion, and reports on the characteristics of an
unselected sample of 154 women who contacted a problem
pregnancy counseling service, and on the subsequent adjustment
of 80 of the 125 who obtained abortions. Findings are consistent
with recent studies that report few negative reactions related
to abortion.*

It is estimated that over one million abortions are induced annually
in this country and that one out of every five pregnancies is terminated
by abortion.[7] With the recent (January 22, 1973) Supreme Court decision declaring restrictive abortion laws unconstitutional, it is anticipated
that the number of women obtaining abortions will continue to increase.

Although a great deal has been written about abortion, many of the
studies were done in other countries or have reported on women who
obtained therapeutic abortions because of psychiatric illness. There has
been a lack of systematic study of women without psychiatric illness who
obtain abortions, especially in regard to their adjustment afterwards.

In reviewing the professional literature from 1934 to 1965 on psychiatric sequelae of abortion, Simon and Senturia[15] reported that the findings
and conclusions ranged from the suggestion that psychiatric illness almost
always is the outcome of therapeutic abortion to its virtual absence as a
post abortion complication. They found that:

> Deeply held personal convictions frequently seem to outweigh the
> importance of data especially when conclusions are drawn.[15]

In comparing the outcome of therapeutic abortion in the European

Elizabeth M. Smith, "A Follow-up Study of Women Who Request Abortion,"
from *The American Journal of Orthopsychiatry*, Vol. 43, No. 4, July, 1973,
pp. 574–585. Reprinted by permission of the author and the publisher.

studies where data was available, Simon[15] reported the findings ranged from 43% of women with severe guilt after abortion and an additional 12% with psychiatric illness,[8] to 11% with serious self reproach and one percent major psychiatric disability,[4] to complete absence of either phenomenon.[1]

Although there was some agreement in the literature that women with diagnosed psychiatric illness prior to abortion continued to have difficulty afterwards, there was a lack of information regarding the effect of time on such responses. Most studies failed to separate psychiatric sequelae of abortion from pre-existing psychiatric illness and to distinguish between "guilt" and psychiatric illness. As a result, there was a lack of conclusive data about the effects of therapeutic abortion on women.

Recent studies (1966–1972) of therapeutic and legal abortion have been more systematic and have reported a consistently low incidence of psychiatric sequelae.

Peck and Marcus[12] followed up 50 psychiatric and non-psychiatric patients who obtained therapeutic abortions in New York and found only one negative reaction related to the abortion. Guilt and depression occurred in 20% of the women but was mild and self-limiting. The psychiatric status of 92% of the women was improved or unchanged.

Patt et al,[11] reporting on 35 patients who obtained therapeutic abortions in Chicago, found that three-fourths of the patients reported a subjective impression of improved emotional status. Twelve patients experienced guilt feelings, but only two would not repeat the procedure. Two patients who were aborted against their will experienced prolonged adverse effects. The researchers concluded that, with rare exceptions, abortion was genuinely therapeutic.

In a study of 46 women after therapeutic abortion in St. Louis, Simon et al[14] found that 35 had improved psychological functioning or were unchanged. Although six women were hospitalized for psychiatric illness afterwards, only one case was as a result of abortion. Four patients had moderate depressive reactions that did not require hospitalization.

Senay[13] reported only one woman who required hospitalization for depression in his follow-up of 150 women who received therapeutic abortions in Chicago.

Studies of patients who obtained abortions in California after the 1967 revision of the Therapeutic Abortion Act have reported few complications. Margolis et al[9] followed up 43 patients, and found that 39 had a positive reaction to abortion or no significant change. Seventeen reported guilt feelings, but only two would not repeat the procedure. Four women experienced negative reactions.

Ford et al[6] studied 22 California women of lower socioeconomic status, and found that although mild depression was common after abortion, the majority had fewer psychiatric symptoms. Fourteen percent of the women were more disturbed following abortion, but all had a history of serious psychiatric problems prior to the procedure.

In Colorado, Whittington[16] reported on 31 patients who obtained therapeutic abortions after liberalization of the abortion law. Only three percent felt subjectively worse after the procedure.

One of the few reports on women who obtained legal abortions in New York state is the Osofskys'[10] short term follow-up study of 250 women. Eighty-five percent of the women were "very happy" to "neutral" after the procedure. Only eight percent reported strong guilt feelings and four percent were objectively distressed.

Most authors seem to agree that mild and self-limiting guilt and depression are common after abortion but that new or lasting psychiatric illness will not result from abortion. In most cases, abortion is genuinely therapeutic if the woman truly desires the procedure.

Unfortunately, few studies have explored the effects of abortion on other aspects of the woman's life. In order to more fully understand the effects of abortion and the immediate and longer range adjustment patterns, it was decided to ask women who had obtained abortions to evaluate their experience and its effect upon them. Their subjective reactions to abortion, their current functioning, relationships with the sexual partner, contraceptive usage, and subsequent unwanted pregnancies were explored.

Information reported in this paper is based on interviews with women who contacted a problem pregnancy counseling service. These women differ from most populations studied in the past. They are not psychiatrically ill, nor are they seeking abortions on mental health grounds. Also, there is a wider socioeconomic sampling, ranging from lower to upper class. The population of women who sought help for an unwanted pregnancy and those who subsequently obtained abortion will be described. Only the follow-up adjustment of women who obtained abortions will be reported in this paper. The small size of the sample who did not abort makes it difficult to compare them with those who obtained abortions.

DESCRIPTION OF AGENCY

All women in this study contacted the Pregnancy Consultation Service (St. Louis) regarding a problem pregnancy. In the state of Missouri, where restrictive laws prevent women from obtaining legal abortions, a crisis-oriented counseling service was developed to provide information regarding where legal abortions can be obtained at reasonable cost. PCS is a non-profit, state-wide agency, staffed primarily by trained volunteer counselors, and is the only agency in Missouri that provides abortion information.

In addition to information regarding where to obtain abortion and the medical procedure, the service provides emotional support at a time of crisis and assists women in exploring all other options, such as single parenthood and adoption, and the resources available for assisting them in these plans. Contraceptive counseling, pregnancy testing, and referral for additional psychological or other treatment are also provided. No fees are charged for counseling services and no financial assistance is available.

METHOD

All women who contacted the Pregnancy Consultation Service during its first year of operation (September 1969 through August 1970) were interviewed by medical students using a structured questionnaire designed to elicit social and psychiatric information as well as attitudes regarding sex, contraception, pregnancy, and abortion.

All women who had obtained abortions were contacted by telephone or letter at least one year and no more than two years later to obtain permission for follow-up interviews. Those who refused or did not respond to the letter were not contacted again. Follow-up interviews were done in person, by telephone, or by mailed questionnaire, depending on the woman's preference and accessibility. The interviews were done by trained counselors using a semi-structured questionnaire. Information was obtained regarding current functioning, relationship with sexual partner, use of contraceptives, subsequent pregnancies, and her evaluation of the effect of the abortion on her life. In addition, she was asked to comment on the counseling she received from PCS prior to the abortion.

SAMPLE

Information was obtained from a complete and unselected sample of 154 women who were interviewed at the time of their first contact with PCS. Although many of the women were under a great deal of stress at the time, all cooperated in the research interview, which required approximately one and a half to two hours. Of these 154 women, 125 subsequently obtained abortions.

Follow-up interviews were obtained from 80 (approximately two-thirds) of the women who terminated their pregnancies. The follow-up questionnaire was completed either in an interview (12), by telephone (42), or in writing (26).

Three who were contacted by telephone refused to be interviewed and 13 who were contacted by mail did not respond. The remaining 29 could not be contacted because letters sent to them were returned due to incorrect address or lack of a forwarding address.

Although follow-up interviews were not easy to obtain because of the difficulty in locating women after a year or more, most of the women who could be found were cooperative. Although the interviewer was a stranger to the women, they talked freely and seemed eager to discuss their experience.

CHARACTERISTICS OF WOMEN SEEKING ABORTION

In this study a great variety of women sought abortion. With an age range of 28 years, various life styles, backgrounds, and reasons for requesting abortion, it often seemed that the only common denominator was an unwanted pregnancy. Table 1 shows a profile of the women seen in this study.

TABLE 1   Profile of total population requesting abortion (N = 154).

CHARACTERISTICS		CHARACTERISTICS	
AGE		**RELATIONSHIP WITH SEXUAL PARTNER**	
Under 20 years	42%	Married	16%
20–29	50	Engaged	6
30–39	7	Steady Dating	16
40–49	1	Friends	53
		Casual	5
MARITAL STATUS		Rape	1
Single	81	Unknown	3
Married	16		
Divorced or separated	3	**CONTRACEPTION USED**	
		None	54
RACE		Rhythm or withdrawal	16
White	92	Pills, diaphragm, foam or condom	28
Negro	8	Type unknown	2
RELIGION		**PREVIOUS UNWANTED PREGNANCY**	3
Protestant	46	**PRIOR PSYCHIATRIC CONTACT**	19
Catholic	27	**PRIOR PSYCHIATRIC DIAGNOSIS**	17
Jewish	12		
None	13	**REFERRAL SOURCE**	
Other	2	Friends	29
		Physicians	23
OCCUPATION		Social Agencies	20
Student	58	School Counselors	15
Professional	14	Ministers	5
Clerical or Sales	14	News Media	5
Housewife	7	Other	3
Semi-skilled	5	**LENGTH OF PREGNANCY**	
Unemployed	2	6 weeks or less	5
		7–12 weeks	71
		over 12 weeks	23
		unknown	1

The majority were single (81%), white (92%), still attending school (58%), and of Protestant (46%) or Catholic (27%) faith. The age range was from 14 to 42 years, with a mean of 21.4 years. The women were generally referred to PCS by friends (29%) or physicians (23%), and 76% were less than twelve weeks pregnant. Ninety-seven percent had not experienced a previous unwanted pregnancy, and 99% had not had a prior abortion.

Over half of the women described their relationship with the sexual partner as "friendship," however, casual sexual contacts were infrequent (five percent). Few of the unmarried women viewed marriage as a realistic option at the time pregnancy occurred. For single women, the two major reasons for choosing abortion were lack of marriage and desire to continue education. Married women requested abortion primarily because of finances or lack of desire for further children.

Fifty-four percent of the women were not using any form of birth control when pregnancy occurred, and another sixteen percent were using unreliable methods such as rhythm or withdrawal. Three-fourths of the non-contracepting women had never used any form of birth control. The majority of women denied that they had consciously wanted to become pregnant and most said they did not really believe that pregnancy would occur even though they were sexually active.

Reasons for not using contraceptives often seemed to indicate a need to deny that there had been a conscious decision to have intercourse. Comments such as, "I didn't plan to have intercourse," or, "I didn't do it that often" and "I just didn't think about it," seemed to indicate that the use of contraceptives implied premeditated sexual activity, and that this was associated with guilt. Some of the women, primarily those who were married, reported dissatisfaction with oral contraceptives but had postponed obtaining or were unaware of other measures.

Most of the contraceptive failures appeared to be related to lack of knowledge regarding use or to misinformation regarding the reliability of the method. Many of the women who were using rhythm as their only form of birth control were unaware of the time in the menstrual cycle when pregnancy was most likely to occur. Most said they were taught little or no practical sexual knowledge either at home (70%) or in school (74%).

The majority of women had never had contact with a psychiatrist. The incidence of pre-existing psychiatric illness was only seventeen percent. Diagnosis was established using Diagnostic Criteria for Use in Psychiatric Research.[5] The most common diagnosis was depression (seven percent), followed by personality disorders (five percent), undiagnosed psychiatric illness (four percent) and drug abuse (one percent). A psychiatric diagnosis was made only when symptoms predated the onset of pregnancy; thus, women who were experiencing symptoms only related to pregnancy were excluded. None of the women in the sample was considered to have symptoms severe enough to meet criteria for therapeutic abortions.

OUTCOME OF PREGNANCY

As might be expected, most (82%) of the women who contacted PCS requesting abortions subsequently did obtain abortions. (Two percent of the women in this group reported self-induced abortions because of lack of money for the procedure.) Three percent of the women reported spontaneous abortions, and one percent stated they did not need abortions because results of initial laboratory tests were incorrect and they were not pregnant. The outcome of pregnancy for six percent of the women was unknown because they discontinued contact with the agency before making a decision.

The remaining women (eight percent) continued their pregnancies and either kept the child (five percent) or placed it for adoption (three percent). Of interest was the fact that all of the women who placed the child for adoption were single, and the majority of those who kept the child were married or had plans to marry in the near future.

Age, race, and religion did not appear to be significant factors in making the decision to continue pregnancy rather than obtain an abortion. However, length of pregnancy at the time of contact with PCS was of importance. All of the women who continued their pregnancies were over twelve weeks pregnant at the time of their initial contact with the agency. This would perhaps indicate that women who seek abortion later in their pregnancies have more ambivalence about terminating the pregnancy than do women who request abortion during the earlier stages of pregnancy.

FOLLOW-UP OF WOMEN
WHO OBTAINED ABORTIONS

The women who were interviewed for follow-up one to two years after their abortions appeared to be representative of the total population who obtained abortions. They were single (61%), white (95%) students (36%) or professional workers (24%) of Protestant (48%) or Catholic (23%) faith. The mean age was 22 years.

Marital status was unchanged for the women who were married at the time they obtained abortions. Twelve of the single women had married after the abortion; eight to the sexual partner and four to others. There was no evidence that the abortion experience had affected the educational or occupational levels of the women. None of the women reported changes in their school or work status as a result of abortion.

PSYCHOLOGICAL REACTIONS

With few exceptions, the women in the follow-up group appeared to be functioning well. Although they frequently mentioned how desperate they felt when they were pregnant, they also indicated that the crisis ended essentially with the termination of the unwanted pregnancy. Negative psychological reactions to abortion were rare immediately afterwards and during the one to two year follow-up period.

As shown in Table 2, 78% of the women denied negative psychological reactions immediately after abortion. Many reported feelings of relief and satisfaction, and few experienced depression, remorse, or guilt. At the time of follow-up, 90% of the women reported they were doing well and were not experiencing any psychological after-effects of abortion. Only four percent were suffering moderate to severe emotional discomfort that they felt was related to the abortion experience.

Ninety-four percent of the women were satisfied with their decision and denied regrets regarding the abortion. Only three percent strongly regretted the abortion; another three percent were ambivalent. The small number of women who regretted their decision felt that they had been influenced by others regarding the abortion. One young woman, who was fourteen years old when she obtained an abortion, stated, "My parents killed my baby." At the time of follow-up, she expressed a great deal of anger at the parents for insisting that she have an abortion and not considering her feelings in the matter. Other women reported more subtle pressure from family or the sexual partner to terminate pregnancy.

TABLE 2   Psychological reaction to abortion immediately afterwards and at time of follow-up ($N = 80$).

Reaction	Immediately afterwards	At follow-up
None	78%	90%
Mild Discomfort	9	6
(noticed by subject but not of real concern to her)		
Moderate Discomfort	7	2
(caused concern to subject and/or others)		
Severe Discomfort	6	2
(prolonged, and impaired functioning)		

Although some authors have indicated that symptoms of depression, guilt, and sexual dysfunction are frequently experienced by women after abortion, this was not confirmed by the present study. The majority of women did not experience these symptoms or other psychological reactions as a result of abortion. During the follow-up period, only eighteen percent of the women had experienced conscious guilt about the procedure, fifteen percent had experienced feelings of sadness and depression, and ten percent had decreased sexual interest or pleasure. In most instances, these symptoms were mild and self-limiting and did not impair functioning or require professional help. There was no evidence of the "post-abortion hangover" observed by Dunbar,[3] which coincides with the time period of the unfulfilled pregnancy and may represent an unconscious carrying-through of the pregnancy. One woman reported a mild reaction at the time delivery would have occurred but denied other difficulties.

Only six percent of the follow-up sample sought psychiatric treatment after abortion. Of these five women, two were treated for depression, one for recurrent dreams about the abortion, one because of school problems, and one for sexual dysfunction and guilt. Although fifteen women in the follow-up group had been given a psychiatric diagnosis on the basis of the initial research interview, only two of these women experienced problems after abortion that required professional help. This data is contrary to previous studies that report that women with pre-existing psychiatric diagnoses continued to have difficulty afterwards. It suggests that abortions have, on the whole, few emotional hazards.

A closer look at the small population of women who did experience post-abortion sequelae revealed several significant factors. All of the women who experienced moderate to severe discomfort afterwards were unmarried, and most were teenagers. Prior to abortion, many of these women had expressed ambivalent feelings about the procedure and approximately one-fifth had predicted that they would have negative reactions afterwards. They often expressed great concern about their ability to have children in the future and mentioned their fondness for children. At the time of follow-up, most of these women had discontinued contact with the sexual partner and few had emotional support from family or friends.

There was no evidence that previous psychiatric history or religious preference influenced the women's adjustment after abortion. Catholic women appeared to have no greater emotional discomfort than did those of other faiths. As mentioned previously, those with previous psychiatric diagnoses did not experience psychiatric symptoms more frequently than did the other women studied. The significance of length of pregnancy at the time of abortion could not be studied because few women terminated their pregnancies during later stages of pregnancy.

EFFECTS OF ABORTION

When asked to evaluate the effect of abortion upon their lives, only two percent of the women reported that it had a negative effect. Forty percent felt that the abortion had a positive effect, and 47% said it had no effect.

Many of the women viewed the experience as a growth producing or maturing process. Others found it a time of discovering "inner resources" they had not realized they possessed. As one young woman said, "I decided that if I could make the decision to get an abortion on my own and then go through it alone that I would be able to handle anything." Some said they had become more tolerant of others. Most young women who had confided in their parents regarding the pregnancy and abortion felt that the experience had brought them closer together and increased communication.

Many reported that the abortion had allowed them to remain in school, to continue working in jobs they enjoyed, or to devote time to their families. One woman, who was recently engaged, wrote, "I would have been married to someone I didn't love and who didn't love me and there would have been a child that neither of us wanted. It's like I was given a second chance at life."

RELATIONSHIP WITH SEXUAL PARTNER

Forty-four percent of the unmarried women had discontinued contact with the sexual partner at the time of follow-up. Four women ended their relationship before the abortion, ten within one to three months afterwards, six after three months, and eight at an unknown time. Thirty-three percent of the women maintained friendship with him, and nine percent were going steady or engaged to the partner. Thirteen percent had subsequently married the man involved and the relationship for two percent of the women was unknown.

Most of the women had talked with the sexual partner about pregnancy and abortion. The majority of the men were supportive, both emotionally and financially, at the time of abortion. It is perhaps for this reason that few of the women expressed negative feelings regarding the partner at the time of follow-up. Sixty-seven percent of the women reported positive feelings toward him, and only eight percent had negative feelings.

All of the women who were married at the time of abortion had talked with their husbands about pregnancy and abortion. All but one were supportive of the women. None of the women reported changes in their marital status or relationships with their husbands as a result of abortion.

SEXUAL ACTIVITY AND
USE OF BIRTH CONTROL

Eighty-one percent of the single women indicated that they had had intercourse since their abortions. Those who were under age 20 had a

TABLE 3   Patterns of contraceptive use before and after abortion.

Contraceptive method	Before abortion (N = 154)	After abortion (N = 80)
None	54	14
Pills	4	49
Diaphragm	1	6
IUD	0	4
Foam	15	4
Condom	8	1
Rhythm	13	0
Withdrawal	3	0
Vasectomy	0	3
Tubal Ligation	0	3
Method Unknown	2	16
	100%	100%

higher rate of abstinence than did their older counterparts. Most mentioned fear of pregnancy as their major reason for avoiding intercourse, two mentioned a loss of interest in sex, and one stated she now preferred homosexual rather than heterosexual relations.

All but three of the sexually active women were using contraception at the time of follow-up. One married woman wanted to become pregnant, and two single women reported infrequent intercourse and did not feel they needed birth control.

Types of birth control measures, as shown in Table 3 indicate that the majority of women were utilizing reliable forms of contraception rather than relying on high risk measures. Forty-nine percent of the women were using birth control pills and none was using rhythm. As one young woman stated, "When I make love I want to be sure that's all I'm making." The majority of women felt they had adequate information regarding birth control, and only eight percent expressed interest in obtaining further information.

All of the women had received contraceptive counseling through PCS prior to the abortion and were contacted by the counselor soon after the procedure and encouraged to obtain a post-abortion check-up and contraceptive prescription. The effectiveness of counseling has also been reported by Dauber[2] in a follow-up study of women who obtained abortions in

California. Nine out of ten women who received counseling prior to abortion returned for their post-abortion check-up and contraceptive prescription and were continuing to use it at the time of follow-up. Only six of ten women who were not counseled returned for medical and contraceptive advice.

SUBSEQUENT UNWANTED PREGNANCY

During the one to two years following abortion, six women (seven percent) had experienced a second unwanted pregnancy. Five of the six had obtained abortions, and one had aborted spontaneously. All but one of the women were single at the time of the second abortion. It is of interest that two-thirds of the women who experienced a repeated unwanted pregnancy had been assigned a psychiatric diagnosis at the time of the research interview.

COMMENTS REGARDING COUNSELING
PRIOR TO ABORTION

The women frequently expressed appreciation for the help they had received from PCS prior to abortion. Eighty-six percent of the women felt that the counseling was helpful to them. Most frequently mentioned were the emotional support provided by the counselor and the information given regarding the abortion procedure. Only seven percent of the women did not feel that counseling was helpful to them.

Those who found counseling least helpful were married or older single women who felt they had adequate information and were receiving emotional support from husband or friends. Younger women and those who had not confided in anyone regarding the pregnancy found the counseling of most value.

Only one woman (the teenager who felt her parents had forced her to have the abortion) felt that the counselor had influenced her decision regarding abortion. The remainder felt the counselor had offered support in whatever decision the woman made.

When asked if there were any suggestions they would like to make regarding the counseling program, several mentioned the need for more information about the actual abortion procedure. Some said they were not prepared for pain, bleeding, or other events that occurred. They felt it would have been helpful to speak with women who had obtained abortions in order to have a better understanding of the procedure.

Many appreciated the opportunity to share their feelings and experiences in the follow-up interview. Some had not talked with anyone about the abortion and felt it might be helpful to provide follow-up counseling immediately afterwards for those who had no one with whom to share the experience.

They felt abortion should be more available, less expensive, and not illegal or shrouded in secrecy. Although they had found abortion an acceptable solution to their unwanted pregnancies, many felt in retrospect that more sex education and birth control information would have prevented them from needing abortions. None viewed abortion as the preferred method of preventing unwanted pregnancies.

DISCUSSION

Women in this study have reported few psychological effects of abortion during the one to two year period following the procedure, and many viewed abortion as a positive experience. That so few women reported negative reactions is perhaps surprising since this study was carried out in a state in which abortion is a matter of criminal law. In spite of the lack of legal and social sanction for termination of pregnancy, the women did not experience excessive guilt or other psychological scarring. It is possible that contact with the Pregnancy Consultation Service may have minimized the criminal aspects and stigma associated with abortion. It also seems possible that, for the majority of women with unwanted pregnancies, abortion does not have grave emotional hazards.

Although few of the women in this study experienced psychological reactions to abortion, further studies are needed to develop methods of predicting women who are prone to developing post-abortion symptoms. Also of concern are the women who obtain repeated abortions or are at risk because of lack of contraceptive use.

Most women who obtain abortions resume sexual activity afterwards. Those working with women who request abortion need to place a high priority on understanding the women's attitudes toward sexuality and birth control practices, as well as providing education and information in this area.

As a result of information received from women who have obtained abortions, PCS is developing a more extensive contraceptive counseling program and has experimented with post-abortion group counseling sessions. Research is now in progress to study women who obtain repeated abortions.

Unwanted pregnancy is a problem of great importance to society and to the individual women who must accept the consequences or seek alternative solutions. Although abortion is not the only solution, it should be available to women who desire it, without stigma or fear of grave psychological effects.

SUMMARY

There have been contradictory reports in the literature regarding the psychological effects of abortion. In order to better understand the effects of abortion it was decided to ask women to evaluate their experience and describe their reactions to abortion. One hundred and fifty-four women who contacted a problem pregnancy counseling service were interviewed prior to abortion. Eighty of the 125 women who subsequently obtained abortions were followed-up one to two years later.

Women in this study who requested abortions were typically single, white students of Protestant faith, in their late teens or early twenties. Less than half were using any form of birth control when pregnancy occurred. Single women sought abortion primarily because of lack of marriage or desire to continue education or employment. Married women requested this because of finances or lack of desire for further children. The majority of women did not have a history of psychiatric problems.

Most of the women reported that they did not experience any emotional discomfort as a result of the abortion. Seventy-eight percent did not experience psychological reactions after the procedure, and 90% denied psychological changes at the time of follow-up. Symptoms of depression, guilt and sexual dysfunction were experienced by a small number of women, and these symptoms were usually self-limiting and did not impair functioning or require professional help. Only six percent of the women sought psychiatric treatment after abortion. Most of the women felt the abortion had a positive effect on their lives, and only three percent strongly regretted their decision.

Most of the unmarried women were sexually active after abortion, and seven percent had experienced a second unwanted pregnancy. At the time of follow-up, the majority of women who were having intercourse were using reliable methods of birth control. Forty-four percent of the women had discontinued their relationship with the sexual partner after abortion, and thirteen percent had subsequently married the partner.

Most of the women felt their contacts with PCS were helpful. Although the women found abortion a necessary solution to their unwanted pregnancies, they did not view it as a preferable means of birth control.

There is a need for further systematic studies of abortion and development of methods of predicting women who are at risk for post-abortion reactions and subsequent unwanted pregnancies.

ENDNOTES

1. Brekke, B. 1958. Other aspects of the abortion problem. *In* Abortion in the United States, M. Calderone, ed. Harper and Row-Hoeber, Inc., New York.
2. Dauber, B., Zalar, M. and Goldstein, P. 1972. Abortion counseling and behavioral change. Fam. Planning Perspectives 4:23–27.
3. Dunbar, F. 1954. The psychosomatic approach to abortion and the abortion habit. *In* Therapeutic Abortion, H. Rosen, ed. Julian Press, New York.
4. Ekblad, M. 1955. Induced abortion on psychiatric grounds: a followup study of 479 women. Acta. Psychiat. Neurol. Scand. Supp. 99:1–238.
5. Feighner, J. et al. 1972. Diagnostic criteria for use in psychiatric research. Arch. Gen. Psychiat. 26:57–63.
6. Ford, C., Castelnuovo-Tedesco, P. and Long, K. 1971. Abortion, is it a therapeutic procedure in psychiatry? JAMA 218:1173–1178.
7. Hardin, G. 1967. *In* The Case for Legalized Abortion Now, A. Guttmacher, ed. Diablo Press, Berkeley, Calif.
8. Malmfors, K. 1958. The problem of women seeking abortion. *In* Abortion in the United States, M. Calderone, ed. Harper and Row-Hoeber, Inc., New York.
9. Margolis, A. et al. 1971. Therapeutic abortion follow up study. Amer. J. Obstet.-Gynec. 110:243–249.
10. Osofsky, J. and Osofsky, H. 1972. The psychological reaction of patients to legalized abortion. Amer. J. Orthopsychiat. 42(1):48–60.
11. Patt, S., Rappaport, R. and Barglow, P. 1969. Follow up of therapeutic abortion. Arch. Gen. Psychiat. 20:408–414.
12. Peck, A. and Marcus, H. 1966. Psychiatric sequelae of therapeutic interruption of pregnancy. J. Nerv. Ment. Dis. 143:417–425.
13. Senay, E. 1970. Therapeutic abortion: clinical aspects. Arch. Gen. Psychiat. 23:408–415.
14. Simon, N., Senturia, A. and Rothman, D. 1967. Psychiatric illness following therapeutic abortion. Amer. J. Psychiat. 124:59–65.
15. Simon, N. and Senturia, A. 1966. Psychiatric sequelae of abortion. Arch. Gen. Psychiat. 15:378–389.
16. Whittington, H. 1970. Evaluation of therapeutic abortion as an element of preventive psychiatry, Amer. J. Psychiat. 126(9):1224–1229.

WHAT DO YOU THINK?

Helen was a very pretty girl whose father was a bluecollar worker and wanted her to marry well. She was going with Harold, a twenty-year-old, an accountant's son who wanted to be "with it"—modern and free. He found Helen to be a good and willing sex partner; in fact, they quit going on dates and spent all their time together in his apartment. When she became pregnant he was shocked, then shouted, "Why did you let this happen?" Helen could not understand his attitude because she was taking pills, and both of them felt this was safe. She wanted to marry Harold and said, "We have to get married." His first thought was, "I'm trapped."

After they verify the pregnancy by a physical examination, what should they do?

Do you think Harold was exploiting a girl from a lower class for sex favors? Was Helen exploiting Harold to get married?

How much exploitation do you think goes on in premarital sex relationships?

Paul learned from experience that if he got too aggressive on the first date, women would not go out with him again. So he behaved well on the first three dates, charmed the women, admired them, and got just a little bit warm. On the fourth date, he found the way clear for heavy petting and coitus. By this time, the woman liked him, trusted him, and could believe him when he said he loved her. Since the woman felt this was mutual love, she responded to him completely. Paul used this line so much he never learned real love, never experienced the depth of feeling associated with love. In fact, he could not believe that there was such a thing as a deep, loyal, sincere, and lasting love.

How could a woman teach a man like Paul that conquest and love are not the same?

What could be done to help Paul gain a better understanding of women?

What will happen to Paul twenty to thirty years from now?

Which of the following statements do you *most* agree with, and why?

I believe it is permissible for males to have intercourse before marriage, but females are bad if they have such experiences.

I think that intercourse before marriage is permissible if the two people love each other.

I feel that intercourse before marriage is permissible if the two people are physically attracted to each other.

I believe that intercourse before marriage is wrong under any circumstances.

Now, substitute the phrase "extramarital intercourse" for "intercourse before marriage," and see how you would respond to each of these statements. Is there any difference? Why or why not?

Zelda is a junior in a large urban college. For the past six months she has been living with Sam, who is in his last year at the same college. Their friends know about the alliance, visit them frequently, and bring them into a variety of couple-activities. They are supported economically by their parents who live several hundred miles away, but have not told them of the "arrangement," in part because they fear that their funds will be cut, but mainly because they do not know how to tell them. Zelda decided she could not continue the deception and would tell her parents when she went home for Thanksgiving. She had always been close to her father and was more apprehensive about his attitude than about her mother's reaction.

Should they tell both sets of parents?

Should Zelda tell her parents about her relationship with Sam or carry on as before?

Should she bring Sam home to help her face the problem?

Should she tell her parents separately or both at once?

Issues of
Intermarriage

Individuals in the United States are expected to be in love with the person they marry. The freedom and opportunity to fall in love, however, are influenced by other considerations thought to be important in America. Such factors as race, ethnic background, religion, and social class are given various degrees of importance in meeting, dating, and finally marrying persons of the opposite sex. "Fall in love, sure; but fall in love with your own kind." "Look for someone you can be comfortable with, who has similar interests, with whom you have things in common." These and similar pieces of advice are often heard, or at least communicated in both formal and informal ways. A substantial proportion of the population, thus, "happens" to fall in love with someone with similar racial, religious, ethnic, and social class characteristics. Others, however, fall in love with and marry someone from a different background. These latter individuals may or may not be just as happily married as those who marry people like themselves.

There have been many arguments for and against intermarriage. The article by Cavan and Cavan discusses these arguments and points to the factors related to endogamy and exogamy. These authors also cover some of the problems that may face an intermarried couple in a society that looks upon such arrangements as being more or less unacceptable.

Religion is one of the most important areas in early marital adjustment. Couples married in a church or temple in a ceremony performed by a clergyman get off to a better start and are more apt to have a stable marriage than are couples who had a civil ceremony. Early in marriage, each couple must decide the amount and type of participation in religious functions they will have. When two people of different faiths marry, they must make extra effort to achieve a satisfactory adjustment in this area. Many dating couples see religion as unimportant, but when they marry—especially when they become parents—religion comes to the fore as a big factor in their lives. Some religious groups are changing their official positions toward interfaith marriages and related matters, and young people need to keep informed about these decisions as they emerge.

Religious convictions are difficult to analyze. If a person in an interfaith marriage refuses to give up his religion, his spouse may see him as stubborn, hardheaded, and rigid rather than as a person with deep faith. On the other hand, the one who converts to his spouse's faith may be seen not as flexible or adaptable, but as shallow, superficial, or wishy-washy.

Religion may be thought by some to be only *one* factor in marital adjustment. However, as Alfred Prince points out, religion may best be seen as culture, something fundamental and pervasive in an individual's life. It can, like culture, penetrate and affect basic values, attitudes, and actions. Interfaith marriages, or intercultural marriages, may therefore produce competing obligations and "role conflicts," which must be resolved to insure stability and happiness of the marriages. These aspects of interfaith marriage are perhaps not considered by interfaith couples who are contemplating marriage.

Cavan discusses Jewish intermarriages in a similar way, as an intersocietal union. She notes, however, that there are differences as well as similarities among Jews, and that some Jews are more inclined than others to marry outside the boundaries of their faith. She predicts a continuing increase in interfaith marriages among the Jewish populations. It may be noted that the growing number of Jewish-Gentile marriages has resulted in attempts to keep young Jews together by organizing social clubs, sponsoring dances, and starting computer dating and matchmaking services for Jews. The effectiveness of such action programs for Jews, or for other religious groups who have had the same experiences, remains to be seen.

The issue of interracial marriage is not new but goes back to early history and can be found in other civilizations besides our own. One of the early American colonies declared the mixture of races illegal but rescinded the law about a half-century later. Some states specified certain races in their laws, while others did not concern themselves with the problem, probably because they had few people of other races in their citizenry. The United States Supreme Court in 1967 declared laws against miscegenation illegal. In other words, people of different races are now legally free to intermarry in this country, although they may still feel social and family pressure to marry within their own group.

13

Ruth S. Cavan and Jordan T. Cavan

Cultural Patterns, Functions, and Dysfunctions of Endogamy and Intermarriage

Endogamy, intermarriage, and quasi-marriage are viewed as parts of the mating system of a society. Endogamy sets boundaries; intermarriage breaches the boundaries and bridges the gaps between endogamous societies; quasi-marriage brings nonlegal and irregular unions within the marital framework. These forms of marriage also may be viewed as types of contact between in-groups. They are related to the general intergroup contacts which are exemplified in forceful military invasion; peaceful intrusion for exploration, trapping, and trading; and immigration for permanent settlement. Each type of marriage has positive functions and also dysfunctions for society and the individual. The intermarried and quasi-married couples are accorded some place in the social framework. They may be absorbed into or rejected by one or both societies involved, may unite with a third society, or may form a new sub-society. Likewise the descendants of an intermarried or quasi-married couple are assigned a place in the social framework.

Endogamy, or marriage within one's own society, and its opposite, intermarriage, may be approached from several points of view. They may be defined as two types of personal relationships between husband and wife. They may be viewed as types of sexual relationships in a framework that includes both endogamy and intermarriage as well as individual sexual relationships outside the bounds of official marriage. Finally, endogamy and intermarriage may be viewed in a context of social organization and

Ruth S. Cavan and Jordan T. Cavan, "Cultural Patterns, Functions, and Dysfunctions of Endogamy and Intermarriage," from the *International Journal of Sociology of the Family*, Vol. I, (Special Issue) May, 1971, pp. 10–24. Reprinted with permission.

intergroup relationships. From the last point of view, endogamy may be defined as a boundary-maintaining device for a specific society or sub-society, whereas intermarriage is a type of contact between distinctive societies or subsocieties. This article concentrates on the sexual framework and marriage as a type of intergroup contact.

FRAMEWORK OF HETEROSEXUAL RELATIONSHIPS

ENDOGAMY AND INTERMARRIAGE

All societies attempt to regulate heterosexual relationships to bring them into the social organization. Nowhere are people completely free to choose their marriage partners on a completely individual basis (Wester-marck, 1922: 35). This does not mean that all heterosexual relationships in a given society fall into one pattern. Regulations may have some flexibility or may differ from one subsociety to another within a society. The most stringent regulations have to do with endogamy, which goes beyond incidental intragroup marriage that may result from lack of contact beyond the society. Endogamy is supported by laws, rules, public opinion, and cultural family pressures, all designed to guide people into marriage within their own society.

Endogamy creates a pool of eligible partners for mate selection. The lines of demarcation between eligible and ineligible marital partners are cultural in origin. Nowhere does there seem to be any innate aversion to sexual contacts between people of different races, religions, castes, political beliefs, languages or other groups based on such cultural factors. Sexual attraction seems to override all differences. The barriers that support endogamy are culturally imposed. Yinger (1968: 104–107) regards the boundary that encloses an endogamous group as a "Socially significant line of distinction . . ." This socially significant line may be regarded as a value or cluster of values to which the society is deeply committed.

The marriage most highly approved by an endogamous society is marriage within its own boundaries, between a man and woman who are already socialized into the society, participate in its activities, and share its values. Such a marriage is given social approval through public recognition. It improves the status of the couple in the society and assigns them new responsibilities as adults.

Endogamous marriage is not the only kind of marriage. Unless a society is physically isolated and contact with members of other societies is impossible, intermarriage occurs. Frazier (1957), interested primarily in race, produces evidence that racial intermixture seems to be worldwide; it sometimes results in a majority of the population being interracial. Intermarriage is the violation of endogamous policies and rules. It occurs when a member ignores the policies and defies the rules in order to marry someone from another society or group whose members are regarded as ineligible for marriage. Endogamy and intermarriage are thus opposites. Endogamy is divisive; it encloses each people within the confines of its culture. Intermarriage is a breaching of these constraining boundaries. Since intermarriage occurs only when endogamous boundaries exist, endogamy is the central term in any discussion of the two types of marriage.

Although intermarriage may not be acceptable to an endogamous society, it is approved by some group; otherwise, it could not be considered a form of marriage with the commitment of husband and wife to the roles and responsibilities of marriage. It may be that only one of the societies is endogamous; the other society may be more permissive and may validate the union as a marriage. If both societies are endogamous, the couple may be able to have their marriage validated by a third society. For example, until recently, in the United States many states had laws that forbade marriage between Caucasians and members of other races. However, an interracial couple could go to a state without such restraining laws and achieve a legal marriage; if they returned to their original state, they were subject to severe penalties. In Italy a law of 1970 swept away certain endogamous laws that had existed for centuries. Under those endogamous laws, the eligible pool of mates was limited to persons who had never been divorced. However, two people, each of whom was already married, could migrate to another country where such restrictions did not exist, secure divorces, and have a legal marriage, which was not however recognized as valid in Italy.

Endogamy may be total, that is, it may forbid anyone to marry outside the society. This situation arises when the society, or a subsociety, is so organized that all needs of the members are satisfied within the society, and there is no need for outside contacts. For example, from 1637 to 1854 Japan was a self-contained society, although previously it had traded with and borrowed foreign cultural elements from both Asian and European countries. Within this closed society complete endogamy was maintained so far as foreign marriages were concerned. Within Japan itself, particularistic rules of endogamy were enforced, especially between social classes; the barriers were upheld by parental and official selection of mates for young people (Welty, 1966: 252; Storry, 1965: 44, 53–54, 62–63, 84). Even after Japan was opened to trade in 1853–54, the society remained essentially endogamous. The period of military occupation after World War II brought in a special type of intermarriage which is discussed later in this paper.

Organized subsocieties within larger societies may approach complete endogamy although they are often dependent for trade on contacts with the larger society. These contacts are controlled by limiting them to older, deeply committed members of the group. In the United States, examples are the Hutterites, a communal society with villages in the Dakotas (Peters, 1965: 41–51) and some communities of Orthodox Jews (Freilich, 1962).

In many other instances, endogamy of subsocieties or less completely organized groups is limited to one or a few phases of culture, while in all other respects, the group makes no restrictions. For example, in the United States, many religions officially prescribe or strongly prefer religious endogamy, with harsh or mild penalties for interreligious marriage. They may have no objection to marriage between races or social classes. Another group may demand racial endogamy but not be concerned about interreligious marriages. These are particularistic kinds of endogamy.

Since certain cultural traits are associated with each other, a marriage that is endogamous in one respect may automatically result in endogamous effects in other respects also. Religious and national background are closely associated; therefore, religious endogamy may result in ethnic endogamy. A certain religious group may consist primarily of a single social class; religious endogamy may then result in social class endogamy.

Conversely, a couple by their marriage might cross all the endogamous lines prevailing in a given society: in the United States, for example, race, religion, national background, and social class. Thus, their marriage would be completely an intermarriage.

Recognition of the complex relationship between endogamy and intermarriage has led to attempts to refine the two concepts. Endogamy may be (1) prescriptive (demanded or required by the society to assure good standing); (2) preferred (given social approval); or (3) permissive (society indifferent) (Merton, 1941; Marcson, 1950). Conversely, the intermarried person would be (1) rejected; (2) disapproved of; or (3) accepted. Since any marriage involves the societies of two individuals, the attitude of both societies must be taken into account. The society of one may accept them, whereas the society of the other may reject them.

A classification of intermarriage into two categories has been made by John Harre (1966: 31) in his study of intermarriage in New Zealand between Maoris (indigenous Polynesian people) and residents of European ancestry. He distinguishes between couples who are racially mixed but share the same culture and those who are fully mixed, that is, both racially and culturally mixed. The latter are more fully intermarried than the former. In addition there would of course be Maoris, and also Caucasians, who were endogamously married as to both race and culture.

Another attempt to measure the degree of intermarriedness has been suggested by Yinger (1968), who points out that two people affiliated nominally with different religious groups, each with its own endogamous policy, may share many cultural values and thus be intermarried only nominally.

The discussion so far has amplified the simple definition of endogamy with which this section started. It has been defined in terms of values and is identified as a boundary maintenance device. In contrast, intermarriage is defined as a breaking through of such endogamous boundaries. Differences in endogamous attitudes of the two societies of the individuals involved in intermarriage create problems as to the validation of the marriage. Special aspects of endogamy include intensity of endogamous principles, total versus particularistic endogamy, and estimation of degrees of intermarriedness.

EXOGAMY

Before the discussion proceeds further, an explanation should be given of a third term, currently sometimes used as a synonym of intermarriage, that is, exogamy. According to its origin, this word is not a synonym for intermarriage; it has a meaning of its own (McLennan, 1886). Exogamy, strictly speaking, is a rule that requires members of a society to marry outside their kinship group, defined as the descendants of a common ancestor; or outside their clan, the members of which are assumed to have descended from a common remote ancestor. Exogamy is not a chance marriage outside of some group but a prescribed marriage supported by laws, rules, enforced customs, and the like (Fairchild, 1964: 111; Theodorson and Achilles, 1969: 138). For example, in the United States exogamy is enforced by state laws that forbid marriage among close blood relatives and in some states, close relatives by marriage (Bell, 1963: 218–219). Another example is India where traditionally, a person had to marry within his caste (endogamy) but outside his village, which was assumed to be composed basically of descendants of the same ancestor (exogamy).

Endogamy and exogamy may exist within the same society. Endogamy sets an outer boundary within which marriage is approved; exogamy sets an inner boundary within which marriage is forbidden. People between the two boundaries are mutually eligible as marriage partners. The rules of exogamy take the person beyond a small inner core but retain him within the endogamous boundaries. Intermarriage has another meaning; it is a violation of endogamous rules and takes the person beyond the society. Substituting the term exogamy for intermarriage destroys the exact meaning of both terms. The present paper is not concerned with exogamy but with endogamy and its violation through intermarriage.

QUASI-MARRIAGE

In addition to endogamy and intermarriage, less binding relationships exist, among which may be mentioned consensual unions, common-law marriage, concubinage, and maintenance of a mistress. These relationships have some degree of duration over time and involve voluntary mutual responsibilities. On a more individual level are temporary sexual relationships such as prostitution and rape, where the contact is physical and temporary in nature.

Consensual or free unions, common-law marriage, and concubinage are quasi-marriages. They are semi-permanent in nature and take on the form of family life with shared living quarters and reciprocal responsibilities, including the birth and care of children.

In the United States, common-law marriage in time received some legal status. Common-law marriage developed in the pioneer period when residence in certain areas preceded the arrival of legal authorities. It was impossible for a couple wishing to marry actually to have a legal marriage. Therefore they said the marriage vows before family and friends and set up a household. Some couples omitted this formality. These marriages tended to be stable and to carry out the functions of a legal marriage. They were accepted locally as valid marriages. Later, many state courts held that they were legally valid marriages in the absence of express statutory prohibition to the contrary, and in 1877 the United States Supreme Court took the same position. State laws are less lenient now, although in the 1960's nineteen states still recognized common-law marriage as legal (Kephart in Christensen, 1964: 950–951). Living together on a voluntary basis continues chiefly in lower socio-economic classes; such unions often are of a temporary nature and scarcely qualify as common-law marriages.

Another example of quasi-marriage that has some validity is the free union of Mexico—a custom of voluntary living together for an undefined period. The union may be dissolved easily by either man or woman, without provision for the support of children. According to Hayner (1966: 113–114), four types of marriage are listed by the Mexican census: legal marriage by civil ceremony; legal marriage by civil and religious ceremony; marriage by religious ceremony only (not legal); and free union, which accounts for 20 per cent of all cases of a man and woman living together as husband and wife. Thus through usage illegal associations came to have a quasi-validity, although their social status was lower than that of a legal marriage.

Concubinage falls into the pattern of quasi-marriage. In addition to a legal wife the man has one or more concubines who often live in the household but whose status is below that of the wife. In the past in China the man who desired a concubine made the arrangement with the parents of the woman, who typically were poor and needed the bride price. Since concubinage was not fully honored as a type of marriage, the girl was usually given to a man from a distant part of the country (Hsu, 1967: 104–106, 256–257, 322–323).

A less permanent and responsible relationship that may be either a substitute for marriage or a supplement is that of the mistress, a woman who is supported by a man who may or may not be married to another woman. The mistress may be recognized as part of the marital and familial system. For instance in Mexico, the children of a mistress as well as those of the legal wife receive public welfare benefits in case of the man's illness or death. However, only the legal wife and not the mistress receives benefits. In Italy during the long period when divorces were not granted many men had mistresses; in their own social circles man and mistress, rather than man and wife, were often invited to social functions, thus giving unannounced recognition that the union existed.

In addition to these forms of marriage and quasi-marriage, individual sexual unions run through many societies. For example, prostitution, which may be permitted legally or by custom, involves no mutual responsibility between man and woman aside from a business like transaction whereby the man buys a freely offered service from the woman. Rape is generally regarded as a highly disapproved relationship, especially by the society to which the woman belongs.

The social significance of these and similar relationships is that quasi-marriage and prostitution as well as endogamous marriage and intermarriage are brought within the limits of some socially organized group or society. Each relationship is recognized, its responsibilities and limitations are defined, and with the possible exception of prostitution, family roles are given a chance to develop.

INTERMARRIAGE, QUASI-MARRIAGE, AND INDIVIDUAL SEXUAL RELATIONSHIPS AS INTERGROUP CONTACTS

Whereas endogamy separates societies, intermarriage and the less formal relationships establish contacts between dissimilar societies. They link societies that do not regard each other as eligible for mate selection.

IN-GROUPS AND OUT-GROUPS

Intersocietal relationships fall into the general pattern of in-groups and out-groups. An in-group (we-group) has been defined as "any association with which one feels identified; to which one belongs—in the sense of longing for when away from it; the members of which are governed by attitudes of loyalty, devotion, sympathy, respect, and cooperation to it, as well as a certain sense of pride. When members are made aware of outsiders, the latter are regarded with indifference, repulsion, and even enmity." (Fairchild, 1964: 135). Whereas in-group refers to a real group, out-group refers to the feeling that in-group members have toward other groups than their in-group. An out-group (they—or others-group) refers to "a group external to the one to which the person in question belongs and toward which he feels such a sense of separation that he would ordinarily use the third person pronoun instead of the first person pronoun in referring to its members. The term is just one of several forms of expressing the emotional distinction between the insider and the outsider, the sympathetic and the antipathetic, the emotional near and far" (Fairchild, 1964: 135). To its own members, the out-group may be an in-group. Out-group refers to a relationship between two in-groups. The out-group relationship expresses social distance, which refers to the unwillingness of individuals or groups to interact with other socially or culturally different groups. When two in-groups feel only slightly distinctive from each other, both out-group feelings and social distance are low: when they feel hostile, out-group feelings are strong and social distance wide.

Relationships between groups are related to types of marriage. The in-group typically is endogamous when its population is sufficient to permit some choice of a marriage partner; this is especially true when the endogamous group has been able to control contacts of its members, and all aspects of life are centered in the in-group, such as in religious communities as the Hutterites and the Hasidic Jews in the United States. Between in-groups marriage is discouraged. However, if there are contacts, attraction between individuals often draws a couple together regardless of the disapproval of their respective in-groups. Such a marriage is an intermarriage. Its status depends on the degree of social distance between the two in-groups and on the total pattern of contacts, of which intermarriage is only one.

When social distance is the central concept, the reciprocal attitudes of the two in-groups are of prime importance (Cavan, 1971). When the groups feel themselves to be distinctive but have friendly contacts with each other, many intermarriages are likely to occur; when one in-group is hostile and the other friendly, a moderate number of intermarriages is likely to occur, when two groups are hostile, the intermarriage rate is likely to be low. In the last situation, each group may reject the idea of intermarriage and both may refuse to validate the marriage. When no third group is available to validate the marriage, the marriage cannot exist. However, as discussed above, if the couple still wishes to establish an intimate and enduring relationship, the way is opened for some form of free union or on a less permanent basis for prostitution and similar contacts.

The various heterosexual contacts are closely related to social distance and the total pattern of contacts between societies or subsocieties. These are related to the impact of one society on the other, of one culture on the other. Changes, including new heterosexual relationships, occur in social organization, government, economics, and religion. Types of contact, out-group relationships, social distance, and type of heterosexual relations form a related cluster of social phenomena. A few illustrations follow.

INTRUSION OF MILITARY FORCES

One type of contact consists of the intrusion of military forces from one society into another. The intruding force typically is composed of young males, either unmarried or separated from their wives and also from other sexual contacts with women of their own society. The relationship is one of mutual hostility and distrust. The invaded society tends to tighten its ideological and social boundaries as well as to defend physical boundaries. If the invaders are defeated they usually withdraw; if they are victorious, contacts between men and women follow, apparently regardless of the degree of hostility or difference in race, language, or culture.

When the conquerors are of superior status in cultural development and sophistication as well as in arms, the initial contact between the conquering males and the defeated females is often on a physical, even brutal basis. The women are seized, used sexually, and discarded.

When this period is followed by occupation or by colonization, another kind of sex relationship develops, on a permanent or semi-permanent basis, while the army remains, perhaps for years, in the conquered country. Roles of husband and wife are adopted; the woman looks after the man's comforts and also provides a ready sexual partner. The man provides for the physical needs of the woman and protects her from other males. Children may draw the pair closer together. The pair may never marry, they may marry in the society that has the less well-defined endogamous rules, or the society with the better organized legal or religious organization may bring pressure on the couple to marry, thus legitimizing the children and giving stability and responsibility to the union. The many types of unions now recognized in Mexico and described above had their origin 450 years ago in the invasion of Mexico by Cortez and his soldiers (Servin, 1970: Chapter 1). Over the centuries the process ran from the seizure of women to their enslavement and concubinage, and finally to free unions or marriage. The resulting intermixture of Indians, Europeans, and later of Negroes now has reached the point that in many regions it is difficult to classify people racially.

Another situation exists when the conqueror and the conquered are of approximately the same level of culture although of very distinctive types. As one example, when the British invaded India, the usual individual kind of sexual relations developed between the soldiers and Hindu women of the lower castes. The Hindu caste rules forbade marrying outside the caste and especially marrying non-Hindus. Lower caste women had little to lose, and perhaps felt they gained some security and protection from some of the hardships of their low status. At first the British encouraged the soldiers to marry the women legally, thinking it would improve relationships between the two societies. However, as soon as British women came to India they strongly opposed such marriages, which were no longer performed. Unlike Mexico, where the mixed population was integrated on a social class basis, in India the Anglo-Indians were rejected entirely by the Hindus but accepted by the British on a lower social-class level (Hedin, 1934). The children of succeeding generations of intermarried Anglo-Indians were provided with an English-type education, admitted into the Anglican church, and provided with low-level civil service positions, but not admitted into British social clubs, permitted to marry British women, or welcomed in Great Britain which the Anglo-Indians considered their "homeland" (Gist, 1967). Gist identifies Anglo-Indians as acculturated to English culture but not socially assimilated and as both culturally and socially alien to Indian society. They form a social island in the vast population of India.

Other population segments of mixed ancestry that remain independent of either parent population are the Anglo-Burmese (Koop, 1960) and the "cape coloured" of South Africa who are a mixture of native African and European stock (Berry, 1958: 329–330).

PEACEFUL INTRUDERS FOR EXPLOITATIVE PURPOSES

When the intruding groups are explorers, trappers, or traders, whose chief motive is to exploit the land and the people by peaceful means, another relationship comes about. They wish to take as much as possible from the land with as little disturbance as possible. In informal agreements between the indigenous population (usually primitive people) and the incoming men of another society, women of the native groups seem to be part of the bargaining process. Journals written by trappers and traders of the nineteenth century on the western plains of the United States include accounts of their various relationships with Indian women from nearby tribes (Abel, 1932: Biddle, 1962; Forbes, 1964). The relationship was understood and accepted on both sides. The Indians had a ready market for furs and a source of supply for tools and weapons. The women who became pseudo-wives had a comfortable place to live, food, clothing, and some luxuries. The men had someone to cook their meals, make or mend clothing, and act as sexual partners. Children were absorbed into the mother's tribe when the men moved into new territory where fur-bearing animals had not been made extinct; the woman returned to her tribe, all without animosity. Nothing other than this had been anticipated. In his new location the man made a new liaison with a woman from one of the nearby tribes. These arrangements were incorporated into the social organization of trapping and trading; some trading posts or forts were constructed with an individual room for each man large enough to accommodate him, his Indian female companion, and a child or two. Men seemed fond of their children, but only occasionally was the child given special care, baptism, or education by the father. Meanwhile the man might have a wife in the east who presumably did not know about his temporary Indian companion, who provided him with some of the comforts of home.

IMMIGRANTS

A third type of sexual union, ending more often in legal marriage than do the above examples, comes with immigration of large numbers of peaceful people into a long settled society with its own strong social organization and a culture accepted by most of the population. The United States is an example par excellence of this type of meeting of societies. With the indigenous Indians pushed into unprofitable corners of the country, the population and the culture were built up from successive waves of immigrants from many countries. The immigrants only gradually were absorbed into the mainline culture which was closely related to the English culture, even in the southwest which originally was strongly influenced by the Spanish influx. The situation in the United States was relatively receptive to the influx of immigrants, whose country of origin changed from decade to decade, depending largely on hardships that developed in their native societies. The early policy of the United States was to receive all comers. Moreover the Constitution of the United States guaranteed freedom of religious belief and practice. Numerous religious groups, feeling oppressed in European countries, came, and new religions quickly sprang up and sometimes almost as quickly died in the culturally tolerant climate. Members of all racial and many language groups arrived, although the racial groups were not as readily received as the religious groups. The result has been a mosaic of racial, ethnic, and religious groups, each of which has been able to retain its endogamous principles and rules, although often with diminishing intensity. With each generation, a gradual weakening of endogamy has accompanied acculturation into the mainstream of American life.

Several articles in this issue are illustrative of endogamous marriage and intermarriage among immigrants and their descendants in the United States: Greeks, Moslems, Jews, and Chinese, each of which represents a distinctive cultural group coming to terms with American culture. In other situations it is the American who enters into another culture and must find his or her place there. The article on Thai-American intermarriage centers on the adjustment of American women to Thai husbands and to Thai culture.

INTERRACIAL CONTACTS

In contrast to the autonomy permitted to ethnic and religious subsocieties in determining their principles and rules of ethnic and religious endogamy, white racial endogamy in several parts of the United States has been enforced through state laws passed by the dominant white racial group. As arbitrarily as the laws had been passed in past decades, in 1967 they all were made invalid by a ruling of the United States Supreme Court.

The dissolving of the laws enjoining endogamy among whites did not result in a rush of white and nonwhite individuals into marriage. The feelings of aversion to each other, based on long years of discrimination against the nonwhites, continued. The background and present status of Black-white intermarriage is discussed in McDowell's paper in this issue.

INTERMARRIAGE AND ASSIMILATION

Intermarriage has sometimes been interpreted as promotion of cultural and social assimilation between differing cultural groups, whose relationship is that of out-group. When the out-group relationship is hostile, individual sexual unions seem to predominate; resentment and disapproval may add to hostility. When the intergroup relationships are friendly, and social distance is low, illicit sexual unions tend to be replaced by intermarriage, tolerated or accepted by the two groups. Intermarriage seems to be a result of friendly relationships rather than initiator of them. As intergroup relationships change, heterosexual relationships also change. Growing hostility and conflict reduce approved sexual contacts, and adjustment of hostility and conflict is accompanied by increased sexual contacts, the trend of which is from individual contacts toward approved intermarriage. If one group is completely absorbed by another, or the two cultures merge, endogamy is the final result.

FUNCTIONS AND DYSFUNCTIONS OF DIFFERENT TYPES OF MARRIAGE

Some of the functions and dysfunctions of the different types of hetero-sexual relationships for the social organization and the needs of individuals have been suggested. This section more directly focuses on these functions and dysfunctions and specifies what aspects of society or individual needs are given support or weakened.

ENDOGAMY

In general endogamy is a conserving force that preserves both the biological lineage and the culture. When successfully enforced, endogamy maintains boundaries that keep the society intact: members are prevented from leaving in order to marry; strangers are prevented from entering the society through marriage; children born to an endogamously married couple clearly are members of the society. Special abilities or talents are retained by the society. Family and kinship ties are strengthened and perpetuated. As a social organization the society remains intact.

Endogamy also legitimates sexual contracts, defines who is a fully accepted member of the society, and controls the way in which property may be inherited. In societies in which property is expected to remain within a family and be inherited intact by succeeding generations, it is of the utmost importance to the society to identify who may inherit. Endogamy is one means to prevent the erosion of this principle of family inheritance.

In many societies preservation of the biological stock is a culturally important value. Biological preservation may be defined in terms of race, but is not limited to race. Continuation of family lineage may be included; thus, one elite of English stock is reported to have said that the best kind of marriage was between cousins. In other societies biological continuity is believed to be closely related to certain deeply rooted values; for example, the belief that God has ordained people of a certain biological lineage to preserve eternal values (the chosen people concept). Closely related is the view of some primitive people that they alone are men; all others are in some way subhuman.

Endogamy also incorporates the individual into an organized and continuing community and socializes him into its values. He is provided with a pool of eligible mates and is protected and guided in his choice. The person who accepts the endogamous group as his social world is relieved of many anxieties and uncertainties.

At the same time that endogamy conserves and stabilizes society, it may restrict the society to the point of maladaptation to the cultural and social changes that are characteristic of the world today. Therefore, from a broader point of view than that of the individual endogamous society, endogamy may be dysfunctional. Some examples follow:

By reducing or eliminating contacts with other cultures, endogamy may lead to impoverishment of the endogamous culture, since cultural exchange is discouraged.

At the personal level, endogamy may restrict the free choice of a mate. If parents and elders accept the responsibility of finding mates, and the principles of endogamy are accepted by young people, free choice may not be expected or even wanted. But absolute segregation is becoming less and less possible. Increasingly, young people in many cultures wish to make their own choices, often outside the endogamous boundaries. Dissension within families and personal disorganization may be a result of strict endogamous rules. Also, the strict enclosure of the young within an endogamous society may lead to formation of a certain type of personality, submissive to family and cultural control. However, with increased communication and wider contacts, another type of personality may be called for, more independent of family and capable of making decisions and of adjusting to changing conditions.

INTERMARRIAGE

Although intermarriage breaches endogamous boundaries and may foster disorganization, it provides an avenue whereby pressures may be relieved, new paths of development opened, and current social movements fostered. In other words, change away from a static rigid social organization may be accelerated in line with the general trends of a given time and place.

In a culturally pluralistic society such as the United States, intermarriage may form links in the accommodation of the segments to each other. When both segments are lenient about accepting outsiders through intermarriage, an exchange of members rather than a gain for one and loss for the other may diminish the threat of extinction of either segment.

Intermarriage bridges cultural and social gaps. In the past more than at present, many royal marriages in Europe were arranged between political rivals to consolidate an alliance or prevent war.

Intermarriage often opens the way for upward social mobility of one member, a commonly accepted social value. In India, where intercaste marriage was formerly forbidden and is still unusual, limited intermarriage between minor divisions of subcastes occurred. The typical pattern was for a woman to marry hypergamously, that is, into a subcaste division higher than her own; she and her parents were subject to some degree of stigma if she married into a lower subcaste division. Since the wife and children took the caste of the husband, a hypergamous marriage constituted upward mobility for the wife and her children and gave vicarious status to her parents (Davis, 1941). Men, however, might marry into a lower subcaste division without loss of status. For some modification of this pattern at present, see the article in this issue by Man Singh Das.

Races often fall into socially superior and inferior classes. Interracial marriage often is also interclass marriage and denotes mobility. In New Zealand (Harre, 1966: 74, 88) where the native Maoris (Polynesians) in general rank lower than the Caucasians of European descent, marriage of a Maori girl to a Caucasian also may elevate her social class position, especially if she has acquired or is able to adopt the cultural earmarks of her husband's culture. Contrariwise, a Caucasian who marries a Maori and adopts the Maori cultural traits becomes identified with the Maoris and loses status.

On the personal side, dissidents who leave an endogamous group by way of intermarriage may find an anchorage in another group which may be more congenial. Intermarriage fits a mobile society in which people of different types mingle freely. Released from the domination of tradition and strict group control, intermarrying couples are left free to develop new personality and family patterns. Intermarriage aids the move away from parochialism and traditionalism toward a modernist, metropolitan, individualistic, and flexible type of life.

Intermarriage may also be an overt expression of the rebellion of youth against parents. Some members of the second generation of immigrants seek through intermarriage to throw off their emotional and cultural bonds to their "old world" parents and the culture they represent.

Intermarriage may contribute to the independence of women. Endogamy is often enforced by parents who keep strict control over the activities of their children, especially girls. Intermarriage is an individual choice of major importance. It signifies independence and a break from strict parental control.

However, the freedom that intermarriage gives from the restrictions of endogamy may be destructive to the endogamous group. For example, Sephardic Jews in the United States, always a small group, have virtually disappeared, presumably in large part through intermarriage and loss of identity with their original group. Likewise all traces of the Indians who occupied Jamaica prior to the coming of Europeans have been lost, either through death or interbreeding with whites and later, Negroes (Carley, 1963: chapter 5).

Personally, intermarriage may alienate the individual from his society.

He may no longer be welcome there. If both partners to an intermarriage are from strictly endogamous societies, both societies may reject them. Then they may be detached from family, friends, and their identity group. They may of course affiliate with still other groups, or they may remain social isolates. Park's concept of the marginal man, developed by Stonequist (1937), may apply to these couples. The marginal person is one who is partially identified with two groups or cultures but not fully incorporated into either. Sometimes the marginal individuals draw together into a marginal group that lives precariously on the borders of two societies, forming a subsociety of its own which is perpetuated by endogamous marriage. Anglo-Indians, already discussed, constitute such a marginal subsociety.

Quasi-marriages and prostitution may serve certain useful functions not provided for in marriage regulations. They break through the rigidity of endogamous and intermarriage rules and may lead to a redefinition of those rules. They provide for sexual expression and often companionship among persons who do not or cannot fit into the accepted social patterns of marriage. An excess of one sex may be drawn into a semblance of family life. Quasi-marriage may also provide a recognized place for persons classified by upper status people as being of low status and unworthy of marriage.

Concubinage serves different purposes in different societies. In traditional China the wealthy man might take one or more concubines for his pleasure, or in the hope of having a son to carry on his lineage when his wife had not produced any, or when he was a widower for his care and companionship. The concubine was provided with more opportunities for herself and her children than she might have had in a marriage in her own social class.

Certain dysfunctions to society also appear. The unvalidated unions may place a strain on the social organization of the society. The individuals involved and their offspring may be rejected by society and become personally demoralized. Children may be stigmatized as bastards and may be unable to inherit from their fathers.

These unacknowledged sexual unions range between endogamous marriage and intermarriage when neither one is possible or desired. Often they provide for persons not acceptable in marriage but allowed entrance into a country. Women who otherwise would become vagrants or thieves in an effort to maintain themselves may be allowed entrance as prostitutes. Irregular unions may also provide for an excess of men or women of a given culture for whom suitable marital partners are not available. As already illustrated, soldiers stationed in a foreign country, distant from their countrywomen, may find comfort in associating with disadvantaged women of the conquered country whose potential mates have been killed in battle.

SOCIAL ABSORPTION OF THE INTERMARRIED COUPLE

The plight of the intermarried couple has been mentioned. If the attitudes of both societies involved are permissive toward intermarriage, the intermarried couple may readily be absorbed into the society of either husband or wife and at the same time retain a friendly relationship with the society of the other mate. Opposition or rejection by only one society may be complemented by assimilation into the society of the other. Opposition by both societies may lead to complete rejection of the couple. They may become social isolates. On the other hand, they may migrate to another society, more accepting of intermarriage, or they may form an exclusive subsociety of their own.

When the intermarriage violates endogamous policies of a subsociety (for example, race or religion) rather than a total society, adjustment may be simplified. The couple may withdraw or be ostracized by one or both of the opposing subsocieties but find acceptance in a third or neutral group within the total society. For example, in the United States if an Orthodox Jew and a Catholic marry (both religions are strongly opposed to marrying outside of the religion) the couple may affiliate with one of the liberal Protestant denominations. If there seems to be no possibility of such affiliation, the couple may simply eliminate all contacts with the groups in which intermarriage is forbidden and identify with other kinds of groups. For example, if a religiously intermarried couple cannot find a religion to accept them, they may establish close ties with some group that is not concerned with the religious affiliation of its members, such as a political or artistic group.

In some societies laws or customary practices determine the affiliation of the intermarried couple. In hypergamous interclass or intercaste marriage, the wife is usually accepted into her husband's class. However, in interracial marriages, the couple usually become associated with the socially inferior race (Zelditch in Faris, 1964: 688–694).

When two societies first meet and sexual contacts or intermarriage are not regularized, the couple may readily be ostracized. Typically as more men and women pair off, some patterns develop, either legally or by custom, to draw the couple into the social framework of one society or the other. Their status may be high or low, but they are accorded a place.

They and others know what their position is and what role they are expected to play in the total society.

CHILDREN OF THE INTERMARRIED COUPLE

The adjustment of the intermarried couple occurs over the lifetime of that couple. They produce children, however, who with their descendants are projected into the future to become a permanent segment of the population. The significance of endogamy in defining the legal status of children and controlling the inheritance of property has already been mentioned. The children of intermarriage also need a defined social status in order to be incorporated into the social structure.

Since the children of intermarriage are not an exact duplication of either parent, they are not automatically absorbed into the culture of either parent. The status and position of descendants of intermarriage call for a cultural solution, a definition of the offspring as belonging to some specific group within society, or as outcasts. The status assigned varies from one society to another and is related both to the general endogamous principles and the identifiability of the offspring as belonging to one parental group or the other.

In some societies the children automatically "belong" to one parent or the other. All children of a Moslem father are considered to belong to the father; among Jews, all children of a Jewish mother are considered to belong to the mother. Of the two societies or groups involved in an intermarriage, one may value retention of the children more than the other. The Catholic Church places the obligation on the Catholic spouse to rear the children as Catholics. A recent study (Salisbury, 1970) shows that children of Catholic-Protestant intermarriages are much more likely to identify with the Catholic than the Protestant religion. If race is a line of demarcation and skin color an identifying symbol of race, children may be absorbed into the race with the least favored skin color. In the United States, mulatto children find adjustment and acceptance more readily in the Negro than the Caucasian society. If they look in the least Negroid, they are classified by the dominant Caucasian society as Negro and, especially in southern United States, are shunned by white children. The same process may occur with cultural differences. A study of Jewish-Gentile children, called mischlings, shows that these children, even though reared by a Gentile mother in a Gentile community, in adolescence often are shunned by Gentile children and find greater acceptance among Jewish children (Berman, 1968: 207–229).

With attachments to two societies through their parents, children may suffer great confusion about their identity and anxiety over rejection or the prospect of rejection if their dual affiliation becomes known. Children who racially or culturally resemble the dominant society may attempt to pass, that is, to leave the society that is ready to accept them and claim full membership in the rejecting society. The very light skinned mulatto may leave his family and Negro friends and enter into white groups, perhaps eventually marrying a white person without revealing his Negro ancestry. The study of the Jewish mischlings spoke of the attempts of some of them to conceal the fact of a Jewish parent and claim full Gentile ancestry, but not without feelings of guilt and anxiety.

In some circumstances, children of mixed parentage form their own subsociety, as is true in India and adjacent countries where there are fairly large groups of Euro-Asians. Once a subsociety is formed, it tends to become culturally distinctive and endogamous. The question of identification of children then is automatically answered: they belong to the subsociety.

Under some conditions the children of mixed parentage are neither absorbed into either parental group nor able to form a subsociety of their own. They are rejected by both parental societies. Such a situation has characterized many of the children of American soldiers and Japanese women, conceived during the period of occupation in Japan after World War II (from magazine and newspaper accounts and personal conversations with educators in Japan). For a time American soldiers were forbidden to marry Japanese or to bring them to the United States. But, as is true of all such situations, American soldiers (both white and Negro) established sexual contacts with Japanese women, sometimes on a purely temporary basis, sometimes through free unions of some permanence, and sometimes with a Japanese marriage ceremony but without registration of the marriage. Many companions, wives, and children were abandoned when soldiers returned to the United States. The children are now young adults who must make their way in an unfriendly (Japanese) society. They are recognizable by Japanese as interracial: the skin is the wrong color; hair texture, features, stature are non-Japanese. It is difficult for them to find work. If they came to the United States they would find similar difficulties. One consequence is that in Japan they tend to find a place in occupations of low status, where their unusual appearance may be an asset. Girls may become prostitutes or entertainers; men may find a place in marginally unethical or illegal work.

The above examples suggest the great variety of ways in which the children of different types of mixed parentage find a place in the total society. The greatest difficulty is suffered when a new type of intermarriage appears, for instance, the American-Japanese after World War II. With successive generations, a pattern develops which puts each child into an assigned status, as is true for the mulatto or the Anglo-Indian.

CONCLUSIONS

This paper is limited to consideration of endogamy, intermarriage, quasi-marriage, and more individualistic unions as parts of a system to bring heterosexual unions into a social framework. Many aspects of controlling the types of marriage are not included, such as socialization of children into marriage norms, control of youth to prevent unapproved types of unions, or penalties for violation of norms. Personal adjustments of husband and wife that are related to intermarriage or quasi-marriage are not discussed.

The forms of marriage are viewed as types of intergroup contact. This approach supports the idea that different types of contact generate different types of marriage or sexual unions. These types may not be approved by all segments of a society. Nevertheless, they serve the society in many positive ways, but at the same time are dysfunctional in other ways.

When two societies make their first contact, heterosexual unions are likely to be individual and often disapproved. In time, however, norms develop for the regulation of these unions. Likewise, the status of children of these unions at first is unorganized and may be demoralizing to the children. In time, the children are fitted into the social organization.

Some more general comments may be in order. Since all societies tend to be endogamous, intermarriage and quasi-marriage develop most rapidly during periods of social change when endogamous boundaries are broken. Members of different societies meet as individuals, no longer under full control of their societies. The nineteenth and twentieth centuries have been periods of widespread dissolution of old traditional patterns of family and social organization and establishment of new ones. Traditional customs often are not fully applicable to urban conditions where individual copes with individual. Men and women meet in impersonal situations of work, travel, recreation, and college, and the old standards of fitting a mate into family and kin are replaced by fitting a mate to one's own needs and desires. As urbanization, migrations, and hostile or peaceful invasions continue or increase, individualism will also increase and with it intermarriage and quasi-marriage. However, research shows that there is a strong desire on the part of members of each society and subsociety to retain a sense of group identity and to avoid assimilation.

REFERENCES

Abel, Annie H. (ed.). 1932, Chardon's Journal at Fort Clark. Iowa City, Iowa: Athens Press.

Bell, Robert R. 1963, Marriage and Family Interaction. Homewood, Illinois: Dorsey Press.

Berman, Louis A. 1968, Jews and Intermarriage: A Study in Personality and Culture. New York: Thomas Yoseloff.

Berry, Brewton. 1958, Race and Ethnic Relations. Boston: Houghton Mifflin Company.

Biddle, Nicholas (ed.). 1962, Journals of the Expedition under the Command of Lewis and Clark, Vols. 1 and 2. New York: Heritage Press.

Carley, Marry Manning. 1963, Jamaica, The Old and the New. New York: Frederick A. Prager.

Cavan, Ruth Shonle. 1971, "Concepts and terminology in interreligious marriages." Journal for the Scientific Study of Religion, (Winter Issue).

Christensen, Harold T. (ed.). 1964, Handbook of Marriage and the Family. Chicago: Rand McNally and Company.

Davis, Kingsley. 1941, "Intermarriage in caste systems." American Anthropologist 43 (July-September): 388–395.

Fairchild, Henry Pratt (ed.). 1964, Dictionary of Sociology and Related Sciences. Paterson, New Jersey: Littlefield, Adams, and Company.

Faris, Robert E. L. (ed.). 1964, Handbook of Modern Sociology. Chicago: Rand McNally and Company.

Forbes, Jack D. (ed.). 1964, The Indian in America's Past. Englewood Cliffs, New Jersey: Prentice-Hall, Inc.

Frazier, E. Franklin. 1957, Race and Culture Contacts in the Modern World. Boston: Beacon Press.

Freilich, Morris. 1962, "Modern shtetl: A study of cultural persistence." Anthropos 57: 45–54.

Gist, Noel. 1967, "Cultural versus social marginality: The Anglo-Indian case." Phylon 28 (winter): 361–375.

Harre, John. 1966, Maori and Pakeha: A Study of Mixed Marriage in New Zealand. New York: Frederick A. Prager.

Hayner, Norman S. 1966, New Patterns in Old Mexico. New Haven: College and University Press.

Hedin, Elmer R. 1934, "The Anglo-Indian community." American Journal of Sociology 40 (September): 165–179.

Hsu, Francis L. K. 1967, Under the Ancestor's Shadow. Garden City, New York: Doubleday and Company.

Koop, John Clement. 1960, The Eurasian Population in Burma. Yale University Southeast Asian Studies. Cultural Report Series, No. 6. Detroit, Michigan: Cellar Book Shop.

Marcson, Simon. 1950, "A theory of intermarriage and assimilation." Social Forces 29 (October): 75–78.

McLennan, J. F. 1886, Studies in Ancient History. London.

Merton, Robert K. 1941, "Intermarriage and the social structure: Fact and theory." Psychiatry 4 (August): 361–374.

Peters, Victor. 1965, All Things Common, The Hutterian Way of Life. Minneapolis: University of Minnesota Press.

Salisbury, W. Seward. 1970, "Religious identity and religious behavior of the sons and daughters of religious intermarriage." Review of Religious Research 11 (Winter): 128–135.

Servin, Manuel P. (ed.). 1970, The Mexican-Americans: An Awakening Minority. Beverly Hills, California: Glencoe Press.

Stonequist, Everett V. 1937, The Marginal Man. New York: Charles Scribner's Sons.

Storry, Richard. 1965, A History of Modern Japan. Harmondsworth, Middlesex, England: Penguin Books, Ltd.

Theodorson, George, and G. Achilles (eds.). 1969, A Modern Dictionary of Sociology. New York: Thomas Y. Crowell Company.

Welty, Paul T. 1966, The Asians: Their Heritage and Their Destiny. Philadelphia: J. B. Lippincott Company.

Westermarck, Edward. 1922, The History of Human Marriage, Vol. 1. New York: Allerton Book Company.

Yinger, J. Milton. 1968, "On the definition of interfaith marriage." Journal for the Scientific Study of Religion 7 (Spring): 104–107.

14

Alfred J. Prince

Attitudes of Catholic University Students in the United States Toward Catholic-Protestant Intermarriage

The purpose of this study was to measure the attitudes of young people, specifically, those of the Catholic faith, toward mixed religious marriages. An attempt was made to ascertain some of the factors which seem to contribute to, and exert an influence upon, the formation of those attitudes. The group selected for study was a systematic sample of all Catholic students attending a coeducational Catholic university in a metropolitan area in the Pacific Northwest in the United States. Three instruments were used to study attitudes toward cross-religious marriages: (1) a comprehensive anonymous questionnaire; (2) Thurstone scale for measuring attitudes toward the church (in abbreviated form); and (3) an attitude scale, constructed for this study, to measure attitudes toward interfaith marriage. An interfaith marriage is more than a union between two people who profess allegiance to different religions. It is a union of two different cultures, or more exactly, the union of two different cultural products. Culture is a pervasive thing, penetrating into every phase of our lives. It reveals itself particularly in those aspects of our lives that are fundamental in the marital relationship. A social role is a unit of culture. It is a pattern of behavior associated with a distinctive social position. A role tells the individual what he ought to do as a father, son, or brother, to whom he has obligations, and upon whom he has a rightful claim. The obligations placed upon an individual by the variety of roles he is expected to play are oftentimes conflicting and difficult to reconcile. Sometimes, there are conflicting pressures and demands within a single role itself.

Alfred J. Prince, "Attitudes of Catholic University Students in the United States Toward Catholic-Protestant Intermarriage," from *International Journal of Sociology of the Family*, Vol. I (Special Issue), May, 1971, pp. 99–126. Reprinted by permission.

Such competing obligations are labeled "role conflicts." Some
social roles are especially susceptible to incompatible expectations.
This is particularly the case with marital roles in interfaith
marriages. In our study, the expressed attitudes of many of the
young people toward mixed religious marriages show a high
potential for "role conflict."

Religion plays a far more important role in marriage than many young persons in love are able to perceive. It may be a uniting force or a disruptive influence. It may make possible a profound sharing in one of the most important areas of life, or it may produce a divergence of interests and possible serious conflict.

A number of empirical studies indicate that there is more instability in mixed religious marriages than in those in which husband and wife share the same faith. In a study of 4,108 mixed and non-mixed marriages among the parents of college students in Michigan, Judson Landis (1949) found that divorce terminated approximately 5 per cent of the marriages when both parties were either Catholic or Jewish, 8 per cent of the Protestant marriages, and 15 per cent of mixed Catholic-Protestant unions. Ashley Weeks (1943), in his study of 6,548 families of public and parochial school children in Spokane, Washington, found a divorce rate of 3.8 per cent among Catholics; 10.0 per cent among Protestants; and 17.4 per cent in mixed marriages. Howard Bell's (1938) analysis of 13,528 families in Maryland showed that the percentage of divorce, separation, and desertion among parents of mixed religious affiliations was over twice as great as it was among parents whose religious affiliations were not mixed. Chancellor and Manahan (1955), in their study of interreligious marriages and divorces in Iowa, noted that mixed-Catholic marriages show a greater proportion of dissolution than marriages in which both parties are Catholic. Burchinal and Chancellor (1962) studied differences in marital survival rates among religiously homogeneous and interreligious marriages in Iowa. They also found that marital survival rates were greater among homogeneous Catholic marriages or homogeneous Protestant marriages than among marriages of Catholics and non-Catholics.

From the viewpoint of family stability, therefore, church authorities appear justified in discouraging young people from marrying outside their faith.

THE CATHOLIC POSITION
ON INTERFAITH MARRIAGE

It is precisely because a religious difference between two people is not trivial, explain Catholic church authorities, that "the Catholic Church has taken such a strong stand against interfaith marriages." (Anon, 1964). Three fundamental reasons why the Church strongly opposes mixed religious marriages are: (1) a mixed marriage hazards the happiness of the marriage itself; (2) a mixed marriage hazards the faith of the Catholic party; and (3) a mixed marriage hazards the faith of the children (Anon, 1964).

A leading family sociologist (Thomas, 1951a: 134) writes:

> For centuries, the (Catholic) Church has been telling its young men and women to marry their own. The Canon Law on marriage lays down positive restrictions against marriage with those not of the faith. Protestant Church leaders warn their young people against marriage with Roman Catholics. Jewish leaders have always condemned marriage with outsiders. Textbooks on marriage show that counselors agree that marriage between people of different religious beliefs is a dangerous gamble. The leaders have spoken, but have our young people heeded their warning?

The Roman Catholic Church strongly advises against the marriage of a Catholic and a baptized non-Catholic and even more strongly discourages the marriage of a Catholic and an un-baptized person.

The Church's disapproval of mixed marriages is not, as some may assume, of relatively recent origin. Saint Paul was not unmindful of the dangers in such unions. A Christian marriage, he held, is a symbol of the union between Christ and His Church. Thus, in writing to the Christians at Corinth, Paul admonished them to marry "only in the Lord," that is, only a Christian (I Cor. 7:39). The Council of Elvira, Spain in 306 forbade Christian girls to marry pagans, Jews, and heretics. The Emperor Constantine in 339 forbade the marriage of a Christian and a non-Christian under penalty of death. And Saint Augustine and Saint Ambrose clearly opposed marriages between Christians and heretics (Thomas, 1956:150; Mihanovich et al., 1952:195).

Present Church legislation concerning mixed marriages is set forth in the Code of Canon law[1] and in various papal encyclicals. (Augustine, 1920:141; Pope Pius XI, 1941:25; Pope Pius XII in Anon, 1939:15; Pope Leo XIII in O'Connor, 1951:40).

Several reasons are advanced for the Church's opposition to mixed marriages. They may be summarized briefly as follows:

(1) differences in religious beliefs furnish the basis for fundamental differences in the individual's value system; (2) the religious training of children can cause conflict in mixed marriages; (3) although the influence of the kinship group is diminishing, there is still considerable pressure exerted by the nearest of kin in regard to religious tolerance; (4) church loyalties and family loyalties frequently clash where there are

divergent beliefs; and (5) the spiritual unity of the marriage is seriously compromised. (Thomas, 1956:152).

Under certain conditions, the Church will permit marriages between Catholics and non-Catholics. These conditions are clearly stated in the Code of Canon Law 1061. The Code states that the Church will not dispense with the impediment of mixed religious marriage unless: (1) there are just and weighty reasons; (2) the non-Catholic party guarantees to remove the danger of perversion from the Catholic party, and both promise to baptize and educate all their children in the Catholic faith; and (3) there is a moral certainty that the promises will be kept (Anon., 1964).

Even when the conditions stated in Canon Law 1061 are met, however, this is not all that suffices for the issuance of a dispensation. The Catholic Church has declared that the conditions in Canon Law 1061 are exacted by the natural and divine law to remove the intrinsic dangers in mixed marriages, but that in addition there must be some grave necessity which cannot otherwise be avoided. The Church will view as a "grave necessity" any of the following: (1) the projected marriage is the only means by which the Catholic education of children born of a former marriage can be safeguarded; (2) danger of civil marriage or complete apostasy from the faith; and (3) grievous scandal can be repaired only by a mixed religious marriage (Augustine, 1920:148).

On March 31, 1970, Pope Paul VI issued motu proprio, the Apostolic Letter Determining Norms for Mixed Marriages (National Conference of Catholic Bishops, 1970). The provisions of this Apostolic Letter, effective October 1, 1970, open the way to an improved pastoral approach in support of couples who are united or who will be united in mixed religious marriages.

The Apostolic Letter recognizes that the canonical discipline on mixed marriages cannot be uniform but must be adapted to the various cases. Also, the pastoral care given to the married people and the children of the marriage also must be adopted according to the distinct circumstances of the married couple and the differing degrees of their ecclesiastical communion.

On January 1, 1971, the National Conference of Catholic Bishops issued a statement on the implementation of the Apostolic Letter on mixed marriages. The Bishops' Conference welcomes the Apostolic Letter and encourages its ready application in the United States.

THE PROTESTANT POSITION

Many Protestant denominations are also opposed to mixed marriages and have sought to dissuade their members from entering such unions. For example, the Presbyterian Confession of Faith, Chapter XXIV, Section III, (Black, 1954:14) reads:

> It is lawful for all sorts of people to marry who are able with judgment to give their consent; yet it is the duty of Christians to marry in the Lord. And, therefore, such as profess the true reformed religion should not marry with infidels, Papists, or other idolaters; neither should such as are godly be unequally yoked, by marrying with such as are notoriously wicked in their life or maintain damnable heresies.

That Protestants of a number of denominations are disturbed at the consequences of mixed marriages with Roman Catholics is increasingly evident in recent discussions and pronouncements. Similar resolutions were adopted by the General Conference of the Methodist Church (Pike, 1954:80), the General Convention of the Protestant Episcopal Church, in 1948, and the Southern Baptist Convention and the International Convention of the Disciples of Christ, in 1950 and 1951, respectively. (Black, 1954:15).

A leading Protestant minister summarizes the reasons why a mixed religious marriage is ill-advised. He writes:

1. A mixed marriage lacks a commonly held and articulated basis of ideas, purposes, and motivations.
2. A mixed marriage lacks the resources of marital health provided by common worship and common involvement in the most significant of all possible interests.
3. A mixed marriage robs the parents of a common relationship with their children on the deepest level, that of spiritual life.
4. In a mixed marriage one of the parents, and sometimes both are robbed of the opportunity of bringing to their children the best spiritual heritage that he or she knows, being barred from discharging this most important aspect of parental responsibility.
5. A mixed marriage (if one of the parties is a Roman Catholic) prevents one of the parties from following his conscience in regard to the planning of parenthood. (Pike, 1954:88).

Despite these indications of opposition to cross-religious marriages, the Protestant Churches generally have no formal rules or regulations binding their members in regard to mixed marriages. The chief concern of these churches is to counsel their young people concerning the difficulties they are likely to encounter should they contract such unions.

NUMBER OF INTERFAITH MARRIAGES

It is difficult at present to ascertain how many marriages in the United States are mixed religious marriages. In Iowa, a state which requires religion to be recorded, 42 per cent of all marriages in which a Catholic was involved in 1953 were mixed marriages. Both valid and invalid marriages are included in this percentage (Chancellor and Monahan, 1955: 233–239).

An analysis of interfaith marriages by John L. Thomas (1956:154) shows that the mixed marriage rate of Catholics for the past number of years has averaged between one-fourth and one-third of all valid Catholic marriages. By dioceses, Thomas (1951a:124–129) found rates ranging from over 70 per cent in Raleigh to less than 8 per cent in the diocese of Corpus Christi.

Thomas (1956:154) also reports many more Catholic girls than boys enter into interfaith marriage, a negative correlation between the proportion of Catholics in an area and the percentage of mixed marriages, and higher mixed marriage rates in the upper socio-economic classes, and lower rates in areas occupied by cohesive ethnic groups.

Thomas (1956:158), sees a strong probability of future increases in interfaith marriages involving Catholics and offers five reasons to support his belief: (1) national groups are gradually fusing with the host culture; (2) Catholic and non-Catholic interaction is increasing; (3) mixed marriages seem to have a cumulative effect in encouraging even more such marriages; (4) there is increasing individualism in the selection of a marriage partner; and (5) the attitude of both Catholic and non-Catholic young people is becoming more tolerant toward mixed marriages.

Ruby Jo Reeves Kennedy (1949), however, in her studies of the New Haven community, found that a triple-melting pot type of assimilation is occurring through intermarriage, with Catholicism, Protestantism, and Judaism serving as the three fundamental bulwarks. Protestants mostly marry Protestants; Catholics mostly marry Catholics; and Jews almost always choose Jewish mates.

Hollingshead (1950) agrees with the triple-melting-pot theory advanced by Kennedy. Hollingshead made a study of the cultural factors in the selection of marriage mates by studying all marriage license data in New Haven, Connecticut for 1948. He found that 91 per cent of the marriages in his sample involved partners from the same religious group. In the case of Jews, this percentage was 97.1; among Catholics it was 93.8 per cent; and for the Protestants it was 74.4 per cent.

John L. Thomas (1951b: 487–491) questions the conclusions drawn from studies of intermarriage in New Haven concerning the extent of religious endogamy. Thomas found in other studies a much higher mixed marriage rate for Catholics. He feels that the formulators of the triple-melting-pot hypothesis were perhaps "overly impressed by the low rate of intermarriage which they discovered in New Haven," a city which Thomas attempts to show is atypical in this respect.

A nationwide study of members of the United Lutheran Church in America (Bossard and Letts: 1956:308–310) showed the percentage of Lutherans marrying outside their church to be high and to be increasing: 46 per cent of those who married during the 1936–40 period; 47 per cent for the 1941–45 period; and 58 per cent for the 1946–50 period. Of those Lutherans who married outside their faith, 57 per cent married other Protestants; 20 per cent married Roman Catholics; 19 per cent married nonchurch members; and 4 per cent married Jews and other non-Christians. Almost twice as many Lutheran women as men married across church lines.

Recall that Thomas (1956:154) also reported more (Catholic) girls than boys contracting mixed marriages. Two explanations have been offered concerning why Catholic girls cross church lines to marry to a greater degree than Catholic men: (1) the choice of the Catholic girl is more restricted than that of the Catholic man because of the passive role assigned to her in courtship; (2) marriage to a non-Catholic man may offer the Catholic girl greater economic security (Mihanovich et al., 1952:204).

Studies on Jewish-Gentile marriages, however, show that Jewish men marry outside the faith more often than Jewish women. This tendency has been explained on the basis of the theory that Jewish boys usually have greater freedom to associate with Gentiles and are not likely to be so carefully supervised as Jewish girls (Baber, 1953:101; Barron, 1946:6–13).

In 1958, the United States Census Bureau (1958) published a nation-wide picture of the extent of mixed religious marriages in the three major religious groups in the United States: Protestant, Roman Catholic, and Jewish. The Bureau found that Protestant-Catholic combinations are by far the most commonly found interfaith marriages. The United States had 2,225,000 Protestant-Catholic married couples in 1958. The census data also show that 58.2 per cent of the Jews who marry outside the faith marry Protestants, and 41.8 per cent marry Catholics. The number of Jewish-Protestant and Jewish-Catholic married couples in 1958 were 57,000 and 41,000 respectively. Of all marriages in the three major religious bodies, 6.4 per cent were mixed.

PURPOSE OF STUDY

The purpose of this study was to ascertain the attitudes of young people, specifically, those of the Catholic faith, toward mixed religious marriages.

An attempt was made to determine some of the factors which seem to contribute to, and exert an influence upon, the formation of those attitudes.

A number of empirical studies have been made to ascertain attitudes of young people toward interfaith marriages (Baber, 1953:119; Landis, 1960; Burchinal, 1960; Wagner and Brown, 1965; Kenkel et al, 1965; Prince, 1956; Weller, 1941; Maier and Spinrad, 1957). A review of the literature, however, revealed three important limitations pertinent to our study.

1. Most of the previously published studies have tried to get at attitudes toward mixed marriages from answers to one or two questions rather than by means of a reliable instrument to measure those attitudes.
2. There have been limited attempts to study thoroughly attitudes toward interfaith marriage held specifically by Catholic students.
3. The sampling methods used by most earlier investigators to select their subjects (Catholics, in particular) do not ensure that a simple random or systematic sample was selected.

In the present investigation, three instruments were used to study attitudes toward cross-religious marriages. They were: (1) a comprehensive questionnaire; (2) the Thurstone (1929) scale for measuring attitudes toward the church;[2] and (3) an attitude scale, constructed for this study, to measure attitudes toward interfaith marriage.[3]

The group selected for study was a systematic sample of all Catholic students enrolled in a coeducational Catholic university located in a metropolitan area in the Pacific Northwest. Enrollment is normally about 2,000 students, approximately 60 per cent men and 40 per cent women.

The hope was that these instruments and the group selected for study would contribute to a more accurate picture of attitudes toward interfaith marriage held specifically by Catholic young people.

HYPOTHESES TESTED

In the present study, 15 hypotheses were investigated.

1. Attitudes toward interfaith marriage are *positively* associated with having parents of mixed religion.
2. Attitudes toward interfaith marriage are *positively* associated with the number of siblings or close friends who have contracted mixed religious marriages.
3. Attitudes toward interfaith marriage are *negatively* related to church attendance.
4. Attitudes toward interfaith marriage are *negatively* related to active participation in religious activities.

5. Attitudes toward interfaith marriage are *negatively* associated with the mother's active participation in religious activities during the subject's formative years at home.
6. Attitudes toward interfaith marriage are *negatively* associated with the father's active participation in religious activities during the subject's formative years at home.
7. Attitudes toward interfaith marriage are *negatively* associated with the perception that the mother would feel "unhappy or disturbed" if the son or daughter contemplated an interfaith marriage.
8. Attitudes toward interfaith marriage are *negatively* associated with the perception that the mother "would try to discourage" if the son or daughter contemplated an interfaith marriage.
9. Attitudes toward interfaith marriage are *negatively* associated with the perception that the father would feel "unhappy or disturbed" if the son or daughter contemplated an interfaith marriage.
10. Attitudes toward interfaith marriage are *negatively* associated with the perception that the father "would try to discourage" if the son or daughter contemplated an interfaith marriage.
11. Attitudes toward interfaith marriage are *positively* associated with the perceived amount of conflict between parents concerning religious questions.
12. Attitudes toward interfaith marriage are *positively* related to the amount of attendance at public secondary schools.
13. Attitudes toward interfaith marriage are *negatively* related to education in parochial schools.
14. Attitudes toward interfaith marriage are *positively* related to length of residence in urban areas.
15. Generalized attitudes toward the church as an institution is *negatively* associated with attitudes toward interfaith marriage.

THE INTERFAITH MARRIAGE SCALE

From a summary of the literature on interfaith marriage, a list of 12 item-pairs concerning the major aspects of such marriages was constructed; for example:

(a) It is as necessary now as it ever was to marry within one's own faith.
(b) It is quite old-fashioned for anyone to object to interfaith marriages.

I feel very strongly (c); quite strongly (d); not at all strongly (e); about this.

The respondent was asked to check the statement, *a* or *b*, which most nearly reflected his own, personal opinion, then to indicate how strongly he felt about this endorsement. The scoring of the items was as follows:

	Score
Approves idea of interfaith marriage and feels very strongly about it	3
Approves idea of interfaith marriage and feels quite strongly about it	2
Disapproves idea of interfaith marriage and feels quite strongly about it	1
Disapproves idea of interfaith marriage and feels very strongly about it.	0

Statement *a* in the above item-pair obviously expresses disapproval of the idea of an interfaith marriage, while statement *b* expresses approval. Only where there were very strong or quite strong feelings about the issue was the item given a score. The overall score for the 12-item scale was obtained by multiplying the mean of the scores on the items for which there was some strength of feeling on the part of the respondent by a constant in order to convert the mean scores to whole numbers after rounding.[4]

ANALYSIS OF RESPONSES TO THE ATTITUDE SCALE ITEMS

As seen in Table 1, a high percentage of both men and women appeared unwilling to contract an interfaith marriage. Approximately 70 per cent of the women and slightly more than 50 per cent of the men agreed with the statement that one should marry within one's faith.

Kenkel, Himler, and Cole (1965:34), however, found that approximately 60 per cent of the Catholic students in their sample were willing to marry outside their faith. Landis (1960:345) and Prince (1965:14) reported that over 70 per cent of the Catholics in their studies said they would contract an interfaith marriage.

The Catholic young people in the sample cited in this paper, therefore, appeared less willing to contract an interfaith marriage than Catholic students studied by most other investigators. For example, one female respondent in our sample wrote:

> I think interfaith marriages should be avoided because I believe religion and one's attitude toward God are the most important

aspects of one's life. If two people do not share the same attitudes on such a basic part of life, I think they are entering marriage with strikes against them.

Another female commented:

Everything I am and do pivots, in some way, around my faith. To marry a non-Catholic would mean the person I am closest to would not share one of the things closest to me.

Another female stated:

I feel that interfaith marriages should be avoided because a difference of religion adds one more problem to an already difficult adjustment of newly married couples. A common religion binds a couple closer together for it gives them the same set of values.

A male respondent wrote:

I feel people are creating unnecessary problems by contracting interfaith marriages. Catholics should, if at all possible, insist upon a Catholic mate or on a person that seriously wants to become a Catholic. This would be best for the children and the partners.

TABLE 1 Strength of belief that one should marry within one's faith by sex of respondent.

| | Sex | | | | |
| | Male | | Female | | |
Belief that one should marry within one's faith	N	%	N	%	Scale value
Very strongly agree	35	20.5	38	33.3	0
Quite strongly agree	52	30.4	41	36.0	1
Quite strongly disagree	27	15.8	13	11.4	2
Very strongly disagree	8	4.7	2	1.8	3
Indifferent	49	28.6	20	17.5	
Total	171	100.0	114	100.0	

$X^2 = 11.12$, $p < .05$.

Table 1 also shows women were significantly ($p < .05$) less willing to cross religious lines and marry than were men. Baber (1953:119), Burchinal (1960:251) and Prince (1956:12) also found women less willing than men to contract an interfaith marriage. Baber and Prince, however, did not analyze the responses of the Catholic and non-Catholic women to this question separately. In the Burchinal study, Catholic students were excluded because of their small number. Burchinal's findings, therefore, hold only for Protestant and religiously nonaffiliated students. Wagner and Brown (1965:90), however, in their study of Newman Club members (a Catholic campus organization), reported that Catholic girls were more willing to cross religious lines and marry than Catholic boys. On the other hand, Kenkel, Himler, and Cole (1965:36), found no significant difference in the response pattern of the Catholic men and women in their sample to the question of willingness to marry outside the faith. Landis (1960:345), noted little difference between the males and females of the Catholic faith in their expressed willingness to contract an interfaith marriage.

Slightly more than one-third (35.4 per cent) of the students believed that everyone, regardless of religious preference, should adhere to the principle of marrying within one's faith. Women appeared slightly more in favor of adherence to this principle than men. The difference, however, was not significant (p > .05).

Also, as shown in Table 2, almost 65 per cent of the women and nearly one-half the men said belonging to the same faith is a necessary part of a successful marriage. Women were significantly (<p.01) more strongly in favor of this statement than men.

More than 60 per cent of the men and over 67 per cent of the women said evidence and common sense support the view that interfaith marriages are undesirable.

In addition, as seen in Table 3, approximately 20 per cent of the men and almost 23 per cent of the women believed that mixed-religious

TABLE 2   Strength of belief that belonging to the same faith is a necessary part of a successful marriage by sex of respondent.

| Belief that belonging to the same faith is a necessary part of a successful marriage | Sex | | | | |
| | Male | | Female | | |
	N	%	N	%	Scale value
Very strongly agree	24	14.0	33	28.9	0
Quite strongly agree	57	33.3	41	36.0	1
Quite strongly disagree	35	20.5	13	11.4	2
Very strongly disagree	19	11.1	5	4.4	3
Indifferent	36	21.1	22	19.3	
Total	171	100.0	114	100.0	

$X^2 = 14.82$, p < .01.

TABLE 3 Strength of belief that interfaith marriages are undesirable even if otherwise successful by sex of respondent.

Belief that interfaith marriages are undesirable even if they are otherwise successful	Sex				
	Male		Female		
	N	%	N	%	Scale value
Very strongly agree	5	2.9	5	4.4	0
Quite strongly agree	28	16.4	21	18.4	1
Quite strongly disagree	57	33.3	32	28.1	2
Very strongly disagree	36	21.1	25	21.9	3
Indifferent	45	26.3	31	27.2	
Total	171	100.0	114	100.0	

$X^2 = 1.20$, $p > .05$.

marriages are undesirable even if seemingly successful. One female student wrote:

My parents are of different faiths and their marriage has been very successful. I can think of at least one more mixed marriage that has been very successful. However, on the whole, I am not in favor of interfaith marriages even in the best of circumstances.

One male student commented:

I have seen a few instances of apparent happiness in a marriage of a Catholic and a Protestant. But I have often wondered, will this endure a lifetime? Do they perhaps feel something is missing?

Over 80 per cent of the men and approximately 77 per cent of the women said differences over religious matters are likely to lead to other marital problems. Student comments on this issue include:

Since I have parents of the same faith who are both devout, I wish to have the same kind of marriage. I have known other families where one parent was of a different faith and there were conflicts over everything from which church to attend to birth control. I feel that unless you agree on religion you will find it difficult to agree on other things.

Religion is more than church services and religious activities. The Catholic religion is a way of life. . . . In marriage, two people cannot live a life together if they do not view life the same.

If your religion is really your way of living, then you cannot divorce it from your marriage.

Marriage entails quite an adjustment on the part of both partners. The fewer areas of disagreement there are the easier the adjustment will be. To me, religion is a very important part of my life; and I would want my spouse to share it with me. If we agree on religion, I think our marriage would have fewer problems.

Does the Catholic party in an interfaith marriage expect the mate to adopt his religion and/or agree to have the children follow the Catholic faith? As seen in Table 4, more than one-half (53.3 per cent) of the students would want the mate to adopt their religion. No significant difference was found between the males and females in the response pattern to this question. As Table 4 shows, almost the same percentage of men as women said the non-Catholic party should adopt the Catholic faith.

TABLE 4   Strength of belief that mate should adopt one's religion by sex of respondent.

| Belief that mate should accept my religion | Sex | | | | |
| | Male | | Female | | |
	N	%	N	%	Scale value
Very strongly agree	47	27.5	33	28.9	0
Quite strongly agree	44	25.7	28	24.6	1
Quite strongly disagree	28	16.4	22	19.3	2
Very strongly disagree	17	9.9	16	14.0	3
Indifferent	35	20.5	15	13.2	
Total	171	100.0	114	100.0	

$X^2 = 3.48$, $p > .05$.

Analysis of the responses to the question of religious training of the children in interfaith marriages showed the majority of students wanted the children to follow their faith. (See Table 5). One female respondent wrote:

I am presently planning to marry someone of the Methodist faith. He respects my views on Catholicism and has agreed to bring up our children as Catholics, although he would certainly prefer that they choose their own religion. My parents would ordinarily not favor such a marriage; but the person I intend to marry is so fine a man that they have given their approval . . . I do not expect him to change his beliefs to mine, since at this time he would find this impossible. I am a devout Catholic; and I would not contract such a marriage if he would not agree to the conditions set down by the Church. If, in the future, he changes his mind and will not agree, I will not marry him, even though I want this more than anything else.

Another female commented:

If I were to marry a non-Catholic, I would not demand that he join my faith. The only demands I would make would be that our children be brought up as Catholics. . . . I have convictions about my faith, and I never want to lose them. I want to give my children these same convictions.

A male respondent stated:

I would contract an interfaith marriage only if my partner agreed to bring up our children in my religion . . . If my partner would not agree to this, I do not believe I would go through with the marriage since this would be a constant tension.

Further study of the data in Table 5 shows that women, more than men, wanted their children to follow their faith. Over 90 per cent of the women compared to approximately 75 per cent of the men wanted the children to follow their religion. This difference was significant ($p < .01$).

A major reason why the Catholic Church opposes interfaith marriages is the belief that a mixed marriage hazards the faith of the Catholic party.

TABLE 5 Strength of belief that children should follow subject's religion by sex of respondent.

Belief that my children should accept my religion	Sex				
	Male		Female		
	N	%	N	%	Scale value
Very strongly agree	96	56.1	88	77.1	0
Quite strongly agree	33	19.3	15	13.2	1
Quite strongly disagree	20	11.7	2	1.8	2
Very strongly disagree	9	5.3	5	4.4	3
Indifferent	13	7.6	4	3.5	
Total	171	100.0	114	100.0	

$X^2 = 14.62$, $p < .01$.

The Church fears that many Catholics who contract a mixed religion marriage attend church irregularly after marriage or lose faith entirely.

As seen in Table 6, more than one-third of the students also felt that interfaith marriages may jeopardize the faith of the partners. Almost one-third of the men and over 40 per cent of the women agreed with the statement that a mixed-religion marriage weakens the faith of the spouses.

TABLE 6   Strength of belief that interfaith marriages weaken the religious faith of the partners by sex of respondent.

| Belief that religious faith is weakened by contracting an interfaith marriage | Sex | | | | |
| | Male | | Female | | |
	N	%	N	%	Scale value
Very strongly agree	18	10.5	16	14.0	0
Quite strongly agree	38	22.2	31	27.2	1
Quite strongly disagree	42	24.6	24	21.1	3
Very strongly disagree	42	24.6	29	25.4	3
Indifferent	31	18.1	14	12.3	
Total	171	100.0	114	100.0	

$X^2 = 3.22$, $p > .05$.

One male student wrote:

Most of the interfaith marriages that I know about have led to the loss or partial loss of one of the partners' faith.

Another male commented:

It is possible that an interfaith marriage could succeed. However, there are so many obstacles for the partners to overcome that the marriage is likely to fail. It would also tend to weaken, possibly destroy, the faith of both partners.

A female student stated:

My faith is very strong. I would never want to risk losing it through an interfaith marriage. I have seen Catholics, even friends of mine, lose their faith this way.

Approximately one student in nine believed it better not to marry than to marry some one of another faith. However, approximately 40 per cent of the men and almost 30 per cent of the women said they would cross religious lines and marry rather than remain single.

A recapitulation of the findings in this section indicates the following:

1. Catholic young people in the sample appeared less willing to contract an interfaith marriage than Catholic students studied by other investigators.

2. Women appeared less willing than men to cross religious lines and marry. This is contrary to Wagner and Brown's (1965: 82–85) findings which showed that Catholic girls were more willing to contract an interfaith marriage than Catholic boys. Kenkel, Himler, and Cole (1965: 30–37), on the other hand, found no significant difference in the response pattern of the Catholic men and women in their sample to the question of willingness to marry outside the faith. Landis (1960: 341–347) noted little difference between the males and females of the Catholic faith in their expressed willingness to contract an interfaith marriage.

3. Slightly more than one-third of the students believed that everyone, regardless of religious preference, should adhere to the principle of marrying within one's faith.

4. Approximately 65 per cent of the students believed that marital happiness is more assured in religiously homogeneous marriages than in mixed-religious marriages.

5. Over one-half of the students, and women more than men, said belonging to the same faith is a necessary part of a successful marriage.

6. More than three out of five students said evidence and common sense support the view that interfaith marriages are undesirable.

7. In addition, approximately one student in five believed that mixed-religious marriages are undesirable even if otherwise successful.

8. Over 80 per cent of the men and approximately 77 per cent of the women said differences over religious matters are likely to lead to marital conflicts.

9. More than one-half of the students would want the mate in an interfaith marriage to adopt the student's religion.

10. In addition, the majority of the students, and women more than men, wanted the children to follow the student's faith.

11. Approximately 18 per cent of the students believed that children of cross-religious marriages are likely to be socially handicapped. Over one-half, however, believed the offspring of mixed marriages are not likely to experience any serious social handicap.

12. More tnan one-third of the students believed that a mixed marriage weakens the faith of the partners.

13. Finally, approximately one student in nine believed it better not

to marry than to marry someone of another faith. However, approximately 40 per cent of the men and almost 30 per cent of the women said they would cross religious lines and marry rather than remain single.

OTHER ASPECTS OF RELIGIOUS AND INTERFAITH MARRIAGE

The data presented in this section are based upon the responses to the general set of questions asked on interfaith marriages.

As seen in Table 7, attitudes toward interfaith marriage are negatively related to church attendance only for the male sample. The hypothesis (3) is partially, supported.

Responses to the question on participation in religious activities (other than church attendance) were categorized as "very active," "participate regularly," and "seldom or never participate." (See Table 8). Over 71

TABLE 7   Correlation between church attendance and attitudes toward interfaith marriage.

Interfaith marriage scale value score	Church attendance					
	Once a week		Two–three times a week		Twice a month or less	
	N	%	N	%	N	%
Males:						
1–2	33	34.0	24	48.9	3	12.0
3–4	42	43.3	21	42.9	10	40.0
5–6	19	19.6	4	8.2	10	40.0
7–8	3	3.1	—	—	2	8.0
Total[a]	97	100.0	49	100.0	25	100.0
Females:						
1–2	22	40.7	29	50.0	—	—
3–4	21	38.9	19	32.8	1	50.0
5–6	9	16.7	8	13.8	1	50.0
7–8	2	3.7	2	3.4	—	—
Total[b]	54	100.0	58	100.0	2	100.0
Both sexes:						
1–2	55	36.4	53	49.5	3	11.1
3–4	63	41.8	40	37.4	11	40.7
5–6	28	18.5	12	11.2	11	40.7
7–8	5	3.3	2	1.9	2	7.5
Total[c]	151	100.0	107	100.0	27	100.0

[a] $X^2 = 18.38$, $p < .01$.
[b] $X^2 = 66.12$, $p > .05$.
[c] $X^2 = 21.66$, $p < .01$.

per cent of the students said they participated actively or regularly in religious activities. This variable, however, was not significantly associated with unwillingness to marry outside the faith. Thus, the hypothesis (4) that attitudes toward mixed-religion marriages are negatively related to active participation in religious activities was not supported.

TABLE 8 Correlation between participation in religious activities and attitudes toward interfaith marriage.

Interfaith marriage scale value score	Participation in religious activities (other than church attendance)					
	Am very active		Participate regularly		Seldom or never participate	
	N	%	N	%	N	%
Males:						
1–2	11	30.6	29	32.9	20	42.6
3–4	11	30.6	44	50.0	18	38.3
5–6	14	38.8	10	11.4	9	19.1
7–8	—	—	5	5.7	—	—
Total[a]	36	100.0	88	100.0	47	100.0
Females:						
1–2	6	33.3	29	46.1	16	48.5
3–4	8	44.5	22	34.9	11	33.3
5–6	2	11.1	12	19.0	4	12.1
7–8	2	11.1	—	—	2	6.1
Total[b]	18	100.0	63	100.0	33	100.0
Both sexes:						
1–2	17	31.5	58	38.4	36	44.9
3–4	19	35.2	66	43.7	19	36.3
5–6	16	29.6	22	14.6	13	16.3
7–8	2	3.7	5	3.3	2	2.5
Total[c]	54	100.0	151	100.0	80	100.0

[a] $X^2 = 9.37$, $p > .05$.
[b] $X^2 = 1.19$, $p > .05$.
[c] $X^2 = 7.41$, $p > .05$.

The relationship between attitudes toward interfaith marriage and mother's participation in religious activities was in the predicted direction. That is, students, women in particular, who said their mothers took an active part in religious functions appeared less willing ($p < .01$) to contract a mixed marriage than those who said their mothers seldom or never participated in church activities. Thus, the hypothesis (5) was supported. (See Table 9).

No statistically significant association was found, however, between father's participation in religious activities and student attitudes toward

TABLE 9 Correlation between mother's participation in religious activities and attitudes toward interfaith marriage.

Interfaith marriage scale value score	Mother's participation			
	Was very active or participated regularly		Seldom or never participated	
	No.	%	No.	%
Males:				
1–2	41	41.0	19	26.8
3–4	38	38.0	35	49.3
5–6	19	19.0	14	19.7
7–8	2	2.0	3	4.2
Total[a]	100	100.0	71	100.0
Females:				
1–2	36	52.9	15	32.6
3–4	18	26.5	23	50.0
5–6	10	14.7	8	17.4
7–8	4	5.9	—	—
Total[b]	68	100.0	46	100.0
Both sexes:				
1–2	77	45.8	34	29.1
3–4	56	33.3	58	49.5
5–6	29	17.3	22	18.8
7–8	6	3.6	3	2.6
Total[c]	168	100.0	117	100.0

[a] $X^2 = 3.80$, $p > .05$.
[b] $X^2 = 6.90$, $p < .05$, $V = .24$.
[c] $X^2 = 9.52$, $p < .01$, $V = .17$.

cross-religion marriages. The hypothesis (6) was not supported. (See Table 10).

Hypothesis (1) predicted that children of a cross-religion marriage would hold tolerant attitudes toward interfaith marriages. Living in a mixed-religion home, these children would not, in general, be exposed to a consistency of religious teachings and perhaps would have acquired a more tolerant attitude toward mixed marriages than children reared in homes where the parents were of one faith. As seen in Table 11, however, the findings do not support this hypothesis. Students whose parents were of different faiths did not appear more willing to contract a mixed marriage than those whose parents were of the same religion. (See also Kenkel, Himler, and Cole (1965: 30–37)).

Although no significant association was found between cross-religion marriage of parents and children's attitudes toward interfaith marriage, many students who were the product of a mixed marriage commented on their feelings toward such a marriage. Some typical comments follow:

TABLE 10   Correlation between father's participation in religious activities and attitudes toward interfaith marriage.

Interfaith marriage scale value score	Father's participation			
	Was very active or participated		Seldom or never participated	
	No.	%	No.	%
Males:				
1–2[a]	30	39.0	29	31.5
3–4[b]	35	45.4	37	40.2
5–6	10	13.0	23	25.0
7–8	2	2.6	3	3.3
Total[c]	77	100.0	92	100.0
Females:				
1–2	18	43.9	33	45.2
3–4	15	36.6	26	35.6
5–6	5	12.2	13	17.8
7–8	3	7.3	1	1.4
Total[d]	41	100.0	73	100.0
Both sexes:				
1–2	48	40.7	62	37.6
3–4	50	42.4	63	38.2
5–6	15	12.7	36	21.8
7–8	5	4.2	4	2.4
Total[e]	118	100.0	165	100.0

[a] One male student who received this scale value score did not answer section on Father's participation in religious activities.
[b] One male student who received this scale value score did not answer section on Father's participation in religious activities.
[c] $X^2 = 3.90$, $p > .05$.
[d] $X^2 = .01$, $p > .05$.
[e] $X^2 = 2.15$, $p > .05$.

Female student:

Being a product of an interfaith marriage, I do not believe in mixed marriages because I know of their disadvantages. Although my parents rarely argue over religious matters, in fact, mother is the one who sees that we attend Mass, etc., the difference is still there. She simply cannot understand our feelings toward our faith, although she has tried.

Male student:

I am the product of a mixed marriage; and I consider my parents' marriage unsuccessful. Had they been of the same religion and

TABLE 11   Correlation between religious faith in which parents were reared and attitudes of students toward interfaith marriage.

| Interfaith marriage scale value score | Parental marriage pattern[a] | | | |
| | Nonmixed marriages | | Mixed marriages | |
	N	%	N	%
Males:				
1–2	32	33.0	18	32.7
3–4	44	45.3	25	45.5
5–6	18	18.6	11	20.0
7–8	3	3.1	1	1.8
Total[b]	97	100.0	55	100.0
Females:				
1–2	27	45.7	22	58.0
3–4	22	37.3	11	28.9
5–6	8	13.6	4	10.5
7–8	2	3.4	1	2.6
Total[c]	59	100.0	38	100.0
Both sexes:				
1–2	59	37.8	40	43.0
3–4	66	42.3	36	38.7
5–6	26	16.7	15	16.1
7–8	5	3.2	2	2.2
Total[d]	156	100.0	93	100.0

[a] Thirty-six students (19 males, 17 females) stated one of their parents was Catholic or Protestant and the other had "no church affiliation." These 36 cases are not included in the table.
[b] $X^2 = .02$, $p > .05$.
[c] $X^2 = 1.35$, $p > .05$.
[d] $X^2 = .62$, $p > .05$.

held the same attitude toward the church, they could very well have made a better adjustment in other areas of their marriage.

Male student:

I have a rather unique situation. My parents contracted an interfaith marriage and my mother adopted my father's religion. My father was later killed in the service; and my mother raised me as a Catholic. She, however, was never active in church activities. Later she remarried a non-Catholic and problems have definitely developed. I would rate my mother's second interfaith marriage as most unsuccessful.

Female student:

My parents' marriage has worked out very well even though they are of different faiths only because they are two very understanding people. Statistics on interfaith marriages show, however, that this is more often the exception. For this reason, I would much prefer to marry a Catholic.

Hypothesis (2) predicted that attitudes toward interfaith marriage would be positively associated with the number of siblings or close friends who had contracted a mixed marriage. This hypothesis was not supported by the findings.

Students who felt their parents would try to "discourage" or "dissuade" them from contracting an interfaith marriage held less tolerant attitudes toward cross-religion marriages than those who did not anticipate opposition from their parents if they contemplated a mixed marriage. (See Tables 12 and 13). The differences, with one exception, were significant (p < .01). The exception, as seen in Table 12, was the correlation

TABLE 12   Correlation between perception that mother would try to discourage son or daughter from contracting a mixed religious marriage and attitudes toward interfaith marriage.

| Interfaith marriage scale value score | "If you wanted to contract an interfaith marriage, how do you think your parents would feel?" | | | |
| | Mother[a] would try to discourage | | | |
	Yes	%	No.	%
Males:				
1–2	36	50.0	15	25.0
3–4	32	44.4	29	48.3
5–6	3	4.2	15	25.0
7–8	1	1.4	1	1.7
Total[b]	72	100.0	60	100.0
Females:				
1–2	26	49.0	9	28.1
3–4	18	34.0	12	37.5
5–6	8	15.1	8	25.0
7–8	1	1.9	3	9.4
Total[c]	53	100.0	32	100.0
Both sexes:				
1–2	62	49.6	24	26.1
3–4	50	40.0	41	44.6
5–6	11	8.8	23	25.0
7–8	2	1.6	4	4.3
Total[d]	125	100.0	92	100.0

[a] Students who stated they did not know how their mother would feel or who did not answer this question are not included in this table.
[b] $X^2 = 15.02$, p < .01.
[c] $X^2 = 4.75$, p > .05.
[d] $X^2 = 17.95$, p < .01.

between the feelings of the women students that their mothers would try to discourage them from contracting a mixed marriage and their attitudes toward interfaith marriage. Hypothesis (10) was supported, and, Hypothesis (8), partially supported.

TABLE 13   Correlation between perception that father would try to discourage son or daughter from contracting a mixed religious marriage and attitudes toward interfaith marriage.

Interfaith marriage scale value score	"If you wanted to contract an interfaith marriage, how do you think your parents would feel?"			
	Father would try to discourage			
	Yes	%	No.	%
Males:				
1–2	24	47.1	14	20.6
3–4	22	43.1	33	48.5
5–6	2	3.9	20	29.4
7–8	3	5.9	1	1.5
Total[a]	51	100.0	68	100.0
Females:				
1–2	25	56.8	6	22.3
3–4	14	31.8	9	33.3
5–6	4	9.1	9	33.3
7–8	1	2.3	3	11.1
Total[b]	44	100.0	27	100.0
Both sexes:				
1–2	49	51.6	20	21.1
3–4	36	37.9	42	44.2
5–6	6	6.3	29	30.5
7–8	4	4.2	4	4.2
Total[c]	95	100.0	95	100.0

[a] $X^2 = 12.50$, $p < .01$.
[b] $X^2 = 12.24$, $p < .01$.
[c] $X^2 = 24.93$, $p < .01$.

Seniors showed less willingness to marry outside their faith than the three other classes. Data in the current study thus corroborate the findings of Kenkel, Himler, and Cole (1965:35), who also noted less willingness on the part of upper-classmen to marry outside their faith than lower-classmen. Thus, the hypothesis (12) was supported.

Hypothesis (13) predicted that type of school attended, whether public or parochial, would be related to attitudes toward interfaith marriage. The findings, however, do not support this hypothesis.

No significant relationship was found between place of residence and attitudes toward interfaith marriage. Students who lived most of their lives in large urban areas did not hold more tolerant attitudes toward mixed marriages than those reared in small cities or rural communities. The hypothesis (14) was not supported.

TABLE 14 Correlation between length of attendance at public school and attitudes toward interfaith marriage.

Interfaith marriage scale value score	Years attendance at public school			
	Years 1–3		Years 4–12	
	No.	%	No.	%
Males:				
1–2	40	35.7	20	33.9
3–4	47	42.0	26	44.1
5–6	23	20.5	10	16.9
7–8	2	1.8	3	5.1
Total[a]	112	100.0	59	100.0
Females:				
1–2	36	49.3	15	36.6
3–4	23	31.5	18	43.9
5–6	11	15.1	7	17.1
7–8	3	4.1	1	2.4
Total[b]	73	100.0	41	100.0
Both sexes:				
1–2	76	41.1	35	35.0
3–4	70	37.8	44	44.0
5–6	34	18.4	17	17.0
7–8	5	2.7	4	4.0
Total[c]	185	100.0	100	100.0

[a] $X^2 = .07$, $p > .05$.
[b] $X^2 = 2.06$, $p > .05$.
[c] $X^2 = 1.20$, $p > .05$.

To test the hypothesis (15), whether generalized attitudes toward the church as an institution are negatively associated with attitudes toward mixed marriages, students' scores on the Thurstone scale were correlated with their scores on the Inter-faith Marriage Attitude scale. Results of the analysis between the two pairs of scores were significant for the men ($r = -.25$, $p < .01$) and for the women ($r = -.19$, $p < .05$), and the hypothesis was supported.

To summarize, the data presented give support to the following hypotheses:

1. Attitudes toward interfaith marriage are *negatively* related to church attendance only for the male sample. (Hypothesis 3).
2. Attitudes toward interfaith marriage are *negatively* associated with mother's active participation in religious activities only for the female sample. (Hypothesis 5).
3. Attitudes toward interfaith marriage are *negatively* associated with perception that mother "would try to discourage" if son or daughter contemplated an interfaith marriage only for the male sample. (Hypothesis 8).
4. Attitudes toward interfaith marriage are *negatively* associated with perception that father "would try to discourage" if son or daughter contemplated an interfaith marriage. (Hypothesis 10).
5. Attitudes toward interfaith marriage are *negatively* associated with perception that mother would feel "unhappy or disturbed" if son or daughter contemplated an interfaith marriage only for the male sample. (Hypothesis 7).
6. Attitudes toward interfaith marriage are *negatively* associated

TABLE 15 Correlation between length of attendance at parochial school and attitudes toward interfaith marriage.

Interfaith marriage scale value score	Years attendance at parochial school			
	Years 1–9		Years 10–12	
	No.	%	No.	%
Males:				
1–2	21	32.3	39	36.8
3–4	31	47.7	42	39.6
5–6	10	15.4	23	21.7
7–8	3	4.6	2	1.9
Total[a]	65	100.0	106	100.0
Females:				
1–2	15	33.3	36	52.5
3–4	21	46.7	20	29.0
5–6	8	17.8	10	14.5
7–8	1	2.2	3	4.3
Total[b]	45	100.0	69	100.0
Both sexes:				
1–2	36	32.7	75	42.8
3–4	52	47.3	62	35.4
5–6	18	16.4	33	18.9
7–8	4	3.6	5	2.9
Total[c]	110	100.0	175	100.0

[a] $X^2 = 1.06$, $p > .05$.
[b] $X^2 = 4.54$, $p > .05$.
[c] $X^2 = 4.22$, $p > .05$.

TABLE 16 Correlation between place of residence and attitudes toward interfaith marriage.

Interfaith marriage scale value score	Have lived most of my life					
	On a farm or small town		In a medium size town		In a large city	
	No.	%	No.	%	No.	%
Males:						
1–2	14	35.9	31	39.7	15	27.8
3–4	17	43.6	34	43.9	22	40.7
5–6	7	17.9	13	16.7	13	24.1
7–8	1	2.6	—	—	4	7.4
Total[a]	39	100.0	78	100.0	54	100.0
Females:						
1–2	10	40.0	22	52.4	19	40.4
3–4	12	48.0	12	28.6	17	36.2
5–6	3	12.0	8	19.0	7	14.9
7–8	—	—	—	—	4	8.5
Total[b]	25	100.0	42	100.0	47	100.0
Both sexes:						
1–2	24	37.5	53	44.2	34	33.7
3–4	29	45.3	46	38.3	39	38.6
5–6	10	15.6	21	17.5	20	19.8
7–8	1	1.6	—	—	8	7.9
Total[c]	64	100.0	120	100.0	101	100.0

[a] $X^2 = 4.57$, $p > .05$.
[b] $X^2 = 3.59$, $p > .05$.
[c] $X^2 = 5.44$, $p > .05$.

with perception that father would feel "unhappy or disturbed" if son or daughter contemplated an interfaith marriage. (Hypothesis 9).

7. Generalized attitudes toward the church as an institution are *negatively* associated with attitudes toward interfaith marriage. (Hypothesis 15).

The following hypotheses were not supported by our data:

1. Attitudes toward interfaith marriage are *positively* associated with having parents of mixed religions. (Hypothesis 1).
2. Attitudes toward interfaith marriage are *negatively* related to active participation in religious activities. (Hypothesis 4).
3. Attitudes toward interfaith marriage are *negatively* associated with father's active participation in religious activities. (Hypothesis 6).

TABLE 17   Correlation between perception that mother would feel unhappy or disturbed if son or daughter contracted a mixed religious marriage and attitudes toward interfaith marriage.

Interfaith marriage scale value score	"If you wanted to contract an interfaith marriage, how do you think your parents would feel?"			
	Mother[a] would feel unhappy or disturbed			
	Yes	%	No.	%
Males:				
1–2	42	50.0	9	18.8
3–4	34	40.5	27	56.2
5–6	7	8.3	11	22.9
7–8	1	1.2	1	2.1
Total[b]	84	100.0	48	100.0
Females:				
1–2	36	52.3	8	30.8
3–4	23	33.3	8	30.8
5–6	9	13.0	7	26.9
7–8	1	1.4	3	11.5
Total[c]	69	100.0	26	100.0
Both sexes:				
1–2	78	50.9	17	23.0
3–4	57	37.3	35	47.3
5–6	16	10.5	18	24.3
7–8	2	1.3	4	5.4
Total[d]	153	100.0	74	100.0

[a] Students who stated they did not know how their mother would feel or who did not answer this question are not included in this table.
[b] $X^2 = 14.18$, $p > .01$, $V = .33$.
[c] $X^2 = .86$, $p > .05$.
[d] $X^2 = 19.70$, $p > .01$, $V = .30$.

4.   Attitudes toward interfaith marriage are *positively* associated with the number of siblings or close friends who have contracted a mixed-religion marriage. (Hypothesis 2).

5.   Attitudes toward interfaith marriage are *positively* associated with perceived amount of conflict between parents concerning religious questions. (Hypothesis 11).

6.   Attitudes toward interfaith marriage are *positively* related to amount of attendance at public secondary schools. (Hypothesis 12).

7.   Attitudes toward interfaith marriage are *negatively* related to education in parochial schools. (Hypothesis 12).

8.   Attitudes toward interfaith marriage are *positively* related to length of residence in urban areas. (Hypothesis 14).

TABLE 18 Correlation between perception that father would feel unhappy or disturbed if son or daughter contracted a mixed religious marriage and attitudes toward interfaith marriage.

| | "If you wanted to contract an interfaith marriage, how do you think your parents would feel?" | | | |
| | Father would feel unhappy or disturbed | | | |
Interfaith marriage scale value score	Yes	%	No.	%
Males:				
1–2	32	45.1	6	12.5
3–4	28	39.4	27	56.2
5–6	8	11.3	14	29.2
7–8	3	4.2	1	2.1
Total[a]	71	100.0	48	100.0
Females:				
1–2	35	61.4	5	20.8
3–4	17	29.8	7	29.2
5–6	4	7.0	9	37.5
7–8	1	1.8	3	12.5
Total[b]	57	100.0	24	100.0
Both sexes:				
1–2	67	52.3	11	15.3
3–4	45	35.2	34	47.2
5–6	12	9.4	23	31.9
7–8	4	3.1	4	5.6
Total[c]	128	100.0	72	100.0

[a] $X^2 = 14.51$, $p > .01$, $V = .35$.
[b] $X^2 = 19.30$, $p > .01$, $V = .49$.
[c] $X^2 = 31.30$, $p > .01$, $V = .40$.

ROLE CONFLICT IN INTERFAITH MARRIAGES

An interfaith marriage is more than a union between two people who profess allegiance to different religions. It is a union of two different cultural products. Culture is a pervasive thing, penetrating into every phase of our existence. It reveals itself particularly in those aspects of our lives that our fundamental in the marital relationship.

A social role is a unit of culture. It is a pattern of behavior associated with a distinctive social position. A role tells the individual what he ought to do as a father, son, or brother, to whom he has obligations, and upon whom he has a rightful claim.

The obligations placed upon an individual by the variety of roles he is expected to play are oftentimes conflicting and difficult to reconcile. Sometimes, also, there are conflicting pressures and demands within a

TABLE 19   Correlation between perceived amount of conflict between parents concerning religious questions and attitudes toward interfaith marriage.

| Interfaith marriage scale value score | Perceived amount of conflict between parents concerning religious questions[a] | | | | | |
| | Very much | | Much | | Little or none | |
	No.	%	No.	%	No.	%
Males:						
1–2	36	32.7	10	37.0	14	42.4
3–4[a]	46	41.9	14	51.9	12	36.4
5–6	23	20.9	3	11.1	7	21.2
7–8	5	4.5	—	—	—	—
Total[b]	110	100.0	27	100.0	33	100.0
Females:						
1–2	25	43.8	13	43.3	13	48.2
3–4	22	38.6	8	26.7	11	40.7
5–6	7	12.3	9	30.0	2	7.4
7–8	3	5.3	—	—	1	3.7
Total[c]	57	100.0	30	100.0	27	100.0
Both sexes:						
1–2	61	36.5	23	40.3	27	45.0
3–4	68	40.7	22	38.6	23	38.3
5–6	30	18.0	12	21.1	9	15.0
7–8	8	4.8	—	—	1	1.7
Total[d]	167	100.0	57	100.0	60	100.0

[a] One male student who received this scale value score did not answer this question.
[b] $X^2 = 3.56$, p > .05.
[c] $X^2 = 3.89$, p > .05.
[d] $X^2 = 1.65$, p > .05.

single role itself. Such competing obligations are labeled "role conflicts." Some social roles are especially susceptible to incompatible expectations. This is particularly the case with marital roles in interfaith marriages.

Two of the most important variables which help determine the degree of role strain that partners in an interfaith marriage experience are (1) the intensity of the couple's individual devotion, and (2) the degree of institutional differences in the two religions.

Role strain is especially acute in the Catholic father-Protestant mother combination. Broom and Selznick (1958:382) offer a possible explanation for this. They write:

. . . a divorce rate three times as high for the Catholic father-Protestant mother combination as for the Protestant father-Catholic mother combination requires special attention. It is likely that the tendency in most Protestant denominations for the father to play a passive role in the religious training of his children lessens conflict with the Catholic mother. When the father is Catholic and the mother Protestant, each is likely to feel strongly that the children's religious training is his own responsibility, increasing the chances of conflict.

Another factor contributing to conflict in the Catholic father-Protestant mother combination is the higher rate of patriarchalism among Catholics. Commenting on this point, Broom and Selznick (1958:383) add:

> The patriarchal husband with an equalitarian wife will have many points of friction. In contrast, the equalitarian husband with a wife accustomed to a more patriarchal family will find his wife less demanding than he expected, while she in turn finds more freedom in marriage than she expected.

Role conflict may also be present in interfaith marriages involving couples whose religious commitment is minimal. In such cases, the source of conflict may be a commitment to one's familial and cultural background. Considerable resistance to giving up one's religion or allowing the children to adopt the mate's religion may emerge, especially if an abandonment of ties to one's familial background is experienced.

In our study, the expressed attitudes of many of the young people toward mixed religious marriages show a high potential for "role conflict." For example, the majority of the students, and women more than men, want the children to follow their religion in a mixed marriage. Controversy over the religious training of the children is perhaps the biggest point of friction in interfaith marriages. It is only natural for both parents to wish to impart to their children some of the religious beliefs they have come to value. However, a Catholic husband married to a non-Catholic wife who expects the children to follow her religion may experience role strain if he meets her expectations. To agree to her religious demands and allow the children to adopt her faith would violate the expectations he, church authorities, and parents hold about his role as a Catholic parent. In addition, he may view the husband's role as the dominant one in a marriage involving major responsibility for all important decisions including the right to decide the religious faith of his children.

Role strain would also be experienced by the Catholic wife who contracts an interfaith marriage and allows her husband to decide the religious faith of the children; by so doing, she would violate the expectations she and others hold about her role as a Catholic mother.

Even though a husband may have disavowed many of his childhood religious beliefs, he may still feel that his children should be brought up in his faith. However, if the husband is Protestant and contracts a mixed marriage with a Catholic, he, as the non-Catholic partner, has agreed not to interfere with the religious training of the children.

A Protestant husband married to a Catholic wife may also feel bewilderment at the complexity of Catholic doctrine and practice and may experience a feeling of isolation from his Catholic spouse and children. Under such circumstances, the father, as the non-Catholic party, may experience difficulty in fulfilling his parental role of leadership and authority in the home.

The possibility of role conflict is great when husband or wife is expected to train the children in ways contrary to his or her religious beliefs. In Catholic-non-Catholic marriages, the spouses will soon discover their marital partners, parents, and church authorities each have differing expectations as to how they should perform their parental role regarding the religious education of their offspring. The more devout, and therefore, committed the spouses are to their different faiths, the greater the role conflict.

More than half the students in our study said they expect the mate to adopt their religion in an interfaith marriage. Such an attitude could lead to role conflict. For example, the Catholic wife who holds this attitude and contracts a mixed marriage is expected in her role as a Catholic to show loyalty to her religion and to try to convert her husband; in her role as wife, however, she is expected to show loyalty to her husband and adopt his faith if this is his attitude; in her role as daughter she is expected to show loyalty to her parents, and they want her to remain faithful to her religion.

Should a husband in an interfaith marriage wish to relinquish his patriarchal role and yield to his wife's domination, especially in regard to religious issues, role conflict may still be introduced by the attitudes of parents and relatives who may feel that the husband should be head of the family and have the final word, especially on such issues as the religion he will follow or the religious education of his children.

Also, when the parental families of a couple who have contracted a mixed marriage are devout in their religion, they may feel strongly that their grandchildren should follow their religious beliefs. The young wife, therefore, who contracts an interfaith marriage is expected, in her role as daughter, to show loyalty to her parents and see that the children follow her faith; in her role as wife, however, she is expected to show loyalty to her husband; she may view a husband's role as involving major responsibility for all important decisions, including the right to decide the religious faith of the children.

Families from some older cultures and ethnic groups also have developed a system of religious worship and practice that is an integral part of their culture. To marry outside the religion of a strong culture group, therefore, would be tantamount to breaking with family tradition and culture. Such a break with one's past can create conflict in some individuals which is oftentimes increased by the pressures exerted by parents and religious authorities to conform to church doctrine and practice. Being at variance with one's family can produce a feeling of guilt and anxiety for some, especially when accompanied by threats of being ostracized by one's family.

In-law interference in interfaith marriages may appear in threats to exclude the son-in-law or daughter-in-law from full acceptance in the family group.

In our study, young people who felt their father would try to discourage them if they contemplated an interfaith marriage expressed unwillingness to cross religious lines and marry. This finding was true for both male and female students.

Men who felt their mother would try to discourage them from entering a mixed marriage also appeared unwilling to contract an interfaith marriage. Women, on the other hand, expressed willingness to cross religious lines and marry even though their mother would feel unhappy and would try to discourage them from contracting a mixed marriage. The potential for role conflict in an interfaith marriage because of parental interference, therefore, appears to be high for the women students in our sample.

The average Catholic has been trained from childhood to identify with and conform to Catholic family standards. Catholic standards impose difficult and exacting obligations upon the faithful. Consequently, the Catholic partner in a mixed marriage who, because of pressure from the non-Catholic spouse or in-law interference, agrees to artificial contraception or does not educate the children in the Catholic faith or fails to conform to other Catholic family standards will experience strain in his religious role.

Catholics possess a concise, authoritatively defined set of principles and precepts covering most aspects of family life. On such moral issues as the use of contraceptives, birth control, the indissolubility of the marriage bond, and the sacramental nature of marriage, Catholics maintain a doctrine somewhat at variance with that held by most non-Catholics. Consequently, the potential for role conflict in mixed marriages involving Catholics is great as the examples in this study illustrate.

CONCLUSIONS

This study attempted to measure attitudes toward interfaith marriage held by Catholic youth. The expressed attitudes of these young people, however, cannot be used to predict whether many of them will actually marry outside their faith. Such factors as differences in the sex ratio, residence, ethnic origin, nationality, socioeconomic status, and personality characteristics of the prospective mate may all play an important part in modifying the influence of expressed attitudes toward cross-religious marriages.

Sometimes, expressed attitudes toward mixed marriages may be in striking contradiction to actual behavior. Then, such attitudes are significant because they may throw light on the extent to which family and/or community attitudes toward mixed marriages influence what one will do when actually faced with the problem of an interfaith marriage.

The Vatican Ecumenical Council has undoubtedly opened the way for a new era of collaboration among the churches. Still, such basic and distinct differences in theological views as the meaning of the Immaculate Conception, the forgiveness of sins, Transubstantiation,[5] Papal Infallibility,[6] and other dogmas held by the various churches continue to serve as barriers to the intermarriage of persons of different faiths who are otherwise compatible.

John J. Kane, Chairman, Department of Sociology, University of Notre Dame, considers interfaith marriages one of the great problems of modern Catholicism. He writes:

> Charity is a virtue to be cultivated by all people. Catholics are directly charged with it by the Church. Yet, in loving all men regardless of race or creed, one should not hesitate to warn against marriage with those not of our faith. Is it not possible to be both charitable and realistic? Nowhere is this more necessary than in the area of mixed religious marriage, one of the great problems of contemporary Catholicism in the United States (Kane).

The Vatican Ecumenical Council has opened the way for a mixed marriage to be blessed by non-Catholic ministers as well as by the Catholic priest who solemnizes the nuptials. The Council has also made it possible for non-Catholics to agree on the Catholic upbringing of children without signing a promise. Nevertheless, most Catholic authorities believe that the Roman Catholic Church will continue to stand by its view that mixed marriages are to be avoided, an attitude shared by many non-Catholic ministers.

ENDNOTES

1. The Sacred Congregation for the Doctrine of the Faith, on March 18, 1966 promulgated an Instruction on mixed marriages, entitled

Matrimonii Sacramentum, which provided that, if the norms laid down therein stood the test of experience, they should be introduced in a definite and precise form into the Code of Canon Law which is now being revised. (See Pope Paul VI, 1970).

2. L. L. Thurstone and E. J. Chave used the method of equal-appearing intervals in constructing a scale to measure attitudes toward the church. The scale consists of 45 statements (Thurstone and Chave 1929: 22–32). In the present study, an abbreviated form of the Thurstone and Chave scale was administered to the students. The shortened form of the scale consisted of items having weights as evenly spaced as was possible over in 11-point continuum.

3. A survey of the literature on interfaith marriage was conducted, and an effort was made to summarize the major issues and risks involved in the interactive and survival aspects of such marriages. From this summary, a list of 12 item-pairs was constructed. The respondent was asked to check the statement which most nearly reflected his own personal opinion, and then to indicate how strongly he felt about this endorsement.

4. An alternate scoring procedure would have been to score the response indicating the subject does not feel at all strongly about an issue in a middle or neutral position. A separate study based on a pre-test sample showed that this scoring scheme correlated very highly $(r = .94)$ with the scoring method actually used.

5. According to Catholicism, the substance of bread and wine becomes the body and blood of Christ by the Consecration at Mass. This change is termed Transubstantiation.

6. Divine assurance that when the Pope, in his official capacity declares and defines Christian dogma, he is immune from error.

REFERENCES

Anonymous. 1939, The Progress and Problems of the American Church. New York: The American Press.

Anonymous. 1964, "The church and mixed marriage." Scope 4, No. 19 (February 2).

Augustine, P. C. 1920, A Commentary on the New Code of Canon Law. St. Louis: B. Herder Book Company.

Barber, Ray E. 1953, Marriage and the Family, second edition. New York: McGraw-Hill Book Company.

Barron, Milton L. 1946, "The incidence of Jewish inter-marriage." American Sociological Review 11 (February): 6–13.

Bell, Howard M. 1938, Youth Tell Their Story. Washington, D.C.: American Council on Education.

Black, Algernon D. 1954, If I Marry Outside My Religion. New York: Public Affairs Committee.

Bossard, James H. S. and Harold C. Letts. 1956, "Mixed marriages involving Lutherans—a research report." Marriage and Family Living 18 (November): 308–310.

Broom, Leonard and Philip Selznick. 1958, Sociology, second edition. White Plains, New York: Row, Peterson and Company.

Burchinal, Lee G. and Loren E. Chancellor. 1962, "Ages at marriage, occupation of grooms, and interreligious marriage rates." Social Forces 40 (May): 348–354.

Burchinal, Lee G. 1960, "Membership groups and attitudes toward cross-religious dating and marriage." Marriage and Family Living 22 (August): 248–253.

Chancellor, Loren E. and Thomas P. Monahan. 1955, "Religious preference and interreligious mixtures in marriages and divorces in Iowa." American Journal of Sociology 61 (November): 233–239.

Hollingshead, August B. 1950, "Cultural factors in the selection of marriage mates." American Sociological Review 15 (October): 619–627.

Kane, John J. "What are your chances in a mixed marriage?" Reprint from Information, a monthly magazine published by the Paulist Fathers.

Kenkel, William F., Joyce Himler and Leonard Cole. 1965, "Religious socialization, present devoutness, and willingness to enter a mixed religious marriage." Sociological Analysis 26 (Spring): 30–37.

Kennedy, Ruby Jo Reeves. 1949, "Single or triple melting-pot? Intermarriage trends in New Haven, 1870–1940." American Journal of Sociology 49 (January): 331–339.

Landis, Judson T. 1949, "Marriage of mixed and non-mixed religious faith." American Sociological Review 14 (June): 401–407.

1960, "Religiousness, family relationships, and family values in Protestant, Catholic, and Jewish families." Marriage and Family Living 22 (November): 341–347.

Maier, Joseph and William Spinrad. 1957, "Comparison of religious beliefs and practices of Jewish, Catholic and Protestant students." Phylon Quarterly 18 (January): 355–360.

Mihanovich, Clement S., Gerland J. Schnepp and John L. Thomas. 1952, Marriage and the Family. Milwaukee, Wisconsin: The Bruce Publishing Company.

National Conference of Catholic Bishops. 1971, Statement on the Implementation of the Apostolic Letter on Mixed Marriages, January 1, Washington, D.C.

O'Connor, John J. 1951, Preparation for Marriage and Family Life. New York: The Paulist Press.

Pike, James A. 1954, If You Marry Outside Your Faith, revised edition. New York: Harper and Row Publishers.

Pope Paul VI. 1970, An Apostolic Letter Issued "Motu Proprio" Determining Norms for Mixed Marriage. Washington, D.C.: National Conference of Catholic Bishops (March 31).

Pope Pius XI. 1941, Casti Connubii. New York: The Missionary Society of St. Paul the Apostle.

Prince, Alfred J. 1956, "Attitudes of college students toward interfaith marriage." Family Life Coordinator 5 (September): 11–23.

Thomas, John L. 1956, The American Catholic Family. Englewood Cliffs, New Jersey: Prentice-Hall, Inc.

1951a, "Are they marrying their own?" Catholic World 174 (November): 124–129.

1951b, "The factor of religion in the selection of marriage mates." American Sociological Review 16 (October): 487–491.

Thurstone, L. L. and E. J. Chave. 1929, The Measurement of Attitudes. Chicago: University of Chicago Press.

United States Bureau of the Census. 1958, "Religion reported by the civilian population of the United States, March 1958." Current Population Reports: Population Characteristics, Series P–20, Number 79 (February 2).

Wagner, Helmut R. and Roger J. Brown. 1965, "Catholic students in non-Catholic colleges." Sociological Analysis 26 (Summer): 82–95.

Weeks, H. Ashley. 1943, "Differential divorce rates by occupations." Social Forces 21 (March): 334–337.

Weller, Forrest L. 1941, "Student attitudes on marriage partners." Sociology and Social Review 26 (September): 512–524.

15   *Ruth S. Cavan*

Attitudes of Jewish College Students in the United States Toward Interreligious Marriage

Intermarriage is one type of contact between societies that do not consider each other's members as eligible marriage partners. In the background of intermarriage are such variables as the stated policies of the societies in question, the expressed attitudes of individuals toward intermarriage, and, related to attitudes, individual commitments and associations with like and unlike minded individuals. Religions may be treated as societies with varying attitudes and policies toward interreligious marriage. These are reflected not only in actual rates of interreligious marriage but also in the attitudes of young people approaching the age for marriage. A questionnaire study of a limited group of college students in the United States sought to distinguish between the attitudes of Reform and Conservative Jewish students, and, when there was no distinction, to discover some variables associated with favourable and unfavourable attitudes toward marriage to non-Jews. The attitudes of Conservative Jewish students closely followed the national policy, endogamy, whereas Reform Jewish students were about evenly divided between marrying within or out of the Jewish faith. When intermarriage with Catholics or Protestants was considered, the Conservative students again were more reluctant than Reform students. Students of both branches were only slightly less reluctant to marry Protestants than Catholics. Various deterrents were associated with the endogamous position, especially disapproval of parents to intermarriage, fear that the intermarriage would not be successful, and concern for the religious training of children. Endogamous attitudes were associated with religious involvement and to a

Ruth S. Cavan, "Attitudes of Jewish College Students in the United States Toward Interreligious Marriage," from *International Journal of Sociology of the Family*, Vol. 1 (Special Issue), May, 1971, pp. 84–98. Reprinted with permission.

slight degree with participation with other Jews. While marked differences can be found between Reform and Conservative Jews, many similarities are found also. The similarities set Jews apart from non-Jews; the differences indicate divisions within Judaism. The differences are sufficient that intermarriage among the branches of Judaism is not freely entered into. For branches studied the movement is away from endogamy as prescribed by the national bodies toward acceptance of non-Jews in marriage provided children are reared as Jews. This movement is operating at the local level and is not validated by the national bodies. It represents diminished control by the national bodies. With the widening social contacts of Jews in the United States intermarriage will probably continue to increase, and eventual national approval seems inevitable. It probably will lead to a new evaluation of Jewish identity and recognition of benefits to both Jews and non-Jews of a balanced interchange of members.

Intermarriage is defined here as one type of contact between societies or groups which do not consider each other as affording suitable mates for their youth. Among the groups that oppose intermarriage are organized religions, most of which have either prescribed or preferential endogamy. Their efforts to prevent intermarriage are not completely successful, and in modern urban settings intermarriage is increasingly difficult to control.

This paper concentrates on one religious group, the Jews in the United States. Their strong sense of identity as Jews, combined with their separation into three branches of Judaism indicative of three forms of acculturation into the United States, provides an unusual opportunity to study various influences on attitudes toward interreligious marriage within one social context—Judaism.

It is known from previously published studies that Jews resist interreligious marriage more strongly than either Catholics or Protestants (Greeley, 1970: 950; summary in Leslie, 1967: 441–444). Moreover, generational studies show that Jewish interreligious marriage is increasing (Goldstein and Goldscheider, 1968: 152–170; Sklare in Rose, 1969; 101–113). This paper accepts these known facts.

These two facts suggest a conflict between the traditional patterns of marriage desired by Judaism itself and the trend of young people of marriageable age. Moreover, the existence of three branches of Judaism suggests that each branch may have some distinctive attitudes while simultaneously adhering to Judaism in a wider context. Specifically, this study explores the attitudes of a limited number of Jewish college students of the Reform and Conservative branches toward marrying into Catholicism and Protestantism and seeks to uncover various deterrents to such interreligious marriages. It also tests attitudes toward intra-Jewish marriage between the branches of Judaism.

The study differs from other, similar studies in that Jews are categorized into the branches of Judaism, whereas usually Jews are treated as one unit. It also looks for deterrents to interreligious marriage, whereas many studies emphasize pressures toward interreligious marriage.

BACKGROUND OF JEWISH INTERMARRIAGE

Although the Jewish religion has firmly fixed historical roots, the many migrations of Jews around the world have led to modifications in interpretation of theological beliefs and in rituals. In the United States three main branches of Judaism are separately organized with numerous small splinter groups. These divisions are not necessarily found in other parts of the world. For an understanding of interreligious marriage of Jews in the United States, a brief historical background is essential.

Interreligious marriage among Jews has existed and been considered a threat to Judaism as far back as the Jews have any written records. Many references in the Bible and other early writings prohibit marriage with members of surrounding tribes worshipping other gods than the God of the Jews. During the Babylonian captivity, earlier prohibitions were reinforced by the belief that the Jews were a "holy people unto the Lord," a unique biological and cultural population with a mission to carry their religion to the world. To protect itself, the Jewish community exiled intermarried Jews and their foreign wives. Later, it was conceded that a person who converted to Judaism was acceptable in marriage to a Jew. This was in the nature of a concession to the intermarriages that took place constantly regardless of prohibitions. From time to time over the centuries and in different localities, rules were changed, but essentially prohibition of intermarriage without true conversion of the non-Jew was maintained and is basic to American Jewish endogamy today (Singer, vol. 6: 610–612).

In time (after 50 A.D.) Jews were dispersed over most of Europe, carrying with them their entire culture. They were not absorbed into the host society nor did they absorb it. They were always strangers, who tended to keep to themselves, and who were rejected socially by the host societies. Christianity also spread through Europe (after about 400 A.D.) as a religious belief imposed on the indigenous people. The political power in one European nation after another adopted Christianity as a part of the national culture, to be enforced on all people. The Jews, committed to their own religion, were the victims of an essentially unsuccessful effort to force them into Christianity. Individuals might defect from Judaism, but the masses of Jews resisted.

Either voluntarily or under compulsion, the Jews lived in compact and sometimes walled communities or ghettos. Their social contacts were within their own community. Marriages occurred there. The Christian society that surrounded them forbade their members to marry Jews. Jews met the Christian society chiefly through commercial contacts of Jewish men, who were permitted outside the ghetto in certain occupations.

Nevertheless, some intermarriages occurred that aroused concern among both the Jews and the Christians. From time to time the very presence of Jews was regarded as intolerable in some nations, depending on the attitudes of those in power and on the conflict between the Catholics and Protestants as each tried to secure dominance and to clear the country of all nonbelievers. Mass migrations of Jews into the Americas were a result of these political and religious conflicts in various parts of Europe.

After the French Revolution (1789) Jews were emancipated in France and gradually in other countries. By 1870 in all European countries Jews were accepted as citizens with retention of their own religion (Blau, 1966: 21–22). As the Jews in Germany came into closer commercial, professional, and to some extent social contact with non-Jews, they gained respect and status. Interreligious marriage increased and received some acceptance, especially in large cities, both in Germany and in other countries (Singer, vol. 6:612). Once the trend toward intermarriage had begun, the rate increased until the time of Hitler, when in some European cities half of Jewish marriages were intermarriages (Barron, 1946:6–13).

During the nineteenth century in Germany, with the decline of ghetto enclosure, urban Jews who were being drawn into secular society found the traditional rules, rituals, and daily customs a stricture on their free movement in German business and social life. A movement toward accommodation to German culture started and eventually grew into the Reform branch of Judaism. While this movement was growing in Germany, solidly orthodox village communities existed in many parts of Europe, each colored to some extent by the culture of the country where it was located and the type of treatment that Jews had received.

SUCCESSIVE MIGRATIONS TO AMERICA

Migration to America came from both urban and village sources. The American pattern of Judaism is not a duplication of either the European Reform or the traditional Jewish religion and culture (Leventman in Rose, 1969:33–55). The original branch of Judaism that came to the United States was the Sephardic Jews who had been forced out of Spain and

Portugal, and after sojourning in other European countries and Brazil came to New Amsterdam (New York) in 1654. The migration was not large and in time was almost completely absorbed into the non-Jewish population or into later migrations of Jews from Europe (Blau, 1966:12, 120; Weinryb, in Sklare, 1958:4). Sephardic Jews are no longer considered as a factor in interreligious marriage.

The second influx of Jews (1815–1880) came from Central Europe (Weinryb, in Sklare, 1958:5, 8), where the Reform movement had already begun to modify some of the traditional interpretations of Jewish beliefs and to adapt to secular urban society. The movement continued in the United States, with many shifts back and forth between orthodoxy and liberalism, but always with a strong bond to Judaism and preservation of a Jewish community. By 1873, Reform rabbis had formed the Union of American Hebrew Congregations, which remains the national organization of the Reform branch of Judaism (Blau, 1966:39f).

At present, Reform Jews no longer live in the compact areas into which newly arrived immigrants typically huddle, but are widely scattered throughout each city, chiefly on a social class basis. They tend to think of their Jewishness as a cultural or historical rather than as a strictly religious bond. Religion resembles an institution whose function is to preserve the Jewish religion and to pass it along in somewhat diluted form to children. They do not wish to lose their identity as Jews or to become assimilated into the larger society, but neither do they wish to restrict their contacts to a traditional Jewish community. Interreligious marriage is not sought as a group goal, but when it occurs it causes less consternation than among the Orthodox Jews.

Immigrants from Eastern Europe, the heart of orthodoxy, began to arrive in the United States during the nineteenth century, and by 1880 had numerically overshadowed the Central European Jews, by then well acculturated to urban United States. The Orthodox Jews coming from villages had to adjust not only to city life and American culture but also to the Reform Jews, many in the second and third generation of residence in the United States. The Eastern European Jews tended to cluster in solidly Jewish communities, but found it imperative to enter into the American culture to earn a living. They were partially rejected by the older Jewish residents who felt them to be a threat to the economic and social status that they had painfully gained over several generations of time. By 1900 the Jews from Eastern Europe felt the need to adapt to American urban culture, but still could not divorce themselves sufficiently from their traditional beliefs and customs to affiliate with the Reform movement. They pulled themselves out of their initial poverty and moved toward middle-class status, and, with American-reared generations, moved into a compromise position that permitted them to remain Jews religiously but still to accommodate to the demands of economic existence. Their movement became known as the Conservative branch of Judaism; by 1913 they had organized the United Synagogue of America, which remains their national organization (Blau, 1966:107–114; Sklare, 1955).

At present Conservative Jews form a sub-society within the larger society. (Sklare, 1955). They live in Jewish neighborhoods, are highly conscious of their identity as Jews, and share many experiences together. Nevertheless, social contacts spread beyond the community and the possibility of interreligious marriage becomes a source of constant worry to parents and religious leaders.

Meanwhile, other Jews have retained their Orthodox position, clinging closely to traditional beliefs and interpretations and daily religious and living rituals and customs. Nationally, they are organized into the Union of Orthodox Jewish Congregations of America. Many Orthodox Jews still tend to live in close proximity to each other and are enclosed within their own institutions so far as possible (Freilich, 1962:45–54). They resemble "total" communities, in which most personal, religious, social, and to some extent educational and economic needs are met within the community; friendships are formed among the members, and marriage follows as a matter of course. (The term "total" community is based on Goffman, in Cressey, 1961: 15–67). Interreligious marriage is less frequent than among Reform or Conservative Jews; it is interpreted as a repudiation of Judaism by the intermarrying Jew, and in extreme cases the old penalty of expulsion from the community may be followed. (Gittleson in Shoulson, 1959: 236–245; Kirshenbaum, 1958:22–124).

The three branches of Judaism represent three stages of adjustment to urban American life, often regarded as steps toward assimilation. However, none of the branches wishes assimilation. It has been suggested that they have a dual identity, socially and intimately as Jews and culturally as Americans. The fear of assimilation always seems to be present, focused on an increasing amount of interreligious marriage from one generation to another (Goldstein and Goldscheider, 1968:152–170; Sklare in Rose, 1969:101–113).

This background statement places religious groups in the framework of in-groups and out-groups, with Jews traditionally enclosed within the endogamous in-group as a result both of their belief in their position as a chosen people and of their reaction to hostility from outside. Social distance attitudes were strong (Bogardus, 1925:1933). However, among groups that moved into the cities of eighteenth century Europe, hostilities decreased and interreligious marriage became a form of accommodation between Jews (especially Reform Jews) and non-Jews.

In the United States the situation is complicated by the concurrent existence of Reform, Conservative, and Orthodox Jews. Reform Jews are well acculturated to American culture, but retain their identity as Jews. Conservative Jews retain an in-group quality but do not approach the "total" community aspect of the Orthodox Jews. Regardless of a general feeling of identity as Jews that pervades all three branches, a certain amount of social distance separates them.

For the sake of contrast the above discussion over-emphasizes the distinctiveness of the three branches. Actually, individuals may pass from one branch to another, from one synagogue to another, from one community to another. While they may be regarded as defectors when they leave a traditional branch for a more secularized branch, usually no strong penalties are imposed.

METHOD

The study of attitudes of Jewish college students toward interreligious marriage was part of a more comprehensive study, called the Midwest Study, made in 1966. The data were gathered by the use of a questionnaire, secured through classroom distribution. However, in the university from which most of the questionnaires were secured, Jews constituted only a small percentage of the total student body. Therefore questionnaires were mailed to all Jewish students enrolled, whose names and addresses were secured from the Jewish campus organization. (The university asked each student at the time of registration to fill out a card giving his religious affiliation for use by the appropriate religious organization.) A 60 per cent return was secured. In addition questionnaires were distributed to selected (mostly social science) classes in a large urban university in the same area. There is no claim that the respondents constitute a random sample of Jewish college students in the area. As a whole they were urban residents, middle class, upwardly mobile, whose family entrance into the United States was by their grandfathers or an earlier generation. The students classified themselves as Reform or Conservative, with too few Orthodox to make it possible to use this group.

The study concerns the current attitudes of the students. An attitude may be defined briefly as a tendency to react favourably or negatively toward some person or thing. Attitudes may be changed. The students expressed their current attitudes toward interreligious marriage. There is no assurance that their attitudes may not change before they actually select a marriage partner. Since the study was anonymous, there was no opportunity for a follow-up to test the durability of their attitudes.

Based on previous studies, hypotheses were set up as to the conditions under which attitudes would favor or reject interreligious marriage. These hypotheses are elaborated in the discussion. Various parts of the questionnaire were geared to specific hypotheses.

One of the major features of the questionnaire was a Dating-Marriage Scale, consisting of a continuum of attitudes toward interreligious marriage, running from complete rejection of a partner of another religion to willingness to become converted in order to make marriage possible (based on Prince, 1956). The Scale is, in reality, a social distance scale, keyed to interreligious marriage (Cavan, 1971a). The items of the Scale are given in Table 2.

The Dating-Marriage Scale forms the chief dependent variable of the study. The student's choice of his placement on the Scale is assumed to rest upon a number of independent variables that preceded this choice in the experience of the students.

The questionnaire also included numerous other questions including a list of statements hypothesized to be deterrents to interreligious marriage and various questions on ideology and on religious and social activities.

HYPOTHESIS 1: INFLUENCE OF RELIGIOUS POLICY

It was hypothesized that students' attitudes would tend to support official marriage policies and rules of their religion. For the three branches of Judaism under consideration, the policy as stated by their national bodies is that marriage should be between Jews; a person converted to Judaism is considered eligible for marriage. Interreligious marriage is not officially approved.

TABLE 1 Percentage of Jewish students in the midwest study who stated they were unwilling to marry outside their faith.

Branch of Judaism	Would not marry out	Would marry out	Total	
			Number	Per cent
Reform:				
Male	42.9	57.1	84	100
Female	51.4	48.6	107	100
Conservative:				
Male	60.8	39.2	102	100
Female	79.1	20.9	110	100

* This Table is included in an article in the American Journal of Sociology for May 1971. Other tables are used in other articles based on different portions of the Midwest Study.

Table 1 supports Hypothesis 1 so far as Conservative Jews are concerned; it is assumed that Orthodox Jews would strongly support this hypothesis. Reform Jews were about equally divided between support of the endogamous rule of their national body and a movement toward tolerance of interreligious marriage.

Rather than showing complete support for Jewish endogamous rules, Table 1 shows a movement away from the traditional position toward a more secular position.

HYPOTHESIS 2: A AND B: INFLUENCE OF SOCIAL DISTANCE ATTITUDES

The data presented so far show the binding of Jews to their religion and point to the strength of Judaism to hold its members. Another aspect of endogamy is the relation to other religions into which intermarriage might be made. Religious groups share with other groups feelings of differentiation or even hostility (social distance) toward other groups, which reciprocate with similar feelings.

It was hypothesized (2a) that Jewish attitudes toward interreligious marriage would vary according to the social distance attitudes held toward specific religions; it was also hypothesized that Conservative Jews would feel greater social distance than Reform Jews, that is, would be more unwilling to intermarry.

The two non-Jewish groups involved are Catholics and Protestants.

Table 2-A shows the attitudes of Reform and Conservative Jewish students, male and female, toward marrying Catholics. The expectation that Conservative students would be more reluctant than Reform students to marry Catholics is borne out for males ($p < .01$); for females the difference is not significant.

Table 2-B gives corresponding information for attitudes of Jewish students toward intermarriage with Protestants. Again, Conservative Jews are more reluctant to intermarry than Reform Jews. The difference in attitude between Reform and Conservative Jews is significant ($p < .05$) for males and $p < .10$ for females).

It was also hypothesized (2b) that both Reform and Conservative Jews would be more unfavourable to marrying Catholics than Protestants because of the longer history of discrimination on the part of the Catholic Church, and also because Catholics have long held a policy forbidding marriage of a Catholic to a non-Christian but making possible marriage to a non-Catholic who nevertheless was a baptized Christian. A comparison of Table 2-A and B, however, shows very little difference, although the

TABLE 2 Attitudes of Jewish university students toward interreligious marriage with Catholics and with Protestants.*

Percentage distribution

| | Dating-Marriage scale | | | | | | | |
| | 1 | 2 | 3 | 4 | 5 | 6 | 7 | |
	Not date	Date, not marry	Marry, if mate converts	Not convert but rear children as Jews	Require neither 3 nor 4	Respondent would convert	No.	Total %
A. *Jewish attitudes toward Catholics***								
a. Reform Jews:								
Males	2	17	33	42	6	0	82	100
Females	8	23	27	29	13	0	105	100
b. Conservative Jews:								
Males	6	18	52	17	7	0	101	100
Females	15	21	36	24	4	0	108	100
B. *Jewish attitudes toward Protestants****								
a. Reform Jews:								
Males	0	15	30	41	13	1	83	100
Females	5	19	26	35	13	2	105	100
b. Conservative Jews:								
Males	5	19	42	23	11	0	102	100
Females	12	19	36	27	4	2	109	100

* The test of significance used for these percentages is the Kolmogorov-Smirnov
2-tailed test.
** The difference in attitudes of Reform versus Conservative Jewish males toward
Catholics is significant ($p < .01$); the corresponding difference for females is not significant ($p > .10$). The difference between males and females of either branch of
Judaism toward intermarriage with Catholics is not significant ($p > .10$).
*** The difference in attitudes of Reform versus Conservative Jews toward Protestants
is significant for males ($p < .05$) and for females ($p < .10$). The difference between
males and females of either branch of Judaism toward intermarriage with Protestants
is not significant ($p > .10$).

difference that exists favors marriage to Protestants. This portion of
hypothesis 2 was not supported.

HYPOTHESIS 3: MOVEMENT
AWAY FROM ENDOGAMY

It was hypothesized that Jewish young people, especially Reform Jews,
are moving away from strict religious endogamy.

The most significant item in the Dating-Marriage Scale for this hypothesis is Number 4, which is the point of departure from traditional rules and practices. Number 4 states that the student would be willing to forego conversion of the non-Jew, provided that the non-Jewish spouse would agree to bring up any children as Jews. There is no provision in official Jewish policy for this compromise. The large percentage of both male and female Jewish students, especially Reform, who were willing to marry a non-Jew under these circumstances shows that young people are moving away from the traditional Jewish policy of no marriage outside the faith. This stand is given strong support by the fact that a minimum— estimated at one-third—of Reform Jewish rabbis will unite in marriage a Jew and a non-Jew who plans to convert to Judaism, or is in the process of conversion, who will keep a Jewish home, and rear children in the Jewish faith (correspondence with Union of American Hebrew Congregations; Gordon, 1964: 208–209). This is as far away from tradition as most Jewish students were willing to go; few would marry without this assurance, and almost no Jewish student would be willing to convert to some other religion to make marriage possible. Since Number 4 preserves the Jewish faith into the following generation, it is essentially in support of endogamy, although the possibility is always present that after marriage, the good intentions might not be carried out.

HYPOTHESIS 4: INFLUENCE OF CERTAIN ATTITUDES AS DETERRENTS TO INTERMARRIAGE

It was hypothesized that concern of students for their future marriage, the objections of family, rabbis, and friends, and certain religious convictions would act as deterrents to interreligious marriage, and more so among Conservative than Reform Jews. Therefore students who said they would not marry out of their faith were asked to respond to a series of statements in support of the hypothesis. Table 3 gives the deterrent statements and the number and percentage of students by sub-group and sex who agreed with the statements.

Differences were slight between students of the Conservative and Reform branches who rejected interreligious marriage. Conservative males slightly exceeded Reform males in number of deterrents; the average number per student was respectively, 4.7 and 4.2. For females the average numbers were 4.7 and 4.9, respectively. As between specific deterrents, Conservative males differed in greater degree and on more deterrents from Reform males than was true for females. Conservative males were more responsive than Reform males on Numbers 1, 2, 4, 6 and 7. Conservative

TABLE 3 Percentage of reform and conservative Jewish students who would not marry out of their faith, who agreed to each deterrent statement, midwest study.

	Reform Jews		Conservative Jews	
Deterrents	Males	Females	Males	Females
1. My parents would object:				
No. of agree answers	28	51	58	84
Per cent of agree answers	78	93	94	97
2. My rabbi would object:				
No. of agree answers	22	38	43	58
Per cent of agree answers	61	69	70	67
3. My close friends would object:				
No. of agree answers	11	23	18	32
Per cent of agree answers	31	42	29	37
4. There is a probability that such a marriage would not succeed:				
No. of agree answers	29	51	56	75
Per cent of agree answers	80	93	90	86
5. It might interfere with the religious training of my children:				
No. of agree answers	32	51	56	81
Per cent of agree answers	89	93	90	93
6. My personal religious conviction is that this would be wrong:				
No. of agree answers	17	34	35	62
Per cent of agree answers	47	62	56	71
7. It would weaken the strength of my religious group for people to marry outside the faith:				
No. of agree answers	17	33	39	53
Per cent of agree answers	47	60	63	61
Total number unwilling to marry out of their faith	36	55	62	87
Percentage unwilling to marry out of their faith	42.9	51.7	60.8	79.1

females were less sensitive than Reform females on Number 4 and more sensitive on Number 6. Conservative males seemed more tradition-bound than Reform males, whereas there was little difference between the two groups of females. The differences throughout, however, were slight.

Although a sharp contrast cannot be drawn between Reform and Conservative Jews, the deterrents merit discussion for the light they throw on the total problem of Jewish interreligious marriage. Parents and rabbis (Numbers 1 and 2) may be regarded both as agents of socialization into the Jewish religion and as adult reference groups whose approval is sought. The objections of both parents and rabbis, but especially of parents, are felt to be strong deterrents to intermarriage, with Conservative Jews being more sensitive to these objections than Reform Jews. These findings may demonstrate the unity of the Jewish family and its strength as a reference group for Jewish beliefs and ideals.

The Midwest Study did not query parents as to their reactions if a son or daughter married out of the faith. A study of Lakeville, a suburb, by Sklare and Greenblum (1967:306–313) asked parents how they would feel if their child married a non-Jew. Twenty-nine per cent said they would be very unhappy, 43 per cent somewhat unhappy, 24 per cent neither happy nor unhappy; only two per cent said they would feel somewhat or very happy. Such parental attitudes no doubt are the corollary to student attitudes rejecting interreligious marriage because parents would object, such as were found in the Midwest Study.

The common assumption that close friends (the peer group) are influential during the teen years led to the inclusion of objections of friends as a deterrent (Number 3). The influence of these objections is mild compared with that of parents and rabbis.

Both Reform and Conservative Jewish students were deeply concerned about the possible effect of interreligious marriage on success of their marriage and on the religious training of children (Numbers 4 and 5).

Religious convictions and fear for the effect of interreligious marriage on Judaism were much less strong as deterrents than statements that had to do with more personal deterrents centered in the family (Numbers 6 and 7).

The hypothesis regarding deterrents was strongly supported by objections of parents, fear that the marriage would not succeed, and interference with religious training of children; moderately well supported by objections of rabbi, personal conviction that interreligious marriage is wrong, and concern for weakening of the religion; but only minimally supported by objections of close friends. Conservative males were most strongly responsive to the deterrents.

HYPOTHESIS 5: IDEOLOGICAL VARIABLES

It was hypothesized that the depth of commitment of students to their religion and the degree of concern for its survival would be positively related to endogamous attitudes.

The questionnaire used in the Midwest Study included items pertaining to attitudes toward Judaism with a choice of responses. Table 4 gives the items, a collapsed form of responses, their relation to an abbreviated form of the Dating-Marriage Scale, and the significance of differences in responses, computed on the original detailed tables. For this part of the analysis Reform and Conservative Jews were combined. The decision to combine was made after it was discovered that the percentage distributions of Reform and Conservative Jews on the items included in Tables 4 and 5 were almost identical. This portion of the study therefore does not show differences between Reform and Conservative branches, but rather their combined responses.

In all instances the more deeply religiously involved students tended more than the uninvolved students to take an endogamous position. However, the difference between the two groups of students is one of degree, since many involved students would marry out of their faith, and many uninvolved would not.

HYPOTHESIS 6: SOCIAL VARIABLES

It was hypothesized that amount of participation of students with other Jews would be positively related to endogamous attitudes. An inspection of Table 5 shows that participating students are more likely than non-participating students to hold endogamous attitudes. However, none of the differences is statistically significant. There is only minimal support for the hypothesis. In comparing hypotheses 5 and 6, ideology outweighs social participation as a determinant of endogamous attitudes. This does not mean that social participation is unimportant. Contacts with non-Jews may socialize the Jew to secular attitudes and thus indirectly be a determinant of non-endogamous attitudes.

INTRA-JEWISH MARRIAGE

The organization of Jews into three distinct branches raises the question of whether there is sufficient compatibility among the three branches to make intra-Jewish marriage feasible. Although the attitudes of Orthodox students are not available, Reform and Conservative students indicated both their attitudes toward marrying each other and toward marrying Orthodox Jews.

Table 6 shows the distribution of responses on the Dating-Marriage Scale. In each combination the mode is that no requirements in the way of conversion or rearing of children would be made; however, less than half of the students are in this category. (See Cavan, 1971b). A small proportion of students would not marry into another branch or would require conversion to their branch. Other than this, students are divided between requiring rearing of the children in the respondent's branch or willingness to convert to make marriage possible. These contrasting attitudes indicate

TABLE 4 The dating-marriage scale and religious attitudes of Jewish students. (Percentage distribution)*

	Dating-Marriage scale				
Attitudes	Not marry or marry only with mate's conversion (nos. 1, 2, 3 from Dating-Marriage scale, Table 2)	Require only that children be reared as Jews, or no requirements, or would himself convert (nos. 4, 5, 6 from Dating-Marriage scale)	Total		
			Number	Per cent	K.S.**
Attendance at religious services during the past year:					
Never	41	59	87	100	.01
Once a month or more	71	29	97	100	
How religious student felt himself to be:					
Mild, indifferent or opposed	48	53	135	100	.01
Moderately or very religious	83	17	46	100	
Student's attitude toward religious beliefs:					
Religious ideals no more important than other beliefs, e.g., political, or has few ideals of any sort	41	59	68	100	.05
Moderately or deeply committed to ideals of his faith	66	34	114	100	
Student's attitude toward status of his faith:					
Falls below many other religions or is one of many religions	47	53	113	100	.01
Has highest degree of religious truth or is only true religion	72	28	68	100	
What student understands to be the official stand of his religion toward intermarriage:					
Indifferent or intermarriage preferred but no penalties	45	55	78	100	.05
Disapproval, or penalties	65	35	106	100	

* This table is for males only. The distribution for females was very similar.
** The Kolmogorov-Smirnov two-tailed test was used to test the significance of the difference between the involved and uninvolved percentage distribution, with the Dating-Marriage Scale in six categories.

TABLE 5 The dating-marriage scale and participation of Jewish students with other Jews.*

Percentage Distribution

| | Dating-Marriage scale | | | | |
| | Not marry or marry only with mate's conversion (nos. 1, 2, 3 from Dating-Marriage scale, Table 2) | Require only that children be reared as Jews, or no requirements, or would himself convert (nos. 4, 5, 6 from Dating-Marriage scale) | | | |
Participation			Total Number	Per cent	K.S.**
Number of Jews among four best friends:					
None, one, or two	46	54	72	100	0
Three or four	63	36	113	100	
Active in Jewish young people's groups in past four years:					
Not at all	48	52	96	100	0
Occasionally attend up to holding an office	65	35	87	100	
Associate with people of other religions:*					
One or more close personal friends	54	46	107	100	0
Various friendly contacts	59	41	78	100	

* This table is for males only. The distribution for females was very similar.
** The Kolmogorov-Smirnov two-tailed test was used to test the significance of the difference between the participating and non-participating percentage distributions, with the Dating-Marriage Scale in six categories.
*** All except three students selected one of the two responses shown here. Other possible responses were belong to some of the same non-religious clubs but have no personal friends, associate only in non-personal ways, or avoid them when possible.

widespread ambivalence among Jewish students toward marriage into a branch other than their own.

Reform students are more willing to convert to Conservative Judaism than to Orthodoxy. Conservative Jews are more willing to marry into Orthodoxy than into the Reform branch. Females are more willing than males to convert to another branch than their own in order to make marriage possible. In most instances the differences are not statistically significant.

When compared with Table 2, Table 6 shows a much greater willingness to marry into another branch of Judaism than to marry a Catholic or

TABLE 6 Attitudes of reform and conservative Jewish students toward intra-Jewish dating and marriage.*

Percentage Distribution

Branch of Judaism	Attitudes toward	1 Not date	2 Date, not marry	3 Marry, if mate converts	4 Not convert but rear children as Jews	5 Re-quire neither 3 nor 4	6 Re-spon-dent would convert	7 Total** No.	%
Reform:	Orthodox								
Male		2	2	9	35	45	7	81	100
Female		1***	7	5	16	49	23	103	100
Reform:	Conserva-								
Male	tive	1	—	2	25	47	25	77	100
Female		—	1	1	6	47	45	102	100
Conservative:	Orthodox								
Male		1	4	13	19	46	16	94	100
Female		1	7	6	10	39	37	104	100
Conservative:	Reform								
Male		—	1	16	33	35	15	94	100
Female		—	—	6	27	40	27	101	100

* This Table is also included in an article in the American Journal of Sociology, May, 1971.
** The totals are less than in Table 2 because of failure of some students to reply to the question.
*** Less than 1 per cent.

Protestant, indicating a marked feeling of Jewish identity. So far as the outer society is concerned, Jews feel as one; within their own religion, however they recognize the three branches as distinctive.

DISCUSSION

It now remains to pull together and interpret these various findings. Those based on the Midwest Study must be considered as limited to the students who participated in the study. However, in order to extend the implications of the study, a more general interpretation is also included.

Regardless of the centuries-long struggle by Jews to control marriage of their members into other religious systems, complete control has not been established. There are indications that interreligious marriage has increased in the United States. It has remained a matter of great concern among Jews.

A study of Jewish culture in the United States and of attitudes of Jewish university students toward interreligious marriage throws some light on present attitudes of Reform and Conservative Jewish students. For the sample used, the following tentative conclusion may be drawn:

1. Jews in the United States represent three stages of acculturation to secular American urban society: Reform Jews are most thoroughly acculturated although not assimilated; Conservative Jews form a sub-society, marginal to both secular society and traditional Judaism; Orthodox Jews are still primarily traditional.

2. The traditional prohibition of interreligious marriage is still the formal position of the national organizations of the three branches of Judaism.

3. Approximately half of Reform Jewish students stated they would not marry out of their faith, compared with about 70 per cent of Conservative Jews. Most Conservative Jewish students therefore support the traditional position on interreligious marriage, whereas Reform Jews only moderately support this position.

4. With reference to interreligious marriage to Catholics and Protestants, Reform Jews were more willing to intermarry than were Conservative Jews, that is, social distance attitudes were weaker.

5. There was little difference in the attitudes of either branch toward intermarriage to a Catholic or a Protestant, despite the longer history of discrimination by Catholics than by Protestants.

6. The attitudes of students show that they are moving away from strict endogamy toward acceptance of a non-Jew in marriage, provided children are reared as Jews. This movement is supported by a minority of rabbis but not by the three national bodies of Judaism.

7. Among students who said they would not intermarry, members of both branches were highly sensitive to fear that an interreligious marriage would not be successful, or that it would be difficult to educate children as Jews. Objection of parents was a strong deterrent; objection of the rabbi was less strong. Only about a third of the students felt that objections of friends would deter them from interreligious marriage. Conservative Jews were more often influenced by these deterrents than Reform Jews, again indicating their closer affiliation with traditional standards.

8. Variables that were associated positively with endogamy were commitment to the Jewish religion, attendance at religious services, and some formal or informal participation with other Jews. However, the students were far from being divided into endogamous and non-endogamous groups on these variables.

9. Jewish students were ambivalent about marriage into a branch of Judaism other than their own, although more willing to make such intra-Jewish marriages than to marry into another religion.

A few tentative general conclusions may be drawn. Over many centuries in Europe and some three hundred years in the United States, Jews have resisted assimilation and maintained a distinctive religious and ethnic culture. Their present status and apparent desire in the United States is to maintain Jewish identity with the three branches of Judaism and at the same time to share in and contribute to American secular life. As shown by the degree of resistance to interreligious marriage, these identities are extremely important. Nevertheless, there are marked indications of ambivalence and of a movement toward greater tolerance of interreligious marriage.

The study shows the inclusiveness and persistence of religion after the purely ethnic differences have yielded to the common pervasiveness of American culture. As one student in the study stated, "A Jew is a Jew regardless of the different branches." At the same time, except for small enclaves of Orthodox Jews, all Jews share the American culture and are incorporated into the American economic, educational, political, and cultural systems.

The study also shows the adaptation of rules of endogamy to the new social situation of the United States, and the process whereby changes may come unofficially at the folkway level (Reform Jews marrying without conversion of the mate) with the informal approval of the rabbis, and with a forecast of formal approval of the national organizations. Unofficial movements of this kind weaken the control of the religion over its members. When the official body accepts the change, it legitimizes the deviant behavior and retains the members, but by so doing, accedes to a weakened endogamous position.

Reform and to some extent Conservative Jews are moving from a prescriptive toward a preferential position on endogamy; they have abandoned the traditional position of expulsion of an out-marrying Jew from family and community. On the other hand, Orthodox Jews cling to the older principle of endogamy. This division of attitudes may threaten a schism between Orthodox Jews and Reform-Conservative Jews.

The movement toward tolerance of interreligious marriage is linked to the continuous enlarging of the social world of the Jews and to increased contacts in non-Jewish institutions, especially those for the young, such as schools and public recreational and cultural facilities.

The Jewish position is moving toward a balance between endogamy and interreligious marriage. Fears for survival are now offset by knowledge that many non-Jews prior to or at the time of marriage become converts to Judaism and seemingly find satisfaction in the religion (Eichhorn in Cahnman, 1963: 111–121). Realization that an amicable union of social identity as a Jew and acculturation into the American culture is possible and beneficial to both Jews and non-Jews is giving a new definition to what it means to be a Jew. The positive functions of interreligious marriage seem to be gaining recognition over the dysfunctions.

REFERENCES

Barron, Milton L. 1946, "Incidence of Jewish Intermarriage in Europe and America." American Sociological Review 11 (February): 6–13.

Blau, Joseph L. 1966, Modern Varieties of Judaism. New York: Columbia University Press.

Bogardus, Emory S. 1925, "Measuring social distance." Journal of Applied Sociology 9: 299–308.

1933, "A social distance scale." Sociology and Social Research 17: 265–271.

Cahnman, Werner J. (ed.) 1963, Intermarriage and Jewish Life. New York: Herzl Press.

Cavan, Ruth Shonle. 1971a, "A Dating-Marriage Scale of religious social distance." Journal for the Scientific Study of Religion 10 (July).

1971b, "Jewish student attitudes toward interreligious and intra-Jewish marriage." American Journal of Sociology 76 (May).

Cressey, Donald R. (ed.) 1961, The Prison, Studies in Institutional Organization and Change. New York: Holt, Rinehart and Winston.

Freilich, Morris. 1962, "The modern shtetl: A study of culture persistence." Anthropos 57: 45–54.

Goldstein, Sidney, and Calvin Goldscheider. 1968, Jewish Americans: Three Generations in a Jewish Community. Englewood Cliffs, New Jersey: Prentice-Hall.

Gordon, Albert I. 1964, Intermarriage: Interfaith, Interracial, Interethnic. Boston: Beacon Press.

Greeley, Andrew M. 1970, "Religious intermarriage in a denominational society." American Journal of Sociology 75 (May): 949–952.

Kirshenbaum, David. 1958, Mixed Marriage and the Jewish Future. New York: Bloch Publishing Company.

Leslie, Gerald R. 1967, The Family in Social Context. New York: Oxford University Press.

Prince, Albert J. 1956, "Attitudes of college students toward interfaith marriage." Family Life Coordinator, 5 (September): 11–13.

Rose, Peter I. (ed.) 1969, The Ghetto and Beyond: Essays on Jewish Life in America. New York: Random House.

Shoulson, Abraham B. (ed.) 1959, Marriage and Family Life, A Jewish View. New York: Twayne Publisher.

Singer, Isidore (ed.). 1902, Jewish Encyclopedia, vol. 2. New York: KYAV Publishing House.

Sklare, Marshall. 1955, Conservative Judaism, An American Religious Movement. Glencoe, Illinois: Free Press.

Sklare, Marshall (ed.). 1958, The Jews, Social Patterns in an American Group. Glencoe, Illinois: Free Press.

Sklare, Marshall, and Joseph Greenblum. 1967, Jewish Identity on the Suburban Frontier. New York: Basic Books.

16   *Charles E. Smith*

Negro-White Intermarriage: Forbidden Sexual Union

FOREWORD

The material in this paper is drawn primarily from my doctoral dissertation on "Negro-White Intermarriage—Metropolitan New York: A Qualitative Case Analysis."* A backdrop to interracial sexual behavior will be
touched upon by employing historical data included in the research study
relating to the Negro's entry upon the American scene during slavery.
In addition, the interactive process between society and the interracial
couples as well as between the married partners themselves will be reviewed.

INTRODUCTION

To some extent a person's family, his community and his larger society
may be viewed in the context of a group. When a person disregards the
group and associates with another who is considered to be undesirable by
group standards because of race, religion, national origin or any other
reason, the group will often bring pressure to bear in an attempt to have
him conform to the standards, mores or ethical code of the group. The
form of pressure or group control utilized to these ends will vary among
groups and will be dependent upon many factors, some of which the group
members may perceive as essential to the cohesion or actual existence of
the group.

    This phenomenon of group control is often rather effective in bringing

Charles E. Smith, "Negro-White Intermarriage: Forbidden Sexual Union."
The Journal of Sex Research, vol. 2, no. 3 (November 1966), pp. 169–177.
Reprinted by permission.
* Columbia University (Teachers College), New York, 1960.

a group member's behavior in line with group thinking. There may be times, however, when the individual continues, despite external pressure, to do that which the group considers to be a violation of its code. Then, almost invariably, conflict arises out of the impact of the group upon the individual, and the latter's reaction to the group.

There are probably few situations which bring this process into focus as vividly as does Negro-white intermarriage. A clearer picture of the impact of group pressure—from family members and others—on the participants in the study cited may evolve from a clearer understanding of the participants' experiences.

BACKGROUND

There is ample evidence of sexual intermixing between Negroes and whites prior to the former's appearance on the American scene. Sexual mixing between the two races in the United States, however, began with the introduction of slavery to this continent. The pattern of racial intermingling in the United States during the Negro's period in bondage, as well as legislation which evolved as a direct result, were all destined to have a more far-reaching effect in shaping the moral and social structure of society concerning the two races than was discernible at the time.

The readily accessible female slaves often served their white masters as sexual partners. These relationships were often forced—but not always —by the white plantation owners and were carried out in a rather surreptitious manner without the advantages of marriage for the female slave and without even the romance or the status which often accompanies "an affair." This practice became so widespread, as evidenced by the large number of mulatto children born to Negro mothers, that laws were enacted against sexual and social associations between the two races. These anti-miscegenation laws still exist in 18 states, which include all of the Southern states, but have been repealed by superior courts in a number of other states. In those states where anti-miscegenation laws still exist, they are apt to be enforced; this is invariably true in the South. States which have repealed their anti-miscegenation laws have done so not to facilitate intermarriage *per se,* but rather to eliminate laws which may represent an infringement of the individual's civil rights, his social equality, or his freedom of choice in marriage. In those states where laws have been repealed, and in those states in which legal restrictions to interracial marriage were never established, there has been no evidence of an overwhelming incidence of Negro-white marriages. Moreover, reliable evidence of any trend regarding Negro-white marriages in the United States is not available because of inadequate data.

With the sexual intermixing between whites and Negroes during slavery as a frame of reference, a number of researchers have described the white man's omnipresent attitude and fear about interracial intermingling as a projection of his own guilt onto the Negro male—a projected symbol. Most of his energy and efforts directed toward keeping the two races separated, by the use of prejudice, discrimination, legal means and acts of violence, are felt to be motivated mainly by anxiety around the possibility of close social interaction and social intercourse between the two races—especially in the case of the Negro male and the white female —some of which may not be merely social in nature. Were the white man not already, himself, a sexual transgressor with the Negro woman and were he not concerned that the Negro man might become similarly involved with the white woman, partly in retaliation, perhaps he would not need to be as concerned as seems apparent about a Negro becoming his son-in-law. Concomitantly, he cannot fully trust his white women perhaps because of his own unfaithfulness. He fears they, too, will succumb to some "inherent weakness" and thereby become interested in Negro men.

Almost every act involving an association between the Negro male and the white female becomes suspect. If it goes beyond suspicion, and often it does not, ". . . it is never proper to suspect the woman" (Simpson, 1958). The presumption of guilt on the Negro's part, especially in the South, is sustained with censure and punishment being meted out. It is expected that, given the opportunity, the Negro will sexually attack the white woman. This feeling is widespread among the white group, the men in particular. "Certainly more Negro women have been attacked or seduced by white men than has been the case with white women and Negro men" (Simpson, 1958). This pattern of denial or appeasement of his guilt, on the part of the white man, is repeated and perpetuated in part by commonly held myths regarding the sexual superiority of the Negro male. The cry of rape is the common charge.

When an alleged or actual rapist is punished, outside the law, lynching is the familiar form of punishment employed. In a number of instances severe mutilation of the victim's body, including the genitalia, is manifest. "The torture which is an accompaniment of modern lynching shows that it is an act of perversion" (White, 1929).

Intermarriage, then, between Negro men and white women becomes a most dreaded fear for white men. Most of the attention in this area is directed toward protecting the white woman from such an eventuality. Despite his expressed attitudes toward Negroes, the white man nevertheless finds the Negro woman an attractive sexual mate. However, the motives involved are probably more complex than sexual interest alone. Dollard (1937) points out, among other things, that the idealization of the white woman in the South makes her tantamount to an "untouchable," whom the white man himself must protect from corruption by Negro men. The Negro woman, then, becomes a natural, already corrupted choice for the white man's sexual desire.

Whatever the reasons, sexual relations and marriages between Negroes and whites are strongly opposed. The opposition is stronger among whites but such marriages are by no means fully accepted by the Negro group. According to Myrdal (1944) and others, the entire caste system is justified by the white man's basic assumption that the Negro's desire for equality is for the sole purpose of facilitating intermarriage. This is seen as a device ". . . to keep the Negroes in a lower status" (Drake, 1945). It is often implemented by the provocative question, "Would you want your daughter to marry a Negro?"

PERSONAL CHARACTERISTICS
AND INTERACTIONS

The participants interviewed for the research study consisted of twenty-two Negro-white married couples residing in metropolitan New York. In thirteen instances the husband was Negro and in nine he was white. The majority of the spouses were born and reared in the northeastern region of the United States. A number of Negro men were born and reared in the South, but no white men came from this region; only two women were born and reared in the South—one from each race.

The couples had a median age of 35.8 when interviewed. The median number of years of marriage for the group was 9.0 and the median child-productivity rate per couple was 2.0 children. Thirteen of the marriages studied (59.1%) represent both interracial and interfaith marriages. When interviewed, 56.8% of the total group professed no religious affiliation, so that actual differences in this area may not be as great as appears.

With respect to education, occupation and social position, the couples rate high. The median numbers of years of school completed for the group was 16.5—college completion. Regarding occupation, 43.2% of those interviewed were professionals. Applying Hollingshead's two factor index of social position (Hollingshead, 1957), the group fell within the second highest position on the five-position scale.

In general, these couples became acquainted through introduction by another person at social functions and gatherings. Not one of the couples reported having met in schools or colleges. The participants and other observers pretty much agree that the white partner in interracial relationships usually accepts the role of initiator in the development of a courtship. The Negro partner in most instances is cautious, having learned well that he is expected to "stay in his place" in relationships between himself and white persons—especially in the case of white women.

The actual period of courtship for these couples varied from two months to five years on either end of the continuum. The mean average for the group was 15.1 months of courtship. They usually dismissed ideas regarding an official announcement of engagement and impending marriage, since most couples felt that society would do a rather thorough job of "publicizing" their marriage anyway. The couples used their informal engagement period to become better acquainted and to test their adjustment to the initial reactions of friends, family members, and society, to their interracial relationship. Most of their friendship patterns remained intact although some breaches with friends were reported and were attributed to the interracial factor of their courtship. Most of the participants' activities as married partners were not dissimilar to what they had been prior to their courtship. A good many of them were involved in interracial civil rights groups. They attended movies, plays, dances, parties and were involved in other activities in the company of friends; on occasion they preferred to be alone. Despite numerous adverse reactions and rebuffs from society, there were no reported incidents of couples going into isolation in an attempt to avoid these or in order to hide the interracial union. Negative reactions from parents were described as the most difficult for the couples emotionally—especially for the white partner. In a number of cases, breaches developed between the white partner and his parents around the time of marriage which were not mended for years after the marriage, if at all; Negro parents for the most part were described as more accepting. Because of expected parental and societal reactions to their impending marriage, couples more often spent a good amount of time discussing the interracial factor in order to decide whether they would be capable of coping with the anticipated problems and conflicts. All of the couples agreed, however, that in the final analysis it was the two personalities that counted most of all and not the families, friends, society or the differences in race.

Individual personality patterns as perceived by the couples were as varied as one might expect. Conflicts which grew out of these differences were considered more important than the interracial differences *per se*. This opinion was universal among the couples interviewed. Yet important racial features did come to the fore for the couples to resolve. It was the white partner who more often came to recognize a larger gap in his experience and knowledge of the Negro than was true in reverse. Myths, stereotypes and "tall tales" had to be met directly. After discussion—and sometimes many arguments later—understanding might evolve. The pattern would be repeated on each new issue regarding racial aspects and the Negro spouse was at times more adamant in these matters than the opposite spouse. One white man summed it up this way: "Negroes don't have to learn to understand the whites as much as the whites must learn to understand Negroes. This has been a sin of omission on our part."

The manner of discussing problems as they arose—which grew in part out of the interracial character of their marriages—was considered by these Negro-white couples to have been an enhancement to marital adjustment. Moreover, the general theme reflected by the couples was that external pressure and skepticism regarding their marriages often proved to be unifying forces in favor of adjustment rather than deterrents. An almost universal reaction among the couples is illustrated by a comment of one Negro woman who said, "We didn't want to give society the satisfaction of our marriage breaking up, so we worked at it harder. . . ." This might be termed an element of defiance in the service of marital preservation.

The sexual adjustments of the Negro-white couples interviewed were explored. No one revealed any sexual experiences which would tend to substantiate the popular beliefs about the existence of unusual sexual attraction between the two races. Several white men expressed a preference for Negro women in terms of general attractiveness. No one else offered a similar observation. Most likely, Negro partners, especially the men, would be more reluctant to verbalize such thoughts regarding attractiveness of whites because of societal stereotypes and emphasis in this direction. But most participants said that they considered beliefs about interracial attraction being based mainly on sex, to be myths grown out of a desire to control racial intermingling. By the same token, the couples generally felt that there is little basis in fact to support the prevailing opinion concerning the alleged greater sexual virility of the Negro male when he is compared to the white male. For the most part, it appears likely that both whites and Negroes are subjected to misconceptions in this area and there are believed to be numerous instances in which both groups perpetuate the sexual myth.

OVERT SOCIETAL REACTIONS

As indicated earlier, overt reaction to an interracial marriage is apt to be considerably stronger and more clear-cut from family members than from friends or associates. At least this was the impression received from the couples interviewed. The friendship patterns and recreational activities established prior to the marriages were similar to those which prevailed afterwards. Likewise, the overt reactions from society were not dissimilar to what they had been during the courtship period. Apparently the initial overt reaction of people to interracial couples has little relationship to whether the couples are actually married or not. After marriage, of course, the reaction from others may be perceived by the couples as more intense and they are then faced with problems arising from community living which they had not heretofore experienced.

Intensive social interaction with community figures as reflected by these couples may begin at the time they set out to find a place to live. With but two exceptions the couples interviewed were faced with many of the same problems which Negroes and other minorities generally meet pertaining to segregated housing. Places which were ordinarily available to whites were not available to them. Although all of the couples preferred an interracial neighborhood, they usually had to accept what was available to them.

The initial entry into a residential community by a Negro-white couple usually provokes a combination of reactions. These may include stares, curiosity, extensions of friendship by a few, patronizing remarks by others and sometimes overt acts of hostility or violence. The same reactions occur outside a couple's residential area. The couples interviewed considered staring to be the most difficult reaction from others to which interracial couples must become accustomed. This was described as a tremendous phenomenon to which to adjust and there were only two couples who departed from this general opinion. In each of the two instances the Negro partner is frequently mistaken for white.

Several couples described having been attacked in the streets by strangers who objected to the couples' interracial relationship. It is a rather common experience for Negro-white couples to be stopped on the highway by curious police officers. Discrimination in public places in the city and in vacation areas was described in detail by the couples. Quite often the female partner in these marriages is thought to be a domestic servant, a victim of abuse or a prostitute; and the male to be a chauffeur, an attacker or a procurer. These stereotypes are common and from the material given by the couples interviewed, it would appear that the possibility of the Negro-white couple being married is the last notion that occurs to the majority of people.

DISCUSSION

The quality of the interaction between married partners is considered to have an important influence upon the marital adjustment of the partners. For interracial couples the personal interaction may involve a higher degree of communication and intimacy than exists in the non-interracial marriage. From the moment of courtship and throughout the subsequent marriage these couples are faced with pressures and obstacles set by society against their intimate association. As a result they often marshal their defenses in order to cope with these barriers and in order to protect their interracial union. To some extent environmental pressures were seen as an actual enhancement to the marriage. The protective reactions on the part of the couples interviewed were clearly illustrated by their comments.

Individual personality characteristics of interracial partners were stressed by the couples interviewed and, as has been described, these were seen as the most important features of their marriage. Reportedly these outweighed the importance of sexual attraction and sexual adjustment for these Negro-white couples who are engaged in a forbidden sexual union.

REFERENCES

Allport, Gordon W. *The Nature of Prejudice.* Cambridge, Mass.: Addison-Wesley Publishing Company, 1954.

Benedict, Ruth F. and Weltfish, Gene. *The Races of Mankind.* New York: Viking Press, 1945.

Dollard, John. *Caste and Class in a Southern Town.* New Haven: Yale University Press, 1937.

Drake, St. Clair and Cayton, Horace R. *Black Metropolis: A Study of Negro Life in a Northern City.* New York: Harcourt, Brace and Company, 1945.

Eisenstein, Victor W. *Neurotic Interaction in Marriage.* New York: The Basic Book Service, 1956.

Golden, Joseph. "Negro-White Marriage in Philadelphia." Unpublished Ph.D. thesis, The University of Pennsylvania, Philadelphia, 1951.

Hollingshead, August B. "Two Factor Index of Social Position." Connecticut: 1965 Yale Station, 1957. (Mimeographed).

Lindzey, Gardner (ed.). *Handbook of Social Psychology.* Cambridge: Addison-Wesley Publishing Company, Inc., 1954.

Myrdal, Gunnar. *An American Dilemma: The Negro Problem and Modern Democracy,* 2 vols. New York: Harper and Brothers, 1944.

Simpson, George E. and Yinger, J. Milton. *Racial and Cultural Minorities: An Analysis of Prejudice and Discrimination.* New York: Harper and Brothers, 1958.

White, Walter. *Rope and Faggot.* New York: Alfred A. Knopf, 1929.

WHAT DO YOU THINK?

It may be argued that intermarriage is good because it will lead to the blending of the population. However, it may also be argued that endogamy is good because it will help maintain a pluralistic society. Which do you agree with, and why?

Which of the following are you most in favor of?

marrying across social class lines
marrying across ethnic lines
marrying across religious lines
marrying across racial lines

Which would you personally *not* consider for your own marriage?

How do you explain the higher divorce rate in mixed marriages?

Should a couple resolve religious differences before marriage or wait until later?

Should children follow the religion of the mother, of the father, or be allowed to choose for themselves?

Why is it more acceptable for females to marry into a higher social class than it is for males?

Oscar was born a Roman Catholic and did not wish to leave his faith. He married Ottilde, a Presbyterian, who had no intention of changing her faith, either. While they were dating, they saw little difference in their points of view, and the wedding was held in her church. Then came the problem of belonging to different denominations, of going to church alone, of belonging to church organizations, and of explaining why the spouse was not there. He wanted to make larger donations to his church than he would give her for that purpose. When the first child was born, her family wanted him to be baptized in her church with her family members as godparents. His family wanted the same.

How can they settle this?

What other problems can crop up in an interfaith marriage?

Issues of Marriage Laws

Two major areas considered in this section are legal aspects of marriage and divorce.

Everywhere, marriage is regulated. Even primitive tribes have rules. In advanced civilizations, laws cover certain aspects of marriage. In this country, each state has its own laws, and even though they are not identical, all these laws concern the welfare of the individual and preservation of the family.

Why is the state interested in marriage? Henry A. Bowman lists these reasons:[1]

to safeguard moral standards;

to protect property rights;

to determine the legitimacy of children;

to protect persons, especially women, from abuse and exploitation;

to guarantee the legality of contracts;

to guard against marriages within prohibited degrees of relationship.

Only two of these reasons deal with property and contracts; the others concern human relationships. Sometimes a person wants to "do his own thing," and considers it no one else's business. But the community is interested in an individual's welfare, and laws are the most explicit statements of community concern.

Issues you may wish to consider after reading the articles by Robert F. Drinan and Norman Robbins include:

Should we have uniform national marriage and divorce laws?
If so, they could be centralized in the federal government. But

---

[1] Henry A. Bowman, *Marriage for Moderns* (New York: McGraw-Hill Book Company, 1970), p. 287.

this might mean more power taken from the states. A start may
have been made when the United States Supreme Court ruled
against laws prohibiting interracial marriages.

When eighteen-year-olds were given the right to vote, they were
considered adults. Some states extend this definition to allow them to marry
without parental consent at this age. However, few young men have
prepared for an occupation by that age or are able to support a wife.
Under present conditions many married women work and must take
lower paying jobs because they lack skills. It is difficult for either party to
attain these abilities before the age of 18, but as far as we could
ascertain there has not been a big rush to the marriage license bureaus to
take advantage of the lower age regulation.

We know that teenage marriages have a high failure rate, but if
marriage has to be postponed too long, other problems crop up. What are
the best ages for marriage?

Laws are not static, however; they are changed as society and modes
of life change. Our society seems to be moving toward more
uniformity of regulations and toward recognizing the need for health,
happiness, and the well-being of all family members. Our constitution
guarantees the right of pursuit of happiness, although it does not say
everyone must be or will be happy! Nevertheless, marriage laws and
divorce laws will, hopefully, be directed toward goals which reflect needs
of the society and also help every person achieve maximum happiness.

Another issue today is that of degree of control by law. We need to
think through many stipulations still on the books. For example, laws
against the marriage of close relatives are still important; but with
modern medicine, are the old health regulations still needed? For example,
tuberculosis is now under control, so we no longer need laws prohibiting
marriage of people who have this disease. At present, the test for
syphilis is the main premarital blood check, but if the test is positive, the
couple may still marry if both know about it. Concern over the increasing
rate of venereal disease may reinforce the value of this type of test. At
least the subjects, by having the test, know whether they have the germ
and become aware of the need for treatment. Thus, the law serves to
educate individuals and to take the first step in preventing the spread of
venereal disease.

Divorce has been with us as long as marriage. Even the Old
Testament gives regulations about divorce. Throughout history, every
culture has set up some means of dissolving a marriage that has gone
sour or that never worked.

Marriage and divorce laws should be designed to protect not just the
couple but also the children. Remarriage after divorce complicates

matters, in that adults select new partners yet the children may or may not be courted in the process, but these are personal problems which are not and should not be controlled by law. Biological parenthood may be accidental, but psychological and social parenthood is purposeful. Adoptive parents select the child and step-parents may adopt the children formally. They thus become adoptive rather than step-parents, a condition which has a much more positive connotation in our culture. Families and communities have the major responsibility for seeing that children have good care, and the law steps in only when there is serious neglect or abuse.

Norman Robbins, an attorney-at-law, is aware of the many problems divorce can bring and points out the positive and negative aspects of no fault divorce. Persons seeking a divorce do not have to blame each other, so no guilt is considered and this does away with airing intimate differences or trumping up charges. Some states allow divorce on no-fault grounds alone, while others have added this to their former list of reasons. Now we have the problem of declaring a marriage irretrievably broken, or dead. Additional difficulties such as child custody, child support, division of property, and others are coming up so that time and experience will be needed before we can be sure that no-fault is the ideal solution.

What happens after divorce? Many individuals experience divorce as a crisis situation which can be serious or have a long-lasting traumatic effect. Rose and Price-Bonham highlighted the results of their review of many studies in their article on divorce adjustment. Their article clarifies many points. Divorce can have a traumatic effect on people, especially on women. As Rose and Price-Bonham show in their analysis of research results, Goode measured the degree of trauma suffered after divorce according to how this affected their sleep, general health, ability to work efficiently, ability to concentrate or to remember, loneliness, and any increase in the amount of smoking or drinking. He found fewer problems if the wife asked for the divorce than if the husband did. Also, if the wife remarried before the husband she showed fewer symptoms of trauma. More will be covered in later chapters, but for now we wish to emphasize that divorce can affect the physical and mental health of the persons involved. So far much of the research has dealt with women, but we need studies of how divorce affects men, the traumatic effects, problems in accepting the economic and legal responsibility for the children of the broken marriage, their attitudes toward the new spouse, and possibly the new family of children.

17 *Robert F. Drinan*

American Laws Regulating the Formation of the Marriage Contract

The only important additions since 1900 to that part of American law which regulates the formation of the marriage contract have been the statutory requirement, in virtually all states, of a premarital test for venereal disease and the banning in 1967 by the United States Supreme Court of legislative restrictions on interracial marriages.[1] Almost all of the other laws regarding such matters as the age at which persons may marry, the right of parents to object to an underage marriage of their children, and restrictions based on affinity and consanguinity have remained almost unchanged during the past fifty years—despite the tidal waves of change which have transformed other areas of American law and American life.

The stability (or stagnation) of laws regulating what society in general would agree is the most serious and fundamental of all of the contracts regulated by law suggests a profound consensus in American society that the state and the law should say as little as possible about who can marry whom. All would agree that there must be some minimal legal regulation of marriage but that this regulation is not to be inconsistent with the conviction that marriage is and should remain the most intimate, personal, and legally unsupervised contract known to the law.

THE FREEDOM TO MARRY ASSUMES CONSTITUTIONAL STATUS

This consensus received a certain constitutional status when a unanimous Supreme Court, writing through Chief Justice Earl Warren in the *Loving* decision of June 12, 1967, stated:

Robert F. Drinan, S.J., "American Laws Regulating the Formation of the Marriage Contract." *The Annals* of the American Academy of Political and Social Science, Vol. 383 (May 1969), pp. 48–57. Reprinted by permission.

The freedom to marry has long been recognized as one of the vital personal rights essential to the orderly pursuit of happiness by free men.[2]

The *Loving* decision ruled that the government, in the exercise of whatever power it might have with respect to the formation of a marriage, may exercise that power only to safeguard some public objective which is demonstrably more important than the diminution of the human freedom to marry a person of one's choice.

The stability as well as the emerging shifts of emphases in American law regarding marriage during the past several decades can be perceived by a review of the following topics:

1. The procedures for the celebration of marriage inherited by America from the ecclesiastical courts and from English law,
2. The impediments to marriage enacted into law in the nineteenth century—many of which are today obsolete,
3. The inducements to marriage which have long been a part of American law and which deserve reconsideration,
4. Proposals and recommendations designed to harmonize the law regulating the formalities of the marriage contract with the contemporary consensus regarding the relationship of law to the formation of the marital union.

PROCEDURES FOR THE CELEBRATION OF MARRIAGE INHERITED BY AMERICA FROM ENGLAND

In 1753 England outlawed all nonceremonial marriages. This action terminated the possibility of legal recognition for all common-law marriages—a procedure by which spouses could become married merely by an unwitnessed oral agreement to be man and wife and a public proclamation of this fact by cohabitation. This form of consensual marriage had been recognized in Europe as valid but illicit by the Catholic Church from at least the year 1215 until its prohibition by the Council of Trent in 1563.

England's abolition of common-law marriages in 1753 did not become the universal law in America, where even in 1969, some fifteen states still permit a common-law or nonceremonial marriage. Almost all American marriages, however, are solemnized by an ecclesiastical or civil official.

Virtually no qualifications are established by American law for the officials who perform marriages or for those who issue licenses to marry. Because of the absence of standards in this area, it would appear that it would be more appropriate to call the procedure for securing a "license" to marry a mere recording or a registration of a marriage.

The casualness and informality with which American law has always treated its marriage procedures has resulted in the phenomenon of the "voidable" marriage. Such a union is neither valid nor void but can be invalidated during the lifetime of both parties if one or more of the formalities required for a marriage have not been complied with. Such formalities, however, must be "mandatory" rather than merely "directory," if they are to be sufficient to void a marriage. Because of all of these distinctions and the maze that they create, married persons seldom petition for a decree of annulment (which would declare the marriage void from its beginning) but seek, rather, a divorce.

PARENTAL OBJECTIONS TO UNDERAGE MARRIAGE

The ambivalence in the law regarding the advisability of being strict in the enforcement of the law's formalities regarding marriage can be seen in the law's handling of parental objections to an underage marriage of their child. The laws in effect in most states, which require parental consent for marriages of girls under 18 or of boys up to the age of 21, generally grant to the underaged spouse the right to void his or her marriage. But only in fourteen states do parents have the right to invalidate those marriages of their underage children for which they had refused their permission.[3] The law of marriage, it would seem, desires simultaneously to maximize the freedom of all to marry when and as they choose, as well as the freedom of parents and of society to insist that only responsible, well-matched couples be permitted to take on the duties of married life. In order to carry out these somewhat contradictory purposes, American law has perpetuated a series of impediments to marriage inherited from ecclesiastical and English law. An analysis of these impediments will show that the American law of marriage embodies, unconsciously and perhaps reluctantly, a synthesis of sacred and secular elements for which, curiously, there exists a broad-based popular consensus.

IMPEDIMENTS TO MARRIAGE IN AMERICAN LAW

The least controversial of all the restrictions on marriage found in American law are those based on consanguinity. Although reliable predictions about defective offspring from marriages between an uncle and his niece, or between first cousins, are difficult if not impossible to obtain, laws forbidding such unions, presumably based on accurate information, hardly ever become a public issue. Nor is there ever any controversy about other restrictions on marriages between persons related by consanguinity—even though the degrees within which marriage is forbidden are taken almost verbatim from Leviticus.

Impediments based on affinity—that is, on legal relationships arising solely from marriage—seem to be indefensible. These restrictions, which exist in twenty states and the District of Columbia,[4] are in the laws of states almost exclusively in the northeastern and southern parts of the nation. It may be that the laws of these states reflect an outdated sectarian point of view predicated, apparently, on the assumption that intra-family harmony could be damaged if persons related by marriage knew that they could marry each other after the death or divorce of the spouse of the person deemed desirable as a marriage partner.

Restrictions upon marriage which are based on physical or mental incapacity are contained in the laws of thirty-four states.[5] In several states, laws forbidding marriages between persons with epilepsy or tuberculosis have now been repealed or are not enforced. The extent to which the many statutes prohibiting the marriage of any person "of unsound mind" are enforced is unknown. These laws appear to be based either on the assumption that a mental disease or defect may be transmitted to one's offspring or upon the assumption that the state should issue a license to marry only to those who have sufficient mental capacity to be adequately responsible parents. Either assumption is open to question and, even if provable, its value must be weighed in relation to the competing ideal of maximizing the freedom of everyone to marry. In this connection, the crucial principle for all thinking on the matter might be Chief Justice Warren's statement in *Loving* that:

> Marriage is one of the basic civil rights of man, fundamental to our very existence and survival.[6]

If one starts with the primacy of each individual's freedom to marry, not a few of the statutory restrictions on the right to marry would be set aside.

Restrictions or, more precisely, mandatory postponements of a person's remarriage after a divorce constitute another and ever more important infringement upon the right to marry. A substantial number of states withhold the right to remarry from divorced persons for a period which may last up to a year.[7] Whether the state has the right of imposing celibacy for even a brief period—and for laudable purposes—is a good question. It would appear that there should be at least some judicial process by which a waiver of the post-divorce waiting period could be secured. This process would be particularly appropriate and helpful for persons divorced because of nonfault grounds such as' the insanity of the other spouse.

The one universal and apparently unquestioned impediment to marriage is, of course, the existence of a valid and undissolved bond of marriage. Monogamy is so firmly rooted in American law that any exception to it or erosion of it seems unthinkable. On four occasions in the last century, the Supreme Court of the United States denied every claim of the Mormons to practice polygamy in the name of religion.[8] No tendency to condone or to make any exceptions for bigamy appears to exist in American law. It may be, of course, that this "absolute" about monogamy is not really too difficult for anyone, since what has been called "successive monogamy" is so readily available because of permissive divorce laws.

The only premarital requirement added to American law during the twentieth century is the test for a venereal disease. Because of advances made in medicine, it is questionable whether the enormous expenses connected with the millions of tests of this nature required each year of prospective spouses can be justified. But the profound reluctance of Americans to tamper with the minimal requirements of the law for would-be marriage partners will probably inhibit anyone from recommending the repeal of the requirement of an examination for a disease which in extreme cases may be communicable to children born of the marriage.

The ambiguous and ill-drafted statutes regarding the requirements for those who desire to be married, accompanied by a relaxed or nonexistent enforcement of these laws, manifest a simple and almost religious faith that any single person over a minimum age, without conspicuous incapacity, should be permitted to marry any person—however ill-advised such a marriage might appear to be. The acceptance of this attitude by most Americans is the result of the convergence of an uncritical reception in America of the English and ecclesiastical law of marriage, along with a popular acquiescence in the romantic notion that two persons who "fall in love" should be able to marry and "live happily ever after."

If law ever seeks to lead, and not to follow, in the area of premarital requirements, the law must first create a climate of opinion which would accept the idea that America's legal institutions should seek to elevate the requirements of marriage and to make it substantially more difficult for some persons to contract a marriage. There appears to be little if any sentiment to support that particular point of view in contemporary American thought about marriage.

INDUCEMENTS TO MARRIAGE
WHICH DESERVE RECONSIDERATION

By a strange paradox, American law, which, as has been seen, rigorously protects the freedom of all to marry, nonetheless simultaneously promotes or induces marriages by means of laws designed to regulate seduction, illegitimacy, and fornication.

Thirty-six states make seduction a crime.[9] In some thirty of these states, the man who allegedly induced a girl to have illicit relations with him, on the strength of a knowingly false promise of marriage, may avoid all criminal penalties by marrying the woman who claims to have been seduced. It is impossible to say how many marriages have been induced by seduction laws, but, clearly, the mere existence of such laws creates a tendency to precipitate marriages.

Statutes regarding illegitimacy and bastardy probably constitute an even more powerful inducement to marriage. Although American law has made substantial progress during the past fifty years in clarifying and guaranteeing the rights of children born out of wedlock, the grim fact remains that in all states except Arizona and Oregon, some disability falls on the illegitimate child.[10] There is therefore a strong inducement to marriage for a couple who have conceived a child out of wedlock. It is amazing, nonetheless, to note that every sixteenth child born in the United States is illegitimate.[11]

The laws in some thirty-five states which make fornication and adultery a crime tend (at least theoretically) to induce marriages, in that they make the male party a likely object of blackmail. Such laws, unknown in England, are obviously designed to protect the integrity of marriage, but their actual operation and their virtual nonenforcement raise the most serious questions as to the wisdom of perpetuating such laws.

A review of the law's restrictions upon and inducement to marriage clearly reveals that the law seeks to impose the least possible regulation on the formation of the marriage contract. The law has, in fact, been unable or unwilling to interject itself into the privacy of the marital institution. The Supreme Court of the United States spoke, almost for the first time, about this attitude in 1965 when, in the *Griswold* case, it declared unconstitutional a Connecticut law banning the sale and use of contraceptives. In eloquent language, the Court exalted the intimacy and privacy which the law should extend to every marriage, and, on that basis, the Court made it clear beyond question that any law restrictive of the freedom of spouses needs an uncontestable justification, if it is to withstand a challenge of its constitutionality.

PROPOSALS AND RECOMMENDATIONS REGARDING AMERICA'S LAW ON THE FORMATION OF THE MARRIAGE CONTRACT

Although many proposals could be made concerning the need for pre-marital education and for the wide availability of marital counseling, these suggestions would be offered more appropriately to religious and educational groups than to the nation's lawmakers. The latter group, pursuant to a broadly held consensus that the law regulating marriage should be minimal, manifests no discernible inclination to have the state or the law decide upon the always complex and controversial questions surrounding the regulation of the formation of marriage.

American law continues to assert two theories, both of which the law took over from ecclesiastical practice. These theories hold marriage as a contract (comparable to but distinguishable from ordinary commercial contracts) and as a status. No one has yet challenged the concept that marriage is a contract from which certain duties and rights automatically arise; all of the elements of a contract are clearly present in the exchange of promises made by spouses on the day of their wedding. But no little confusion exists with respect to the meaning of the term "status" as applied to marriage. The law of divorce has generally insisted that marriage is a status or an institution which cannot be rescinded or dissolved by the mutual desires of a married couple. The law has affirmed that the contract of marriage is "tripartite" with the state as the third party. Permission for divorce from the state, consequently, has always been required. Such permission is given only after the presentation of adequate evidence that the reasons for divorce, as designated by the state, have been met. These reasons or grounds, until recently, have almost always been based upon the fault of one of the parties; in every state, for example, adultery, cruelty, and willful desertion are grounds for divorce. These fault-grounds, however, have been eroded in practice, and sometimes broadened by statute, to include non-fault-grounds such as incompatibility, living apart for a specific period, and insanity.

If American divorce law in the near future formally endorses the idea that spouses may rescind their contract of marriage by mutual choice and without any allegation or proof of fault, American law may well have explicitly or implicitly rejected the concept of marriage as a status or as an institution. Inevitably, this new concept of marriage as a mere contract rescindable at the will of the parties will have an enormous influence upon whatever American law may decide to do in order to regulate the formation of such a contract. For if the marriage contract is seen as an agreement between a man and a woman, which can be dissolved by mutual wish or even unilaterally by one spouse without fault on the part of the other spouse, then the law need not reassert and seek to implement all those safeguards now present in the law, most of which clearly presuppose that the marriage contract is made for life, that one of its primary purposes is to form a family unit in which children can be educated, and that only in extreme cases will the state permit the dissolution of any marriage bond which has been created in compliance with all the dictates of the law.

It can be seen, therefore, that the dilemmas confronting American law with respect to the soundest policies by which divorces should be granted are, to some extent, the same problems which American law has been reluctant to face in connection with the formation of marriage. How long American society and American law can continue to disregard these basic dilemmas is hard to predict. But, apart from these fundamental issues of public policy which the law is apparently unwilling to resolve, are there some less fundamental, but nonetheless important, reforms or modernizations which the law could and should introduce? Four such modernizations are here suggested: (1) the establishment of a uniform marriage registration act, (2) the enactment of laws which would make marriages valid or void but not voidable, (3) a new emphasis on the rights of minors and of children, and (4) the adoption by the law of a philosophy of marriage which is based on those moral values which are common to the people of a pluralistic nation.

(1) *A uniform marriage registration act:* Although persons applying for a "license" to marry may not feel any particular resentment at the fact that the state cannot really grant permission or a "license" to exercise a fundamental human right, it would nonetheless be more appropriate to have a marriage registration act rather than a marriage license law. A modern registration law, moreover, should be on a statewide or even federal basis. It should, moreover, be able readily to pick up impediments to a marriage and should provide for a judicial process by which a request for a waiver of certain impediments could be expeditiously granted or denied.

The present system of securing a license to marry in the town where one resides is obviously obsolete. Such a system makes it almost impossible to prove the existence or nonexistence of a marriage in a nation of two hundred million highly mobile people. A comprehensive and computerized method of marriage registrations would bring benefits to those whose unions are thus systematically recorded, to the children of these marriages, and to the 800,000 spouses who each year secure a divorce. A national uniform registration of marriage might also stimulate the fifteen states which still recognize consensual, nonceremonial marriages to require registration of all marriages—at least prospectively.

(2) *Marriages should be valid or void, and not voidable:*   A uniform registration of all marriages would make it much more feasible to eliminate from the American law of marriage the substantial number of marriages in which the spouses retain a right to void their marriage because of some noncompliance with legal procedures or formalities. The concept of the voidable marriage was almost unknown in ecclesiastical law, since that system included a method by which a dispensation from some but not all impediments to marriage could be obtained prior to the marriage. The civil law of marriage in America, for historic reasons which are not clear, adopted the ecclesiastical law of marriage almost in its entirety but without its processes to grant dispensations from impediments to marriage. As a result, certain marriages in America, as, for example, those of underaged persons or of dubiously divorced spouses, may be voided at the option of one of the parties to the marriage. Certainty about the validity of all marriages is surely desirable. A far greater certainty about the validity of all American marriages can be obtained by the enactment of laws which would practically eliminate the concept of voidability.

(3) *Marriage law and a new emphasis on the rights of minors and children:*   Despite the fact that the median age at which Americans marry is now the lowest in history, the law regulating the creation and dissolution of marriage places little emphasis on the rights of those under the age of twenty-one. The most obvious example of this deficiency is evident in the laws pertaining to the marriages of underaged youth. These laws often seem to have been written to protect parents rather than their children. The law does not provide, for example, for a hearing to be granted to a minor whose parents object to his marriage. The law somehow assumes that an "unemancipated" youth (that is, one under twenty-one or eighteen who lives at home and is financially dependent on his parents) has no right to be heard when his desire to marry is contrary to the wishes of his parents. Similarly, those states which permit parents to prevent the marriage of their underage children grant no right to be heard to a pregnant underaged daughter who desires to marry in order to legitimatize her future child.

In regulating the remarriage of those who have children by their former spouse, marriage law should also become more sensitive to the rights of children. If there is any reason which might justify a state requirement of a postponement of a marriage, it is the presence of children whose rights may well be adversely affected if their divorced mother or father remarries. A clash between the right of a divorced parent to remarry and the right of this parent's child to have some type of hearing on the question is one of the conflicts which Americans are not even ready to recognize, much less discuss. But teenage children who, without being consulted, have been placed by the law in the custody of their mother and who subsequently are required by the law, again without being heard, to live in a household with their mother's second husband, can legitimately complain that the law of marriage treats children as persons without rights and with lives whose disposition depends almost entirely on the marital successes or failures of their parents. It is therefore not impossible that the law will soon confront a challenge brought by young people who have not been heard in judicial proceedings settling their custody and who have absolutely no option except to acquiesce in the remarriage of their custodian parent and to continue to live in the same household with their stepfather. It may seem unthinkable to suggest that such young people should have *some* right to be heard on matters which affect their life so profoundly. But it must be at least recognized that a whole new and vast class of youths have been created by easy divorce, a group profoundly affected—for better or for worse—by the law's attitude that any validly divorced adult should, regardless of his or her existing commitments to children or to an ongoing family, be entitled to marry with the same absolute ease as do persons who have never been married before. It will be seen, therefore, that the "hands-off" attitude of the law with regard to the formation of the marriage contract has profound and unexplored consequences when it is automatically extended to all prospective spouses regardless of their previous marital history or their obligations to children by previous marriages.

American law during the past few decades has been increasingly sensitive to rights of children who are born out of wedlock or are adopted or retarded or delinquent. A whole new class of children is beginning to attract the law's attention—the children of divorce. Whether an adequate response can be made to the needs and rights of these children without some change in the law's attitude of permitting a second marriage with the same liberality as a first marriage remains to be seen. But if any substantial change in the law's traditional attitude of permissiveness with regard to the formation of almost all marriages is to occur, it seems safe to predict that it will have application only to the remarriages of divorced persons with minor children.

(4) *Toward a philosophy of law based on moral values generally accepted by a pluralistic nation:*   It is possible that the contemporary

satisfaction and consensus with regard to the law's minimal regulation of marriage may continue for an indefinite period of time. Convictions about the indispensability of monogamy, coupled with the desirability of maximum human freedom concerning marriage, are, after all, central to Western culture. A legal system based on these two principles may go on for a long time after the religious bases of these principles have been discarded. It would appear, however, that the concepts and procedures which the American law of marriage continues to employ, almost all of which had their origin in ecclesiastical canon law, may tend eventually to break down, because, in the nature of things, they cannot reflect the reality or regulate the substance of modern marriage and divorce.

If it becomes necessary for the law to adopt a new approach to marriage, the crucial question will be the choice of those moral or social values which the law should primarily emphasize. One could select as a point of departure, for example, the idea that the law of marriage should concentrate on the prevention of the birth of defective or retarded infants. With the coming explosion of knowledge in genetics, it may be possible, as never before, to achieve such an objective; the consequent restrictions on the freedom to marry are clear.

If, on the other hand, one assumes that the law should seek to prevent the marriages of persons who are clearly ill-suited for each other and whose union will almost certainly end in disaster, the conclusions of the sociologists of marriage would become the major premise of the law. If one adopts a theory that only those marriages should be permitted which give promise of providing a suitable family life for children, then a different major objective would be the primary purpose of the law.

No one of these theories or even any combination of them will necessarily furnish a philosophy of marriage law which will be satisfactory to all of the significant elements of American society. But it is ever more important to formulate and to discuss the role of law in establishing guidelines for the institution of marriage. Although laws in America concerning the formation of the marriage relationship appear not to have changed radically during the twentieth century, the ambiguous approach of the law to the question of the extent to which easy divorce should be accessible indicates that the law in America may be required, perhaps sooner than anyone anticipates, to formulate an approach to marriage which reinforces those values to which most persons adhere, but also to set forth some challenging and controversial principles designed to protect the eroding solidarity of marriage as an institution. If American law is to be successful in developing a new law of marriage for the citizens of a free and pluralistic society, the time has come to rethink and rewrite the archaic statutes by which marriage is regulated in modern society.

ENDNOTES

1. Loving v. Virginia, 388 U.S. 1 (1967).
2. *Id.* at 12.
3. VERNIER, AMERICAN FAMILY LAWS 251 (1931); 150 A.L.R. 2nd 609 (1944).
4. Drinan, *The* Loving *Decision and the Freedom To Marry,* 29 OHIO ST. L.J. 358–398 (1968). Drinan, *supra,* Apps. A, B, and C, at 380–389, contains a compilation of all state laws on consanguinity and affinity.
5. *Id.* at 389–396.
6. Loving v. Virginia, *supra* note 1, at 12.
7. See Kingsley, *Remarriage after Divorce,* 26 So. CAL. L. REV. 280 (1953).
8. Reynolds v. United States, 98 U.S. 145 (1878); David v. Beason, 133 U.S. 333 (1890); Mormon Church v. United States, 136 U.S. 1 (1890). See also Miles v. United States 103 U.S. 304 (1880).
9. For a list of the statutes, see Wadlington, *Shotgun Marriage by Operation of Law,* 1 GEORGIA LAW REVIEW 183 (1967).
10. For a complete review of the law of illegitimacy, see Krause, *Equal Protection for the Illegitimate,* 65 MICH. L.R. 477 (1967).
11. Krause, *The Nonmarital Child—New Conceptions for the Law of Unlawfulness,* 1 Family Law Quarterly (June, 1967).

18 Norman N. Robbins

THERE OUGHT TO BE A LAW!
Have We Found Fault in
No Fault Divorce?

The no fault doctrine, as applied to divorce matters, has been tested recently in fourteen different states in this country. Our experience to date indicates that not only is this doctrine workable, but it has gone a long way to alleviate some of the trauma and suffering usually associated with finding guilt and placing before the public eye the alleged marital indiscretions of spouses.

In 1969 the State of California took the first major step in revising divorce laws that were based upon ecclesiastical doctrines dating back to the seventeenth century. The doctrine that one must come into court with clean hands in order to obtain a divorce, or the theory that one spouse was innocent of wrong-doing proved to be mythical, immoral, and unworkable. The fraud and injustice perpetrated by the need to find fault before a divorce could be granted became so apparent to some legislative bodies that in a period of four years fourteen states have enacted a partial or complete revision of their domestic relation laws so as to incorporate the "no fault" doctrine.

Under the "fault doctrine" it was necessary to prove that some specific act detrimental to the opposite spouse or the marriage had occurred, such acts as physical beating, threatening, desertion, an act or acts of adultery, non-support, a previously undissolved marriage, alcoholism, indignities, cruelty, etc., were the requirements *in toto* or in part of many states. Under the no fault doctrine proof that the marriage corpus is no longer viable, that there has been an irretrievable breakdown with no reasonable likelihood of a reconciliation is all that is required. In theory the new doctrine

Norman N. Robbins, "THERE OUGHT TO BE A LAW! Have We Found Fault in No Fault Divorce?" from *The Family Coordinator*, July, 1973, pp. 359–362. Reprinted with permission.

attempts to do away with evidence of specific acts of fault. Is this theory working in our trial courts?

There is a complete deficiency of Supreme Court decisions defining the breakdown of marriage, the words irretrievable or irreconcilable, objects of matrimony, or what evidence is needed to prove that a marriage is dead. Therefore, each trial court is left with the prerogative to make its own definitions and interpretations. As expected, courts differ in their understanding of the law. Some judges are satisfied that there is a dead marriage when the plaintiff testifies that he or she will no longer live with the spouse in a marital relationship. Other judges still demand testimony eliciting the specific acts of fault before making their decisions.

Many serious questions arose in regard to no fault divorce legislation. Was it constitutional or was it an unlawful delegation of authority by the legislature to the courts? What amount and type of testimony is required to obtain a divorce under this doctrine? Must you prove if a marriage has irretrievably broken down, or prove why a marriage is irretrievably broken down? Perhaps one of the most difficult questions that arose was whether fault should be a factor in determining the question of alimony, support, and division of property between the parties.

There was no difficulty in determining the constitutionality of no fault divorce legislation. The amount and type of testimony required is still unsettled in many jurisdictions. In a number of states, it depends upon the policies of the individual jurists and will remain that way until a higher court sets the standards. Where the court is merely interested in finding out if the marriage has broken down it is usually sufficient for the party applying for the divorce to give the following answers to the following questions:

Question: Why are you applying for a divorce?
Answer: My marriage is dead. I no longer wish to live with my spouse. I will never again live with my spouse. I don't love my spouse. My spouse and I have irreconcilable differences and the marriage is irremediably broken down.
Question: Is there a chance for a reconciliation?
Answer: None whatsoever. (Please note that the type of questions vary from state to state and this is merely a composite example. There are usually other questions such as establishing jurisdiction, date and place of marriage, number of children, property involved, custody, alimony, support, etc.)

Where the court desires to determine why the marriage has broken down, then we must go into the old fault type of questions and answers as follows:

Question: Why are you applying for a divorce?
Answer: Our marriage is dead.
Question: Why is your marriage dead?
Answer: My spouse has been unfaithful; my spouse drinks heavily; my spouse doesn't support me; my spouse struck me; etc. (Please note again that this is merely a composite example and many other questions and answers are equally given.)

Whether the court should consider the fault of the parties in determining alimony, support for children, or in dividing the assets has been resolved in Iowa by two recent landmark decisions. In the case of In re the marriage of Williams (199 NW 2339) the court said

Fault concept as a standard for granting dissolution of marital relationship has been definitely eliminated by statute. Fault is not a factor to be considered in awarding property settlement, or an allowance of alimony or support money under statute governing dissolution of marital relationship.

This case was decided in June 1972 and sets a precedence that should be followed by other no fault divorce jurisdictions. This ruling, of course, does not affect community property states. In California, when a party starts a divorce action he or she knows immediately that the judgment of divorce will automatically divide equally all property accumulated by the parties during their marriage.

In a later Iowa case (In re marriage of T. Jaden—199 NW 2d 475) the court gave further credence to the earlier ruling. This court stated:

Under dissolution of marriage, procedure effective July 1, 1970, fault concept was eliminated as standard for granting dissolution of marital relationship and evidence of conduct of parties, insofar as it tended to place fault for the marriage breakdown on either spouse, also had to be rejected as a factor in awarding property settlement or an allowance of alimony or support money.

There is a consensus that we no longer have to look at the question of guilt. The real difference occurs between the court that delves into the questions "Is there a breakdown of the marriage" and the court that asks, "Why is there a breakdown in the marriage."

Now, we must distinguish guilt from fault. Though as stated, guilt is not a factor, fault is still sought by some courts at this date. It is certainly conceivable that a spouse may admit living with another person in an illicit relationship, or being alcoholic, or not performing marital duties and be granted a divorce. Here the court is not interested in determining who is guilty of the breakdown of the marriage, but merely that there is a breakdown because of the fault of one of the parties; and the court wants to know what factors broke up the marriage.

All states require whatever admissable evidence necessary in determining custody of minor children conflicts. Certainly the conduct of the parties, if relevant will be admissable in such hearings whether it is a no fault divorce state or not. The welfare of the minor child or children usually being the paramount consideration the court will not refuse testimony as to the fitness of the parties to have custody.

The fourteen states that have some type of no fault divorce proceeding that has been enacted within the past four years are as follows:

Alabama:	(1972) Irretrievable breakdown of the marriage and that further attempts at reconciliation are impractical or futile and not in the best interests of the parties or family.
Arkansas:	(1969) Living apart and separate for three (3) consecutive years regardless of fault; voluntariness immaterial; guilt considered only when wife seeks alimony or property settlement.
California:	(1969) Irreconcilable differences which have been caused by the irremediable breakdown of the marriage. (Incurable insanity)
Colorado:	(1972) Irretrievable breakdown of the marriage.
Florida:	(1971) Irretrievable breakdown of the marriage. (Mental incompetence three years)
Iowa:	(1970) Breakdown of the marriage relationship to the extent that the legitimate objects of matrimony have been destroyed and there remains no reasonable likelihood that the marriage can be preserved.
Michigan:	(1971) Breakdown of the marriage relationship to the extent that the objects of matrimony have been destroyed and there remains no reasonable likelihood that the marriage can be preserved.
New Hampshire:	(1971) Irreconcilable differences which have caused the irremediable breakdown of the marriage.
North Dakota:	(1971) Irreconcilable differences.
Oregon:	(1971) Irreconcilable differences between the parties have caused the irremediable breakdown of the marriage.

South Carolina: (1970) Living apart for three (3) consecutive years.

Texas: (1970) Without regard to fault if the marriage has become insupportable because of discord or conflict of personalities that destroys the legitimate ends of the marriage relationship and prevents any reasonable expectation of reconciliation.

Virginia: (1970) Living separate and apart without cohabitation uninterruptedly for two years (no recrimination or *res adjudicata*).

Washington: (1970) Living apart for two or more years without regard to fault in separation.

Only California, Colorado, Florida, Iowa, Michigan, and Oregon have merely one no fault ground for divorce whereas the other states have added a no fault ground to their existing fault grounds (with the exception of the ground of insanity in California and Florida).

We have had over 150 years of "fault" divorce in our country (with a few exceptions), and we have had literally thousands of decisions, defining and circumscribing its intent and content. Now, I presume, we must wait for a number of years to pass before we fully understand how "no fault" divorce matters will be uniformly treated by our courts. The tip of the iceberg in sensible and humane family law has been sighted. What use we make of this sighting is now up to our courts.

19

Vicki L. Rose and
Sharon Price-Bonham

Divorce Adjustment:
A Woman's Problem?

Research in the area of postdivorce adjustment is reviewed and the major findings are presented. Trauma resulting from divorce is discussed in relationship to several variables. The major emphasis of the paper, however, is divorce adjustment, in terms of its relationship to a number of factors, including trauma, friends, children, dating, and other activities. Remarriage as a form of adjustment to divorce, as well as readjustment in remarriage, is discussed.

INTRODUCTION

Waller's (1967) *The Old Love and the New*, initially published in 1930,[1] constituted the only major research dealing with adjustment after divorce until the publication of Goode's (1956) study of divorced women in Detroit. Since Goode's study, research in the area of divorce has been concerned only tangentially with the problem of adjustment. The primary purpose of this paper, therefore, is to review the literature and consolidate the major findings relative to divorce adjustment. Even though volumes have been written regarding the impact of divorce on children, the topic will be considered only insofar as it might affect the adjustment of the divorcing spouse-parent.

The concept of adjustment is applied to many aspects of social behavior. Adjustment is defined as a basic requirement of social participation (Bell, 1967). However, it is among the most controversial concepts dealt with in the study of the family. Divorce adjustment has been used in a variety of ways. It is beyond the scope of this paper to define divorce adjustment. However, it is necessary to caution the reader there is no stated

Vicki L. Rose and Sharon Price-Bonham, "Divorce Adjustment: A Woman's Problem?" from *The Family Coordinator*, July, 1973, pp. 291–297. Reprinted with permission.

275

consensus upon the usage of the term in the works which are cited in this paper.[2]

It is also pertinent that articles dealing with the general topic of divorce affect the general adjustment of women more than that of men. Likewise, Goode (1956) in his survey of postdivorce adjustment interviewed only mothers (95 percent had custody of their children) as he assumed that greater hardship is involved for the divorced woman with children than for the divorced man.

THE DIVORCE

A divorce often comes as a crisis, even if desired by both spouses. Burgess, Locke, and Thomes (1963) contend that a crisis may not be experienced when the emotional involvement between the spouses is relatively weak, while it may be experienced as an extreme crisis when there is strong community opinion against it. Bernard wrote:

> . . . the whole trend in current social life is in the direction of demands for *laissez faire* in personal relationships. The issues that do arise will tend to be in the direction of making divorce as nontraumatic as possible for partners and for children (1970, 28–29).

Gurin et al. (1960) reported that persons who were relieved by divorce often suffered ample disorganization to the degree that they sought professional help. The trauma resulting from divorce includes both personal disorganization and behavior definitions such as unhappiness generated by conflict and the "unraveling of marital habits," which in turn affect the actions of divorcees (Goode, 1956, 185).

Goode (1956) measured the degree of trauma (high, medium, low) experienced by women in his study according to behavior items including difficulty in sleeping, poorer health, greater loneliness, low work efficiency, memory difficulties, increased smoking, and increased drinking. Using these criteria Goode found higher trauma to be positively related to: (1) having the husband first suggest divorce; (2) being given a short time for consideration of divorce; (3) having the idea of divorce come unexpectedly; (4) continuing to have attachment or emotional involvement with the ex-spouse after the divorce; (5) possessing a desire to punish her former husband; (6) being ambivalent about obtaining a divorce; (7) being personally disapproving of divorce; (8) having divorce disapproved of by her reference groups (family and friends); (9) experiencing discrimination as a divorcee; (10) coming from a rural background; and (11) her former husband having a middle or upper class occupation. In regard to age, Goode found the degree of trauma varied according to the length of time the divorcee had been married:

> . . . for younger people there is an association between a long marriage and a higher trauma index. However, for older people this pattern is reversed; a long marriage seems to be less traumatic . . . the possibility that in the case of older people the marriage has itself become somewhat stale and there are relatively few attractions in it for them . . . when the marriage is a short one, there is little association between age and trauma (1956, 193).

Goode also found that the decision to divorce was generally a reluctant decision which was reached over a long period of time, ". . . on the average of about two years" (1956, 137). For the *Significant Americans*, divorce was viewed as an "end of the rope" decision after a period of three or four years or even as long as ten or twelve years (Cuber and Haroff, 1965, 90). As a result of the fact that the decision to divorce is reached over a long period of time, it can be assumed that much of the adjustment relative to the divorce occurs before the divorce decree is granted. Therefore, Goode's (1956) finding that the greatest amount of trauma occurred at the time of the final separation rather than following the final decree was not unexpected.

Similarly, Bohannon distinguished between "emotional divorce" which is the deterioration of a marital relationship, and the "legal divorce":

> . . . the legal processes do not provide an orderly and socially approved discharge of emotions that are elicited during the emotional divorce and during the early parts of preparation for the legal processes (1970a, 48).

Several authors have stressed the fact that many times it is the adversary legal system that increases the trauma experienced by divorcing and divorced couples. Davis (1957) pointed out that the gap between theory and practice is perhaps greater in the field of divorce law than in any other area of legal practice. According to Hunt (1966) the grounds for divorce are molded to fit with the permissible grounds in any given state, and the charade-type nature of the suit is recognized by all who participate. In addition, Hunt contended that the laws require the divorcing spouses to become adversaries. The law's insistence on an adversary system tends to exacerbate the conflict (Kay, 1970), with disastrous moral and emotional consequences for everyone concerned (Lasch, 1966, 58). This adversary system could result in detrimental consequences for adjustment to divorce.

Several parallels have been drawn between loss of a spouse by divorce and loss of a spouse by death, as trauma and loneliness result from the loss of an intimate tie in either case. Weiss (1969) advised that new relationships be established; Hunt (1966) advocated "divorce work" to alleviate "role disturbance" including tears, reflection, and talk, therefore discharging feelings and slowly modifying one's habits and expectations in order to establish a new life. However, several students of divorce (Bernard, 1956; Bohannon, 1970a; Davis, 1957; Goode, 1956; Hunt, 1966; and Waller, 1967) noted differences between the two. Even though structural factors in the positions of the widow and divorcee are similar, the widow generally receives greater sympathy and support (Goode, 1956). According to Bernard ". . . no one . . . can take the sting or heartache out of divorce. That can perhaps never be institutionalized, as bereavement can" (1970, 16–17). In addition, loss of a spouse by divorce "involves a purposeful and active rejection by another person, who, merely by living, is a daily symbol of the rejection" (Bohannon, 1970a, 42).

Goode (1956) concluded that while society permits divorce, post-divorce institutional arrangements are inadequate. He outlines the failure of the kinship structure to provide unambiguous arrangements after divorce in material support, emotional support, readmission into the kinship structure, formation of families, and proper behavior and emotional attitudes. Society affords no clear definition as to the proper relationship between the divorced spouses. In spite of feelings of bitterness, love, or defeat, divorced persons "are obliged by convention to behave as though they were indifferent to it all" (Bernard, 1956, 202). Goode also noted the lack of prescriptions regarding reaction to divorce. Hunt agreed "the novice FM[3] does not know with any certainty what is expected (of him)" (Hunt, 1966, 46). Bohannon (1970a) contended that because of this ignorance concerning the requirements of divorce, the adjustment is more likely to be difficult.

Thus we see that difficulty in adjusting to a divorce may be largely a result of the ambiguous status of the divorced person because of the lack of institutionalized norms. The individual's attitudes toward their status as a divorcee will have an influence upon their adjustment and upon the performance of their new role as a divorced person (Bell, 1968).

Goode (1956) found a higher degree of adjustment after divorce among the women who: (1) had been the first to suggest divorce in their previous marriage; (2) held an attitude of indifference toward their former spouse; (3) could depend on regular child support payments from their former spouse; (4) had a full time job (thereby affording opportunities for meeting people); (5) had greater opportunities to date and develop new social relations. In addition, themes of complaint against the ex-husband were analyzed for their relationship to adjustment, but "other items, such as . . . age or dating behavior will shape . . . post-divorce experience far more definitely" (Goode, 1956, 131).

Hunt suggested "it is what the FM sees or believes about his own case that most affects his . . . adjustment or maladjustment to his new status" (1966, 25). However, Goode pointed out that a realistic "definition of the situation" facilitated adjustment.

A redefinition of identity was seen as required by Bohannon. New activities and behavior change his focus from past to present to future. The "psychic"[4] divorce, described as "the separation of self from the personality and the influence of the exspouse" is difficult, but "personally constructive" (1970a, 60).

The implication is clear; opportunities to date and meet new people are all-important for adjustment to divorce. Therefore, the approval of one's circle of family and friends is significant for the adjustment of the divorcee, as they will be helpful in meeting new people (Goode, 1956). Goode also reported that friends' acceptance of and reflection back to the divorcee of her new self-identity will facilitate her adjustment. Goode also found that divorcees who have some divorced or divorcing friends are slightly more likely to fall into the low trauma classification.

Bohannon (1970a) and Cuber and Haroff (1965) reported divorcing persons often find themselves "dropped" by their married friends as they are viewed as introducing problems in social activities. Hunt (1966) pointed out that this alienation of the divorced person from married friends is at least partially because of difference in interests. He introduced the concept of "the world of the formerly married"—a subculture of the divorced and separated with its own rules, market mechanism, and adjustment patterns. "In general . . . continued relationships with friends and their children can make the disrupted home a less lonely and sad one" (Miller, 1970, 85).

CHILDREN

Children are involved in the majority of divorces and the custody of children is generally awarded to the mother. Children are often viewed as greatly complicating their mothers' postdivorce adjustment (Bernard, 1970). In contrast, Burgess, Locke, and Thomes (1963) suggest that the custodial parent experiences less crisis than does the parent who is cut off from his children.

Nearly all divorcing parents are concerned with the possible ill effects divorce may have on children, and according to Bohannon, "We do not know very much about it" (1970a, 55). In Goode's study the higher trauma group of women more often reported there had been some period during the divorce when the children had been harder to manage. At the same time, most of the mothers felt that the divorce had not been detrimental to their children; almost all believed that their children were "no worse off after the divorce than before" (1956, 318).

Kay (1970) and Bernard (1970) agree that research indicates that children of divorced homes suffer less than children living in homes torn with constant conflict. Bernard (1970, 12) continued: "To a woman concerned about the effect of divorce on her children, such findings are reassuring," and therefore, should have a positive effect upon her adjustment to divorce.

DATING AND OTHER NEW ACTIVITIES

Dating as an index of adjustment indicates a willingness to start a new life and serves as both "an introduction and stimulus to that new life" (Goode, 1956, 258). Hunt (1966) viewed the dating experience as one of reevaluation and one which renews self-esteem.

Friends and/or relatives provided help in meeting eligible suitors for almost half of Goode's respondents, while Hunt's respondents found such "conventional" methods to be of limited value and were willing to try more "unconventional" methods. Hunt concluded, "it is part of the way of life of the Formerly Married to violate conventions and take risks in order to increase the changes of readjustment and the opportunities for remarriage" (1966, 108).

Activities such as dating or taking a new job have similar beneficial effects. In either context, the divorcee's primary status is redefined; in the dating situation or work situation, the divorcee is "courted" or treated as a "co-worker" rather than someone's "ex." Likewise, even though the divorcee is strongly ambivalent in regard to loving again, both casual sex and love affairs are viewed as potential forms of aids in repairing the ego and leaving the individual more ready for remarriage (Hunt, 1966).

REMARRIAGE AS A FORM
OF ADJUSTMENT

The statistics as to the rate and rapidity of marriage after divorce vary according to the source.[5] However, within any age group the divorced have a better chance for remarriage than either the widowed or the never married (Bernard, 1956; Goode, 1956).

Bell (1968) reported that the majority of the divorced view remarriage as the best means of postdivorce adjustment; and Goode (1956) concluded that remarriage represents a solution to the ambiguous status of the divorced. Hunt noted that his respondents who even considered themselves reasonably successfully divorced "will not consider themselves wholly successful until they remarry" (1966, 285). Furthermore, it is held that "contemporary community attitudes appear to be receptive toward remarriage . . . for the divorced" (Bernard, 1956, 36). Reasons for remarriage include the fact that American adult society allows little latitude for the unmarried person, especially unmarried female parents; and social pressures for remarriage, though they may vary in intensity, are recurrent and include the couple-based nature of our society, the symbolic threat which the divorcee represents, the idea that children need two parents, and pressures from the children themselves (Goode, 1956).

Although Bernard (1956) reported that dependent children had a negative effect on the eligibility of women, Goode stated that "the remarriage rate of divorced mothers is not much lower than that of female divorcees generally" (1956, 207). Goode (1956) found that the number of children seemed to have no significant effect on the divorcee's courtship activities. However, women with fewer children did not remarry as rapidly as did those with more children.

Earlier remarriage was found more often among those women who (1) deliberated a longer period of time between first serious consideration of divorce and filing of the lawsuit; (2) experienced greater loneliness during the period of separation; (3) experienced high trauma; and (4) reported being in love with another man prior to divorce. Remarriage will be discussed only in the light of how it may affect the overall postdivorce adjustment.

BONDS BETWEEN EX-SPOUSES

Divorce, although it legally terminates the husband-wife relationship, never completely severs the ties between the individuals involved (Bohannon, 1970a; Burgess, Locke, and Thomes, 1963; David, 1957; Mead, 1970; Hunt, 1966; Schwarz, 1968). Marriage has been referred to as "terminable and interminable" (Hunt, 1966) and the divorce process, just as it begins prior to the decree, "so may continue long afterwards" (Goode, 1956, 286). Vestigial bonds remain between the pair, especially when the marriage produced children:

> . . . our present divorce style often denies the tie between the child and one of the parents, and it permits the parents to deny that— through their common child—they have an irreversible, indissoluble relationship to each other (Mead, 1970, 120–121).

This relationship with the ex-spouse could definitely affect adjustment in a remarriage. Bohannon refers to the chaotic situation in households of remarriage, i.e., the pattern of "divorce chains." These "chains" are "pseudokinship groups . . . formed on the basis of links between the new spouses of ex-spouses" (1970b, 129), and are not uncommon, particularly when children are present as mediating influences. For example, ex-spouses are linked to each other as parents and as part of a kind of extended family, and a man's present wife and his ex-wife may become friends.

On the other hand, bitterness—or civility, at best—may characterize the relationship between ex-spouses. Hunt (1966) stated that continuing anger is more often found among divorced women than among divorced men. Goode's divorcees were most unhappy if their ex-spouses had remarried when they had not and least unhappy when they themselves had remarried while their ex-husbands had not. Thus, "in a certain sense, it may be said that the cost of a successful second marriage after divorce is often borne by the unmarried spouse" (Bernard, 1956, 203).

It is frequently the case that the crisis experienced by one member of the divorcing couple is prolonged by his attachment to the ex-spouse (Burgess, Locke, and Thomes, 1963). Although the general concession that some form of ties remain between the divorced spouses, it is at the same time true that disengagement from emotional involvement with the ex-spouse is imperative if adjustmental progress is to be made (Hunt, 1966).

ADJUSTMENT OTHER THAN REMARRIAGE

The divorced persons who do not eventually remarry are in the minority. They are described as "long-terms" by Hunt (1966) and "hard core divorced" by Bernard (1956). The tendency of "long-terms" to remain in the "world of the formerly married" is explained by Hunt in terms of their more severe trauma and their need to progress through the process of adjustment more slowly; he further suggests the possibility of a "comfortable long-term adjustment to divorced life" (1966, 266).

NEED FOR FURTHER RESEARCH

This review of literature quickly reveals that much research is needed in the area of postdivorce adjustment.

It is evident that although Goode asserted, "the distortions created by interviewing only the wife are not extensive or many" (1956, 26) and the work of Bernard (1956), Hunt (1966), and Bohannon (1970) provide insights as to the postdivorce adjustmental process among men, research dealing with the male divorcé is very much needed. An investigation of divorcing and divorced *couples*, even though it may involve many prohibitive factors, would provide invaluable information. Likewise, the possibilities for cross-analysis of such data are extensive. In addition, it has been nearly a quarter of a century since the collection of Goode's data; this is approximately the same amount of time which passed between the publication of Waller's and Goode's studies. Also, replication of Goode's work would provide much information, especially in terms of empirical support (or lack of support) for possible changes in attitudes toward divorce and divorcees.

We must agree with Bernard that "no amount of research can wholly eliminate the emotional price exacted by divorce" (1970, 140). However, if, as she further alleges, research can "help lighten the load (and) . . . mitigate the accompanying feeling of guilt and shame" (1970, 104), then, clearly, more research in this area can do much to facilitate the process, as well as the understanding, of postdivorce adjustment.

ENDNOTES

1. Although Waller's study is certainly a classic in the field and provides "an untapped source of hypotheses pertaining to personal adjustment" (Farber), it should not be included in the present paper. *The Old Love and the New* may more properly be considered an historical backdrop for more contemporary studies. The reader is referred to the 1967 edition in which Professor Bernard Farber, in the introduction, provides a valuable analysis of Waller's contribution to the study of postdivorce adjustment in terms of indicating the extent to which later investigation confirmed, denied, or modified Waller's hypotheses. Implicit in Farber's discussion are the limitations of any current application.
2. See Bell, 1967; Goode, 1949; Waller, 1967; Bernard, 1956; Locke, 1951; Goode, 1956; Hunt, 1966; Burgess, Locke, and Thomes, 1963.
3. Hunt utilizes the abbreviation FM to denote "the Formerly Married," a category including both the separated and the divorced, but omitting the widowed.
4. The reader will note that Bohannon's concept of the "psychic divorce" and its outcome is closely in line with Goode's definition of postdivorce adjustment in terms of a reorientation to the divorcee's present and future status.
5. See Hunt, 1966; Bernard, 1956; Locke, 1951; Goode, 1956; Rollin, 1971.

REFERENCES

Barnett, James H. and Rhoda Gruen. Recent American Novels, 1938–1945: A Study in the Sociology of Literature. *Social Forces*, 1948, 26, 322–327.

Bell, Robert R. *Marriage and Family Interaction*. Homewood, Illinois: The Dorsey Press, 1967.

Bell, Robert R. (Ed.) *Studies in Marriage and the Family*. New York: Thomas Y. Crowell Company, 1968.

Bergler, Edmund. *Divorce Won't Help*. New York: Harper and Brothers, 1948.

Bernard, Jessie. *Remarriage: A Study of Marriage*. New York: Dryden Press, 1956.

Bernard, Jessie. No News, but New Ideas. In Paul Bohannon (Ed.) *Divorce and After*. Garden City, New York: Doubleday and Company, Inc., 1970, 3–29.

Bitterman, Catherine. The Multimarriage Family. *Social Casework*, 1968, 49, 218–221.

Bohannon, Paul. The Six Stations of Divorce. In Paul Bohannon (Ed.) *Divorce and After*. Garden City, New York: Doubleday and Company, Inc., 1970(a), 33–62.

Bohannon, Paul. Divorce Chains, Households of Remarriage, and Multiple Divorcers. In Paul Bohannon (Ed.) *Divorce and After*. Garden City, New York: Doubleday and Company, Inc., 1970(b), 127–139.

Bohannon, Paul. Some Thoughts on Divorce Reform. In Paul Bohannon (Ed.) *Divorce and After*. Garden City, New York: Doubleday and Company, Inc., 1970(c), 283–299.

Bohannon, Paul (Ed.) *Divorce and After*. Garden City, New York: Doubleday and Company, Inc., 1970.

Bossard, James H. S. Previous Conjugal Condition. *Social Forces*, 1939, 18, 243–247.

Bowerman, Charles E. Assortive Mating by Previous Marital Status: Seattle, 1939–1946. *American Sociological Review*, 1953, 18, 171.

Burgess, Ernest W., Harvey J. Locke, and Mary Margaret Thomes. *The Family*. New York: American Book Company, 1963.

Chen, Ronald. The Dilemma of Divorce: Disaster or Remedy. *The Family Coordinator*, 1968, 17, 251–254.

Cuber, John F. and Peggy B. Harroff. *Sex and the Significant Americans*. Baltimore, Maryland: Penguin Books, 1965.

Davis, Kingsley. Divorce and its Effects. In Morris Fishbein and Ruby Joe Reeves Kennedy (Eds.) *Modern Marriage and Family Living*. New York: Oxford University Press, 1957, 100–113.

Gebhard, Paul. Postmarital Coitus among Widows and Divorcees. In Paul Bohannon (Ed.) *Divorce and After*. Garden City, New York: Doubleday and Company, Inc., 1970, 89–106.

Glick, Paul. First Marriages and Remarriages. *American Sociological Review*, 1949, 14, 726–734.

Goode, William J. Problems in Postdivorce Adjustment. *American Sociological Review*, 1949, 14, 394–401.

Goode, William J. *Women in Divorce.* New York: The Free Press, 1956.

Goode, William J., Elizabeth Hopkins, and Ellen M. McClure. *Social Systems and Family Patterns: A Propositional Inventory.* Indianapolis: Bobbs-Merrill, Inc., 1971.

Gurin, Gerald, Joseph Veroff, and Sheila Feld. *Americans View their Mental Health.* New York: Basic Books, Inc., 1960.

Hunt, Morton M. *The World of the Formerly Married.* New York: McGraw-Hill Book Company, 1966.

Ilgenfritz, Marjorie P. Mothers on their Own—Widows and Divorcees. *Marriage and Family Living*, 1961, 23, 38–41.

Jacobson, Paul H. *American Marriage and Divorce.* New York: Rinehart and Company, Inc., 1959.

Jourard, Sidney M. Reinventing Marriage: the Perspective of a Psychologist. In Herbert A. Otto (Ed.) *The Family in Search of a Future.* New York: Appleton-Century-Crofts, 1970, 43–50.

Kay, Herma Hill. A Family Court: the California Proposal. In Paul Bohannon (Ed.) *Divorce and After.* Garden City, New York: Doubleday and Company, Inc., 1970, 243–281.

Kushner, Sylvia. The Divorced, Noncustodial Parent and Family Treatment. *Social Work*, 1965, 10, 52–58.

Landis, Judson T. The Pattern of Divorce in Three Generations. *Social Forces*, 1956, 34, 213–216.

Lasch, Christopher. Divorce and the Family in America. *Atlantic Monthly*, 1966, 218, 57–61.

Levinger, George. Marital Cohesiveness and Dissolution: An Integrative Review. *Journal of Marriage and the Family*, 1965, 27, 19–38.

Litwak, Eugene. Three Ways in which Law Acts as a Means of Social Control: Punishment, Therapy, and Education: Divorce Law a Case in Point. *Social Forces*, 1956, 34, 214–223.

Locke, Harvey J. *Predicting Adjustment in Marriage: A Comparison of a Divorced and a Happily Married Group.* New York: Holt, Rinehart and Winston, 1951.

Locke, Harvey J. Predicting Marital Adjustment by Comparing a Divorced and a Happily Married Group. *American Sociological Review*, 1947, 12, 187–191.

Mead, Margaret. Anomalies in American Post-divorce Relationships. In Paul Bohannon (Ed.) *Divorce and After.* Garden City, New York: Doubleday and Company, Inc., 1970, 107–125.

Miller, Arthur A. Reactions of Friends to Divorce. In Paul Bohannon

(Ed.) *Divorce and After.* Garden City, New York: Doubleday and Company, Inc., 1970, 63–86.

Mills, C. Wright. *The Sociological Imagination.* London: Oxford University Press, 1959.

Monahan, Thomas P. How Stable Are Remarriages? *American Journal of Sociology,* 1952, 58, 280–288.

Monahan, Thomas P. The Changing Nature and Instability of Remarriages. *Eugenics Quarterly,* 1958, 5, 73–85.

O'Neill, William L. *Divorce in the Progressive Era.* New Haven, Connecticut: Yale University Press, 1967.

Otto, Herbert A. *The Family in Search of a Future.* New York: Appleton-Century-Crofts, 1970.

Popenoe, Paul. Remarriage of Divorcees to Each Other. *American Sociological Review,* 1938, 3, 695–699.

Rollin, Betty. The American Way of Marriage: Remarriage. *Look Magazine,* 1971, 35, 62, 64–67.

Schlesinger, Benjamin. Remarriage: An Inventory of Findings. *The Family Coordinator,* 1968, 17, 248–250.

Schlesinger, Benjamin. *The One-Parent Family.* Toronto, Ontario: University of Toronto Press, 1970.

Schwarz, Anne C. Reflections on Divorce and Remarriage. *Social Casework,* 1968, 49, 213–217.

Waller, Willard. *The Old Love and the New: Divorce and Readjustment.* Carbondale, Illinois: Southern Illinois University Press, 1967.

Weiss, Robert S. The Fund of Sociability. *TransAction,* 1969, 6, 36–43.

WHAT DO YOU THINK?

What are some valid reasons why people who are closely related should not marry each other?

Under what conditions would a trial marriage be considered a common-law marriage in your state?

Would you change our laws so that marriage would be harder to get into and easier to get out of? Would you have a longer waiting period, older age at marriage, allow divorce on request and without grounds?

What do you think about establishing a legal requirement that each marriage contract be renewed periodically?

What would be the advantage of allowing polygamy in our society? Remember that this has two sides: Polygyny allows a man to have two or more wives, and polyandry allows a woman to have two or more husbands.

When a marriage is annulled, it means that no valid marriage ever existed. Some people would like to get rid of this form of dissolving a marriage and have all such action under the laws of divorce. What are the benefits of annulment rather than divorce? How is divorce better?

If a marriage is annulled, what is the social status of the children even if they are declared legitimate? Do they take the father's name? Who is responsible for them? Can they inherit from the father and mother or other relatives?

When does a marriage become valid: at the wedding ceremony, the honeymoon, the legal recording of the signed document, or at some other point?

Should parents who give their written consent to the children's marriage be held legally responsible for that marriage? Why? For how long?

List the ways a marriage is defined as a legal contract, and show how a marriage contract differs significantly from other legal contracts.

If you obtain a marriage license, why does the state also require a marriage ceremony?

Issues of Marital Adjustments

The honeymoon is usually the first stage of marriage. Couples sometimes feel they will make their major adjustments in this period, when in fact, the really important changes are made when they settle in their own home. They may well suffer a "honeymoon letdown" when they realize this.

The O'Neills are a husband and wife team with two grown sons, so they can look at marital adjustment from a personal as well as a professional point of view. Their book, *Open Marriage: A New Life Style for Couples* aroused a great deal of interest. Other publications on this subject have been well received and the suggestions they give in the article reprinted here can be helpful to newlyweds and to people who have been married a long time. One reason for boredom with the marriage, the job, the neighbors, the way of life in general may be tunnel vision. The man who sees his job as his main mission in life is not a whole person. He needs skills in interacting and communicating with his family and others. In a similar fashion the woman who is trained only to be a mother and homemaker is too specialized in her outlook. We see people like this who are utterly lost when these functions are no longer needed. On the other hand, women who are trained for a career without education in home and human relationships lack the balance needed for multiple role-taking. The concept of open marriage may free both parties to be more alive as persons and marriage partners.

Sexual adjustment in marriage has often been considered an area where responses come naturally and adjustments are automatic. But studies show this is not true. The entire gamut of previous attitudes, values, and experiences influence a sexual relationship, and these attitudes depend to a large extent on the social class background of each individual. As in the total marital relationship, the sex roles of men and women differ, and each partner has a different response pattern.

Very often couples turn to "marriage manuals" or "sex manuals" for advice and assistance with their sexual adjustment. These manuals, which have been on the market for decades, have probably been helpful. However, as Gordon and Shankweiler point out, the manuals may also help perpetuate a sexist viewpoint of marital sex. After examining marriage manuals written in the last two decades, the authors conclude that the "expert advice" still assumes that females have less interest and experience in sex, and that they will rely on males to initiate, cultivate, and dominate their sex lives. The manuals generally ignore recent research, which suggests that females are just as capable as males of initiating, experiencing, and enjoying sex.

Although the "New Morality" may still expect marital fidelity of both partners, one mode of sexual adjustment tried by some couples is that of "swinging" or mate swapping. Much of the literature, as Denfeld points out, attempts to demonstrate the positive effects that swinging may have on the marriage. There may be some problems in swinging, however, that need to be considered. Swinging may have negative as well as positive results. Further, swinging (like marriage manuals) may reflect a masculine wish rather than a feminine or an equalitarian desire. As Denfeld concludes, the husband appears to be the one who initiates the swinging activity, while the wife is the one who first wants to drop out. These differences between husbands and wives may reflect more general distinctions between the sexes. Males have more difficulty than females in establishing an emotional relationship and in viewing sex as an integral part of that relationship.

Balswick and Peek propose that a basic difference between males and females is in expressing emotions. Husbands, it is suggested, simply have more difficulty in expressing emotions than do wives, and this difficulty may be more pronounced at the lower class level, as the article by Rainwater shows. If, however, men become more capable of expressing emotions with women in the future, marriages may not necessarily become more stabilized. As Balswick and Peek conclude, we shall have to wait to see the full impact of the liberalization of males.

Although sex is an important area of marital adjustment, other areas must also be considered.

One area of early adjustment concerns relatives. Time spent with friends does not seem to reduce the amount of time couples spend with relatives; socially inclined young people make room for both groups. The main relatives are the in-laws—the parents, brothers, and sisters of the new husband and wife. In-laws appear to present particular adjustment difficulties, especially if they are strangers to the new spouse. The bride's family is more apt to know the groom, or to know him better, than his family is to know the new wife, because the man was more likely to have called at her home when they were dating. This often means the biggest adjustment will be between the groom's mother and the new bride, who have to make an extra effort to become acquainted. This brings up the simple but vital issue of what to call each other. What do young people call their new parents-in-law?

Young people today have more in-laws and will have them longer than was ever true before, due to the life span being increased by about twenty-five years during the last century. It is important that a couple establish a good mutual relationship with their in-laws, because these relationships will last a long time. Friends and relatives are equally important in ensuring a good marriage.

It has been estimated that at least 25 percent of the population of the United States is moving up the social scale, and only about 5 percent move down. In marriage, the wife usually shares the husband's status; and if she marries a man of a higher class, she may have to make major adjustments in her values. An example may illustrate these points more clearly:

> Bill Jones is a recent college graduate and plans to enter law school. His father is a professional man, and his mother is a college graduate who spends her time making a home for the family, doing volunteer work at the hospital and other social activities. His father and mother belong to several business and social clubs and often attend meetings and social functions together. They are companions and help each other in many ways, talk over family plans, and discuss major purchases. They belong to the same church, and the children learned values and human relationships from their parents and church. Bill experienced warmth and acceptance at home and wants the kind of relationship in his marriage that existed at home. He learned from his father that a man can enjoy cooking, taking care of children, sharing time with them, and gain rather than lose status as a man.

> Mary Smith came from a family of second-generation Americans of middle-European background. Her father is the patriarchal head of the family, and what he says is the law. He finished eighth grade, had various jobs, and finally went to work in a factory where his work is monotonous but not really heavy. When he comes home he likes silence at supper, then settles down to watch television. He would not think of helping with the dishes or doing anything in the house, because that is "woman's work." His wife takes care of the house and does most of the child-rearing. Mr. Smith belongs to a union but seldom attends meetings and is somewhat indifferent about going to church. He does not allow his wife to belong to any clubs, not even the missionary society of the church. When his paycheck comes, he turns over to his wife

enough money to run the household, but there is very little joint planning. Companionship between husband and wife is nonexistent, and there is little warmth in their relationship even though they do not fight and do not disagree very often. Mary learned that a wife must defer to her husband and must "do her duty" as a wife. Her parents agreed to allow her to go to college to become a teacher, provided she worked to earn her way.

Bill and Mary became friends at the university and want to marry. Both families are reluctant to approve. Even though they find each other interesting, they will have to make many adjustments in their attitudes and values. Mary is somewhat mobile in an upward direction, but can she learn to become a companion to her husband rather than a subservient wife? She will have to learn to be a member of groups, to work for the good of the community without being paid, and to become a mother who can play with the children and be concerned with their social and emotional development. This might put a strain on her and make it difficult for her to enjoy the social and sexual sharing characteristic of her husband's status group. How patient will Bill be with her?

Another early marriage problem is finances. A great deal has been written about the mechanics of handling money, but very little has been said about the attitudes and values connected with it. How do people learn to handle money? Does it mean love and security, or does it serve to develop status or power? Can young people do without things they want in order to have more later on? The article by Edith G. Neisser discusses emotional and social values attached to money and how these attitudes can affect marriage.

20

Nena O'Neill and George O'Neill

Open Marriage: Implications for Human Service Systems*

The authors of Open Marriage *reiterate the meaning and possibilities of the open marriage concept and advance suggestions for change in the areas of residence, work, child care, and educational patterns. Human service systems must search out the universal values to be maintained in all human relationships. Editor.*

We, ourselves, as individuals from two different backgrounds, as developing personalities with distinct identities, as husband and wife, and as mother and father of two grown sons, have in the half century of our lives witnessed the profound alterations in our social and technological organizations. They have influenced us in a deeply personal manner as individuals, as parents, as a family, and as members of our society, just as they have influenced other individuals and families living in a world of rapid social change. For many, these changes have raised questions concerning commitment to marriage. The meaning of commitment in marriage and family life today *is* being modified and both the individuals and the systems that service their needs require review as to the meanings and goals of their mutual involvement in the institution of marriage.

In response to the rapid changes in our social, psychological and physical environment, many variant and experimental family and marriage forms have emerged, not all of them monogamous. We frankly believe that monogamy provides the potential for the most fulfilling of human relationships. It is to this potential that we addressed ourselves in our book, *Open Marriage: A New Life Style for Couples* (O'Neill and O'Neill, 1972a, 1972b).

Nena O'Neill and George O'Neill, "Open Marriage: Implications for Human Service Systems," from *The Family Coordinator*, October, 1973, pp. 449–456. Reprinted with permission.
* Slightly revised version of a paper presented at the Annual Meeting of The Groves Conference on Marriage and the Family, Dallas, Texas, May 6, 1972.

In researching contemporary marriage since 1967, we found that many of the expectations for traditional monogamy, which we term "closed marriage," limited this potential and were out of step with changes in a contemporary world where technological and sociological conditions had inevitably altered our needs for flexibility and had changed our perspectives on human equality. The rigidities of a patriarchal and monolithic style of marriage, based on an agrarian past with husband and wife roles solidified into stratified positions, did not readily permit growth or change. In our contemporary world many factors including a longer life span, education, greater mobility, and technological innovations have changed the position of women and have created new needs for greater parity in marriage and in man-woman relationships.

Open Marriage presents a model for a marital relationship that *is* based on equality and that is flexible enough to not only permit but encourage growth for both partners. It is directed to the individuals upon whom the marital relationship depends—the husband and wife. Inherent in this model is our belief that individuals can and ought to be the focus for change. Also inherent in the way we have presented *Open Marriage* is our belief that in a complex and bureaucratic society the best human service system may well be your own.

While *Open Marriage* attempts to demythologize the unrealistic ideals and expectations of our traditional closed marriage, its primary objective is to delineate the elements that contribute to a more vital and egalitarian marital relationship and to outline some methods and skills for attaining such a relationship. The open marriage model offers insights and learning guides for developing more intimate and understanding marital relationships.

Open marriage can be defined as a relationship in which partners are committed to their own and to each other's growth. Supportive caring and increasing security in individual identities makes possible the sharing of self-growth with a partner who encourages and anticipates his own and his mate's growth. It is a relationship that is constantly being revised in the light of each one's changing needs, through consensus in decision-making, by acceptance and encouragement of individual development and in openness to new possibilities for growth.

The first step is for partners to reassess the marriage relationship that they are in or hope to achieve, in order to reevaluate expectations for themselves and for their partner. Former expectations, such as the belief that woman's primary role is wife, mother, and child-raiser and that man's primary role is provider and part-time father, limit both spouses in their full expansion into personhood. Another major expectation of closed marriage—namely, that one partner will be able to fulfill *all* of the other's needs—presents obstacles to growth and attitudes that foster over-dependency and conflict between partners. Awareness of these expectations and a realignment more in accord with a realistic appraisal of each partner's capabilities is fundamental to instituting change and to solving problems in the relationship.

The open marriage model embodies eight guidelines for achieving more openness and growth in the marriage relationship. Living for now involves relating to self and partner in the present rather than in the past or in terms of future goals which are frequently materialistic rather than emotional or intellectual ones wherein growth is possible. The granting of privacy is essential for examination of self and for psychic regeneration. A way out of the role-bind involves working toward greater role flexibility, both in terms of switching roles temporarily or on a part-time basis and as a therapeutic device for greater understanding of self, the other, and the dynamics of their interaction. Open and honest communication is perhaps the most important element in an open relationship. Lack of communication skills creates a formidable barrier between husband and wife, yet these skills are the most important in sustaining a vital relationship, promoting understanding and increasing knowledge of self. Open companionship involves relating to others, including the opposite sex, outside the primary unit of husband and wife as an auxiliary avenue for growth. Equality involves relating to the mate as a peer in terms of ways to achieve stature, rather than in terms of the status attached to the traditional husband and wife roles. Identity involves the development of the individual through actualizing his own potentials rather than living through the mate or the child. Trust, growing through the utilization of these other guidelines and based on mutuality and respect, creates a climate for growth. Liking, respect, sexual intimacy, and love grow through the dynamic interaction and use of these elements.

Each progressive guideline becomes increasingly abstract. The system can be seen as an expending spiral of evolving steps in complexity and depth in the marital relationship. The system operates on the principle of synergy, which means that two partners in a marriage, or in any relationship, can accomplish more personal and interpersonal growth together while still retaining their individual identities, than they could separately. Synergic buildup is the way in which the growth of both partners, women as well as men, provides positive, augmenting feedback that can continuously enhance mutual growth and fulfillment. It is not assumed that most couples can or would want to utilize all of these guidelines simultaneously. Open marriage, then, can best be understood as a resource mosaic from which couples can draw according to their needs and their readiness for change in any one area.

What then are the implications of this new and revitalized open relationship in monogamy for human service systems? We believe they will develop in two directions. One is the way service systems can help effect and support more egalitarian marriage relationships, and the other is the effect an increasing number of open marriages will have on these service systems, thus setting up a feedback situation based on cybernetic dynamics. We feel that open marriages and the values they engender are conducive to building healthier, more dynamic, and stronger family units. In this way we see social change occurring through micro-cultural changes which stem from the strength of the basic family unit. It can happen in three ways.

First: Open marriage is designed to strengthen the marriage and at the same time strengthen the individual in the marriage. A more vital and understanding marital relationship gives more meaning to shared commitment. Rather than harboring deep-seated resentments or splitting when problems arise, couples may be able to resolve differences, to cope with change, and to find greater joy and challenge in sharing life together.

Second: We feel that the children of open marriages will tend to be responsible, confident, self-reliant individuals. If husband and wife grow in emotional maturity through open marriage, and if their relationship is one of equality, respect, mutual problem-solving through consensus, and supportive love, these values can then be transmitted to the child. Through an enculturation process that emphasizes the values of respect for individual differences, personal responsibility, self-actualization, and growth in interpersonal relationships, family ties will be more meaningful, thus providing the foundation for creating an open family. Utilizing the elements and themes of open marriage within the family should encourage dialogue between generations and minimize the conflict and gaps in understanding.

Third: Because couples have an open marriage they can open up to other families. By being open within, they can be more open without. Because they have established the meaning of commitment to each other within the family, they can better relate to other couples and families and explore the meaning of mutual commitment and a greater intensification of humanness with others. They can create strong local groups which might be called "initiator groups" and increase community solidarity in terms of goals and thus provide the foundation for creating family-based social networks. In this way they can direct their strength toward obtaining needed services and toward dealing with bureaucratic inadequacies in existing services.

However, the reality today is that no matter how open some marriages, families, and communities are, they still operate in a societal context where human service systems have not caught up to their needs and where substantial structural revisions are necessary to meet these needs. We have mentioned the need for supportive structures in our book: "While each of us can modify roles to suit our needs, the success of sharing parenthood and interchanging husband and wife roles will depend on the creation of new patterns in work and family arrangements which offer broader bases than the nuclear family for sharing and mutual support" (1972a, 158). Obviously it will be difficult for couples to achieve an open marriage in a society that does not provide means or opportunities for individual growth for both partners at the same time that the needs of children and family life are considered.

What can human service systems do in innovative ways to help effect greater parity in the marriage relationship, to provide for developing individual potential for all members of the family, and at the same time encourage closer family ties and greater community support? Change can occur on two levels: one concrete, the other in value orientation.

We shall mention some of the concrete proposals first, many of which have already been suggested by members of this group and others (Osofsky and Osofsky; Rossi 1970, 1972a, 1972b; Steinem, 1972; Stoller, 1970; Sussman 1971a). They occur primarily in the area of change in residence, work, child care, and educational patterns. Some are directed toward facilitating the movement of women into the mainstream of American life, some toward sharing parenthood and family responsibilities, and others for changes in education.

1. An expansion of equal opportunities for women in education, jobs, and professions, including, of course, equal salaries.
2. Minimization of sex role stereotyping in all media and in our educational institutions.
3. Networks of child care centers under voluntary, private, community, industrial, university, and other institutional auspices. We have excluded state auspices from this list because of the recent proposals for 24-hour nurseries. We do not endorse group child care during the crucial first two years of infancy, since our interpretation of developmental and primate studies indicates that a one-to-one or one-to-two relationship of close physical intimacy and affectionate response provides optimum benefits for the infant. Whether this care is maternal, paternal, or surrogate or whether it occurs in a nuclear, single, or extended family context does not seem to be as significant as the maintenance of the quality of intimacy and the level of interaction and response. After these early years, the benefits of broader socialization patterns are clearly acknowledged.
4. An upgrading of the nurturing professions and the increasing utilization of men and older men and women in teaching and child-care facilities.
5. An expansion of opportunities for continuing and alternating sequences of education throughout life.
6. Encouragement of arrangements and innovations conducive to shared parenthood between husband and wife and community.

There have been many suggestions in this area; some are for time off with pay, alternating work weeks or days, or interchangeable jobs, such as those which are being experimented with in Scandinavia where the same job is held by husband and wife who alternate weeks at work and home.

7. Decentralization of many delivery systems. The new telecommunications inventions (Goldmark 1972) may well facilitate mechanical delivery of services to the families of the future, but in the present we still need more personalized and direct service. The mechanical communications revolution and the implications it has for the loss of intimacy and for fragmentation may result in an even greater necessity to focus on the fulfillment and depth that interpersonal relationships have to offer.

8. Dissemination of contraceptive and sex information both to reduce the number of unwanted children and to encourage responsible family planning.

9. Education for parenthood, sex, human biology, and infant development. This education need not be in terms of how the child is to be raised, which may be unduly restrictive, but could be in the areas of imparting knowledge about the relevant biological and cognitive stages of child and adolescent development, and basic elements in the role of parenting.

10. The establishment of parity for men and women in legal codes affecting marriage, sex, and human rights, including those of the child. Upon ratification, the new Equal Rights Amendment will have far-reaching effects on marriage and parenthood. Until such parity is effected, persons entering marriage should be made aware of the implicit legal aspects of the marriage contract they are signing and of the legal statutes affecting their rights in marriage.

11. A movement of women into policy-making positions on governmental and institutional levels.

12. A change in work and residence patterns designed to effect more family contact hours and contiguity between work and family living.

13. A revamping of the policies of industry and employers regarding job offers and job relocation will be necessary in order to accommodate an increasing number of dual-career families and couples.

14. An increase in planned built-in environments accommodating many life styles and encouraging community interaction, solidarity, and support. Suburban sprawl and anonymous urban cubicles isolate the family and its members from facilities as well as community support.

15. Encouragement of kin and non-kin peer family networks for mutual aid and support.

16. Encouragement of discussion groups and experiential therapy for

. couples. Six years ago, Dr. Clark Vincent (1967) suggested that marital health become a legitimate field of specialization. In line with his suggestion, there could be an increase in couple counseling as well as an increase in discussion groups for couples who may not need therapy but who want to clarify issues and attain better relationship skills.

17. An increase in creative premarital counseling.

18. In general, non-directive counseling designed to reduce the pressure of conformity to traditional role expectations in marriage, and to help couples and individuals to clarify their own goals and to understand and maximize the choices available to them. Many systems could focus on providing the individual, the marital couple, and the family unit with new coping mechanisms for meeting change in life events through experimental and emotional education. Coping mechanisms, however, should evolve into more positive ways of providing creative and growth experiences.

19. Changes in home maintenance and housework patterns. The answer is not to put every husband in an apron and a lunch bucket or executive pen in every wife's hand, but to encourage everyone to share in home maintenance, including our children who currently expect Mom to do it all. Less of an emphasis on material possessions and goals would contribute to a more relaxed style of living and housekeeping that values creative work and play arrangements. Certainly our technological know-how could be applied to making household maintenance simpler and more efficient instead of grinding out dubious technological marvels and an avalanche of material possessions that threaten to bury us all in ecological overkill.

20. A deliberate focus on the problems of men in adjusting to our new equalities. Ten years of the women's movement and, of course, other conditions in our society have brought many changes and have altered our conceptions of marriage and the role of men and women in it. Its impact has prepared many women for new adjustments, but little has been actively initiated to help men adjust to the changes in masculine and feminine expectations, or to promote the man's understanding of these changes. Both men and women as well as therapists report the doubts, conflicts, and confusion centering around current changes in the concepts of masculine and feminine identity. Although courses in women's studies now number 670 across the country (Rossi 1972b) there has been no similar expansion in the number of courses dealing with both masculine and feminine role changes. A new course designed to explore the problems of both men and women in adjusting to new role expectations might be helpful for both sexes. In addition, there could be an emphasis on education, research, and modes of therapy in this area.

We have two additional suggestions in the area of education which are closer to the heart of the matter and have implications far beyond marriage. One of these is education for a full life for everyone. By this we mean a man is not a full person if he is educated just for a career or job, and a woman is not a full person if she is educated just for the expectation of homemaking and raising children or careers which are in conflict with these roles. All of us anticipate multiple roles in career, family, social, civic, and leisure areas. Our life span is too long, too varied, and too subject to change today for education to be devoted to rigid role specialization and to be limited only to the early years. There should be education for the whole person. Spontaneity, innovation, and creativity should be encouraged in addition to the acquisition of skills needed for specific careers.

Effort should be made to make a child's education more participatory and relevant to his experiences and needs in our culture. The recent Foxfire project in Georgia (Johnston, 1972; Wigginton, 1972) is one example of how this can be done, while the free school movement is another expression of this need. In preliterate, small-scale societies, a child's education for living and parenthood is coeval with growing up. In ours it is not. Therefore we should educate our population for a new kind of thinking that incorporates the whole person and that is devoted to maximizing individual potential and responsibility. Education should provide individuals with experience and skills in dealing with the problems of the world we live in. Experiential training should and can be combined more effectively with didactic methods. In a recent article Alice Rossi (1972b) made some suggestions along this line for incorporating in the school curriculum specific training for young people in carrying combined home, civic, and school responsibilities.

Another suggestion we have in this area is to implement courses in human relations in our school systems from primary grades through college. This education would not only be valid as preparation for marriage, but would be basic for conducting any human relationship—that between person and person, child and adult, and person and group.

The need to learn skills in conducting interpersonal relationships and to maintain those values we consider most important to being human is paramount in today's world. Many of our satisfactions and dissatisfactions in life hinge on our ability to sustain and benefit from rewarding interpersonal relationships. Certainly there are factors in our mass technological society which are beyond an individual's control yet which affect his personal development, growth, and fulfillment. As Useem has commented: ". . . people are in trouble if that with which they are imprinted does not enable them to live emotionally satisfying lives in those social conditions which are blueprinted" (1971, 223). Obviously there are problems today in both the imprinting and the blueprinting process—both of which need comprehensive revision. Although individuals may feel that they have little direct control over social conditions or the blueprinting process, they *can* improve their own interpersonal relationships. Change in this area, whether gained through individual motivation and efforts or in school curricula could have widespread effects. The seed from which social responsibility grows can be found in how we care for and relate to others. As David McClelland (1970) has suggested, even leadership and power can have an S-power or social component, i.e., a concern for the welfare of others.

If we can educate our young in career and literacy skills, certainly it should be possible to educate them in acquiring skills for conducting beneficial and synergic human relationships which could be more emotionally satisfying and growth enhancing. Logically, parents could impart these skills beginning in the home with the new infant, but husband and wife are frequently caught in emotional and habitual patterns of relating and communicating carried over from their own parental, kinship, and social models. Without re-education in relationship skills, parents perpetuate the negative aspects of their childhood models in raising their children. We have tried to provide guidelines in *Open Marriage* for achieving awareness and relationship skills, but the exercise of these requires strong motivation and, most important, practice. So there is a need for experiential training, not only for couples in a marriage relationship, but at an age much earlier than when marriage occurs.

The elements and content of such training and courses would not be difficult to define once value orientations were stated and kept clearly in mind. The major focus could be on re-education and communication skills. We do not mean the techniques of persuasion and manipulation so popular in our advertising-dominated media and too frequently mirrored in our interpersonal relations. We do mean the skills of true dialogue and of competence in distinguishing between such elements as feeling, intention, interpretation, and expression in communication (Miller, Nunnally, Wackman, 1971) which lead to knowing one's self and others and helps in working out differences in constructive ways. Over and over, our research pointed out this pressing need for skills in communication, not only in marriage but in other areas as well (O'Neill, 1964). Misunderstanding and lack of skills in communication repeatedly impeded understanding and the attainment of mutual goals. In our days of an astounding revolution in communication technology we are still living in the dark ages of personal, face-to-face communication. Billions of dollars are invested in new communication marvels, yet few are invested in teaching husband and wife, parent and child, worker and employer, or person and person to communicate in ways that clarify feelings, encourage mutual decision-making, and promote self-esteem, human dignity, respect, and compassion.

Many of these needs have been ignored through the imperatives of our technological and market-oriented society. To counteract this there should be a positive thrust for education in those values we consider to represent humanness. Although man is born with the capacity to be human, he nevertheless has to be taught to be human. The emphasis in this kind of education would not be on what types and forms of human relations people should have, but only on how to conduct the ones we do have so that everyone's needs are considered and the relationship can provide optimum benefits for all.

These suggestions for education for human relationships thus have ramifications for many social problems in our society, most of which are simply not subject to technological solutions. In the face of computer projections, such as those of the Club of Rome (Meadows, 1971), which demonstrate the possible fate of a technological and overpopulated future, it is apparent that we need both technological *and* human solutions. Better and more responsible human relations would certainly contribute a new factor and parameter for the computer calculations, and incidentally might help us in designing a different future.

All of which brings us to the value orientation we spoke of earlier. Since we live in a pluralistic society, the effectiveness of our human service systems will be a function of their capacity to become more flexible, to acknowledge new directions, and yet to keep intact certain basic core values. For instance, the emphasis of human service systems could be less on favoring only one dominant family form and more on discovering those values which are universal to all family forms, both variant and experimental. (For a review of these forms see Sussman 1971b). In marriage, the emphasis could be less on perpetuating a dominant mode of marriage which favors one partner, and more on discovering the values and needs of both partners in a marriage.

One of the ways in which this can be done is to facilitate a closer interaction between service systems and the people they service. The flow in the past has been from the top of the service pyramid—that is, from the institution and blueprinters—down to the individual. The flow must be reversed from the individual upwards in a synergistic process between individuals and institutions. Individuals can and do shape their culture, but they cannot do it effectively against institutional rigidities or against blueprints they did not help design. People on all levels must be drawn into the decision-making process that directly affects their lives and their interpersonal relationships.

Wherever we start, whether on an individual level as in open marriage or on an institutional level, the priorities are the same: an emphasis on human values that encourage cooperation through recognition and acceptance of individual differences and needs. Perhaps our human service systems could profit from a new focus on what we call "people systems." Quite realistically people systems would be expected to be inefficient and creative human systems rather than direct analogs of mechanical and thermodynamic models so favored by the systems analysts. While "trade off," "payoff," "input," and "output" might occasionally be valuable systems terms in analyzing interpersonal and group dynamics, we prefer to believe that there is something more to human relationships than input and output and that there are values that are not efficiency-oriented. A recognition of people systems would enable human service systems to concentrate on helping individuals integrate their multiple roles and to deliver services with an understanding that human interaction is more than a sum of its parts.

The concept of open marriage both explicitly and implicitly delineates and spells out certain basic values in the marital relationship. Perhaps our central message is that human service systems will also and necessarily have to do the same: they will have to search out the universal values to be maintained in all human relationships. We believe that certain fundamental values are common to any good human relationship no matter the variety or form. That these basic values revolve around equality, responsible freedom, personal growth, respect for self and others, and a desire for more rewarding interpersonal relationships appears self-evident. Once having declared these values, both individually and institutionally, we can then perhaps more clearly see that there are many routes to perpetuating them and upholding them, and that there are many paths to joy, sharing, and cooperation in an open world that has a place for everyone.

REFERENCES

Goldmark, Peter C. Tomorrow We Will Communicate to Our Jobs. *The Futurist*, 1972, 6 (2), 55–58.

Johnston, Donald. 'Foxfire': They Learned, and They Loved It. *The New York Times*, April 9, 1972.

McClelland, David D. The Two Faces of Power. *Journal of International Affairs*, 1970, 24, 29–47.

Meadows, Donella, Dennis L. Meadows, Jorgen Randers and William W. Behrens, III. *Limits to Growth*. New York: Universe Books, 1971.

Miller, Sherod, Elan W. Nunnally and Daniel B. Wackman. Awareness and Communication Training for Engaged or Married Couples. Presented at the Annual Conference of the American Association of Marriage and Family Counselors, Salt Lake City, Utah, October, 1971.

O'Neill, George Caracena and Nena O'Neill. *Vocational Rehabilitation Needs of Disabled Puerto Ricans in New York City: A Pilot Study.* New York: Puerto Rican Social Services, Inc., 1964.

O'Neill, Nena and George O'Neill. *Open Marriage: A New Life Style for Couples.* New York: M. Evans and Co., 1972a.

O'Neill, Nena and George O'Neill. Open Marriage: A Synergic Model. *The Family Coordinator,* 1972b, 21, 403–410.

Osofsky, Joy D. and Howard J. Osofsky. Androgyny as a Life Style. *The Family Coordinator,* 1972, 21, 411–418.

Rossi, Alice S. Equality Between the Sexes: An Immodest Proposal. In Mayer Baresh and Alice Scourby (Eds.). *Marriage and the Family.* New York: Random House, 1970, 263–309.

Rossi, Alice S. Family Development in a Changing World. *American Journal of Psychiatry,* 1972a, 128, 1057–1066.

Rossi, Alice S. Letter to The Editor under heading "Practicing Beliefs," in *The New York Times Magazine,* April 9, 1972b, 6, 8, 18.

Steinem, Gloria. What it Would Be Like if Women Win. In Frank D. Cox (Ed.). *American Marriage: A Changing Scene?* Dubuque, Iowa: Wm. C. Brown, 1972, 214–219.

Stoller, Frederick H. The Intimate Network of Families as a New Structure. In Herbert A. Otto (Ed.). *The Family in Search of a Future.* New York: Appleton-Century-Crofts, 1970, 145–159.

Sussman, Marvin B. The Experimental Creation of Family Environments. Presented at the Annual Meeting of The Groves Conference on Marriage and the Family, San Juan, Puerto Rico, May 8, 1971a.

Sussman, Marvin B. Family Systems in the 1970s: Analysis, Politics, and Programs. *The Annals of the American Academy of Political and Social Science,* 1971b, 396, 40–56.

Useem, Ruth Hill. The New Woman. In Paul B. Horton and Gerald R. Leslie. (Eds.). *Studies in the Sociology of Social Problems.* New York: Appleton-Century-Crofts, 1971, 217–228.

Vincent, Clark E. Mental Health and the Family. *Journal of Marriage and the Family,* 1967, 29, 18–39.

Wigginton, Eliot. (Ed.). *The Foxfire Book.* New York: Doubleday, 1972.

21 *Michael Gordon and Penelope J. Shankweiler*

Different Equals Less: Female Sexuality in Recent Marriage Manuals*

Eighteen bestselling marriage manuals of the past two decades were examined to see if changes had occurred in the portrayal of female sexuality since the beginning of the century. It was found that the woman is still assumed to have less sexual interest and experience than the man, who is ascribed the instrumental role of cultivating his wife's sexuality. While greater female initiative and "cooperation" in sex is advocated, the male continues to be the dominant partner. Radical implications of research on the multiorgasmic potential of women are virtually ignored in these books. These findings are interpreted as indicating the ideological nature of much of the advice proffered in this form of adult-education literature.

Coitus can scarcely be said to take place in a vacuum; although of itself it appears a biological and physical activity it is so deeply within the larger context of human affairs that it serves as a charged microcosm of the variety of attitudes and values to which the culture subscribes. (Millett, 1970:23)

This quotation from Kate Millett's *Sexual Politics* reveals the theme of the present paper. We are in agreement with her thesis that what takes place between men and women in the bedroom has something to tell us

Michael Gordon and Penelope J. Shankweiler, "Different Equals Less: Female Sexuality in Recent Marriage Manuals," from *Journal of Marriage and the Family*, August, 1971, pp. 459–466. Reprinted with permission.

* This study is part of a larger project dealing with changes in American marital education literature, published between 1830 and 1970, that the first author began in 1969. It was supported, in part, by a University of Connecticut Research Foundation grant, and a Temple University Faculty grant.

about the relationship that prevails between them in the world at large. While Millett draws primarily upon the work of three major novelists to document this thesis we will use non-fictional sources, more specifically marriage manuals published in the last two decades.[1] This form of literature was chosen because we feel it contains the currently regnant views on human sexuality, and also because it receives reasonably wide circulation (e.g., David Reuben's *Everything You Always Wanted to Know About Sex* has already sold over a million copies in the hard-bound edition alone).[2] Furthermore, the experts, often self-proclaimed, who write these manuals influence the views of those who provide sexual counseling in our society. Whether these books influence behavior in any important sense is moot, but at the very least they do help create the sexual expectations of those directly or indirectly exposed to them.

We see this as a study in sexual ideology. As traditionally defined, ideology refers to the body of beliefs and values which legitimate the status quo, an important aspect of which may be a dominant group's position vis-à-vis other groups in a society. If women are conceived of as a "minority" group it then becomes important to explore the ideology which perpetuates this status. It is our contention that a significant dimension of this ideology is the manner in which women have had their sexuality *defined* for them. Women have had specific boundaries imposed on the expression of their sexuality. To be sure, the same is true of men, but the constraints have been looser and fewer. Moreover, these boundaries are the creations, for the most part, of male "experts," whose opinions and advice have reflected the interests of a patriarchal society. We will begin by examining the manner in which female sexuality has been depicted in the manuals published in the period between 1830 and 1950.[3]

FEMALE SEXUALITY, 1830–1950

Stereotypes do on occasion reflect a considerable degree of the reality they generally simplify and distort. The popular image of nineteenth century, middle-class society being one in which the professed values placed sex in the category of an unfortunate procreative necessity is for the most part substantiated by the contents of the marriage manuals published during this period. Such books generally advocate a policy of sex for reproduction only, as is attested to by continence being the most frequently recommended form of contraception. Women are granted any form of sexual desire so begrudgingly that for almost all intents and purposes it is nonexistent.

As a general rule, a modest woman seldom desires any sexual gratification for herself. She submits to her husband, but only to please him; and, but for the desire of maternity, would far rather be relieved from his attentions. The married woman has no wish to be treated on the footing of a mistress (Hayes, 1869:227).

However, as the century draws to a close one can see the *beginnings* of an acceptance of non-procreative marital sexuality, as well as female sexual desire, in some of the manuals.

In the early years of the twentieth century what was hinted earlier becomes the prevailing view, *viz.*, sex in the context of marriage is not only right and proper, but an important aspect of married life as well. As one might expect, this point of view is tied to a reorientation toward female sexuality. Its existence is now recognized, but in a form which distinctly sets it apart from male sexuality:

> It is the complexity of woman's sex nature you have not understood. A wife needs the affection of attention, interest. With her it is not merely a craving for carnal pleasures; it is something deeper, something of a spiritual nature which sweetly blended with her physiological demands (Howard, 1912:22).

> To a great percentage of men a strictly monogamous life is either irksome, painful, disagreeable or an utter impossibility. While the number of women who are not satisfied with one mate is exceedingly small (Robinson, 1917:325).

These two excerpts, which are typical of the period, are related to one another in an important fashion. One might say that the ideas contained in one almost logically flow from the other. Women are presented with a definition of their sexuality that conveniently excludes the possibility of engaging in the kind of non-marital sexual behavior men are granted. Here, then, we have one rationale for the "double-standard" that has been with us so long, and that is only now beginning to break down.

Another important dimension of the conception of female sexuality that arose at the beginning of the century is its alleged dormancy. That is to say, in contrast to the male who from puberty on is confronted by imperious sexual impulses females supposedly do not experience strong desire until sex is initiated—in the marriage bed, of course.

> No doubt women differ greatly, but in every woman who truly loves there lies dormant the capacity to become vibrantly alive in response to her lover, and to meet him as a willing and active participant in the sacrament of marriage (Gray, 1922:145).

What is of significance here is that female sexuality becomes a male creation, without his intercession it remains incipient at best, and nonexistent at worse.

Once a woman's sexual desire has been "awakened" by her husband, its satisfaction, not surprisingly, falls on his shoulders, and in a specific way, *viz.*, coitus culminating, ideally, in simultaneous climax. Writing in 1926 Margaret Sanger had the following to say on this matter:

> Experience will teach the husband to watch for and recognize in his beloved the approach of the culminating ecstasy. Not until this point is attained may he release his own emotions from control so that both together at the same moment may yield themselves for the final ecstatic flight (Sanger, 1926:142).

Such statements are encountered as early as 1900; by the 1930s their number has reached such proportions that it has been described as "a cult of mutual orgasm" (Gordon, in press). This emphasis on a particular form of orgasmic ordering is noteworthy because it defines the appropriate mode for sexual satisfaction in terms of the male's orgasmic potential.[4]

Thus, while the very recognition of female sexuality at the beginning of the century was in itself revolutionary, it was presented in invidious terms: not only was it different and less clamorous than that of the male, but essentially dependent upon him for its arousal and satisfaction. We hope to show that new evidence and knowledge is beginning to lead to a reappraisal of female sexual potential, but that the idea of male domination continues to be as firmly entrenched in the sexual sphere as it is in male-female relationships in the society as a whole.

THE MANUALS

The eighteen manuals on which this study is based were for the most part the bestsellers of the 1950–70 period.[5] This is not to say that all of them were first published during these two decades. Some appeared earlier in the century, e.g., Chesser's *Love Without Fear* (1947), but continued to sell in large number through the sixties.[6] We have adopted this selection procedure rather than sampling systematically from the manuals published in this two decade interval because we were not concerned with the views that were most representative of this type of literature, but rather with the views the greater number of people were being exposed to, and which thus could be viewed as being the most influential. In discussing this material we shall first explore what we see as indications of a broad changing sexual ethic and then focus on the treatment of female sexuality in this context.

FINDINGS

THE NEW SEXUAL ETHIC

One of the most notable shifts in the recent manuals is the growing acceptance, often implicit, of nonmarital sex for women. As we have already noted, men in the past have been granted more sexual license than women and it was expected that they would engage in a certain amount of pre- or extramarital sex. This view holds through the 1950s with most writers appearing to direct their books to couples entering marriage with the wife a virgin and the husband furtively experienced. In the 1960s we notice not only a less critical attitude toward premarital sex for women but the appearance of books which provide instruction for its successful pursuit as well. Among the earliest of these, and certainly the most widely read was Helen Gurley Brown's *Sex and the Single Girl* (1962).[7]

> Nice, single girls *do* have affairs, and they do not necessarily die of them! They suffer sometimes, occasionally a great deal. However, quite a few "nice" girls have affairs and do not suffer at all! (Brown, 1962:225)

The cheering can stop. While Helen Gurley Brown did openly and approvingly discuss nonmarital sex she was committed to the status quo insofar as male-female relationships are concerned. The same holds true of *The Sensuous Woman*, a recent best seller that graphically explores the frontiers of sexual behavior while clinging to conventional notions of broader relationships between the sexes. This book might have been appropriately subtitled, *How to Get to a Man's Heart Through His Genitals.*

It should be stressed that the acceptance of premarital experience in the majority of the manuals is much less explicit than in the books discussed above. For the most part, even throughout the sixties, sex is assumed to take place within the social context of love and marriage, the latter being "the most precious and deeply satisfying relationship we know" (Calderone, 1960:13). Even those writers most deeply committed to sensuality still subscribe to the idealized view of sex as a sacrament, a means of communicating love for another person and ideally in a marital setting.

In view of such a sentiment it is not surprising to find that extramarital affairs are almost overwhelmingly rejected in the books included in the study, and concomitantly, a major concern is with improving marital sex so as to avert this eventuality. Some authors assume that the basic recipes have been mastered and "a couple who will not be content with a static love, even if it is a satisfying love, will have to keep up a constant search for ways of introducing a freshness into their sexual experience" (Chartham, 1970:27). Moreover, it is expected that the approach of old age will not mark the end of the couple's sexual life. Increasingly we are finding books containing sections on what we might call gerontological sex. Masters and Johnson's (1966) finding on the abilities of the elderly, when in good health, to function adequately sexually has lent support to this position.

Part of the concern with reinvigorating marital sex is manifested in the growing interest in what we might call "gourmet" sex as is indicated by the titles of books such as *Sex for Advanced Lovers* (1970) and *Sophisticated Sex Techniques* (1967). These books are usually less programmatic than earlier ones such as, for example, Van de Velde's *Ideal Marriage* (1930). While the latter, as did similar books in the 1930s and 1940s, presented a demanding sexual regimen involving the specification of appropriate behavior at all stages of the sex act, more recent books in general seem to place more emphasis on spontaneity and the willingness to experiment. Alternative forms of sexual expression such as oral-genital and anal-genital, while previously either ignored, or relegated to foreplay, are now beginning to be elevated to ends in their own right, and represent part of a generally freer orientation toward recreative sex. The boundaries of human sexuality are slowly being expanded. Hedonism within the context of marriage is the new norm.

An important illustration of the rejection of the stress on technique and rationality in sex and the new hedonism, as well, is the reappraisal of simultaneous climax in the past two decades. In the first half of the century and particularly since the 1930s, "mutual orgasm" had been presented as the ultimate in sexual bliss. Recently some voices have been raised in opposition to this view. On the one hand there are those who feel it has created standards that most couples find difficult to meet:

> In many books of sexual enlightenment, simultaneous orgasm or almost simultaneous orgasm is put forth as being the normal, common and desirable thing. It is, however, a lie that has caused much damage in the course of time because it has resulted in many couples feeling abnormal or 'no good' without reason (Hegeler and Hegeler, 1963:196).

Others criticize it on what we may call aesthetic grounds:

> Although there is certainly no denying that mutual simultaneous orgasm is very enjoyable, there is also something to be said for consecutive orgasm. Since the precise moment of orgasm usually brings on a lapse of consciousness, neither man nor woman is able to enjoy the orgasm of their partner (Reuben, 1969:56).

Still others raise questions which relate to female sexuality:

> This pursuit of a fanciful notion will operate to maintain a woman
> at a single-orgasm level, a loss of completion far more to be de-
> plored than that resulting from separate orgasm (Street, 1959:67).

The last excerpt was written in the year that Masters and Johnson began
their research. Ironically enough, in the years since their research has
been published we have not seen similar critiques.

THE NATURE OF FEMALE SEXUALITY

In the context of a growing emphasis on pleasure and spontaneity
there is occurring a gradual change in ideas about female sexuality. In
the books published between 1950–1965 men are perceived as having
greater sexual needs than women, whereas in those appearing in the
1965–70 period the predominant idea is that men and women are equal
in sexual desire but the nature of their sexuality is, in a variety of ways,
different. The latter is witnessed by statements such as the following: "men
can enjoy sex, in an animal sort of way, without love. Women can't, so
remind her of your love often, in some way or another" (Hall, 1965:12).
Female sexuality is still seen as more emotional and idealized than its
male counterpart, something which grows out of love rather than physical
desire.

What is important here is the persistence of a restrictive definition of
female sexuality. If one is continually told that one has to care for, if not
love, a man in order to sleep with him, then it can act as a self-fulfilling
prophecy, and lo and behold many women find truth in David Reuben's
words ". . . before a woman can have sexual intercourse with a man she
must have social intercourse with him" (Reuben, 1969:103).

Furthermore, women are portrayed as likely to be negative about sex.
In discussions of sexual maladjustment and experimentation it is generally
the woman who is seen as the problematic partner. While socialization is
frequently viewed as the source of female inhibitions, other differences are
seemingly attributed to biological factors. Thus, Greenblat maintains:

> . . . in many women, as a result of physical development and social
> training, the desire for actual sexual intercourse as distinct from
> kissing and petting may develop somewhat later than in young
> men. However, it is also true that the greater complexity of the
> woman's sexual organs makes possible a much deeper and more
> lasting physical emotional [sic] response. This response is not
> easy to sum up in a few words and not easy to achieve or to satisfy

in the few seconds or minutes of sexual activity that would satisfy most males (Greenblat, 1956:8).

Here we see the persistence of the belief in the dormancy and slow development of female sexuality. In fact, women are believed to reach sexual "maturity" 10 to 12 years later than men, who are at the peak of their desire and performance at eighteen, a point to which we will return later in the paper.

In general, men are presented as simple creatures sexually whose desire is as easily satisfied as it is aroused. They are supposedly capable of responding to what they think, imagine or see, while women are thought to be "touch" creatures who have to be slowly stimulated by gentle kisses and caresses. One author expresses concern that men should not base their idea of what "normal" women are like sexually on their experiences with women who:

> because of their unusually high sex and endowments are prone to have many voluntary and non-prostitutional premarital affairs. Such females are frequently so easily aroused and satisfied sexually that their male partners receive the erroneous impression that all normal females are, or should be, the way the minority of females behave (Ellis, 1966:19).

Reservations such as these notwithstanding, the prevailing view is that once a woman is aroused her desire is as strong as a man's—some books even mention the female capacity for multiple orgasm, but almost all fail to discuss its implications.

It is important to assess the extent to which such views of female sexuality are based on ideology. The findings of Masters and Johnson (1966) lend support to the position that while there are differences in the sexual response cycles of men and women, with the exception of orgasmic capacity, they resemble each other more than they differ. That is to say, the excitement, plateau, orgasmic and resolution phases are essentially similar. One does, of course, have to consider the degree to which cultural overlay masks some of these similarities. For example, a recent study carried out by the Institute for Sex Research at the University of Hamburg found that when exposed to erotic photographs women tend to judge them to be less arousing than do men but "the women showed almost the same degree of sexual-physiological reactions and activation of sexual behavior as the men" (Sigusch et al., 1970:23). The importance of the Hamburg findings is that they indicate the extent to which women are responding to cues that define socially appropriate and inappropriate situations calling for a sexual response, rather than their own bodies.

The Masters and Johnson (1966) study has been iconoclastic in a number of ways. Not only have their findings raised serious doubts about the differences between male and female response cycles, but, as is well known, they have also toppled the oft-proclaimed distinction between vaginal and clitoral orgasms, and with this have prepared the ground for the emergence of a new view of female sexuality.[8]

The impact of their work has not been strongly felt in the marriage manuals. A number of recent manuals do discuss the findings on the clitoris and gerontological sex, but they generally fail to explore the implications of the findings on the multiorgasmic capacities of women not only for sexual technique, but for the broader relations between men and women as well. Only one book even broaches the latter topic. In commenting on Masters and Johnson's findings on multiple orgasm Robert Chartham notes:

> If multiple-orgasm becomes a widespread experience however, the whole sexual relationship with regard to the sensual content of swiving [coitus] is likely to go reverse. Whereas in the past men have taken it for granted that theirs was the superior experience, since they could never bring an episode of swiving to its natural ultimate conclusion without coming off, now though they will still have this advantage, their responses are bound to be inferior to the multiple-orgasm partner (Chartham, 1970:85).

Others, have carried such ideas much further, most notably Mary Jane Sherfey in her masterful essay on female sexuality.

Dr. Sherfey reviews the findings of Masters and Johnson and concludes that:

> . . . the more orgasms a woman has, the stronger they become; the more orgasms she has, the more she *can* have. To all intents and purposes, *the human female is sexually insatiable in the presence of the highest degrees of sexual satiation* (Sherfey, 1966:99).

Moreover, she views monogamous marriage as something which men have never fully accepted and women have been coerced into accepting: ". . . women's inordinate orgasmic capacity did not evolve for monogamous, sedentary cultures" (Sherfey, 1966:118).

Another point raised by Sherfey that is important for our understanding of prevailing views of female sexuality is that of the differential sexual "maturation" rate of males and females. That is to say, men and women reach the height of their responsiveness at different times. The source of this view is the Kinsey study:

We have pointed out that the male's capacity to be stimulated sexually shows a marked increase with the approach of adolescence, and that the incidences of responding males and the frequency of response to the point of orgasm, reach their peak within three or four years after the onset of adolescence. . . . On the other hand, we have pointed out that the maximum incidences of sexually responding females are not approached until some time in the late twenties and in the thirties. . . (Kinsey *et al.*, 1953: 714–715).

This has been frequently commented upon in the marriage manuals and plays an important role in defining current notions of women's sexual uniqueness. In the words of Maxine Davis woman "is an early-leafing but late-flowering plant" (Davis, 1963:88). Sherfey explores what others had hinted at: The roots of this difference may be more social than biological.

Less than one hundred years ago, and in many places today, women regularly had their third or fourth child by the time they were eighteen or nineteen, and the life span was no more than thirty-five to forty years. It could well be that the natural synchronization of the peak periods for sexual expression in men and women have been destroyed only in recent years (Sherfey, 1966:118–119).

One would have to interpret this to mean that with the postponed age of marriage in industrial societies and the differential sexual license granted men and women, natural synchronization has broken down. Or, to put it differently the reason women are "maturing" more slowly than men is they have less opportunity to engage in heterosexual relations and perhaps more importantly they are socialized in such a way as to suppress rather than encourage the expression of their sexuality early in adolescence in autoerotic forms.

What makes all of this especially interesting is the new data that is becoming available on changes in rates of premarital intercourse for college students. The studies of Bell and Chaskes (1970) and Christensen and Gregg (1970) found that between 1958 and 1963 there was an increase in female premarital sex. Bell and Chaskes also found that the context in which sexual intercourse had first occurred had changed with the dating and going steady settings increasingly replacing engagement. Moreover, there is in general a growing convergence of the rates for men and women with this being especially notable in Denmark where Christensen and Gregg report 95 percent of the men and 97 percent of the women having had premarital coitus. Findings such as these suggest that as the differences between male and female premarital experience rates begin to decrease, we may also see a growing convergence in sexual "maturation" rates.

MALE AND FEMALE SEXUAL ROLES

Even the growing number of authors who are advocating an "equal but different" image of female sexuality still subscribe, for the most part, to a belief in the importance of male leadership and initiative. Brisset and Lewis in their study of sex manuals note that "between three and four times as many prescriptions for behavior are directed to the male as to the female" (1970:42). Nevertheless, a common theme is the encouragement of female initiative as means of improving the couple's sex life. "The bride should overcome her modesty and let him know which caresses are most desirable and the manner of their performance" (Levine, 1950:5). What this and similar authors are trying to do is have women overcome the passivity they feel impedes sexual pleasure, but the focus is always on the man:

> In lovemaking your body is your instrument. You shouldn't settle for less than the best. An Arthur Rubenstein or Van Cliburn is not going to select a clunky, unresponsive, out-of-tune piano on which to perform his artistry ("J", 1969:28).

The metaphor here is a rather revealing one.

For a number of authors the importance of male control takes on the character of an imperative for general domestic as well as sexual adjustment:

> Manly self-assertion can be *tempered* with gentleness and consideration, but both your sex life and your marriage suffer if you allow it to be smothered or overrestrained by such qualities. Emotionally and physically, your wife needs the assertiveness of a masculine figure to make a good marital adjustment. The highest form of considerateness in the long run is to become such a figure in her eyes (Eichenlaub, 1968:82).

So we see that while the trend toward what we have earlier called "gourmet" sex may have contributed to the emergence of a more active conception of the woman's role, it has not altered more fundamental sexual behavior. There is nothing irreconcilable between the feminine mystique and a woman who plays a more active role in bed, as long as control resides with the man.

CONCLUSION

We trust that our discussion of the manner in which female sexuality has been depicted in the marriage manuals of the past two decades has revealed the ideological overtones of such literature. Women in this century have been granted the right to experience sexual desire and have this desire satisfied, but always with the man calling the tune. This we have suggested is a manifestation of the minority group status of women. Given their primary roles of wives and mothers their sexuality is something which has been subject to masculine definitions of its purity, spoilage, ruination and so on. Women have been given the sop of sexual spirituality in return for the sexual freedom they have been denied. In short, they have been offered a conception of their sexuality that has not allowed it to follow its underlying physiology.

We see this as an ideology reflecting the prevailing social relations between the sexes. As James Coleman notes:

> . . . when [a woman's] status and ultimate position do not depend greatly on her husband she need not be so cautious. Her sexual activity may now be a pleasure to be enjoyed more nearly for its own sake, without regard for its loss in value through promiscuity and loss of 'reputation.' Her sexual activity is not so much a commodity by which she establishes her ultimate social position, and she need no longer withhold it for exchange purposes. She becomes more like the male in this regard, having less reason to maintain her sexual activity as a scarce good in a market, more reason to consume it for its direct enjoyment (Coleman, 1966: 217).

Since women are not independent in this regard, it is not surprising that the changes that have occurred in recent sex manuals do not represent a dramatic reorientation toward female sexual roles. The new findings on female sexuality appear to be poured into the old bottles of male-female relationships. If women have been encouraged to take more initiative it is in order that they might give more pleasure to their husbands rather than achieve more autonomy in the sexual realm.

ENDNOTES

1. We use the term marriage and sex manuals interchangeably in this paper, though a good argument can be made for the point that the term sex manuals is best left reserved for those books which focus almost exclusively on sex education, in contrast to marriage manuals which focus on a broader spectrum of domestic life. By this definition books used in this study are sex manuals.
2. In order to understand just how impressive this figure is, one must

realize that Van de Velde's *Ideal Marriage* (1930) has not in the American edition sold as many copies in the forty years it has been in print, and it is one of the most popular marriage manuals ever published.

3. For a more complete discussion of the literature of this period the reader is referred to Gordon (in press) and Gordon and Bernstein (1970).

4. Some people have seen Freudian influence in the development of "the cult of mutual orgasm." As we have indicated, there were writers advocating this well before Freud had written on any topic bearing on this subject. However, in the 1920s and 1930s his conception of "mature" female sexuality being vaginal sexuality probably was a factor accounting for the growth of those recommending this form of orgasmic ordering, and, of course, was the source of what Koedt has called "the myth of vaginal orgasm."

5. In the first author's earlier studies the manuals were selected differently. Because of their small numbers an attempt was made to locate the total universe of nineteenth century manuals, and 63 were ultimately found to be useable. Twentieth century manuals were selected by means of representative sample of manuals published in each decade of the century.

6. Furthermore, several of the books included in this study have gone through innumerable printings and several editions and revisions. The year given for a book is usually that of its most recent revision, where it was possible to establish this date.

7. This book is not a sex or marriage manual and is thus not included in the enumeration of manuals in this study. Its discussion is felt to be warranted because of the radical character of its theme.

8. It should be pointed out that Kinsey and his associates in *Sexual Behavior in the Human Female* (1953:582–583) discussed evidence that seriously if not irrefutably questioned the possibility of a "vaginal orgasm." Interestingly enough this was virtually ignored while other sections of the book such as the differential sexual "maturation" rate of the sexes was frequently commented upon by authors of marriage manuals. This would seem to be a case of facts being widely disseminated which can be reconciled with prevailing beliefs and those which cannot, dismissed or ignored.

REFERENCES

Bell, Robert R. and Jay B. Chaskes. 1970, "Premarital sexual experience among coeds, 1958 and 1968." Journal of Marriage and the Family 32 (February): 30–35.

Brissett, Dennis and Lionel Lewis. 1970, "Guidelines for marital sex: An analysis of fifteen popular marriage manuals." The Family Coordinator 19 (January) : 41–48.

Brown, Helen Gurley. 1962, Sex and the Single Girl. New York: Bernard Geis.

*Butterfield, Oliver M. 1967, Sexual Harmony in Marriage. New York: Emerson Books.

*Calderone, Mary S. 1960, Release from Sexual Tensions. New York: Random House.

*Chartham, Robert. 1970, Sex For Advanced Lovers. New York: New American Library.

*Chesser, Eustace. 1947, Love Without Fear. New York: Roy Publishers.

*Chesser, Eustace. 1970, Love and the Married Woman. New York: New American Library.

Christensen, Harold T. and Christina Gregg. 1970, "Changing sex norms in America and Scandinavia." Journal of Marriage and the Family 32 (November) : 616–627.

Coleman, James S. 1969, Letter to the editor. American Journal of Sociology 72 (September) : 217.

*Davis, Maxine. 1963, Sexual Responsibility in Marriage. New York: Dial Press.

*Eichenlaub, John E. 1961, The Marriage Art. New York: Dell.

*Eichenlaub, John E. 1968, New Approaches to Sex in Marriage. New York: Dell.

*Ellis, Albert. 1966, The Art and Science of Love. New York: Bantam Books.

Gordon, Michael. In press "From an unfortunate necessity of a cult of mutual orgasm: Sex in American domestic education literature, 1830–1940." In James Henslin (ed.), The Sociology of Sex. New York: Appleton-Century-Crofts.

Gordon, Michael and M. Charles Bernstein. 1970, "Mate choice and domestic life in the nineteenth-century marriage manual." Journal of Marriage and the Family 32 (November) : 665–674.

Gray, A. H. 1922, Men, Women and God. New York: Association Press.

*Greenblat, Bernard R. 1956, A Doctor's Marital Guide for Patients. Chicago: Budlong Press Company.

*Hall, Robert E. 1965, Sex and Marriage. New York: Planned Parenthood.

Hayes, A. 1869, Sexual Physiology of Woman. Boston: Peabody Medical Institute.

* One of the 18 books on which the present study is based.

*Hegeler, Inge and Sten. 1963, An ABZ of Love. New York: Medical Press of New York.

Howard, William Lee. 1912, Facts for the Married. New York: Edward J. Clode.

*"J." 1969, The Sensuous Woman. New York: Lyle Stuart.

Kinsey, Alfred *et al*. 1953, Sexual Behavior in the Human Female. Philadelphia: Saunders.

*Levine, Lena. 1950, The Doctor Talks with the Bride and Groom. New York: Planned Parenthood.

Masters, William H. and Virginia E. Johnson. 1966, Human Sexual Response. Boston: Little, Brown.

Millett, Kate. 1970, Sexual Politics. New York: Doubleday.

*Reuben, David. 1969, Everything You Always Wanted to Know About Sex . . . New York: David McKay.

Robinson, William J. 1917, Woman, Her Sex and Love Life. New York: Eugenics Publishing Company.

Sanger, Margaret. 1926, Happiness in Marriage. New York: Blue Ribbon Books.

Sherfey, Mary Jane. 1966, "The evolution and nature of female sexuality in relation to psychoanalytic theory." Journal of the American Psychoanalytic Association 14 (January): 28–127.

Sigusch, Volkmar *et al*. 1970, "Psychosexual stimulation: Sex differences." Journal of Sex Research 6 (February): 10–24.

*Stone, Hannah and Abraham. 1953, A Marriage Manual. New York: Simon and Schuster.

*Street, Robert. 1959, Modern Sex Techniques. New York: Lancer Books.

*Van de Velde, Th. H. 1930, Ideal Marriage. New York: Random House.

Woodward, L. T. 1967, Sophisticated Sex Techniques in Marriage. New York: Lancer Books.

Jack O. Balswick and
Charles W. Peek

The Inexpressive Male:
A Tragedy of American
Society*

*The position is taken in this paper that inexpressiveness is a
culturally produced temperament trait which is characteristic of
many American males. It is suggested that in growing up, boys
are taught that expressiveness is inconsistent with masculinity.
Inexpressive males come in two varieties: the cowboy who,
although he does have feelings toward women, does not or
cannot express them; and the playboy who is a non-feeling man
void of even unexpressed emotional feelings toward women.
In light of the increase in importance of the companionship and
affection function in marriage, across-the-board inexpressiveness
of married males (that is, inexpressiveness toward all women,
wife included) can be highly dysfunctional to their marital
relationships, while selective inexpressiveness (that is,
inexpressiveness toward women other than their wives) may be
just as functional to maintaining these relationships.*

The problem of what it means to be "male" and "female" is a problem which is faced and dealt with in its own way in every society. Through
cross-cultural research one now surmises that culture rather than "nature"
is the major influence in determining the temperamental differences between the sexes. It may be no accident that a woman, Margaret Mead, did
the classic study demonstrating that temperamental differences between the
sexes are explained very little in terms of innateness, but rather in terms
of culture. In her book, *Sex and Temperament,* Mead reported on the
differences in sex roles for three New Guinea societies. Using ethnocentric

Jack O. Balswick and Charles W. Peek, "The Inexpressive Male: A Tragedy
of American Society," from *The Family Coordinator,* October, 1971, pp. 363–
368. Reprinted with permission.
* A revised version of a paper read at the meetings of the American Sociological Association, Washington, D.C., September, 1970.

western standards in defining sex roles, she found that the ideal sex role for both the male and female was essentially "feminine" among the Arapesh, "masculine" among the Mundugumor, and "feminine" for the male and "masculine" for the female among the Tchambuli. The Tchambuli represents a society that defines sex roles in a complete reversal of the traditional distinctions made between masculine and feminine roles in the United States.

It is the purpose of this paper to consider a particular temperament trait that often characterizes the male in American society. As sex role distinctions have developed in America, the male sex role, as compared to the female sex role, carries with it prescriptions which encourage inexpressiveness. In some of its extreme contemporary forms, the inexpressive male has even come to be glorified as the epitome of a real man. This will be discussed later in the paper when two types of inexpressive male are examined.

THE CREATION OF THE INEXPRESSIVE MALE

Children, from the time they are born both explicitly and implicitly are taught how to be a man or how to be a woman. While the girl is taught to act "feminine" and to desire "feminine" objects, the boy is taught how to be a man. In learning to be a man, the boy in American society comes to value expressions of masculinity and devalue expressions of femininity. Masculinity is expressed largely through physical courage, toughness, competitiveness, and aggressiveness, whereas femininity is, in contrast, expressed largely through gentleness, expressiveness, and responsiveness. When a young boy begins to express his emotions through crying, his parents are quick to assert, "You're a big boy and big boys don't cry." Parents often use the term, "he's all boy," in reference to their son, and by this term usually refer to behavior which is an expression of aggressiveness, getting into mischief, getting dirty, etc., but never use the term to denote behavior which is an expression of affection, tenderness, or emotion. What parents are really telling their son is that a real man does not show his emotions and if he is a real man he will not allow his emotions to be expressed. These outward expressions of emotion are viewed as a sign of femininity, and undesirable for a male.

Is it any wonder, then, that during the most emotional peak of a play or movie, when many in the audience have lumps in their throats and tears in their eyes, that the adolescent boy guffaws loudly or quickly suppresses any tears which may be threatening to emerge, thus demonstrating to the world that he is above such emotional feeling?

THE INEXPRESSIVE MALE AS A SINGLE MAN

At least two basic types of inexpressive male seem to result from this socialization process: the cowboy and the playboy. Manville (1969) has referred to the *cowboy type* in terms of a "John Wayne Neurosis" which stresses the strong, silent, and two-fisted male as the 100 percent American he-man. For present purposes, it is especially in his relationship with women that the John Wayne neurosis is particularly significant in representing many American males. As portrayed by Wayne in any one of his many type-cast roles, the mark of a real man is that he does not show any tenderness or affection toward girls because his culturally-acquired male image dictates that such a show of emotions would be distinctly unmanly. If he does have anything to do with girls, it is on a "man to man" basis: the girl is treated roughly (but not sadistically), with little hint of gentleness or affection. As Manville puts it:

> "The on-screen John Wayne doesn't feel comfortable around women. He does like them sometimes—God knows he's not *queer*. But at the right time, and in the right place—which he chooses. And always with his car/horse parked directly outside, in/on which he will ride away to his more important business back in Marlboro country." (1969, 111)

Alfred Auerback, a psychiatrist, has commented more directly (1970) on the cowboy type. He describes the American male's inexpressiveness with women as part of the "cowboy syndrome." He quite rightly states that "the cowboy in moving pictures has conveyed the image of the rugged 'he-man,' strong, resilient, resourceful, capable of coping with overwhelming odds. His attitude toward women is courteous but reserved." As the cowboy equally loved his girlfriend and his horse, so the present day American male loves his car or motorcycle and his girlfriend. Basic to both these descriptions is the notion that the cowboy does have feelings toward women but does not express them, since ironically such expression would conflict with his image of what a male is.

The *playboy type* has recently been epitomized in *Playboy* magazine and by James Bond. As with the cowboy type, he is resourceful and shrewd, and interacts with his girlfriend with a certain detachment which is expressed as "playing it cool." While Bond's relationship with women is more in terms of a Don Juan, he still treats women with an air of emotional detachment and independence similar to that of the cowboy. The playboy departs from the cowboy, however, in that he is also "non-feeling." Bond and the playboy he caricatures are in a sense "dead" inside. They have no emotional feelings toward women, while Wayne, although unwilling and perhaps unable to express them does have such feelings. Bond rejects women as women, treating them as consumer commodities; Wayne puts women on a pedestal. The playboy's relationship with women represents the culmination of Fromm's description of a marketing-oriented personality in which a person comes to see both himself and others as persons to be manipulated and exploited. Sexuality is reduced to a packageable consumption item which the playboy can handle because it demands no responsibility. The woman in the process, becomes reduced to a playboy accessory. A successful "love affair" is one in which the bed was shared, but the playboy emerges having avoided personal involvement or a shared relationship with the woman.

The playboy, then, in part is the old cowboy in modern dress. Instead of the crude mannerisms of John Wayne, the playboy is a skilled manipulator of women, knowing when to turn the lights down, what music to play on the stereo, which drinks to serve, and what topics of conversation to pursue. The playboy, however, is not a perfect likeness; for unlike the cowboy, he does not seem to care for the women from whom he withholds his emotions. Thus, the inexpressive male as a single man comes in two types: the inexpressive feeling man (the cowboy) and the inexpressive non-feeling man (the playboy).

THE INEXPRESSIVE MALE AS A MARRIED MAN

When the inexpressive male marries, his inexpressiveness can become highly dysfunctional to his marital relationship *if* he continues to apply it across-the-board to all women, his wife included. The modern American family places a greater demand upon the marriage relationship than did the family of the past. In the typical marriage of 100 or even 50 years ago, the roles of both the husband and the wife were clearly defined as demanding, task-oriented functions. If the husband successfully performed the role of provider and protector of his wife and family and if the wife performed the role of homemaker and mother to her children, chances were the marriage was defined as successful, both from a personal and a societal point of view. The traditional task functions which in the past were performed by the husband and wife are today often taken care of by individuals and organizations outside the home. Concomitant with the decline of the task functions in marriage has been the increase in the importance of the companionship and affectionate function in marriage. As Blood and Wolfe (1960, 172) concluded in their study of the modern American marriage, "companionship has emerged as the most valued aspect of marriage today."

As American society has become increasingly mechanized and depersonalized, the family remains as one of the few social groups where what sociologists call the primary relationship has still managed to survive. As such, a greater and greater demand has been placed upon the modern family and especially the modern marriage to provide for affection and companionship. Indeed, it is highly plausible to explain the increased rate of divorce during the last 70 years, not in terms of a breakdown in marriage relationships, but instead, as resulting from the increased load which marriage has been asked to carry. When the husband and wife no longer find affection and companionship from their marriage relationship, they most likely question the wisdom of attempting to continue in their conjugal relationship. When affection is gone, the main reason for the marriage relationship disappears.

Thus, within the newly defined affectively-oriented marriage relationship male inexpressiveness toward *all* women, wife included, would be dysfunctional. But what may happen for many males is that through progressively more serious involvements with women (such as going steady, being pinned, engagement, and the honeymoon period of marriage), they begin to make some exceptions. That is, they may learn to be *situationally rather than totally inexpressive*, inexpressive toward women in most situations but not in all. As the child who learns a rule and then, through further experience, begins to understand the exceptions to it, many American males may pick up the principle of inexpressiveness toward women, discovering its exceptions as they become more and more experienced in the full range of man-woman relationships. Consequently, they may become more expressive toward their wives while remaining essentially inexpressive toward other women; they learn that the conjugal relationship is one situation that is an exception to the cultural requirement of male inexpressiveness. Thus, what was once a double *sexual* standard, where men had one standard of sexual conduct toward their fiancee or wife and another toward other women, may now be primarily a double *emotional* standard, where men learn to be expressive toward their fiancee or wife but remain inexpressive toward women in general.

To the extent that such situational inexpressiveness exists among males, it should be functional to the maintenance of the marriage relationship. Continued inexpressiveness by married males toward women other than their wives would seem to prohibit their forming meaningful relationships with these women. Such a situation would seem to be advantageous to preserving their marital relationships, since "promiscuous" expressiveness toward other women could easily threaten the stability of these companionship-oriented marital relationships.

In short, the authors' suggestion is that situational inexpressiveness, in which male expressiveness is essentially limited to the marital relationship, may be one of the basic timbers shoring up many American marriages, especially if indications of increasing extramarital sexual relations are correct. In a sense, then, the consequences of situational inexpressiveness for marital relationships do not seem very different from those of prostitution down through the centuries, where prostitution provided for extramarital sex under circumstances which discouraged personal affection toward the female partner strong enough to undermine the marital relationship. In the case of the situationally inexpressive husband, his inexpressiveness in relations with women other than his wife may serve as a line of defense against the possible negative consequences of such involvement toward marital stability. By acting as the cowboy or playboy, therefore, the married male may effectively rob extramarital relationships of their expressiveness and thus preserve his marital relationship.

The inexpressiveness which the American male early acquires may be bothersome in that he has to partially unlearn it in order to effectively relate to his wife. However, if he is successful in partially unlearning it (or learning a few exceptions to it), then it can be highly functional to maintaining the conjugal relationship.

But what if the husband does not partially unlearn his inexpressiveness? Within the newly defined expressive function of the marriage relationship, he is likely to be found inadequate. The possibility of an affectionate and companionship conjugal relationship carries with it the assumption that both the husband and wife are bringing into marriage the expressive capabilities to make such a relationship work. This being the case, American society is ironically short changing males in terms of their ability to fulfill this role expectation. Thus, society inconsistently teaches the male that to be masculine is to be inexpressive, while at the same time, expectations in the marital role are defined in terms of sharing affection and companionship which involves the ability to communicate and express feelings. What exists apparently, is another example of a discontinuity in cultural conditioning of which Benedict (1938) spoke more than 30 years ago.

CONCLUSION AND SUMMARY

It has been suggested that many American males are incapable of expressing themselves emotionally to a woman, and that this inexpressiveness is a result of the way society socialized males into their sex role. However, there is an alternative explanation which should be explored, namely, that the learning by the male of his sex role may not actually result in his inability to be expressive, but rather only in his thinking that he is not supposed to be expressive. Granted, according to the first explanation, the male cannot express himself precisely because he was taught that he was not supposed to be expressive, but in this second explanation inexpressiveness is a result of present perceived expectations and not a psychological condition which resulted from past socialization. The male perceives cultural expectations as saying, "don't express yourself to women," and although the male may be capable of such expressiveness, he "fits" into cultural expectations. In the case of the married male, where familial norms do call for expressiveness to one's wife, it may be that the expectations for the expression of emotions to his wife are not communicated to him.

There has been a trickle of evidence which would lend support to the first explanation, which stresses the male's incapacity to be expressive. Several studies (Balswick, 1970; Hurvitz, 1964; Komarovsky, 1962; Rainwater, 1965) have suggested that especially among the lowly educated, it is the wife playing the feminine role who is often disappointed in the lack of emotional concern shown by her husband. The husband, on the other hand, cannot understand the relatively greater concern and emotional expressiveness which his wife desires, since he does not usually feel this need himself. As a result of her research, Komarovsky (1962, 156) has suggested that "the ideal of masculinity into which . . . (men are) . . . socialized inhibits expressiveness both directly, with its emphasis on reserve, and indirectly, by identifying personal interchange with the feminine role." Balswick (1970) found that males are less capable than females of expressing or receiving companionship support from their spouses. His research also supports the view that inadequacy of expressiveness is greatest for the less educated males. Although inexpressiveness may be found among males at all socioeconomic levels, it is especially among the lower class male that expressiveness is seen as being inconsistent with his defined masculine role.

There may be some signs that conditions which have contributed toward the creation of the inexpressive male are in the process of decline. The deemphasis in distinctiveness in dress and fashions between the sexes, as exemplified in the "hippy" movement can be seen as a reaction against the rigidly defined distinctions between the sexes which have characterized American society. The sexless look, as presently being advanced in high fashion, is the logical end reaction to a society which has superficially created strong distinctions between the sexes. Along with the blurring of sexual distinctions in fashion may very well be the shattering of the strong, silent male as a glorified type. There is already evidence of sharp criticisms of the inexpressive male and exposure of him as constituting a "hangup." Marriage counselors, sensitivity group leaders, "hippies," and certainly youth in general, are critical of inexpressiveness, and candid honesty in interpersonal relations. Should these views permeate American society, the inexpressive male may well come to be regarded as a pathetic tragedy instead of the epitome of masculinity and fade from the American scene. Not all may applaud his departure, however. While those interested in more satisfactory male-female relationships, marital and otherwise, will probably gladly see him off, those concerned with more stable marital relationships may greet his departure less enthusiastically. Although it should remove an important barrier to satisfaction in all male-female relationships via an increase in the male's capacity for emotional response toward females, by the same token it also may remove a barrier against emotional entanglement in relations with females outside marital relationships and thus threaten the stability of marriages. If one finds the inexpressive male no longer present one of these days, then, it will be interesting to observe whether any gains in the stability of marriage due to increased male expressiveness *within* this relationship will be enough to offset losses in stability emanating from increasing displays of male expressiveness *outside* it.

REFERENCES

Auerback, Alfred. The Cowboy Syndrome. Summary of research contained in a personal letter from the author, 1970.

Balswick, Jack O. The Effect of Spouse Companionship Support on Employment Success. *Journal of Marriage and the Family*, 1970, 32, 212–215.

Benedict, Ruth. Continuities and Discontinuities in Cultural Conditioning. *Psychiatry*, 1938, 1, 161–167.

Blood, Robert and Donald Wolfe. *Husbands and Wives: The Dynamic of Married Living*. Glencoe, Illinois: The Free Press, 1960.

Cox, Harvey. Playboy's Doctrine of Male. In Wayne H. Cowan (Ed.) *Witness to a Generation: Significant Writings from Christianity and Crisis (1941–1966)*. New York: Bobbs-Merrill Company, 1966.

Hurvitz, Nathan. Marital Strain in the Blue Collar Family. In Arthur Shostak and William Gomberg (Eds.) *Blue-Collar World*. Englewood Cliffs, New Jersey: Prentice-Hall, 1964.

Komarovsky, M. *Blue-Collar Marriage*. New York: Random House, 1962.

Manville, W. H. The Locker Room Boys. *Cosmopolitan*, 1969, 166 (11), 110–115.

Mead, Margaret. *Sex and Temperament in Three Primitive Societies*. New York: William Morrow and Company, 1935.

Popplestone, John. The Horseless Cowboys. *Transaction*, 1966, 3, 25–27.

Rainwater, Lee. *Family Design: Marital Sexuality, Family Size, and Contraception*. Chicago: Aldine Publishing Company, 1965.

23 *Duane Denfeld*

Dropouts From Swinging

A report from marriage counselors who have worked with swinging dropouts, this paper delineates some of the problems encountered.

The literature on swinging, or mate swapping (an agreement between husband and wife to permit sexual relations with other people usually at the same time) has portrayed this behavior as supportive of the marriage. Bartell (1971) reported that swinging appeared to contribute positively to the marital adjustment of a substantial number of his 350 Chicago area respondents. The Smiths (1969) came to a similar conclusion in their study of more than 500 California swingers. A review of all the serious literature on swinging noted that every study reported finding positive contributions in swinging (Denfeld and Gordon, 1970).

Another research finding is that swingers tend to be socially conservative and conforming and do not fit the stereotypical image of deviants. Swingers tend to be otherwise conventional citizens of the community. Although swingers as young as eighteen and as old as 70 have been discovered, the most common age group is 25–35. They are not rebellious youth who have substituted a new value system, but rather people who grew up in the 1940s and 1950s were exposed to the values of the time which included the importance of sexual fidelity and guilt following sexual infidelity. Swingers, nevertheless, report little difficulty in overcoming or replacing values concerned with marital fidelity.

The findings that the consensual exchange of partners can be accomplished without feelings of guilt and without threatening the marriage are surprising to many people including some social scientists. Swingers respond that they have discovered more honest and genuine values and have developed strategies and rules that insure the protection of their marriages and, additionally, serve to give new life and variety to their marital rela-

Duane Denfeld, "Dropouts From Swinging," from *The Family Coordinator*, January, 1974, pp. 45–49. Reprinted with permission.

330

tionship. For example, they view the sexual relationship of the marriage as one of love and of emotion and the consensual extramarital relationship as physical. They drop out of swinging if the wife desires to get pregnant in order to insure that the husband is the child's father. Jealousy is avoided by giving the marriage paramount loyalty and by avoiding emotional attachments to others.

The old sexual values are replaced by new ones with the swingers. It is rationalized that most couples violate the rule of marital fidelity at some time, which results in lying and cheating. Swingers argue that lying and cheating are the damaging aspects in extramarital sex and that if these are removed, non-emotional extramarital sex can be beneficial to the marriage because it can provide excitement and variety without threatening the marriage.

The failures in swinging, or swinging dropouts, have not found their way into studies because of the research designs. Studies of swinging have involved snow-ball samples (the location of one swinger who names others who name further swingers) which are limited to active swingers; the unsuccessful have dropped out. There has not been a study of swingers using a probability sample which would include past, present, and future swingers. The number or proportion of swingers who dropout is unknown.

MARRIAGE COUNSELORS AND SWINGERS

What kinds of problems do swinging dropouts have? What are their reasons for dropping out? On the assumption that at least some swingers who dropout will consult marriage counselors, a questionnaire was sent to 2,147 marriage counselors, all of those listed in the directories of the American Association of Marriage and Family Counselors and the California Association of Marriage and Family Counselors.

Nine hundred and sixty-five questionnaires were returned. Four-hundred and seventy-three counselors had counseled at least one dropout couple. They had seen a total of 1175 couples, an average of 2.5 couples per counselor. Among the remaining counselors who responded, 368 had never counseled a dropout couple, and 125 more indicated that they were retired, inactive, or in specialized practice that would give them no opportunity to counsel swinging dropouts.

It was not entirely clear why one active counselor in general marital practice and not another had counseled swinging dropouts. Some counselors in small cities, for example, had counseled swinging dropouts, but some counselors in cities as large as San Francisco or Los Angeles had not done so. Pastoral counselors had rarely treated ex-swingers and believed it was because the former swingers feared censure or criticism on religious grounds.

Follow-up telephone calls were made to 50 non-responding counselors. Results from the telephone contacts suggested that other counselors had had similar experiences to the respondents. Although the return rate does not permit generalizations about all counselors in the two associations, it is possible to use the returns as a means of gaining some insight into the problems that cause swingers to dropout.

PROBLEMS OF DROPOUTS

Counselors were asked to discuss the histories of clients who had dropped out of swinging. The problems cited by the counselors from the reports of their clients contain no major surprises. The major problems that were reported were:

Jealousy (109).   Jealousy was cited as a reason for dropping out by 109 couples. A typical explanation was that "the husband (or wife) could not handle the jealousy rising out of his (or her) mate having sex with another person." Husbands reported more jealousy than wives. A number of husbands became quite concerned over their wives' popularity or sexual performance (for example, endurance capabilities), or feared that their wives were having more fun than they were. When wives reported jealousy it was more likely related to fear of losing their mate. These findings suggest the influence of the double standard; the emphasis of the husband is on his pleasure and satisfaction as compared to that of his wife, whereas the emphasis of the wife is on the maintenance of the marital unit.

Guilt (68).   This was named as a problem for 68 couples.

Threat to the Marriage (68).   Guilt and jealousy may also be a part of the third most cited problem, the threat to the marital bond (68 couples). Dropout couples report that swinging weakened rather than strengthened the marriage. Swinging can lead to other marital problems. Fighting and hostilities became more frequent after swinging.

Development of Outside Emotional Attachments (53).   Swingers attempt to protect against the development of emotional attachment by swinging only once with another couple and also avoiding expressions of personal feelings such as "I care for you." In spite of these efforts swinging couples have become emotionally attached to people with whom they swing. The emotional attachment to swinging partners in a number of cases led to divorce and sometimes to new marriages. For example, a counselor reported that

"wife A and husband B got divorced and married each other. The husbands couldn't handle it any longer."

In some cases the new emotional attachment in the swinging relationship lasted a short period or led the swinger(s) to a marriage counselor.

Lying, cheating, another violation of swinging rules, was also uncovered, and when clandestine meetings in violation of swingers rules were discovered, conflict or separation resulted. Swinging for those couples did not destroy the interest in extramarital affairs or the possibility of development of emotional attachment.

Boredom and Loss of Interest (49).   The next two reasons cited for dropping out can be described as a gap between fantasy and reality. Swinging for many couples was boring; it did not always provide the excitement that the couple fantasized.

Disappointment (32).   For some other couples swinging did not offer the anticipated benefits and was a disappointment. Complaints included: "did not live up to expectations as to improved relationships with spouse; did not meet emotional needs or social needs; strong dislike for other participating person." Other swinging dropouts said it became boring and uninteresting. The main reason cited for the gap between fantasy and reality was the absence of seduction and emotion necessitated by a swinging relationship.

Divorce or Separation (29).   Divorce or separation was mentioned as a reason for dropping out by 29 couples.

Wife's Inability to "Take It" (29).   Very frequently one partner was more troubled or upset than the other partner. The wife was most likely the one to respond that she could not take it or threatened divorce. These findings bring into question some additional notions concerning swinging. The first belief brought into question is that swinging emphasizes sexual equality (Denfeld and Gordon, 1970) and greatly benefits the wives. Anne-Marie Henshel (1973) has questioned the finding that swinging favors the "wives as much as, and in certain respects, more than their husbands" (Bartell, 1971; Smith and Smith, 1970). Ms. Henshel discovered in her Canadian swinging group that husbands initiated swinging activities 58.7 percent of the time. Wives were the initiators in only twelve percent of the cases. In the other cases the decision was mutual.

If wives are hesitant to swing and have less interest, one can expect more women to initiate the dropping out. Some writers have argued, however, that women, once they "get their feet wet," enjoy swinging more than men. The findings here do not support that view; dropping out was initiated by the wives 54 percent of the time, by the husbands 34 percent, and mutually twelve percent of the time.

The marriage counselors suggested that wives were considerably more bothered by swinging than husbands. Wives expressed such feelings as disgust or repulsion. Husbands were more likely to initiate dropping out not for reasons of distaste but because they were bothered by their wife's popularity.

Wives were forced into swinging as a promise or commitment to the marriage. Husbands were described as "children with new toys." One counselor expressed a common finding: "In all my cases (3) the men initiated the swinging and the women forced the termination."

The enthusiasm of the men was not matched by a similar feeling by the women. Swinging was a way for some of the men to have sexual variety, but they needed their wives to accomplish it. In such cases the double standard and exploitation of women is very much a part of the arrangement. Wives were forced into swinging for the husbands' benefit. Swinging also demonstrated male dominance in terms of male impotence resulting from their contact with "aggressive women" and an inability to accomplish sexual intercourse.

Fear of Discovery (15).   Another problem experienced by swingers was the fear of discovery by the community or their children of their swinging activities. Swinging couples dropped out to satisfy neighbors who had discovered their swinging activities. The white collar or professional backgrounds of swingers makes discovery a threat to their business and social reputation. A number of counselors reported that couples dropped out because their children were beginning to question their activities. This was particularly true for couples with teenage children. In cases where the children had discovered the swinging activity family functioning was seriously disturbed. Because the parents had kept their swinging activities a secret from their children, discovery came as a shock to the children.

CURRENT SWINGERS

Counselors were also asked to discuss clients who are presently engaged in swinging. Of the 620 counselors who responded to this question, 192 were counseling couples who were presently swinging. A comparison of the problems experienced by current swingers and dropouts was undertaken. The two lists were very similar, with jealousy, guilt, and threat to marriage leading both lists. The major difference between the two lists was the greater presence of "fears" in the current swingers' list of problems. Active swingers report fears of discovery by children and the community, venereal disease, and rejection. This difference is not surprising because the dropouts had already been discovered or had avoided detection and would not report this as a fear. It would appear that the fears exceeded the real dangers, although a number of dropouts had been discovered by neighbors or had been infected with venereal disease.

That contemporary swingers in this study reported problems is not surprising since they were taking part in counseling, but it also is important to note that all but 25 of the active swingers linked their problems to swinging. Swinging difficulties for many active swingers were the problems that brought them to the marriage counselor.

IMPROVED MARITAL RELATIONS

Not all of the results of swinging were reported as negative. Of the 425 couples for whom such information was available, 170 reported improvement in the marital relationship. A number of those couples, however, discovered that the improvement was temporary.

The reasons given by the couples—with the number of couples cited—were as follows: excitement (49), sexual freedom (36), greater appreciation of mate (35), learning of new sex techniques (35), sexual variety (34), and better communication or openness between partners (20).

To such persons, swinging seems to deliver its promises in terms of excitement, sexual freedom, and variety, and to provide a safe and non-threatening method of experiencing a sexual revolution. Some swingers are able to find exciting if only temporary sexual intercourse with a number of different partners and at the same time maintain a permanent relationship. The dropouts, however, are troubled by jealousy, guilt, and the development of emotional ties to swinging partners.

CONCLUSION AND IMPLICATIONS

This report from marriage counselors does not allow a rejection of the optimistic view of swinging. It does, however, raise some questions as to the extent of positive outcomes and portrays some of the problems associated with the consensual exchange of marriage partners. Previously, problems of swinging received little attention because only successful swingers were likely to be included in the research studies. There is also the possibility that some swinging researchers have been "swinging" researchers and advocates, sometimes with a missionary zeal, of swinging as a positive activity.

The delineation of problems may add some balance to the understanding of swinging. It is clear from the marriage counselors' reports that many couples left swinging hurt and psychologically damaged. The positive image previously presented may have encouraged couples to engage in swinging. The indications are that some couples are not emotionally capable of or prepared for swinging. Knowing these things should give pause to anyone who is inclined to recommend or imply that swinging will help a couple's marriage.

The results of the reports also challenge the argument that swinging demonstrates the realization of equality of the sexes. Husbands often forced wives into swinging and wives were more dissatisfied with swinging and more frequently initiated the dropping out. Rather than being equalitarian, swinging is more likely to be a truly "sexist" activity.

REFERENCES

Bartell, Gilbert. *Group Sex,* New York: Wyden, 1971.

Denfeld, D. and Michael Gordon. The Sociology of Mate Swapping. *Journal of Sex Research,* 1970, pp. 85–100.

Henshel, Anne-Marie. Swinging: A Study of Decision Making in Marriage. *American Journal of Sociology,* January, 1973, 78:4, pp. 885–891.

Smith, J. R. and L. G. Smith. Co-Marital Sex and the Sexual Freedom Movement. *Journal of Sex Research.* 1969, 6, pp. 131–142.

24 *Edith G. Neisser*

Emotional and Social Values Attached to Money

When economists and sociologists discuss money, they view it as a serviceable tool used by sensible men. As Freud and his circle first pointed out, money has in addition to its objective significance a variety of subjective aspects, both individually and culturally, which have a forceful impact on personality.[1]

"To date there has been no adequate research on the complicated relationship between the psychological and economic factors in living in a money world," Feldman asserts.[2] Advancing knowledge of the dynamics of behavior has made it clear that money plays an important role in the emotional and social adjustment and, therefore, in the development of values of individuals and families no matter where they stand financially.

In different phases of his development and at different levels of his experience the young adult has been coping with various meanings of money since his earliest childhood, as Ferenczi and Taeuber set forth.[3]

THE BEGINNINGS OF MONEY

In prehistoric times all social relations, including economic activities, were regarded as religious acts. The origin of money in Western culture, Desmonde suggests, may be traced to the animal sacrifices in Greece and Crete.[4] The ritual of the common meal on the sacred sacrificial bull or cow was an early form of obtaining and distributing food. The communal

Edith Neisser, "Emotional and Social Values Attached to Money." *Marriage and Family Living*, vol. 22, no. 2 (May 1960), pp. 132–138. Reprinted by permission.

Adapted from a paper "The Many Faces of Money" presented at the conference of the National Council on Family Relations, Ames, Iowa, August 20, 1959.

feast also represented mother's milk. The wish to incorporate oneself within the bull goddess who symbolized the mother was another element in these ceremonies.

In addition, or perhaps because of its religious importance, the bull became, further along in the development of Greek society, the unit of value. Still later, when gold came into circulation, its value was based upon the value of the cow.[5]

The psychoanalysts make a connection between the acquisition of money and finding the security of a mother substitute. The sacred bulls and cows were related to the mother goddess. These animals were then converted into monetary units. In acquiring money, therefore, one unconsciously gained the protection of the mother.[6]

Medals, which gradually came to be used as coins, began as amulets having magic powers, Desmonde and Garnet maintain.[7] In the sacrificial system of antiquity an offering was frequently made for the purpose of propitiating dead parents. He who offered up the animal was customarily rewarded by the chief with an amulet. This honor signified, among other things, the good opinion of the ruler.

Indirectly it was the equivalent of the approval of parents; so we may infer that in the earliest social groups the desire to acquire money was motivated by the wish for paternal love.

A different theme also runs through primitive myths, to which Freud calls attention.[8] Frequently in the fairy tales the devil presents his admirers with gold. Then he disappears and the gold turns to filth. The devil in these tales may be equated with the unconscious. We speak of someone being "filthy rich," as Jones reminds us,[9] nor have we entirely discarded the Roman proverb *pecunia olet*.[10]

The formulators of psychoanalytic theory tell us that the beliefs and practices of prehistoric cultures have a parallel in the symbols which occur in the mental life of the individual. "The renunciation of the instinctual gratifications which took place as man became civilized are approximated as the young child becomes domesticated," was Freud's statement quoted by Desmonde.[11]

The Freudian principle that during the second year of life an infant goes through the anal-erotic phase of his psycho-sexual development is sufficiently familiar to need no elaboration. Freud states that the value attaching to money is a "direct continuation of the value the infant attaches to his own excrement. . . . Between the most valuable substance a man possesses and the least valuable, there is a strong association."[12] In the consciousness of the adult, this value is replaced by opposite feelings, but in the unconscious, the equation of money with feces continues.

The individual who in infancy becomes unduly concerned with withholding feces, may become the parsimonious, indeed, the miserly person in adulthood.[13] Extreme saving, collecting, and hoarding are associated with gratification in holding back excrement.

Ferenczi traced the sequence from infantile pleasure in fecal matter to an interest in mud, as the infant learns that certain odors are unacceptable.[14] Then delight in sand replaces absorption in mud. This, in turn, is replaced by a fascination with pebbles, marbles, buttons, and (if we may bring Ferenczi up-to-date) bottle tops. Finally, coins themselves become objects to be acquired as the child sees that adults consider these superior to his treasures.

Fenichel explains that the function money usually performs in the realm of reality reinforces the anal-erotically conditioned instinct of accumulation for "there is a reciprocal interaction between the basic instincts and the social system."[15]

Feelings about money, then, go deep, both in the history of the race and in the unfolding of personality.

CHILDREN AND MONEY

Young people come to college with attitudes toward money derived from direct experiences with it, from explicit teachings in their homes and the implicit teachings of the culture. The total emotional tone of the family plays a part in the values its members develop about money. In Prevey's study of middle class high school students,[16] she found that satisfactory emotional relationships in childhood tended to be of some significance in the ability to manage money in early adulthood.

Children who grow up in homes where parents have been unable to meet their need for love may use money as a substitute for affection. Inner anxiety may drive them to overvalue possessions, especially dollars and cents. Emotional deprivation has long been familiar to the personnel of child guidance clinics as a prime cause of stealing. The overvaluing of money may show up either in hanging on tightly to everything or quite the other way: these lonely children may lavish inappropriate gifts on everyone and give away anything they have in an effort to purchase the affection they sorely miss.

Actual poverty, parental unemployment, and acute economic insecurity usually heighten the worries and bafflements of childhood.[17]

As Lauterbach affirms, "The economic failure of parents, siblings or other prominent childhood figures has an important emotional effect on the child. It either leads to hostility or rejection toward the parents, which may not come out in the open until later in life, or to hidden guilt feelings, which likewise may warp emotional development."[18] The guilt feelings stem from childish fantasies of omnipotence which result in a child's convincing himself that his own conduct or spoken or unspoken wishes brought misfortune on the household.

That acute poverty may engender either vaulting ambition or apathy is a familiar concept, but the effects of an economy of abundance on personality, as set forth by Potter have fresh and provocative implications. The thesis of *People of Plenty* is that for the first time in the history of mankind, we in the United States have had a sufficiency—in land, in natural resources, in opportunities for work and, it also follows, in money. To a greater degree than in other cultures and other eras "work calling urgently for workmen," rather than "the worker seeking humbly any kind of toil," has been the prevailing pattern. "As a suppliant to his superiors, the worker under scarcity accepted the principle of authority. . . . Such a man naturally transferred the principle of authority to his own family."[19]

Authoritarianism's wane in the family, then, is to be attributed not only to the findings of clinics and consulting rooms, but to the fact that it was possible to earn or to hope for a decent portion, not merely crumbs and scraps.

Against this socio-economic background, let us survey the wide range of approaches to children's monetary experiences in vogue today, which, in turn, may throw light on the values evidenced by the college student.

"The dole system" for giving children spending money sets no fixed amount to be dispensed at given intervals. As a result, the children become adept at managing their parents rather than their pennies. They learn how to wheedle, cajole, and browbeat their elders for quarters and half dollars, but they learn little else.

Some parents insist children should earn every cent they receive, lest they grow up believing one gets something for nothing. In these families the children are generally paid for helping with household tasks. They grow to regard everything and everyone as having a price, while cooperation, mutual aid, and similar values which make for emotional depth and richness tend to go undeveloped.

A school of thought akin to this one uses money as a tool for discipline and as a reward for virtuous or at least tolerable behavior. This may lead to an improvement in conduct, but, as Gruenberg demonstrated, it may also lead to a deterioration in social values.[20]

A variation of this plan is to give an allowance but to institute an elaborate system of fines and penalties. The fallacy here is that a boy or girl absorbs the notion that cash payments amply atone for misbehavior or negligence and social responsibility tends to be vitiated.

Then there are the families, and, from what one observes, their tribe *is* increasing, who give their children a modest, regular, noncontingent allowance, the amount and scope of which is increased through the years. These children carry responsibility for making family life more comfortable without being paid. Opportunities are offered to earn extra sums by doing additional tasks. Children in such families stand a better chance of learning that money is a medium of exchange which can buy goods and services, but it is not synonymous with virtue, nor can it absolve a person from obligations to his fellows.[21]

The Prevey study of family practices in regard to money indicated that "the kinds of experience offered in using money bore little relationship to independence at the high school level, but was positively related to the ability to utilize financial resources in early adulthood."[22]

Among the notions which children glean from adult conversation, radio, TV, and the movies is the belief that those things which cost the most are worth the most. Some children fantasy that all who have wealth have obtained it by magical or by dishonest means. Many of those who grow up surrounded by industrious adults gain the impression that those who work hardest will have the most money.

An unfortunate approach to values, from the writer's observations, seems to be resulting from the practice of setting up in the elementary grades, right down to kindergarten, savings accounts for children. Deposits are brought to school at stated times and credited, through the bank which sponsors the scheme, to a child's own savings account. Children are not learning thrift in this way, for, as Jordan points out, "Financial education comprehends far more than the accumulation of credit entries."[23] Usually it is not even money they have saved which they so proudly bring to school. The insidious pressure exerted to bring a good round sum, leads to wheedling it from a mother, who may even find this a convenient way to put aside a dollar or two. What is more, accumulation, not wise spending, is stressed as the ultimate value, and the irrational hoarding which often characterizes the years of middle childhood is given support.

Most children are rigorously taught not to steal money from an individual, but cheating a corporation is condoned in many families. Conflicts in values arise, too, because what is encouraged as promising business acumen in one situation is berated as unethical in another setting. It is not easy for a child or even an adolescent to distinguish between the co-operatively oriented group such as the family, the Scout troop, and so forth, and the market place where profit taking is the very reason for entering into a business venture.

The adolescent's values in regard to money are one complex aspect of his struggle to find his identity, Feldman explains.[24] His tendency to be highly critical of his parents' spending and saving, and of their standard of living, is part of his repudiation of parental ways in order to establish his own.

According to Potter, the adolescent's conflicts are multiplied by our custom of delaying his economic responsibility and urging his pseudo-sophistication and social activities. This dichotomy arises out of the economy of abundance, for only in a culture of plenty could young persons be indulged with the dubious advantage of an excessive amount of play and a minimal amount of work.[25]

Some adolescents use money as one more weapon in their arsenal for attacking their parents. Others, with whom the demand for money always outruns the supply, are unconsciously equating money with love. Their demand is really to know they are still accepted, and in receiving money they *feel* they are gaining proof that such is the case.

MONEY AND THE CULTURE

Each individual will have a different combination of meanings which he attaches to money, selected consciously or unconsciously from among those current in the community. These meanings might be thought of as occurring in overlapping, contiguous layers like the leaves of a cabbage. They may not always dovetail as neatly as do cabbage leaves, for one may contradict the other.

In the outside "layer" human worth equals financial success, Feldman, Gorer, Landis and Lauterbach agree.[26] Horatio Alger is still the culture hero and "to make good" the object in life.

Packard explains that one reason why money is a source of prestige may be found in the geographical mobility of the average American family, which moves once every five years.[27] Tangible possessions and the kind of job one holds establish who and what one is to a far greater degree than would be the case in a community where everyone was well acquainted with the ancestry, background and achievements of his neighbor.

Prestige in one's own eyes constitutes another "layer" of attitudes about finances. For some individuals money which can be used for consumer goods is almost synonymous with self-respect.

Money also stands for power, a third layer of meaning. The member of the family who pays the rent is admired and catered to. Many of those who hang on tightly to their money fear that in relinquishing any of it, or surely the control of it, they will relinquish power.

Packard claims that frequently men of substantial means are careful to deny that they possess either wealth or power.[28] Does this perhaps go back to the distant past of the race when stating a name or a fact out loud robbed it of its magic potency?

On another less openly acknowledged level the ownership of dollars is a sign that one is worthy of love, just as the achievement of good grades in childhood at school guaranteed parental approval.[29]

On a deeper level the possession or the spending of money may take the place of love.[30] This is particularly likely to happen to young adults on their own for the first time. Some may become extremely frugal, because funds in the bank represent emotional even more than financial security. Others spend more than they should, lavishing unnecessary luxuries on themselves, as if they were giving themselves the affection others seem to be denying them.

For a man the earning of money may equal competition, Lauterbach says.[31] It stands consciously or unconsciously for the abandonment of the security of childhood. There is a type of personality who is afraid of assuming his place as a strong, independent male, who prefers to continue to be the good child cared for by indulgent parents. He may repeatedly maneuver himself into a situation where he will lose his job, thus relieving his anxiety about competing and his fear of the dangers of success.

Those to whom competition is more congenial find money and what it buys to be the means, par excellence, of proving one is ahead. The struggle to equal or, preferably, to surpass one's fellows has its roots in early rivalries at home. To see one's neighbor possess what one had not been able to acquire, or has not even thought of acquiring, is painful. One therefore makes haste to acquire it, and "one man's consumption becomes another man's wish," as Galbraith phrases it.[32]

Currently, keeping down with the Joneses has become even more important than keeping up with them, as Whyte's studies have shown.[33] The young couple who could afford to furnish their home more comfortably, drive a better car or take a more interesting vacation than their neighbors or fellow employees hesitates to do so. As for making it appear that one could afford as much or more than the family in the next higher echelon at the office or the plant—that would be a fatal error.[34]

In the higher economic brackets new possessions or ostentatiousness are regarded as vulgar, in the real sense of that word or as being "for the crowd," while inconspicuous consumption becomes the hallmark of superiority.[35] The simplicity which only money can buy or wealth give the courage to maintain is expressed in a bit of folklore about the two psychiatrists who were discussing the car one of them was about to purchase. "Why don't you get a Cadillac? It's a good car and you drive a lot." "No," was the answer, "I'm not sick in that way."

GUILT-EDGED SECURITY

These socio-economic values attached to money in our culture may be more or may be less acknowledged, more or less unconscious in different individuals. There are also deeper layers in the superego attributing guilt-tinged meanings to money and tending to create conflicts within the individual. Lauterbach describes these as, first "The continued influence of pre-capitalistic values in a capitalist world . . . and the medieval aesthetic negation of personal gain . . . [which] may plague the apparently money-mad individual with opposing values."[36]

The disapproval of early Christianity and other religions of the accumulation and especially the borrowing and lending of money constitutes another layer in conscience.

The Calvinistic tradition of hard work and thrift compose still another layer of superego attitudes.[37] Frugality and the accumulation of capital were essential to the economy of scarcity in a frontier nation. With present pressures to "go now, pay later," "visit your friendly loan company" and to "have the house (or the boat, or the figure, or the TV set) of your dreams today, no down payment," some agonizing reappraisal is required to square current customs with puritan economic teaching. The sacred character of savings is neatly caricatured in the apocryphal story of the New England spinster who took to street-walking, "Because," she said, "returns on investments are so slight nowadays, and, of course one wouldn't want to dip into capital."

Whether or not one agrees with all its tenets, the very existence, let alone the popularity of John Kenneth Galbraith's *The Affluent Society*[38] attests to the profound influence of eighteenth and nineteenth century economics on present day thinking and feeling. One need not be explicitly aware of the doctrines of Riccardo or William Graham Sumner to be relieved when someone makes the reassuring statement, as Galbraith does, that it is not sinful to behave in a fashion contrary to their economic principles. A book devoted to proving that eighteenth and nineteenth century psychology, much less physics or medicine, are outmoded would hardly be a revelation. Yet when an economist sets at naught the classic teaching of his discipline, the reading public, which presumably includes the college student, is awestruck.

Another layer of guilt feelings interprets the financial reverses and crises the individual encounters as punishment for too much emphasis on making money.[39]

Finally "reform movements which set up definite noneconomic values," says Lauterbach, "tend to generate guilt about measuring personal success in financial terms."[40]

Individuals in reasonably good mental health may have a number of these layers, conscious or unconscious, in their emotional repertoire. A functioning ego may keep a working balance and make it possible for the individual to cope effectively with money in his daily life. When one or another of these attitudes becomes a person's only approach to finances and colors his entire outlook on other matters as well, then difficulties are likely to arise.

MONEY IN A MARRIAGE

The husband and wife each brings to the partnership his experiences, his own hopes and anxieties about money as well as values derived from his ethnic, social, and economic background. The symbolic meanings family finances take on, together with the real problems of making ends meet and obtaining satisfactions each finds important results in "money being the major problem area of married couples today," according to Paul H. Landis.[41]

The research of Judson T. Landis found money difficulties second only to problems of sex adjustment in eight categories checked by 409 sets of parents of college students. Fifty percent of these successfully married husbands and wives said in reply to a questionnaire that money matters had been satisfactorily handled from the beginning, but the remainder said it had taken months or even years to come to terms with financial matters.[42] Revealing as is this testimony in itself, its implications in the light of the experiences of caseworkers and counselors are still more important.

Family counselors, as Feldman pointed out, find that while money may precipitate quarrels, it is not the basis of domestic difficulties as frequently as the marital partners themselves tend to believe.[43] In a marriage in which mutual trust and willingness to compromise predominate, normal differences about money do not necessarily lead to neurotic difficulties over income and outgo.[44] In a good marriage, the amount of money a couple has, and even how it is budgeted and spent, do not weigh as heavily in the harmony of the relationship as how the couple feel about financial matters.

Terman found in his studies of factors in marital happiness, that there was no correlation between the amount of income a couple had and their satisfaction in their marriage.[45] Counselors are aware that two couples may have the same income and similar obligations—indeed, similar backgrounds, too—yet one couple consider themselves well provided for while the other couple are in debt and bemoan their inadequate funds.

Katona's level of aspiration elucidates this dichotomy.[46] Somewhere between what a person can achieve and his ideal for achievement lies a point which would satisfy him at that moment. This highly individualized level of aspiration goes up with success and down with failure.

When a couple are not making a satisfactory adjustment, feelings originating in other areas often are transferred to money, for "money is a device through which a subtle struggle for power and dominance may be waged," says Paul H. Landis.[47] One may deny a wife or husband the right to use money when unconsciously one is refusing to give love. It is far more acceptable socially to complain that a wife is extravagant than to admit that she is slovenly; to berate a husband for being niggardly than to face the fact that he is a crashing bore. Economic matters may be a safety valve too. Quarrels about money may drain off animosity generated in other aspects of living.

Money may also be a weapon for attacking a marital partner.[48] The man who fears his wife is dominating him may spend an unwarranted sum on his hobbies or in gambling, in contrast to his usual conservative habits, because he is determined to show "who is boss."

The woman who feels neglected by her husband typically goes out and spends more than she should, thus acting out her resentment and giving herself the attention she would like to be getting from him. Wild extravagance is often the unconsciously selected device of the person who is extremely dependent on his or her parents. Abraham discussed the wife who, away from her parents, becomes anxious or depressed and strives to relieve her anxiety by random buying.[49] She is proving, symbolically, through her aimless buying that she can direct her psychic energy where she pleases, and that she really is not tied to her parents after all.

WORKING WIVES

With one-fourth of the students on campuses currently married,[50] two aspects of the financial situation which are heavily weighted emotionally for young couples are working wives and parental subsidies. According to Glick, 40 percent of the wives in the general population were working in the period immediately following World War II.[51]

For a well integrated young man and woman who appreciate the necessity and the value of a wife providing income, there may be practical difficulties to solve, but the fact that a wife is gainfully employed outside her home is not an impediment to a happy marriage, according to Burgess and Cottrell.[52] It is when a woman's being an earner carries unfavorable meanings for either partner that conflict arises.

The very idea of his wife as an income producer may be an affront to the man who is not completely secure in his role as protector and provider. If he is nagged by guilt because his wife is carrying the burden, he may become overbearing, critical, and demanding just when his wife feels he should be appreciative.

Wives have also been known to feel cheated if the role of the dependent partner comes too easily to a man.

A woman may consciously or unconsciously, openly or secretly, resent the fact that she must hold a job to finance her husband's education. Her resentment may lead her to be dominating or deprecating, or perhaps to treat him indulgently like "a good little boy."

Quite the other way, some girls welcome the more readily recognized productivity of a paid position. Does this indicate that they are being competitive with men? If it does, then perhaps paid employment for them is a useful channel for draining off competition.

Unfortunately, being an earner sometimes reinforces competitive feelings. "My money" in contradistinction to "our money" or "your money" becomes another tool for proving superiority.

PARENTAL HELP

No well-established custom decrees how or to what extent parents shall assist their married sons and daughters. A wide range of helping patterns has been found workable, and various rationalizations are invoked to justify withholding or refusing to accept assistance.

The success or failure of any arrangement rests far more on the relationship of the persons involved and what giving or receiving financial aid signifies to each, than on the economic need or the amount or kind of subsidy.

Subsidies or frequent gifts may appear to be a threat—a way of continuing a dependent state—or be realistically a welcome source of temporary assistance. Such help can be granted as a bribe, withheld as a punishment, or given freely as a token of confidence. The values of parental assistance can only be assessed in the context of the total relationship.

Sussman, in his investigation of helping patterns in middle class New Haven families, found that the regular stipend was far less acceptable from the older generation than assistance in the form of presents on appropriate occasions or service when an extra pair of hands was needed. He also found that parents expected to stand by their children after marriage.[53] Hollingshead, who also carried on research in New Haven, found that the young families he studied usually started with about $1400 worth of cash or merchandise; so whether they realized it or not, they were actually receiving help.[54]

WHAT CAN BE DONE, SPECIFICALLY?

On the basis of the multiple meanings money has and has had for young people, what can be done in college to support constructive values?

Is it possible that in discussing money in courses in marriage, more interpretation of its emotional significance might be in order? Techniques of budgeting and of using banking and credit facilities might be explained as more useful when one is aware of what may lie beneath overt behavior. For instance, many of the excellent college texts[55] speak of the stereotype of the extravagant woman and the more conservative man. The productive orientation of the man and the woman's orientation toward consumption are explained on the basis of role. Might our students be able to grasp an interpretation of the dynamics of some women's dependency needs which lead to overspending, as well as the equating of the financial control with masculinity in some men? Further insight might help students evaluate their goals and understand their prejudices.

Both in counseling and in the classroom, Lauterbach's comment has some thought provoking implications: "Is it asking too much of the educator not to take the social framework and the norms of his own period for granted, not to interpret his role toward the student as an attorney for the social order, even though the teacher, like the therapist, represents 'society' in a formal and clinical sense?"[56]

Outside the classroom—and the writer is aware that this is even more dangerous ground to tread—can we attempt to create an atmosphere which does not stress either keeping up or down with those fearsome Joneses? A college community is uniquely situated for demonstrating to its inhabitants what money is really good for and what you cannot buy with it.

Perhaps the best preparation for the market place in which most of our students will spend their lives is not to make the campus a microcosm of that market place. Could we offer through academic and extracurricular activities a release from market-place pressures and the overvaluing of market-place personalities?

If college campuses were to be, as they were originally intended to be, a working demonstration of a community bound together by common interests with a common purpose of more than a pedestrian nature, we might grow values that would make it possible for many of our students to understand and cope with the many faces of money in our culture, rather than being confused and beguiled too often by the false smile some of those faces present.

ENDNOTES

1. Otto Fenichel, "The Desire to Amass Wealth," *Collected Papers of Otto Fenichel*, New York: Norton, 1954; Sandor Ferenczi, "Onto-genesis of the Interest in Money," *Sex in Psychoanalysis*, Boston: Badger, 1922; Sigmund Freud, "Character and Anal Eroticism," *Collected Papers*, Vol. II, London: Hogarth Press, 1949.
2. Frances Lomas Feldman, *The Family in a Money World*, New York: Family Service Association, 1957, p. 160.
3. Ferenczi, *op. cit.*; Walter Taeuber, "Psychologie des Geldes," *Journal Psychologie und Psychotherapie*, No. 1 (1953), pp. 14–36.

4. William H. Desmonde, "Origin of Money in the Animal Sacrifice," *Journal of Hillside Hospital*, Vol. 6, No. 1 (1957), pp. 7–23.
5. *Ibid.*
6. *Ibid.*
7. William H. Desmonde, "Anal Origin of Money," *American Imago*, 10 (1953), pp. 375–378; Louis Garnet, "La Notion Mythique de la Valeur en Grece," *Journal Normal et Pathologique*, 41 (1948), pp. 415–462.
8. *Op. cit.*
9. Ernest Jones, "Anal Erotic Character Traits," *Papers on Psychoanalysis*, 5th ed., Baltimore: William and Wilkins, 1948.
10. Sandor Ferenczi, "Pecunia Olet," *Further Contributions to Theory and Technique of Psychoanalysis*, London: Hogarth Press, 1926.
11. Desmonde (note 7), p. 376.
12. "Character and Anal Eroticism," (note 1), p. 50.
13. Jones, *op. cit.*
14. "Ontogenesis of the Interest in Money," (note 1).
15. *Op. cit.*, p. 90.
16. Esther E. Prevey, "A Quantitative Study of Family Practices in Training Children in the Use of Money," *Journal of Educational Psychology*, 36 (1945), pp. 411–428.
17. Feldman, (note 2).
18. Albert Lauterbach, *Men, Motives, and Money*, Ithaca: Cornell University Press, 1954.
19. David M. Potter, *People of Plenty*, Chicago: University of Chicago Press, 1954, p. 205.
20. Sidonie M. Gruenberg and Hilda S. Kretch, *Pennies in Their Pockets*, Chicago: Science Research Associates, 1955.
21. Edith G. Neisser, *The Many Faces of Money*, New York: Mental Health Materials Center, 1958.
22. *Op. cit.*, p. 421.
23. David J. Jordan and Edward F. Willet, *Managing Personal Finances*, New York: Prentice-Hall, 1951.
24. *Op. cit.*
25. *Op. cit.*
26. Feldman, (note 2); Geoffrey Gorer, *The American People*, New York: Norton, 1948; Paul H. Landis, *Making the Most of Your Marriage*, New York: Appleton, 1951; Lauterbach, *op. cit.*
27. Vance Packard, *The Status Seekers*, New York: McKay, 1959.
28. *Ibid.*
29. Gorer, *op. cit.*
30. Feldman, (note 2).
31. *Op. cit.*, (note 18).
32. John Kenneth Galbraith, *The Affluent Society*, Boston: Houghton Mifflin, 1958.
33. William H. Whyte, *The Organization Man*, New York: Simon and

Schuster, 1956; William H. Whyte, "How the New Suburbia Socializes," *Fortune*, 48 (July, 1953), pp. 84–89, 156–160.

34. Whyte, *ibid.;* see also Packard, *op. cit.*

35. Galbraith, *op. cit.;* and Packard, *op. cit.*

36. *Men, Motives, and Money* (note 18), p. 140.

37. Lauterbach, *op. cit.*

38. Galbraith, *op. cit.*

39. Lauterbach, *op. cit.*

40. *Ibid.*, p. 141.

41. *Making the Most of Your Marriage*, p. 367.

42. "Adjustment After Marriage," *Marriage and Family Living*, 9 (1947), pp. 32–34.

43. *Op. cit.*, (note 2).

44. Neisser, *op. cit.*

45. Louis Terman, *Psychological Factors in Marital Happiness*, New York: McGraw-Hill, 1939.

46. George Katona, *Psychological Analysis of Economic Behavior*, New York: McGraw-Hill, 1951.

47. *Op. cit.*, p. 368.

48. Feldman, (note 2).

49. Karl Abraham, "The Spending of Money in Anxiety States," *Selected Papers of Karl Abraham*, London: Hogarth Press, 1927.

50. William M. Smith, Jr., personal communication to the author, 7/9/59.

51. Paul Glick, "The Life Cycle of the Family," *Marriage and Family Living*, 17 (1955), pp. 1–39.

52. Ernest Burgess and Leonard Cottrell, *Predicting Success and Failure in Marriage*, New York: Prentice-Hall, 1939.

53. Marvin B. Sussman, "Helping Patterns in the Middle Class Family," *American Sociological Review*, 18 (February, 1953), pp. 22–28.

54. August B. Hollingshead, *Elm Town's Youth*, New York: Wiley, 1949.

55. Howard F. Bigelow, *Family Finances*, Philadelphia: Lippincott, 1936; Robert O. Blood, *Anticipating Your Marriage*, Glencoe: Free Press, 1953; Robert G. Foster, *Marriage and Family Relationships*, New York: Macmillan, 1950; Jordan and Willets, *op. cit.;* Paul H. Landis, *op. cit.;* Robert F. Winch, *The Modern Family*, New York: Holt, 1952.

56. (Note 18), p. 298.

WHAT DO YOU THINK?

Ray was the youngest of ten children, all married with children. His parents, two grandparents, and one great-grandparent lived in the same city and were very close. When he married Roberta, who was an only child whose parents and only one uncle and aunt lived in the city, his family rallied around her and took her into the clan with such enthusiasm that they absorbed all of her time. The couple spent nearly all their social time with Ray's family, saw Roberta's relatives only once or twice a year, and had no outside friends. Roberta did not protest at first, but later she wanted to spend more time with her own family. Ray was uncomfortable with his in-laws and felt it was the woman's place to fit into the man's side of the family. As long as they had relatives, they did not need other friends.

What should the husband know about his wife's need for social life?

How could the couple distribute their social time between the two sides of the family?

Where could Ray have developed the attitude that his side of the family is more important than Roberta's?

Sally and Samuel have been married two years and are expecting their first child. The members of both their families keep talking about the baby as "he," and all the baby gifts are blue. There is no particular reason why a boy is so important to the family, as the family name will be carried by other members. Sally thinks it would be nice to have a girl but would not dare mention this to Samuel or any other member of the family.

How does prejudice against having a girl affect wives? How might it affect daughters?

When Walter and Wendy were dating, they only went out to dinner a few times. These were special occasions, and they enjoyed each other's company. However, after they married, Walter became the silent dinner partner at home. He enjoyed the food but only grunted when Wendy tried to talk. She had come from a family in which dinner was the time to visit with other members, tell the things that had happened during the day, and generally have fun. But Walter's father had been silent and insisted the children refrain from unnecessary talk. They were not aware of this basic difference in philosophy before they married.

What do you see as the best way to adjust to the problem?

It takes longer to eat if you talk at the same time. What are the good points of each plan? Which would you select for your family?

When Tim and Thora were married, they had no money saved. Tim brought home about $700 per month, and they had no trouble getting credit, so they bought good furniture and other household equipment. Then one evening Tim came home in great excitement. He had traded their old car for a new, expensive sports car. His other car covered the down payment, and he arranged for 36 months to pay the rest. When they paid the rent of $200 per month and made all the credit payments, there was nothing left to live on. Tim insisted that Thora go to work and help to support them. Thora said, "We agreed we would talk over any big expenses before buying anything." Tim replied, "But I am the head of this family, and you have the furniture. I think I deserve something, too."

How could they have avoided this muddle?

How much credit can they afford on his salary?

What does this tell you about the maturity of both Tim and Thora?

Vern and Vera knew each other's families before they married. At that time, they addressed the parents of the other as Mr. and Mrs. Now these people had become in-laws and deserved a term which indicated the closer relationship. Vera said, "I don't know what to call your mother and father. Mr. and Mrs. sound so formal, and I don't know them well enough to give them nicknames." Vern suggested, "Why don't you call them what I do, Mom and Pop?" "They may think these names belong to you and that I would be trying to get too familiar," said Vera. Vern got an idea: "For that matter, what do I call your parents?" Vera replied, "Well, I call my father Daddy, but that is my own name for him."

They did not come to an agreement about what to call the new parents-in-law. How would you settle this problem?

How can the names affect good in-law relations?

Our language needs a term for in-laws. What should this be for the father-in-law? For the mother-in-law?

As the son-in-law or daughter-in-law, what would you like to be called?

Issues of Marital Problems

The "live happily ever after" theme is deeply imbedded in our culture. But any two people can disagree, especially if they live together constantly or live in close quarters. Marriage is not so much a state reached as a continuing process—a meshing of two people into a unit without complete loss of individual personalities. This process can produce conflicts, or at least differences of opinion. One person should not give in to the other constantly, to deny completely his own ideals or ideas, nor should he force the other to give in all the time. The modern development of companionship in marriage rules out complete absorption by one spouse of the personality of the other.

How do we maintain the delicate balance between individuality and cooperation in marriage? Evelyn M. Duvall and Reuben Hill show how mutual acceptance and respect can be reinforced when each person's feelings gain expression. They emphasize that both parties have a right, and even the responsibility, to recognize negative aspects building up in the relationship, and either partner may initiate the process of solving problems or differences. In other words, either spouse can "start a fight." Whether negative feelings are mutual or one-sided, giving vent to these feelings opens the path for solutions, for negative feelings may snowball and become serious issues. When bad feelings are out of the way, the good ones are left; now there is room for cooperative efforts.

Among the issues that crop up—early or late—in marriage are those of how husbands and wives treat each other. Paul Popenoe investigated this and found that wives in several countries had these complaints about husbands:[1]

1. They lack tenderness. It seems to be easy to complain but hard to compliment and hard to use words of endearment.

[1] Paul Popenoe, *Sex, Love and Marriage* (New York: Belmont Books, 1963), pp. 144–146. Used by permission of the author.

2. They forget to be polite. Perhaps they see this only as company behavior, but developing and maintaining patterns of courtesy can pay dividends.

3. They may refuse to be sociable at home. The husband who is a great social person at the office may come home and scarcely talk to his wife or children.

4. They lack patience. They may give way to their own feelings and fail to understand that wives and children also have moods or peculiarities, that they may not always feel just right.

5. They are unfair about money. The dole system seems to be the main source of irritation, when the husband gives the wife less money than is needed for running the household.

6. They often ridicule and humiliate their wives. Some husbands do this when visitors or relatives are present or even in front of the children. In private they may completely reverse themselves but this does not take the sting out of the more public ridicule or deprecation.

7. They should be more honest. Husbands sometimes try to deceive their wives when they would not dream of being dishonest in business or with their fellow workers. Wives say it is difficult to love a man who cannot be trusted.

The roles of American wives are changing rapidly, so the husbands' criticisms of wives will change, too. However, a rather universal past and present complaint is that wives nag. Paul Popenoe has a short test which points up the characteristics of nagging and also gives an opportunity for self-evaluation:

Test yourself. Circle the 0 for never or not at all; circle 1 for sometimes; and circle 2 if you frequently do this:

1. If my husband does not accede to some request, I repeat it over and over.   0 1 2

2. I tell my husband that I have a great need for various things which we do not have and cannot afford to buy.   0 1 2

3. I express regret that we don't have a more expensive automobile.   0 1 2

4. I complain that I am overworked.   0 1 2

5. I compare my husband with other women's husbands—to his disadvantage—when we have an argument.   0 1 2

6. I point out to my husband, in a restaurant, that the food he is ordering will not be good for him.   0 1 2

7. If my husband does not want to do something, I remind him that it is his "duty" to do it.   0 1 2

8. When telling him something unpleasant, I add some such statement as, "I don't like to say this, but it is for your own good."   0 1 2

9. I comment on the fact that I enjoyed advantages, before marriage, which I do not have since I married him.   0 1 2

10. I am guilty of "love-nagging." (Do you really love me? You don't act as if you loved me. I don't believe you love me as much as you used to. If you really loved me you would etc., etc.)   0 1 2

Add all of the numbers you circled. If your score is less than 10, you are probably not a chronic nagger. If it is above 10, watch it!

We would like to see a similar test for husbands—not as naggers but as gripers.

Our society has an ambivalent, if not negative, viewpoint toward divorce. As Judson T. Landis points out, we use two criteria to judge a marriage: happiness and stability. The ideal is a happy, stable relationship. In some marriages, however, people are not happy. Should they stay in this situation or have another chance even if it means divorce? At least divorce frees individuals to marry again, and studies show the majority of second marriages work out well. There are intact marriages in which the spouses feel trapped and unhappy but tolerate their lot in life. Landis shows some of the factors that influence this decision, such as family background, education, religiosity, occupation, and the mother's employment.

If people had a choice, would they elect stability in marriage or happiness? When we say everyone should have a chance at happiness, and divorce is good if it gives people another try, we get negative reactions. Even modern young people appear to see divorce as bad. But when we ask whether it is better to divorce than be unhappy, many people answer yes. Thus, there are many ambivalent feelings about this problem even among young moderns. The reader will be challenged by the Landis's and Bohannan's articles to examine his own attitudes about divorce and divorced people.

Divorce may sometimes seem like the only solution to marital problems. Divorce, however, is by no means a simple solution, but as Bohannan points out in his article, is a complex set of experiences that relatives and friends are not always willing or able to facilitate. Ambivalence, if not more negative attitudes toward divorce, makes individuals feel like they are going through these procedures alone. Clear recognition, understanding, and appreciation of these "Six Stations of Divorce" may enable us to be of greater assistance to others who are going through these experiences. Divorce, after all, is not necessarily the end, but may actually be the beginning—the beginning of a second and more successful marriage.

25 *Evelyn M. Duvall & Reuben Hill*

How Can You Cope with Conflict Constructively?

Destructive quarrels are those that leave fewer assets in the relationship than it had before. Destructive quarreling is directed at the person and succeeds in destroying the illusions and fictions by which the person lives. It is a type of conflict which concentrates on the other's ego. It is of the belittling and punishing variety. Destructive quarrels lead to alienation as the love object is transformed into a hate object, and separation is thereby made possible. Destructive quarrels have at least one value. They succeed in alienating incompatible couples so that engagements are broken, or if marriage has occurred, so that early divorce follows.

Productive quarrels are those that leave the marriage stronger through a redefinition of the situation causing the conflict. Productive quarreling is directed at an issue, and leads to more complete understanding. Issues, problems, and conditions rather than the person himself tend to be the object of productive quarrels. Ideally, the quarrels tend to become fewer and less violent as the marriage progresses and basic routines and solutions to problems are established. Gradually the couple learn the techniques for handling conflict, so that for problem-solving purposes it is not so violent nor so painful. The informed couple learn to recognize the source of their differences early and to relay to one another the message that excitement is brewing.

Most conflict situations find one party the aggressor and one the defendant. Married people need to know how to play both roles well to get the most out of a quarrel. They may have to change roles in the middle to keep things moving to a satisfying climax in which tensions are fully released. There is sometimes what appears to be a bit of perverse interdependence, the aggressive one needing the defensive and the defensive

Reprinted by permission of the publisher, from E. M. Duvall and R. Hill, *Being Married* (Lexington, Mass.: D. C. Heath and Company, 1960), pp. 284–289.

needing the aggressive, to carry the quarrel through to a satisfactory conclusion. Both would feel cheated and disappointed if either party retired from the fray too soon.

THE COURSE OF CONFLICT

Unless the newly married couple have had a background of constructive conflict in their respective parental families, they may be devastated by their first quarrels. In time they come to recognize that conflict has a pattern and runs a course that is predictable.

A typical marriage quarrel has three stages: (1) the buildup, (2) the climax, and (3) the movement toward reconciliation.

During the build-up stage there is often petulant irritability and jittery nagging on the part of the wife, if she is the aggressor. If the husband is the aggressor, the symptoms of tension express themselves in emotionally toned growling, griping, and overcritical comments on the sloppy house, the overdone steak, or the bill from the hairdresser. The aggressor is readying himself to take out his accumulated frustrations on the partner, who takes it just so long and then begins to fight back.

The privilege of initiating the conflict is available to the party who develops the irritability first. He or she has a chip on the shoulder and is looking for trouble. The aggressor role includes, therefore, the insight to recognize in oneself feelings of malaise, uneasiness, or frustration and the willingness to do something about it. The marital sparring partner who plays the defendant role has a special responsibility. If the irritability of the aggressor seems due to hunger, sickness, fatigue, pregnancy, menstrual blues, or tensions aggravated by other physiological dysfunction, the situation may call for hearing it out, for reassurance and sympathy rather than active opposition. The person who has been emotionally wounded in his workaday contacts may need the same understanding and sympathy. Humiliations and personal defeats may be offset by the understanding of the partner.

The second stage is the battle royal itself. It consists of one or more of the efforts discussed earlier to manipulate the partner around to one's own position: coercion, coaxing, name-calling, accusations, arguing, and various forms of masking and pretending. This is the time when cards are put on the table and both husband and wife clarify their values and express their feelings so that the other may get the point without question.

Constructive quarreling calls for skill on the part of both husband and wife in avoiding sensitive spots in the other. It requires skill in identifying and letting the other know the particular sore spots in one's make-up that might be hurt in the verbal jabbing. Much as fighters in the ring are expected to "fight fair," husband and wife must learn not to aim foul blows at each other in their quarreling.

For the wife to jeer at her husband's inability to make money or to become president of the firm would be for most men a blow below the belt, because she aims at the area over which he has least control. Likewise for a man to taunt his wife about her inability to have children may be such a cruel jab that she will never quite recover. In time the sparring partner learns to anticipate the hidden weaknesses and finds where to aim his blows to get the maximum release of tension with a minimum damage to the personality.

You fight fair when you—

Spell out exactly what you don't like, and how you want things changed.

Stick to the point and avoid side issues.

Stay with it until you thrash things out.

Go on to some simple next step for improvement.

Get it out, don't let it fester.

Attack the problem rather than each other.

Avoid dragging in your relatives.

Give each other cues as your tension lets up.

This second stage may be relatively short, a matter of minutes when the issue is trivial and the partners are competent in handling their conflicts. It may last in a relatively non-violent form for hours into the night, depending on the issues, the nature of the tensions, and the ability of the pair to proceed into the process of reconciliation.

The third stage of a quarrel starts as one or both of the partners recognize what the other is driving at, and communicates his understanding: "I'm beginning to see what this means to you . . ." This may elicit some mutual role reversal as each tries to feel the issues as the other does. Now comes the joking with the release of tension, and the first random efforts to find a possible solution to the problem.

If the issue is a poor meal or an evening's disappointment the quarrel may end here. If something of greater value and permanence is involved the process of making-up has to continue through further exploration of causes and possible ways out of the situation. This may include an agreement to seek help through marriage counseling, the local family service bureau, or mental health clinic. This plan for further action mutually agreed upon is usually enough to bring peace for the time being.

It is important that the conflict be brought to a genuine conclusion. "It does not suffice merely to abandon an attitude of hostility and resume an attitude of tenderness. The whole episode must be given an artistic consummation. The dispute which ends when one person slams the door and walks out, to return when the storm is blown over, is probably not ended at all. Even if they kiss and go to bed they may be leaving their quarrel half done, like a play which does not go beyond the second act. When it is said that the quarrel must be brought to a conclusion, this does not mean that the substance of the dispute must be settled one way or the other, once and for all, but only that the episode of the dispute must be so stage-managed that it will become, in retrospect, a pleasant memory."[1]

If the quarrel has been a good one, both husband and wife are purged of their earlier tensions, resentments, fears, and anxieties. Suddenly the world seems bright again, and each, a little sheepishly at first, grins with satisfaction upon the other. Now the marriage seems sturdier than ever with the realization that "If we can take this, we can take anything!"

Skillful couples realize that conflict is not something to fear, but something to utilize to strengthen their relationship when tensions and misunderstandings arise. One of the benefits of productive quarrels is that they reveal to the married couple how strong their relationship really is. Some men and women, deluded by the romantic notion that love must have left when monotony came in, are surprised at the force of love emotions that arise as a result of a quarrel. Quarreling thus helps to stabilize the marriage by reminding the couple, as they kiss and make up, of the depth of their love.

SKILLFUL HANDLING OF CONFLICT

Opposition in marriage is universal and normal, but skillful handling of marital conflict must be learned. The channels of communication between husband and wife can be kept open during conflict only if they each use gestures of acceptance of the other as they differ. In the old West there was a saying "Smile when you say that, pardner; them's fighting words!" In marriage, opposition is less likely to arouse animosity if the partner prefaces his assertions with a family gesture of acceptance. Heat in an argument, and animosity directed against the person are joined in some conflicts, but they need not be threatening if the combatant is secure, knows he is loved, and realizes that the love is not conditionally dependent upon his agreeing with the spouse.

Two people can afford to be genuinely honest with each other, and share fully their feelings as well as their ideas when their relationship is based upon unswerving loyalty. "You are a thoughtless brute. You walk all over my feelings. But, mean as you are, I love you and always will," suggests the kind of basic security that allows for differences and for the expression of hurt and hostility without threatening the marriage.

The handling of conflicts in marriage is helped by previous experience with conflict in one's parental family or with one's peers. There needs to be a deeply held conviction that problems can be solved and that consensus is possible. A happy by-product of observation of successful quarreling in one's parental family is the absence of fear when conflict looms in later marriage. People who are afraid of combat are often the first to get hurt.

There are other ways of handling tensions than the forthright methods described above. In the film *Who's Boss*, the husband warns his wife upon arrival home that he has had a hard day and may prove irritable during the evening by *twirling his hat*, and his wife has a signal just as voiceless; she *wears her apron astern*. With this advance notice, the partner less fatigued can take some responsibility for providing a sounding board for the day's tensions. The wife may give her husband a snack, if supper is going to be late, knowing that hunger complicates any tensions which may have arisen. The husband may whisk out the children from under foot, knowing that preparing a hot meal requires coordination that demanding children can upset.

Some married partners who perceive conflict brewing attempt to drain out their tensions first on the woodpile, or with a golf club, or in bowling. The wife may scrub the floors or pound Sibelius out on the piano. When they return to face each other the original conflict is probably still unresolved but they are better prepared to deal with it, now that the most intense feelings of unpleasantness have subsided. The widespread interest in baseball, wrestling, murder mysteries, and western stories suggests the almost universal need in our culture to drain off excessive aggressions before they become explosive.

In time, the two marriage partners get well enough acquainted so that they can recognize trouble brewing between them, and dissipate the tensions without the intensity of their earlier quarrels. Short cuts to understanding, to communication, and to coping with conflict are learned so that the earlier struggles to get through to each other are no longer necessary.

One immeasurably helpful attitude toward conflict of all kinds is to see its roots and its meanings within the person. "See him as the child he was. Behind the pomp or the rudeness, beneath the crust of meanness or coldness, begin to perceive the wistful little boy (or girl) who is hurt and disappointed and determined to strike back at the world. Or the little boy who is frightened, and tightens his jaw and clenches his fist to ward off some overwhelming fear that hovers deep in the dark past . . . Only in this way can we guard ourselves against responding in kind, against re turning pettiness to the petty and cruelty to the cruel."[2]

An attitude of humility within oneself as an individual is similarly helpful. The person who realizes that he is not always right, that he has been profoundly influenced by forces over which he had little control, that he has to live with himself in the best way he can, such a person can seek professional help without shame, and start on a program of self-improvement with pride.

ENDNOTES

1. Robert C. Binkley and Frances Williams Binkley, *What is Right with Marriage*, New York: Appleton, 1929, pp. 227–228.
2. Sidney J. Harris, "See Him as the Child He Was" in *Strictly Personal*, syndicated feature, September 17, 1956.

26 Judson T. Landis

Social Correlates of Divorce or Nondivorce Among the Unhappy Married

Kirkpatrick has pointed out that many couples who divorce have had happier marriages than other couples who remain married.[1] This position seems plausible although it has not yet been verified by empirical investigation. Marriage counselors and others working closely with families have observed that some couples experience a series of crises in their marriages and yet they continue married, whereas other marriages are quite brittle in that a much less serious crisis may result in their divorcing. Our earlier research found that if there is a history of divorce in the family, couples are more likely to divorce than if there is no history of divorce.[2]

In our society, marriages are assessed according to two norms: happiness and stability. When happiness is not achieved, strain results. Part of the strain is conflict over whether to go against the societal norm of stability in marriage and the family. This research attempts to differentiate those families which do and do not take the step of divorce when a certain "strain" point has been reached.

The working hypothesis for the present research is that: given equal strain or unhappiness there are significant social variables that differentiate between unhappy marriages that end in divorce and unhappy marriages that remain intact.

METHOD

To test the hypothesis, information gained from a previous study of the maturation and dating of 3,000 students from eleven colleges and uni-

Judson T. Landis, "Social Correlates of Divorce or Nondivorce Among the Unhappy Married." *Marriage and Family Living*, Vol. 25, No. 2 (May 1963), pp. 178–180. Reprinted by permission.

versities was used. Each student had been asked to give the marital status of his parents at the time the questionnaire was completed and also his rating of the happiness of his parents' marriage up to the time the respondent was 15 years of age. The reporting of the parents' marital status should be reliable since all respondents would know whether parents were married or divorced. The rating of the parents' marital happiness would necessarily be as the child viewed it, and this might not agree with the parents' view of the marital happiness. In a few cases (28) students reported the parents' marriage had been happy and also the parents' marital status as divorced. These 28 cases were eliminated from the sample. We also eliminated 43 men and 81 women who were too young at the time of the parents' divorce to give any rating of the parents' happiness. This left a total of 2,865 respondents for the analysis, 1,995 reporting happy marriages, 667 reporting unhappy, nondivorced marriages, and 203 reporting unhappy divorced marriages.

In analyzing our data we have compared the "average" group with the unhappy groups and found that the average group tends to have the characteristics of the unhappy groups rather than of the happy group. Since the American ideal emphasizes happiness it seems that when people rate a marriage as "average" they are saying, in substance, that it is an unhappy marriage. Those marriages rated as happy stand apart and differ significantly from those rated as average to very unhappy. Therefore we combined the happy and very happy into one group, *the happy;* and average, unhappy and very unhappy into another, *the unhappy.*

Although our interest here is in comparing the family variables of unhappy nondivorced and unhappy divorced we have included percentage distributions on all tables for the happy, married.

FINDINGS OF THE STUDY

Table 1 summarizes the percentage distributions of the reported family characteristics on ten variables. It will be observed that there are differences between the unhappy nondivorced and the divorced in age at marriage. Men who had married at age 21 and under and women who had married at 19 and under tended to end an unhappy marriage through divorce more often than people who married at later ages. Men who married at 30 and over tended to remain in the nondivorced group even though unhappy.

In comparing the happy marriages with the two groups of unhappy marriages it will be noticed that the happy marriages tended to be for men in the age-groups at marriage of 22 to 29 and for women 20 to 23.

TABLE 1 Percentage distribution of family characteristics as reported by men and women from happy, divorced and unhappy nondivorced parental marriages.

Family characteristics	Happy	Unhappy nondivorced	Unhappy divorced
Father's Age at Marriage*	N = 1995	N = 664	N = 203
21 and under	13%	11%	19%
22–25	41	37	40
26–29	28	26	23
30 and over	18	26	18
		$X^2 = 11.73$	P < .01
Mother's Age at Marriage	N = 1957	N = 666	N = 203
19 and under	19	22	31
20–23	47	40	37
24–27	25	27	21
28 and over	9	11	11
			N.S.
Father's Occupation	N = 1880	N = 632	N = 190
Professional	19	15	20
Business	43	35	34
White Collar	14	14	16
Skilled/semi-skilled	14	23	24
Unskilled	1	3	2
Farm manager/owner	9	10	4
			N.S.
Father's Education*	N = 1840	N = 628	N = 185
Grammar School	16	29	14
High School	32	37	39
College	36	25	28
Graduate School	16	9	19
		$X^2 = 23.59$	P < .01
Mother's Education*	N = 1827	N = 617	N = 187
Grammar School	9	21	13
High School	45	44	42
College	40	30	37
Graduate School	6	5	8
		$X^2 = 9.87$	P < .05
Mother's Employment*	N = 1943	N = 664	N = 202
Employed	26	33	64
Not Employed	74	67	36
		$X^2 = 59.50$	P < .01
Family Religiosity*	N = 1964	N = 667	N = 202
Devout	41	25	18
Slightly religious	47	50	41
Indifferent	12	25	41
		$X^2 = 19.61$	P < .01
Parental Interaction	N = 1944	N = 662	N = 122
Father dominant	29	40	47
50–50	60	30	31
Mother dominant	11	30	22
			N.S.

* Statistically significant.

Several other studies have found these ages to be associated with a higher degree of success in marriage.

The occupation of the husband did not seem to be closely associated with whether an unhappy marriage ended in divorce or continued as an unhappy marriage. Percentage-wise the professional men in this study who were reported to have unhappy marriages tended to end the unhappy marriages through divorce, while men in the farm-manager or owner classification tended to remain in their unhappy marriage.

Level of education was associated with whether unhappy marriages had been terminated through divorce. Unhappy married men and women with a grammar school education tended to remain married, while men and women with college and graduate school educations tended to divorce if their marriage was unhappy. It will be observed (Table 1) that more happy marriages were reported for those couples with a college or graduate education than among those with a grade or high school education.

In considering the employment status of the wife, it was found that a far larger percentage of the divorced women had worked full or part time outside the home than had the unhappy nondivorced women. It is difficult to assess our data on the employment of the wife (mother of the student reporting) since we do not know whether her employment was before or after the divorce.

Findings given in Table 1 show that people who are indifferent to religion tended to end unhappy marriages through divorce while more of those who are devout continued in unhappy marriages.

The patterns of parental dominance in the home did not differ significantly between the unhappy nondivorced and the divorced, although the percentage direction was in the direction one might predict. The unhappy, father-dominated marriage was slightly more likely to have ended in divorce, and the unhappy, mother-dominated marriage was slightly more likely to have remained intact. The most interesting comparison in this table is the preponderance of 50—50 dominance patterns in happy marriages compared with the two dominance classifications of unhappy marriage.

One other analysis was made of faith groups to see whether members of any one faith showed a tendency to remain married even though unhappy. It might be theorized that since the Catholic church takes a strong stand against divorce, a larger percentage of unhappy Catholic marriages would remain intact than would be true of other faiths. Our data gave no support to this belief. Jews were most likely to be found among those who remained in unhappy marriages, and people of no religious faith were least likely to be found among those who remained in unhappy marriages. Catholics and Protestants fell between the two extremes.

DISCUSSION

This research tends to support the hypothesis that given equal strain or unhappiness, other variables emerge as significant in differentiating between unhappy, nondivorced marriages and divorced marriages.

The findings suggest that those who marry at very young ages and who find themselves in an unhappy marriage tend to get out of the marriage through divorce. Possibly this means that those who marry young have greater confidence that they can remarry after divorce than those who marry at a later age. However, if we look at the other extreme we will observe that it is the men and not the women married at the later age, who tended to remain in the unhappy marriage. Men can remarry more easily at an older age because of the favorable sex ratio. It is the woman who has the greater disadvantage in remarrying as she gets older.

The findings on occupation and education suggest that people in the higher educational-occupational levels are more prone to end an unhappy marriage through divorce. Possibly professional people and more highly educated people recognize the damage that may be done to children in an unhappy marriage, or they may have a wider choice of alternatives available when they consider their future if they divorce. Women with a college or graduate education may have more confidence that they can find work and earn a living if they do divorce.

Full or part-time work outside the home characterized those wives who had divorced. We cannot be sure whether a wife's outside work may have contributed to dissatisfaction with her marriage, whether her undertaking an outside job may have been the result of an already existing dissatisfaction with her marriage, or whether she was forced to take an outside job after her divorce. In some cases getting a job may be the first step toward divorce. It is possible that some of the full-time homemakers remain in unhappy marriages because they have no alternative if they lack the skills or the initiative to hold a job. This notion is suggested by the finding that more of the full-time homemakers had a grammar school education only. However, we can only conjecture on these points since we do not know at what time the wives began doing outside work. A fairly safe assumption is that all of the factors mentioned above have a part in explaining why the divorced woman had a work history when compared with the unhappy, nondivorced.

That more of the religiously devout remained married even though unhappy has two possible explanations: Religious scruples may rule out divorce, or it may be that those who divorce become indifferent or antagonistic to religion after they end a marriage. Both reasons may contribute to the finding. Further research might attempt to answer these and many other questions about family background characteristics and intrafamily relationships of those who do and do not divorce when unhappily married.

ENDNOTES

1. Clifford Kirkpatrick, *The Family as Process and Institution,* New York: The Ronald Press Company, 1953, p. 518.
2. Judson T. Landis, "The Pattern of Divorce in Three Generations," *Social Forces,* 34 (March, 1956).

27 *Paul Bohannan*

The Six Stations of Divorce

Divorce is a complex social phenomenon as well as a complex personal experience. Because most of us are ignorant of what it requires of us, divorce is likely to be traumatic: emotional stimulation is so great that accustomed ways of acting are inadequate. The usual way for the healthy mind to deal with trauma is to block it out, then let it reappear slowly, so it is easier to manage. The blocking may appear as memory lapses or as general apathy.

On a social level we do something analogous, not allowing ourselves to think fully about divorce as a social problem. Our personal distrust of the emotions that surround it leads us to consider it only with traditional cultural defenses. Our ignorance masquerades as approval or disapproval, as enlightenment or moral conviction.

The complexity of divorce arises because at least six things are happening at once. They may come in a different order and with varying intensities, but there are at least these six different experiences of separation. They are the more painful and puzzling as personal experiences because society is not yet equipped to handle any of them well, and some of them we do not handle at all.

I have called these six overlapping experiences (1) the emotional divorce, which centers around the problem of the deteriorating marriage; (2) the legal divorce, based on grounds; (3) the economic divorce, which deals with money and property; (4) the coparental divorce, which deals with custody, single-parent homes, and visitation; (5) the community divorce, surrounding the changes of friends and community that every divorcee experiences; and (6) the psychic divorce, with the problem of regaining individual autonomy.

The first visible stage of a deteriorating marriage is likely to be what

psychiatrists call emotional divorce. This occurs when the spouses withhold emotion from their relationship because they dislike the intensity or
ambivalence of their feelings. They may continue to work together as a
social team, but their attraction and trust for one another have disappeared.
The self-regard of each is no longer reinforced by love for the other. The
emotional divorce is experienced as an unsavory choice between giving
in and hating oneself and domineering and hating oneself. The natural
and healthy "growing apart" of a married couple is very different. As
marriages mature, the partners grow in new directions, but also establish
bonds of ever greater interdependence. With emotional divorce, people
do not grow together as they grow apart—they become, instead, mutually
antagonistic and imprisoned, hating the vestiges of their dependence. Two
people in emotional divorce grate on each other because each is disappointed.

In American society, we have turned over to the courts the responsibility for formalizing the dissolution of such a marriage. The legislature
(which in early English law usurped the responsibility from the church,
and then in the American colonies turned it over to the courts) makes the
statutes and defines the categories into which every marital dispute must be
thrust if legal divorce is possible. Divorce is not "legalized" in many
societies but may be done by a church or even by contract. Even in our
own society, there is only one thing that a divorce court can do that cannot be done more effectively some other way—establish the right to remarry. As long as your spouse lives, you cannot legally remarry until
you are legally divorced. Because of the legal necessity of this one aspect,
several other aspects of divorce are customarily taken care of by lawyers
and judges. However, legal divorce itself does nothing but create re-
marriageability.

The economic divorce must occur because in Western countries husband and wife are an economic unit. Their unity is recognized by the law.
They can—and in some states must—own property as a single "legal
person." While technically the couple is not a corporation, they certainly
have many of the characteristics of a legal corporation. At the time the
household is broken up by divorce, an economic settlement must be made,
separating the assets of the "corporation" into two sets of assets, each belonging to one person. This is the property settlement. Today it is vastly
complicated by income tax law. A great deal of knowledge is required to
take care of the tax positions of divorced persons—and if the lawyer does
not have this knowledge, he must get assistance. Although the judges may
ratify the property settlement, they usually do not create it unless the
principals and lawyers cannot do so.

The coparental divorce is necessary if there are children. When the
household breaks up, the children have to live somewhere. Taking care of

the children requires complex arrangements for carrying out the obligations of parents.

All divorced persons suffer more or less because their community is altered. Friends necessarily take a different view of a person during and after divorce—he ceases to be a part of a couple. Their own inadequacies, therefore, will be projected in a new way. Their fantasies are likely to change as they focus on the changing situation. In many cases, the change in community attitude—and perhaps people too—is experienced by a divorcee as ostracism and disapproval. For many divorcing people, the divorce from community may make it seem that nothing in the world is stable.

Finally comes the psychic divorce. It is almost always last, and always the most difficult. Indeed, I have not found a word strong or precise enough to describe the difficulty or the process. Each partner to the ex-marriage, either before or after the legal divorce—usually after, and sometimes years after—must turn himself or herself again into an autonomous social individual. People who have been long married tend to have become socially part of a couple or a family; they lose the habit of seeing themselves as individuals. This is worse for people who married in order to avoid becoming autonomous individuals in the first place.

To become an individual again, at the center of a new community, requires developing new facets of character. Some people have forgotten how to do it—some never learned. The most potent argument against teen-age marriages is that they are likely to occur between people who are searching for independence but avoiding autonomy. The most potent argument against hurried remarriage is the same: avoidance of the responsibilities of autonomy.

Divorce is an institution that nobody enters without great trepidation. In the emotional divorce, people are likely to feel hurt and angry. In the legal divorce, people often feel bewildered—they have lost control, and events sweep them along. In the economic divorce, the reassignment of property and the division of money (there is *never* enough) may make them feel cheated. In the parental divorce they worry about what is going to happen to the children; they feel guilty for what they have done. With the community divorce, they may get angry with their friends and perhaps suffer despair because there seems to be no fidelity in friendship. In the psychic divorce, in which they have to become autonomous again, they are probably afraid and are certainly lonely. However, the resolution of any or all of these various six divorces may provide an elation of victory that comes from having accomplished something that had to be done and having done it well. There may be ultimate satisfactions in it.

Divorce American style is a bewildering experience—so many things are happening at once. We have never been taught what we are supposed to do, let alone what we are supposed to feel. I know a divorced man who took great comfort in the fact that one of his business associates asked him, when he learned of his divorce, "Do I feel sorry for you or do I congratulate you?" He thought for a moment and said—out of bravado as much as conviction—"Congratulate me." It was, for him, the beginning of the road back.

THE EMOTIONAL DIVORCE AND
THE PROBLEM OF GRIEF

One of the reasons it feels so good to be engaged and newly married is the rewarding sensation that, out of the whole world, you have been selected. One of the reasons that divorce feels so awful is that you have been deselected. It punishes almost as much as the engagement and the wedding are rewarding.

The chain of events and feelings that lead up to divorce are as long and as varied as the chain of events that lead up to being selected for marriage. The difference is that the feelings are concentrated in the area of the weak points in the personality rather than the growing points of the personality.

Almost no two people who have been married, even for a short time, can help knowing where to hit each other if they want to wound. On the other hand, any two people—no matter who they are—who are locked together in conflict have to be very perceptive to figure out what the strain is really all about. Marital fights occur in every healthy marriage. The fact of health is indicated when marital disputes lead to a clarification of issues and to successful extension of the relationship into new areas. Difficulties arise only when marital conflict is sidetracked to false issues (and sometimes the discovery of just what issue is at stake may be, in itself, an adequate conclusion to the conflict), or when the emotional pressures are shunted to other areas. When a couple are afraid to fight over the real issue, they fight over something else—and perhaps never discover what the real issue was.

Two of the areas of life that are most ready to accept such displacement are the areas of sex and money. Both sex and money are considered worthwhile fighting over in American culture. If it is impossible to know or admit what a fight is all about, then the embattled couple may cast about for areas of displacement, and they come up with money and sex, because both can be used as weapons. Often these are not the basis of the difficulties, which lie in unconscious or inadmissible areas.

These facts lead a lot of people to think that emotional divorce occurs over money or over sexual incompatibility just because that is where the overt strife is allowed to come out. Often, however, these are only camouflage.

MONEY AND THE EMOTIONAL DIVORCE

One of the most tenacious ideas from our early training is "the value of a dollar." When in the larger society the self is reflected in possessions, and when money becomes one mode of enhancing the self—then we have difficulty with anybody who either spends it too lavishly or sits on it more tightly than we do.

Money is a subject about which talk is possible. Most middle-class couples do talk about money; most of them, in fact, make compromises more or less adequate to both. But in all cases, money management and budgeting are endlessly discussed in the American household. If communication becomes difficult, one of the first places that it shows up is in absence of knowledge about the other person's expenditures.

I interviewed one divorced woman who blamed her ex-husband's spending practices and attitude toward money as a major factor in their divorce. She said that he bought her an expensive car and asked her to leave it sitting outside the house when she was not driving it. *She* announced that *he* could not afford it. He asked her to join a golf club. She refused, although she was a good golfer and liked to play—because *she* told him *he* could not afford it. Whenever he wanted to use her considerable beauty and accomplishments to reflect a little credit on himself for being able to have captured and kept such a wife, she announced that he could not afford it. After the divorce, it continued. Then one day, in anger, she telephoned him to say that she was tired of making sacrifices—this year she was going to take the children on a transcontinental vacation and that he would simply have to pay for the trip. He did not explode; he only thought for a minute and said that he guessed that would be all right, and that he would whittle down his plans for the children's vacation with him, so that it would come within the budget.

This woman told this story without realizing what she had revealed: that her husband was not going to push himself or them into bankruptcy; that he did indeed know how much things cost, and that he could either afford or otherwise manage what he wanted to give her. There was doubtless a difference of opinion about money—she, it appears, preferred to save and then spend; he preferred, perhaps, to spend and then pay. She, for reasons I cannot know from one extended interview, did not recognize his feelings. She *did* announce to him, every time that he wanted to spend money on her, that he was inadequate. I suspect it was her own fear that she would let him down. Without knowing it, she was attacking him where it hurt him and where her housewifely virtue could be kept intact, while she did not have to expose herself or take a chance.

I am not saying that there are not spendthrift husbands or wives. I am saying that if differences that lie beyond money cannot be discussed, then money is a likely battleground for the emotional divorce.

SEX AND THE EMOTIONAL DIVORCE

Among the hundreds of divorcees I have talked to, there is a wide range of sexual attitudes. There were marriages in which sexual symptoms were the first difficulties to be recognized by the couple. There were a few in which the sexual association seemed the only strong bond. I know of several instances in which the couple met for a ceremonial bout of sexual intercourse as the last legitimate act before their divorce. I have a newspaper clipping that tells of a man who, after such a "last legal assignation," murdered his wife before she became his ex-wife. And I know one divorce that was denied because, as the judge put it, he could not condone "litigation by day and copulation by night."

Usually, when communication between the spouses becomes strained, sexual rapport is the first thing to go. There are many aspects to this problem: sexual intercourse is the most intimate of social relationships, and reservations or ambivalences in the emotions are likely to show up there (with unconscious conflicts added to conscious ones). The conflicts may take the extreme form of frigidity in women, impotence in men. They may take the form of adultery, which may be an attempt to communicate something, an unconscious effort to improve the marriage itself. It may be an attempt to humiliate the spouse into leaving. Adultery cannot sensibly be judged without knowing what it means to a specific person and to his spouse in a specific situation. Adultery is a legal ground for divorce in every jurisdiction in the United States, and indeed in most of the record-keeping world.

Because sexuality is closely associated with integration of the personality, it is not surprising that disturbance in the relationship of the spouses may be exposed in sexual symptoms. Except in some cases in which the marriage breaks up within a few weeks or months, however, sexual difficulties are a mode of expression as often as they provide the basic difficulty.

GROWING APART

Married people, like any other people, must continue to grow as individuals if they are not to stagnate. Only by extending themselves to new experiences and overcoming new conflicts can they participate fully in new social relationships and learn new culture. That means that no one, at the time of marriage, can know what the spouse is going to become. Moreover, it means that he cannot know what he himself may become.

Some of this growth of individuals must necessarily take place outside of the marriage. If the two people are willing and able to perceive and tolerate the changes in one another, and overcome them by a growing relationship directly with the other person, then the mutual rewards are very great, and conflicts can be resolved.

Inability to tolerate change in the partner (or to see him as he is) always lies, I think, at the root of emotional divorce. All marriages become constantly more attenuated from the end of the honeymoon period probably until the retirement of the husband from the world of affairs. That is to say, the proportion of the total concern of one individual that can be given to the other individual in the marriage decreases, even though the precise quantity (supposing there were a way to measure it) might become greater. But the ties may become tougher, even as they become thinner.

When this growing apart and concomitant increase in the toughness of the bonds does *not* happen, then people feel the marriage bonds as fetters and become disappointed or angry with each other. They feel cramped by the marriage and cheated by their partner. A break may be the only salvation for some couples.

In America today, our emotional lives are made diffuse by the very nature of the culture with which we are surrounded. Family life, business or professional demands, community pressures—today all are in competition with one another for our time and energies. When that happens, the social stage is set for emotional divorce of individual couples, because the marriage relationship becomes just another competing institution. Sometimes emotional divorce seems scarcely more than another symptom of the diffuseness.

EMOTIONAL DIVORCE AND GRIEF

Emotional divorce results in the loss of a loved object just as fully—but by quite a different route of experience—as does the death of a spouse. Divorce is difficult because it involves a purposeful and active rejection by another person, who, merely by living, is a daily symbol of the rejection. It is also made difficult because the community helps even less in divorce than it does in bereavement.

The natural reaction to the loss of a loved object or person (and sometimes a hated one as well) is grief. The distribution of emotional energy is changed significantly; new frustration must be borne until new arrangements can be worked out. Human beings mourn every loss of meaningful relationship. The degree depends on the amount of emotional involvement. Mourning may be traumatic—and it may, like any other trauma, have to be blocked and only slowly allowed into awareness. Mourning may take several months or years.

Divorce is even more threatening than death to some people, because they have thought about it more, perhaps wished for it more consciously. But most importantly—there is no recognized way to mourn a divorce. The grief has to be worked out alone and without benefit of traditional rites, because few people recognize it for what it is.

When grief gets entangled with all the other emotions that are evoked in a divorce, the emotional working through becomes complicated—in a divorce one is very much on his own.

THE LEGAL DIVORCE AND
THE PROBLEM OF GROUNDS

Judicial divorce, as it is practiced in the United States today, is a legal post-mortem on the demise of an intimate relationship. It originated in Massachusetts in the early 1700s as a means for dealing with the problems that emotional divorce caused in families, at the same time that all going households could continue to be based on holy matrimony. Legal divorce has been discovered and used many times in the history of the world, but this particular institution had no precursors in European history. The historical period in which it developed is important. In those days it was considered necessary that the state could profess its interest in the marriage and the family only in the guise of punishing one of the spouses for misconduct. Thus, the divorce itself was proclaimed to be the punishment of the guilty party. Whether divorce as a punishment was ever a commonsensical idea is a moot point—certainly it is not so today. Yet, our law still reflects this idea.

Thus, if the state is to grant divorces to "innocent" spouses as punishment to offending spouses, it must legalize certain aspects of the family—must, in fact, establish minimal standards of performance in family roles. Marriages break down in all societies; we have come, by state intervention, to solve some of these breakdowns with the legal institution of divorce. Until very recently, no country granted its citizens the clear right to divorce, as they have the clear right to marry. The right is always conditional on acts of misbehavior of the spouse, as misbehavior has been legally defined and called "grounds." Whatever the spouse does must be thrust into the categories that the law recognizes before it can be grounds for divorce.

This way of handling divorce has some strange and unintended effects.

It has made lawyers into experts in several aspects of divorce; there are no recognized experts in other aspects of divorce. Therefore, lawyers are called upon to assume responsibility for more and more aspects of the institution—and in many they have no training, in others there is no possible legal base from which they can operate. The difficulty in legal divorce in America seems to lie in two related situations: the uncertainty of the population and even of the legal profession about what the lawyers are supposed to do, and the absence of institutions paralleling the legal institutions to handle the non-legal problems.

DIVORCE LAWYERS AND WHAT THEY DO

If you want a physician, you look in the yellow pages and find them noted, most of them with their specialties spelled out. With lawyers it is not so—there is only a list. It is an unfortunate by-product of the ethical commitment of the American Bar Association not to advertise that attorneys cannot list their special competences. It is my opinion that, at least as far as family lawyers are concerned (the only exception now allowed is patent law), this ruling should be changed.

The legal profession is committed to the proposition that any lawyer— or at least any firm of lawyers—should be able to handle any sort of problem. Legally, divorce is indeed a simple matter; that is part of the trouble. Any competent lawyer can indeed write the papers and make the necessary motions. The difficulty comes in the counseling aspect of divorce practice.

Every divorcing person must find his lawyer—and it may be difficult. It may be done through friends, business associates, clergymen, but it is surprisingly often done in the yellow pages. Perhaps there is no other situation in our country today in which a person in emotional distress is so faced with buying a pig in a poke. Clients who are inexperienced may not realize that they can fire a lawyer faster than they can hire him. They worry along with a lawyer they neither like personally nor trust professionally.

Because lawyers are for the most part untrained in family psychology and sociology, and because there is no practice—not even the criminal law —in which they are dealing with people in such states of emotional upset, divorce becomes a "messy" or "dirty" kind of practice—these are their words. In the hierarchy of lawyers by specialties (and there is a rigid and fairly overt hierarchy), the divorce lawyer and criminal lawyer rank approximately at the bottom—allowing, of course, for such considerations as ethics, financial success, social rank, and the like. My own opinion is that the more emotional the problems a lawyer handles, the further down the lawyers' pecking order he ranks. Corporation lawyers are at the top; corporations have no emotions. Divorcees and criminals have little else.

Lawyers also dislike divorce practice because it is not lucrative. Many divorcees think lawyers take advantage and overcharge them. In most divorce cases, the legal fees—both of them—are paid by the husband, and are set by the judge at the time of the divorce hearing. Many lawyers think that the fees that the court sets are ridiculously low—another reason that they do not like to take divorce cases. Many lawyers make additional charges for the many other services they perform for divorcees. Divorce lawyers tend to work on an hourly rate, though probably all of them adjust the rate to the income of their client.

Most divorcees, on the other hand, do not appreciate how much work their lawyers actually put in. Because the court hearing seldom takes more than a few minutes, and because the papers are often not a thick bundle, the assumption is that comparatively little effort went into it. The divorce lawyers I know earn their fees; the good ones always contribute a lot of personal advice, care, and solace without charge.

Many divorce cases do not end when the decree is final. Money must be collected; ex-husbands may use non-payment of alimony as the only sanction they have over ex-wives; financial positions and obligations change. For these and many other reasons, the divorcee may come back to the lawyer sooner or later. One divorced woman summed it up, "Every divorcee needs a good firm of lawyers."

But the greatest difficulty arises from the fact we started with: divorce lawyers are forced, in the nature of the law, to put the "real situation," as they learn it from their clients, into language that the law will accept. If a divorce action is to go to court, it must first be couched in language that the courts are legally permitted to accept. Both marriage counselors and lawyers have assured me that reconciliation is always more difficult after grounds have been discussed and legal papers written than when it is still in the language of "reasons" and personal emotion. Legal language and choice of grounds are the first positive steps toward a new type of relationship with the person one of my informants called "my ex-to-be." Discussion of grounds often amounts, from the point of view of the divorcing person, to listing all the faults that the spouse ever committed, then picking one. Since everyone has faults, this is not difficult to do. (There is an old joke that goes the rounds of divorce lawyers about the conscientious young man who came to his lawyer and said he wanted a divorce, but was not sure he had grounds. The cynical lawyer raised his eyes and asked, "Are you married?")

We all know that grounds and reasons may be quite different. The divorcing person usually feels that he should not "tattle" and selects the "mildest" ground. Yet, every person who institutes a suit for divorce must wonder whether to use "adultery" if in fact it occurred, or to settle for the more noncommittal "mental cruelty." Does one use drunkenness when divorcing an alcoholic? Or desertion? Or does one settle for "incompatibility?"

WHAT THE COURT DOES

The judges in a divorce court are hard-working men who must become accustomed to a veritable chaos of emotional confusion. Some of them do the job well, with great knowledge and commitment. Others feel that they have themselves been sentenced, that no human being should be asked to stand very much of it, and hope to be in some other court soon.

The usual divorce in court takes only a few minutes—sometimes as little as two or three and seldom more than fifteen or twenty. Many divorcees are disturbed to discover this fact, having thought all their grievances would be heard and, perhaps, they would "get some justice." Many report, "It's a weak-kneed system. I don't feel that it really did the job." Others are constantly aware that they perjured themselves—about grounds, about residence, perhaps about facts. Some divorcees feel virtuous for using "mental cruelty" as a ground and tell all their friends "the real reason"—thereby alienating friends. Others take a pragmatic attitude about the legal proceedings: "What do I care? I got what I wanted, didn't I?"

The court action seems short and ineffective at the time—not traumatic. Most divorcees, in retrospect, cannot remember the details of it; in part, I think, because there is little to be remembered. Divorce dockets are crowded in all American cities. Judges do not have time to give each case the thought and time the divorcing parties think it deserves—realizing that one's monumental troubles are not worth the court's time can often act as a restorative, but sometimes as a depressant. Many judges agree that they would like to have more time to make specific investigations and suggestions in each case—to convince themselves that attempts have been made to discover whether these two people should in fact be divorced— whether divorce is a reasonable solution to their problems. Though judges do take time with some cases, most would like to be able to take more.

One of the reasons that the divorce institution is so hard on people is that the legal processes do not provide an orderly and socially approved discharge of emotions that are elicited during the emotional divorce and during the early parts of preparation for the legal processes. Divorces are "cranked out" but divorcees are not "cooled out."

THE ECONOMIC DIVORCE AND
THE PROBLEM OF PROPERTY

The family household is the unit of economic consumption in the United States. As such, middle-class households must have a certain amount of domestic capital equipment besides personal property such as cars and television sets. In most households, these items "belong to the family," even though they may be legally owned in the name of one of the spouses. There are (at the time of writing) six states in the United States that declare all property owned by either spouse to be "community property" except for what they owned before the marriage and what they inherit. California is the most thorough and noteworthy example of a community-property state; many states are in process of changing their laws—some of them toward stricter community-property principles, some for a "better break" for one partner or the other. Any list is soon out of date.

Behind the idea of fair settlement of property at the time of divorce is the assumption that a man cannot earn money to support his family if he does not have the moral assistance and domestic services of his wife. The wife, if she works, does so in order to "enhance" the family income (no matter how much she makes or what the "psychic income" to her might be). Therefore, every salary dollar, every patent, every investment, is joint property.

In most states, the property settlement is not recorded in the public records of divorce, so precise information is lacking. However, in most settlements, the wife receives from one-third to one-half of the property. As one sits in a divorce court, however, one realizes that in many divorces the amount of property is so small as to need no settlement or even to cause any dispute. Judges regard settlement as the province of lawyers, and generally agree that the lawyers have not done their jobs if the matter comes to court.

Many wives voluntarily give up their rights to property at the time they become ex-wives. Some are quite irrational about it—"I won't take *anything* from *him!*" Sometimes they think (perhaps quite justly) that they have no moral right to it. Others, of course, attempt to use the property settlement as a means of retaliation. The comment from one of my informants was, "Boy, did I make that bastard pay." It seems to me that irrational motives such as revenge or self-abnegation are more often in evidence than the facts of relative need, in spite of all that judges and lawyers can do.

The property of the household is never, in the nature of household living, separable into two easily discernible parcels. Even in states that lack common-property laws, the *use* of property is certainly common within the household and subject to the rules of the household, of course,

but (except for clothes or jewelry or tools) usually not the exclusive property of any specific member of the household. Whose, for example, is the
family car? Whose is the hi-fi? Whose is the second-best bed? And whose
is the dog?

ALIMONY

The word "alimony" is derived from the Latin word for sustenance,
and ultimately from the verb which means "to nourish" or "to give food
to." The prevailing idea behind alimony in America is that the husband,
as head of the family, has an obligation to support his wife and children,
no matter how wealthy the wife and children may be independently.

At the time of divorce, the alimony rights of the wife are considered
to be an extension of the husband's duty to support, undertaken at the
time of marriage. Therefore, alimony means the money paid during and
after the divorce by the ex-husband to the ex-wife (rarely the other way
around).

There is, however, another basis on which some courts in some American jurisdictions have looked on alimony—it can be seen as punishment of
the husband for his mistreatment of the wife. Where this idea is found,
the wife cannot be entitled to alimony if she is the "guilty party" to the
divorce. In most states, the amount of alimony is more or less directly
dependent on whatever moral or immoral conduct of the wife may come
to the attention of the court. A woman known to be guilty of anything the
court considers to be moral misconduct is likely to be awarded less than an
"innocent" wife. The law varies widely on these matters; practice varies
even more.

The most important thing about the award and payment of alimony
is that it is done on the basis of a court order. Therefore, if it is not paid,
the offending husband is in contempt of court. The institution of divorce is
provided, as we have seen before, with only one formal sanction to insure the compliance of its various parties. And that is the court.

The amount of alimony is set by the court, on the basis of the wife's
need and the husband's ability to pay. Both her education and training
and his may be taken into account; the state of health may be relevant.
Sometimes the length of the marriage is a consideration—a short period
entitling the wife to less alimony. The age of the children, the moral behavior of each spouse, the income tax position—all these things and undoubtedly many more will affect the court's decision about alimony.

Either ex-spouse may petition the court to have alimony arrangements
changed, upon any change in either the ex-wife's need or the ex-husband's
ability to pay. It cannot, however, be changed on the basis of the postmarital behavior of either party. Some courts listen with sympathy to an

ex-husband's request to reduce alimony at the time of his remarriage; almost all alimony is arranged so that it stops entirely at the time of the ex-wife's remarriage.

CHILD SUPPORT

Courts and citizens are both much clearer about child support than they are about alimony. The principle is obvious to all: as long as he is able to do so, the responsibility for supporting children lies with their father. Whether a man is morally and legally obliged to support his children depends only on one factor: his ability to do so. In assessing child support payments, the court looks simply at his ability to pay, including his health, and to the needs of the child. The amount may be set by the court; it is always ratified by the court.

The principles behind the idea of child support are simple. However, the functioning of the child support aspects of the divorce institution are anything but simple. The difficulty arises, again and as usual, because of the lack of sanctions aside from the court, and from the further fact that court action is expensive and usually slow. The father who does not pay the stipulated child support is in contempt of court, and can be brought back into court on that basis. In order to avoid clogging the courts, some states have found various ways in which the payments can be made to the state and forwarded to the mother or other guardian of the children. This, too, is expensive. There seems to be no really adequate means, as yet, of dealing with men who do not make support payments.

Some mothers try to stop the visitation of fathers who do not make support payments—and some courts uphold them. Although most divorced parents realize that "fighting through the children" is harmful to the children, not all succeed in avoiding it.

THE COPARENTAL DIVORCE AND
THE PROBLEM OF CUSTODY

The most enduring pain of divorce is likely to come from the coparental divorce. This odd word is useful because it indicates that the child's parents are divorced from each other—not from the child. Children do not always understand this: they may ask, "Can Father divorce *me?*" This is not a silly or naïve question; from the standpoint of the child what was a failure in marriage to the parents is the shattering of his kinship circle.

The children have to go somewhere. And even when both parents share joint legal custody of the child, one parent or the other gets "physical custody"—the right to have the child living with him.

The word "custody" is a double-edged sword. It means "responsibility for the care of" somebody. It also means "imprisonment." The child is in the custody of his parents—the criminal is in the custody of the law. When we deal with the custody of children in divorces, we must see to it that they are "in the care of" somebody, and that the care is adequate— we must also see that the custody is not punitive or restricting.

Legal custody of children entitles the custodial parent to make decisions about their life-styles and the things they can do which are developmentally important to them—educational and recreational and cultural choices. In the common law, the father had absolute property rights over the child—the mother had none, unless she inherited them at the death of the father. About the time judicial divorce was established in America, custody preferences shifted until the two parents were about equal. With the vast increase in the divorce rate in the early third of the twentieth century, the shift continued giving the mother preference in both legal and physical custody. We rationalize this practice by such ideas as mother love, masculine nature, or the exigencies of making a living.

Custody of the children, once granted to the mother will be taken away from her by the courts *only* if she can be shown to be seriously delinquent in her behavior *as a mother*. Her behavior *as a wife* may be at stake in granting the divorce or in fixing the amount of the alimony—but not in granting custody. A woman cannot be denied her rights as a mother on the basis of having performed badly as a wife, or even on the basis of her behavior as a divorcee if the children were not threatened physically or morally. Similarly, a man cannot be penalized as a father for his shortcomings as a husband.

The overriding consideration in all cases is that the court takes what action it considers to be "in the best interests of the child." The rights of children as human beings override, in our morality and hence in our laws, all rights of the parents as parents, and certainly their rights as spouses. We have absolutely inverted the old common law.

It is generally considered that a child's best interests lie with his own parents—but if they do not, what is called "third-party custody" can be imposed by the court. Courts do not like to separate children from at least one parent—but sometimes there is no alternative "in the best interests of the child."

A man is always, either by statute law or by common law, obliged to take financial responsibility for his minor children. If there are overriding circumstances that make it impossible for him to work, then that responsibility devolves on their mother. Sometimes a mother refuses her ex-husband the right to support his children as a means to deny him the right to see them—some men accept this, but few would be forced by a court to accept it if they chose to question its legality.

The rights of the parent who has neither legal nor physical custody of the child are generally limited to his right of visiting the child at reasonable times. This right stems from parenthood and is not dependent on decrees issued by a court. The court may, of course, condition the rights of visitation, again in the best interests of the child.

CHILDREN AND ONE-PARENT HOUSEHOLDS

Children grow up. The association between parent and child and the association between the parents change with each new attainment of the child. The child grows, parents respond—and their response has subtle overtones in their own relationship. In divorce, their responses must necessarily be of a different nature from what it is in marriage. In divorce, with communication reduced, the goals of the spouses are less likely to be congruent—the child is observed at different times and from different vantage points by the separated parents, each with his own set of concerns and worries.

Coparental divorce created lasting pain for many divorcees I interviewed—particularly if the ex-spouses differed greatly on what they wanted their children to become, morally, spiritually, professionally, even physically. This very difference of opinion about the goals of living may have lain behind the divorce. It continues through the children.

The good ex-husband/father feels, "My son is being brought up by his mother so that he is not my son." A divorced man almost always feels that his boy is being made into a different kind of man from what he himself is. Often, of course, he is right. The good ex-wife/mother may be tempted to refuse her ex-husband his visitation rights because, from her point of view, "He is bad for the children." This statement may mean no more than that the children are emotionally higher strung before and after a visit, and therefore upset her calm. But the mother may think the father wants something else for the children than she does, thus putting a strain on her own efforts to instill her own ideals and regulations.

It is difficult for a man to watch his children develop traits similar, if not identical, to those he found objectionable in their mother and which were among those qualities that led to the emotional divorce. The child becomes the living embodiment of the differences in basic values. A man may feel that "she" is bad for the children even when he has the objectivity to see also that the children will not necessarily develop unwholesome personalities, but only different personalities from those they might have developed through being with him.

The problem for the mother of the children is different—she has to deal with the single-parent household, making by herself decisions, which she almost surely feels should be shared. She does not want somebody to tell her what to do, as much as somebody to tell her she is right and make "sensible suggestions." Like most mothers, she wants support, not direction.

There is a traditional and popular belief that divorce is "bad for children." Actually, we do not know very much about it.

Although social scientists no longer put it this way, there is still in the general population a tendency to ask whether divorce "causes" juvenile delinquency. Obviously, if the child's way of dealing with the tensions in the emotional divorce of his parents is to act out criminally, he has turned to delinquency. But other children react to similar situations with supercompliance and perhaps ultimate ulcers. The tensions in divorce certainly tell on children, but the answers the children find are not inherent in the institution of divorce.

The more fruitful question is more difficult: "How can we arm children to deal with themselves in the face of the inadequacies and tensions in their families, which may lead their parents to the divorce court?" At least that question avoids the scapegoating of parents or blaming it all on "society"—and it also provides us a place to start working, creating new institutions.

TELLING CHILDREN ABOUT DIVORCE

It is a truism today that parents should be honest with their children, but parents apparently do not always extend this precept to being honest with their children about divorce. One of the most consistent and discouraging things found in interviewing American divorced persons came in response to my question, "What have you told your child about the nature of divorce in general and your own in particular?" The question was almost always followed by a silence, then a sigh, and then some version of, "I haven't told them much. I haven't had to. They know. You can't kid kids."

It is true, generally, that children are not easily deceived. But it is not true that they know instinctively why something is happening. Children today are comparatively sophisticated about divorce—until they are involved in it.

Children who live in and with the institution of divorce have a lot to learn that other children may never have to learn. The most important ideas to be communicated to them deal with the nature of the new life they will lead. It may be reasonable, in some cases, not to acquaint them with the facts of the emotional and legal divorces. But the new situation—custody, visitation, the new division of labor in the household—can be explained quite clearly so that the child can do his adjusting to a fairly predictable situation.

Of equal importance, they must be taught purposefully and overtly some of the culture of the family that does not occur in the ex-family. That is to say, children in divorce must pick up by instruction what they would have learned by habituation or osmosis in an unbroken healthy home.

The children must learn how to deal with the "broken orbit" of models for the roles they will play in life. A boy cannot become fully a man—or a girl a woman—if they model themselves only on the cues they pick up from one sex alone. A woman cannot teach a boy to be a man, or a girl a woman, without the help of men. And a man cannot teach either a boy to be a man or a girl to be a woman without the help of women.

All of us interact with members of both sexes. Our cues about the behavior of men come from the responses of women, as well as from the responses of men. Children—like the rest of us—must have significant members of both sexes around them.

Obviously, children of even the most successful homes do not model themselves solely on their parents, in spite of the importance parents have as models. There are television models (boys walk like athletes or crime busters) ; there are teachers, friends, storekeepers, bus drivers, and all the rest. But the child who lives in a one-parent home has to adjust to a different mixture of sex-role models. The big danger may be not so much that a boy has no father model in his home, but that his mother stops his walking like Willie Mays or a television cowboy because she doesn't like it. And worst of all, she may, without knowing it, try to extinguish in him the very behavior patterns he has learned from his father: especially, if she does not want to be reminded of his father.

Children who live in one-parent homes must learn what a husband/ father is and what he does in the home—and they have to learn it in a different context from children of replete homes. They must learn what a wife/mother is in such a home. Children are taught to be husbands and wives while they are still children. In the one-parent home the children have to be taught actively and realistically the companionship, sexual, coparenting, and domestic aspects of marriage.

It is important to realize that these things can be taught. Yet, it is in this very process of teaching the child that the parent may reveal a great deal of bitterness and hostility toward the ex-spouse. The good parent has to teach the child without denigrating or idealizing the other parent.

A noted psychoanalyst has told me that in her opinion there are only two things children learn in two-parent homes that cannot be taught in one-parent homes; one is the undertone of healthy sexuality that is present in a healthy home. Nothing appears on the surface save love—but the sexual tone of married love permeates everything. Even in the most loving one-parent home this is something that can, perhaps, be explained to children, but something that they will have trouble feeling unless they experience it elsewhere. The other thing that is difficult to teach, she says, is the ambivalence of the child toward both parents. When the relationship of father-child is none of the business of the child's mother, or the relationship of mother-child outside the ken and responsibility of the child's father, then the illusion can be maintained by the child that father is wholly right and mother wholly wrong, or father wholly unjustified and mother completely innocent. It is seldom true.

In short, the ex-family must do many of the things that the family ordinarily does, but it does them with even more difficulty than the family. It is in the coparental aspects of the divorce that the problems are so long-lasting—and so difficult. And the reason, as we have seen, is that a child's mother and father are, through the child, kinsmen to one another, but the scope of activities in their relationship has been vastly curtailed.

THE COMMUNITY DIVORCE AND THE PROBLEM OF LONELINESS

Changes in civil status or "stages of life" almost invariably mark changes in friends and in significant communities. We go to school, and go away to college. We join special-interest groups. When we are married, we change communities—sometimes almost completely except for a few relatives and two or three faithful friends from childhood or from college.

When we divorce, we also change communities. Divorce means "forsaking all others" just as much as marriage does, and in about the same degree.

Many divorcees complain bitterly about their "exfriends." "Friends?" one woman replied to my question during an interview, "They drop you like a hot potato. The exceptions are those real ones you made before marriage, those who are unmarried, and your husband's men friends who want to make a pass at you."

The biggest complaint is that divorcees are made to feel uncomfortable by their married friends. Little need be said about this here because Doctor Miller's chapter in this report covers the matter decisively.

Like newly marrieds, new divorcees have to find new communities. They tend to find them among the divorced. Morton Hunt's book, *The World of the Formerly Married*, provides a good concise report on these new communities. Divorcees find—if they will let themselves—that there is a group ready to welcome them as soon as they announce their separations. There are people to explain the lore that will help them in being a divorcee, people to support them emotionally, people to give them information, people to date and perhaps love as soon as they are able to love.

America is burgeoning with organizations of divorced people. The largest, and a vastly admirable organization, is *Parents Without Partners,* which has many branches throughout the country. Here, as Doctor Bernard mentioned in the first section, a divorced person can find information and friends. The character of this organization varies from one of its chapters to another. I know one chapter—over a third of its membership widows—that is quiet to the point of being sedate. I know other chapters that devote themselves to public works, largescale picnics and parties that include all their children, and the kind of "discussion" of their problems that enables people "to get to know each other well enough to date seriously rather than experimentally."

There are, of course, some people who avoid other divorcees. Such people tend to disappear into the population at large, and hence are more difficult to find when we study their adjustments.

But the community divorce is an almost universal experience of divorcees in America. And although there are many individuals who are puzzled and hurt until they find their way into it, it is probably the aspect of divorce that Americans handle best.

THE PSYCHIC DIVORCE AND
THE PROBLEM OF AUTONOMY

Psychic divorce means the separation of self from the personality and the influence of the ex-spouse—to wash that man right out of your hair. To distance yourself from the loved portion that ultimately became disappointing, from the hated portion, from the baleful presence that led to depression and loss of self-esteem.

The most difficult of the six divorces is the psychic divorce, but it is also the one that can be personally most constructive. The psychic divorce involves becoming a whole, complete, and autonomous individual again— learning to live without somebody to lean on—but also without somebody to support. There is nobody on whom to blame one's difficulties (except oneself), nobody to shortstop one's growth, nobody to grow with.

Each must regain—if he ever had it—the dependence on self and faith in one's own capacity to cope with the environment, with people, with thoughts and emotions.

WHY DID I MARRY?

To learn anything from divorce, one must ask himself why he married. Marriage, it seems to me, should be an act of desperation—a last resort. It should not be used as a means of solving one's problems. Ultimately, of course, most people in our society can bring their lives to a high point of satisfaction and usefulness only through marriage. The more reason, indeed, we should not enter it unless it supplies the means for coping with our healthy needs and our desires to give and grow.

All too often, marriage is used as a shield against becoming whole or autonomous individuals. People too often marry to their weaknesses. We all carry the family of our youth within ourselves—our muscles, our emotions, our unconscious minds. And we all project it again into the families we form as adults. The path of every marriage is strewn with yesterday's unresolved conflicts, of both spouses. Every divorce is beset by yesterday's unresolved conflicts, compounded by today's.

So the question becomes: How do I resolve the conflicts that ruined my marriage? And what were the complementary conflicts in the spouse I married?

Probably all of us marry, at least in part, to defend old solutions to old conflicts. The difficulty comes when two people so interlock their old conflicts and solutions that they cannot become aware of them, and hence cannot solve them. Ironically, being a divorced person has built-in advantages in terms of working out these conflicts, making them conscious, and overcoming them.

WHY WAS I DIVORCED?

Presumably the fundamental cause of divorce is that people find themselves in situations in which they cannot become autonomous individuals and are unwilling to settle for a *folie à deux*. Divorcees are people who have not achieved a good marriage—they are also people who would not settle for a bad one.

A "successful" divorce begins with the realization by two people that they do not have any constructive future together. That decision itself is a recognition of the emotional divorce. It proceeds through the legal channels of undoing the wedding, through the economic division of property and arrangement for alimony and support. The successful divorce involves determining ways in which children can be informed, educated in their new roles, loved and provided for. It involves finding a new community. Finally, it involves finding your own autonomy as a person and as a personality.

AUTONOMY

The greatest difficulty comes for those people who cannot tell autonomy from independence. Nobody is independent in the sense that he does not depend on people. Life is with people. But if you wither and die without specific people doing specific things for you, then you have lost your autonomy. You enter into social relationships—and we are all more or less dependent in social relationships—in order to enhance your own freedom and growth, as well as to find somebody to provide for your needs and to provide good company in the process. Although, in a good marriage, you would never choose to do so, you *could* withdraw. You could grieve, and go on.

These are six of the stations of divorce. "The undivorced," as they are sometimes called in the circles of divorcees, almost never understand the great achievement that mastering them may represent.

WHAT DO YOU THINK?

Don and Denise have been married over a year but are having troubles. The same old themes keep cropping up; Don talks about them all of the time while Denise keeps quiet; in fact, you could say they really do not communicate. Denise wants them to go to a marriage counselor but Don refuses. What do you suggest?

Shall Denise go to the counselor alone?

Shall she keep after Don to go?

Shall she just continue to keep quiet?

Should she get a divorce?

What other suggestions do you have?

Two divorced people marry each other. Jake mentions his former wife in his conversations constantly, while June never even mentions her former husband and refuses to discuss the time they spent together. What do you think?

Is it better to discuss the former marriage, the positive as well as the negative aspects?

Is it better never to mention the former spouses?

Is it better to act as though that part of life never existed?

Is it good to let Jake talk about his former spouse and let Jane keep quiet about hers?

Think about these problems:

What is the difference between an argument and a fight?

If the man is the big boss at home and his wife is the meek "Yes, Dear" type, will the marriage have a minimum of problems? Why or why not? Are they apt to be happy? Why or why not?

Look at the test for naggers. What would you include if this were a test for male naggers only? How do men nag?

Popenoe investigated the complaints of wives. What would you include in a list of complaints about husbands?

Issues of Parenthood

Parenthood is certainly a general expectation in our society. "That's why you got married," we may hear, or, "A marriage is not complete without children." This expectation may sometimes be sensed as pressure, and young couples may be pushed into starting a family: "Well, what are you waiting for? When are you going to have a baby?" Couples may feel they became parents before they had a chance to adjust to each other or to consider various aspects of parenthood discussed in this section.

George J. Hecht, in his article "Smaller Families: A National Imperative," makes cogent statements about the need for limiting family size. He emphasizes that this is not only the responsibility of the poor, but also of people in better circumstances. At one time college graduates were having four or five children and thus added to the population explosion. The danger of overpopulation is so great that everyone should be aware of it and concerned about the consequences.

Childlessness was once considered a tragedy or a shame. Now we see that couples have a right to remain childless if they prefer this. The old ideas held that parenthood is a social responsibility, that the child is an extension of the self, and claimed that women do not feel fulfilled unless they bear a child—or that becoming a father established masculinity for men. Some couples want to avoid parenthood because they have strong convictions regarding children, may not really like them, or prefer to be free of encumbrances. J. E. Veevers who has been studying this problem points out that some childless women did not have parents who took child-care roles, and know mothering only from being the recipient. They may feel uncomfortable or inadequate around children. The one-child family could foster this reaction, but the oldest girl from a large family may have had heavy mothering duties to perform and want no more of it.[1]

Gustavus and Henley made a detailed study of childless couples who

[1] J. E. Veevers, "The Child-Free Alternative: Rejection of the Motherhood Mystique," *Women in Canada*, Maryles Stephenson (ed.) Toronto: New Press, 1973, pp. 183–187.

applied for sterilization. The main reasons given included a simple statement that they did not want children, concern regarding overpopulation, poor health of one of the partners, career interests, and age factors. Parents do not rear children without some help and one source of guidance is popular literature. Dr. Bigner made an analysis of the advice given in three women's magazines between 1950 and 1970, and shows how the philosophy regarding child-rearing as well as the recommendations shifted from teaching children to conform to helping them become self-actualizing individuals.

The one-parent family may be headed by a person who is widowed or divorced. Or, in cases of desertion, the parent may function alone because the partner (usually the husband) is gone but the marriage is legally intact. Benjamin Schlesinger outlines the conditions of lone parenthood and suggests what society could do to help parents without partners.

Among the issues we need to face today is the amount of social isolation the lone parent experiences. American society is run mainly by married couples, who have a three-way access to the social life of a community: the man's membership, the woman's membership, and as a couple. The lone parent is forced to cope with the single-access road, often fraught with obstacles. Even friends and relatives are often blind to the dilemmas of the 12 percent of Americans cut off from certain avenues to social life, and who are raising children alone.

Schlesinger's analysis of the problems is still valid, but he referred to 1960 Census data. The most recent figures we have concerning the number of lone parents in the U.S. show that there were 8,838,000 families with children under 18 years living with the mother, and 796,000 living only with the father.[2]

There are many arguments regarding the optimal time to begin a family, desirable number of children, and appropriate spacing of childbirths. These considerations are among the topics discussed in an article by Harold T. Christensen.[3] His major conclusion is that the degree to which a couple can control family planning to their own satisfaction is more important for their marriage than are the number and spacing of children. A major question, then, is whether the number and spacing of children corresponds with a couple's desires. If things do not work out as planned, are the parents able to alter their desires and be satisfied with

---

[2] U.S. Bureau of the Census, *Current Population Reports*, Series P–20, No. 242, "Marital Status and Living Arrangements: March, 1972," U.S. Government Printing Office, Washington, D.C., 1972, p. 25.

[3] Harold T. Christensen, "Children in the Family: Relationship of Number and Spacing to Marital Success," *Journal of Marriage and the Family*, Vol. 30, No. 2 (May 1968), pp. 283–289.

their family? What happens when husband and wife disagree over family planning? How will that affect birth control and marital happiness?

There is still some debate over whether parenthood is a crisis. Most studies indicate that parents must make changes in their behavior in order to accommodate the needs of children. The question that remains is how parents feel about these necessary changes; for their attitudes, and perhaps their adaptability, may help or hinder their transition from a marital to a family relationship. As Arthur P. Jacoby has suggested, however, the crisis of parenthood depends on the life styles of the various social classes.[4] Some parents see their children as intruders, while others feel children make their lives more complete.

One issue confronting parents is how to maintain a satisfactory marital relationship while achieving a successful relationship with the children. Is it possible to be the parent you want to be and to be the ideal marriage partner at the same time? Think about it, in detail. How would you work out the difficulties you have noted?

Raising children is seen as a natural process. But, on second thought, a parent-child relationship is a two-way street, and the ways children influence parents are as natural as the ways parents influence children. Children affect the marriage when they are born, and Geraldine M. Devor notes, children continue to influence their parents as they grow up. The parents' personalities, their marriage, and their child-raising philosophies are some of the things changed by children. The study by Devor, of course, deals only with conscious aspects. What about the numerous subtle and unconscious ways children influence and change parents? What are the limits to which parents should let themselves be influenced by children?

There are many kinds of parents. Also, there is no one-and-only ideal parent, as the work by E. E. LeMasters shows. He points out numerous models, each with some good and some bad points. The very fact that he wrote it for the counselor gives some idea of how parents can be helped. People go to a dentist when they have a toothache, to a physician when they are ill. Does it not make sense to have parents go to a counselor when they need help being parents? LeMasters has had a great deal of experience with parents, and his examples are vital. He shows that there is freedom in our society for people to decide what kind of parents they want to be.

[4] Arthur P. Jacoby, "Transition to Parenthood: A Reassessment," *Journal of Marriage and the Family*, Vol. 31, No. 4 (November 1969), pp. 720–727.

28 *George J. Hecht*

Smaller Families: A National Imperative

Economists, educators, demographers, and other experts concerned with the problems of population control have called attention—in many magazines and newspapers and on radio and TV—to the frightening statistics concerning our already overpopulated world. To the readers of Parents' Magazine, such statistics have very special significance.

Overpopulation has given rise to our environmental crisis and to a host of related social problems. Half the world is hungry now; this year, 4,000,000 people will die of starvation; millions more will be stunted mentally or physically by deprivation.

The most eminent scientists advise us that if world population continues to grow at its present rate, there will be twice as many people on earth—more than 7 billion people—by the year 2000. That's only 30 years away. At its present rate, the population of the United States will grow 50 percent, reaching a total, by the year 2000, of 300 million people. If you think the streets of our cities are crowded now, and that our education, sanitation, and housing facilities are inadequate, imagine what they will be like 30 years hence.

In this short editorial I shall limit the discussion to the problem of the United States:

> *For 25 million Americans who are poor, overpopulation helps make their poverty a life-long prison. It slams the door on decent housing, higher education, and better jobs.*
>
> *The poor know all about overpopulation. One of their major problems is that they have more children than they want. There are*

George J. Hecht, "Smaller Families: A National Imperative," from *Parents Magazine* and *Better Family Living*, July, 1970, pp. 24f. Reprinted with permission.

too many mouths to feed, bodies to clothe, minds to educate. [Italics added.]

But it isn't only the poor in this country who know the meaning of overpopulation.

Look at what is happening in our cities. They are turning into enormous traffic jams. You crawl along so-called "expressways," fight your way through traffic snarls. And when you finally reach your destination you find there's no place to park.

Besides the endless traffic, there are overcrowded schools and overburdened public facilities . . . there are over-loaded telephone lines, power failures, and water shortages. There is inadequate housing yet high-rise buildings sprout like weeds surrounded by urban blight.

The only way to limit the population growth of the United States, and the overpopulation that threatens it, is for families to have fewer children than they do now.

The more intelligent families should set an example to the others. It is extremely urgent that from now on families should have no more than two children. This should apply to the wealthy as well as to the poor. Limiting families to two children has advantages in addition to checking overpopulation. Couples with no more than two children are more likely to have the energy, the spirit, and the money to raise their children well and happily.

We all know that few couples will limit the number of children they have just because they don't want the U.S. to grow too fast. Everyone is tempted to think that increasing population is someone else's problem. Before a young couple can be persuaded not to have a third or fourth child, they must first understand the advantages of a small family.

In a small family, obviously, there is more time for the adults to spend with each child—which means more love and appreciation to go around. A richer life can be led by each member when that family is smaller. A life that involves, for the children, such important extras as music lessons, vacations, camps, travel.

In point of fact, three children simply cannot be brought up as cheaply as two. The Institute of Life Insurance not long ago came up with some rough calculations of what it costs to raise a child. The Institute estimated that a family with two children and an average income of about $6,000 would spend around $24,000 to raise each child from infancy to 18 (before college). For a four-member family with an annual income of $15,000, an 18-year outlay could go as high as $59,000 per child.

As those figures help show us, family planning isn't just for poor people. There is an ethical obligation on the part of the well-off to limit their families, for theirs are the children who not only cost more to rear but who become in turn the greatest consumers—thus swelling the totality of goods produced and used in this country.

Family planning should be a concern of every parent interested in his child's future, in the possibilities that his child will have to enjoy all the things that give life value and meaning. The enjoyment of nature is one that is increasingly endangered. If our population growth continues, the Population Reference Bureau makes this grim prediction: "Outdoor recreation in these United States will have become a nostalgic memory, even perhaps before the babies born today have children of their own."

Our society's efforts to provide birth control information and services to the economic groups who most need it must be stepped up. Certainly the federal government should increase financial assistance to local poverty areas for birth control education and supplies. A good percentage of the poor and less educated people of this country do not want an excessive number of children but do not know how to prevent conception.

When couples freely decide to have children, the whole quality of family life is different. If considerations of health and well-being for the child and the mother—for the entire family—are paramount, each individual not only leads a better life but faces a more hopeful future.

Too many of us are, on the whole, poorly informed and little concerned about our nation's population problems. Too many of us tend to think that such problems only relate to the underdeveloped countries.

In the United States, it is a question of changing the general view of what constitutes the ideal family. About 85 percent of our population in the reproductive age bracket is acquainted with and uses birth control devices. But as long as this 85 percent regards a three or four child family as ideal, we will not be able to check our dangerous population growth. Nothing less than a change of social attitude has to take place, a change that would confer approval on the one or two child family.

I have long maintained that parents who really love children can and should do a better job with two than they could possibly do with more. If they feel they must have three and can afford to raise them, there are always adoptable children who need love and a good home.

There is a choice: we can have intolerable overcrowding in cities and suburbs, higher taxes, too few schools, inadequate housing, insufficient—perhaps polluted—water, insurmountable traffic problems, and little unspoiled land left for outdoor recreation. Or we can check our population growth by making small families the American ideal.

29

*Susan O. Gustavus and
James R. Henley, Jr.*

Correlates of Voluntary
Childlessness in a
Select Population*

For several decades, social scientists and demographers interested in
population processes have focused research efforts on the formation of
attitudes toward childbearing. Many variables, including race, religious
preference, social class, and social mobility have been found to be instrumental in the formation of these attitudes and in the subsequent fertility
experienced by the couples. However, little data can be found on what
factors predispose a couple to negative fertility attitudes, that is, to desire
to have no children.

The lack of attention given to the voluntarily childless couple, and indeed to the childless couple in general, probably stems from several
factors. Firstly, the phenomenon of childlessness, whether voluntary or
involuntary, is increasingly rare. Table 1 shows the percent of ever-married
women who were childless at selected ages and dates from 1940 to 1967.
The total age group, as well as selected age categories within the total
group, have experienced steady declines in childlessness. But to assume
that this trend will continue may be an error. With increasingly effective
means of contraception available, with abortion laws undergoing examination and change, and with increasing concern with, and publicity over,
growing population, this trend may very well reverse itself.

Secondly, the neglect of the voluntarily childless couple may be a result of the tendency to view childlessness as just another quantitative state
of parity. It would seem that there are important qualitative differences

Susan O. Gustavus and James R. Henley, Jr., "Correlates of Voluntary Childlessness in a Select Population," from *Social Biology*, Vol. 18, No. 3, pp. 277–
284. Reprinted with permission.
* Paper prepared for presentation at annual meetings Southwestern Sociological Association, March 25–27, 1971, Dallas, Texas.

TABLE 1   Per cent of women childless at selected ages and selected dates, noninstitutional population of the United States.

Age	1967	1965	1962	1960	1957	1952	1950	1940
15–44	13.3	14.2	14.4	15.0	15.9	20.7	22.8	26.5
20–24	28.0	28.0	23.4	24.2	26.9	30.9	33.3	39.9
30–34	6.4	7.2	9.9	10.4	11.3	14.7	17.3	23.3
40–44	8.9	11.0	12.8	14.1	14.1	19.8	20.0	17.4

Source: Figures for 1967 taken from U.S. Bureau of the Census, 1969, Table 7. Figures for all other dates taken from U.S. Bureau of the Census, 1969, Table 1.

associated with childless and childed states, since those who are presently childless are in violation of the statistical and social norm to have children.

Finally, were the above problems to be ignored or deemed not prohibitive, the design of a systematic study of voluntarily childless couples is a formidable task. Where would such couples be found? How could the researcher be sure that the childlessness was voluntary?

MATERIALS AND METHODS

In an attempt to bridge this research hiatus and to begin to cope with the difficult problems of sampling, this paper deals with the seventy-two childless couples who during the last two years applied to the Association for Voluntary Sterilization (AVS) for help in obtaining surgical sterilizations. Such couples, of course, are not representative of the total population of voluntary childless couples in the country. It might be maintained that these couples are more dedicated to the idea of remaining childless than other couples might be, since they are willing to take this frequently irreversible step.

Undoubtedly there are couples who have had such operations for the purpose of preventing conception without the aid of AVS. But the couples who come to AVS are sometimes from communities where it is difficult to obtain such operations. As one applicant stated rather bitterly: "I have tried to obtain a vasectomy locally but Puritanism is still strong in this part of the country and no consideration whatsoever is given to private individual judgments and wishes." If this is often the case, these couples may be the most flagrant norm violators of all.

They are described here, then, not as a representative or probability sample of all voluntarily childless couples. Instead they constitute an availability sample. In fact, they might best be treated as a separate population since there is little basis for estimating the degree to which even gross demographic characteristics of the national population of voluntarily childless couples are represented by these seventy-two couples. Nevertheless, it is hoped that detailed description of their characteristics will provide theoretical and research leads for further investigations of negative fertility attitudes.

DATA AND RESULTS

Table 2 gives preliminary descriptive data on the applicants to AVS. The vast majority of these applicants are males, presumably since a vasectomy is a simpler operation than a tubal ligation would be. Most of them come from the northeastern region of the United States. Table 2 also shows that most of these couples come from large urban areas. Indeed, while 12% of them seem to come from very small communities this is probably an overstatement of the numbers actually from isolated small communities since some of the small places included in that category are in fact suburbs of very large metropolitan areas.

The mean number of years these couples have been married is 5.2, but half of them have been married for less than four years and two-thirds have been married for less than six years before applying to AVS for assistance. Finally, most of the couples heard about AVS through some form of mass media, including radio or TV, magazines, and newspapers. While most of the applicants for the actual operations were males, the magazines most frequently mentioned as sources of information about AVS, were *McCalls*, *Redbook*, and other magazines traditionally thought of as women's publications.

Table 3 shows the age, religion, and socioeconomic status of both husbands and wives, as measured by their occupation, education, and income. Also shown are comparable data for the United States population at selected dates. This enables some comparison of these voluntarily childless couples with the general population on at least four of these characteristics.

The mean age of husbands in this sample is 32 and of wives 29—the traditional three-year difference in age found in most populations. Over 50% of both husbands and wives are less than 30. The decision to be sterilized in order to prevent conception is apparently an early one. However, 17% of the husbands and 10% of the wives are over 40, so that this decision is not exclusively confined to extremely young couples by any means.

Perhaps the most theoretically interesting finding concerning the characteristics of these couples is the disproportionate number among them who have no religion whatever. Forty per cent of the husbands and 36% of the wives fall into this category, as opposed to 4% and 1% of U.S. males

TABLE 2   Percentage distribution of childless applicants for voluntary sterilization by selected characteristics.

Characteristic	%
Sex	
Male	95
Female	4
Nonresponse	1
Total	100
Residence	
Northeast	61
North Central	17
West	10
South	12
Total	100
Size of place	
Less than 2,500	12
2,500 to 10,000	17
10,000 to 50,000	25
50,000 to 100,000	6
More than 100,000	40
Total	100
Number of years married	
One or less	24
Two or three	25
Four or five	18
Six or seven	8
Eight or more	25
Total	100
$\bar{X}$	5.2
Source of referral to AVS	
Other agency	20
TV or radio	19
Magazine	33
Newspaper	10
Friend or relative	4
Other	13
Nonresponse	1
Total	100

and females respectively. Catholics are under-represented among these couples in comparison with their proportion in the population, as might be expected given the prohibition against birth control and the value placed on children in this religion. But other religious groups are also under-represented among the childless couples, with two exceptions. Jewish men, who comprise 11% of the childless husbands, constitute only 4% of the general population. Secondly, both sexes in the "Other Protestant" category are somewhat over-represented among the 72 couples when compared to national proportions.

TABLE 3 Percentage distribution of religion, age, occupation, education, and income of childless couples requesting voluntary sterilization, and of the United States population at selected dates.

Characteristic	Childless Couples		United States	
	Husbands	Wives	Male	Female
Age				
25 or less	22	32	...	...
26–30	29	33	...	...
31–35	21	11	...	...
36–40	7	10	...	...
41 or more	17	10	...	...
Nonresponse	4	4	...	...
Total	100	100	...	...
X̄	32	29	...	...
Religion*				
Catholic	6	6	28	28
Jewish	11	4	4	4
Baptist	3	4	15	15
Methodist	6	7	13	14
Presbyterian	4	6	6	6
Other Protestant	30	37	28	30
No religion	40	36	4	1
Total	100	100		
Occupation†				
0–29 (low)	1	3	20	...
30–59	15	14	41	...
60–79	14	28	25	...
80–99 (high)	62	28	14	...
No occupation	8	27	...	...
Total	100	100	100	...
X̄	78	70		
Education‡				
Less than 8th grade	...	...	23 (17)	20 (14)
Some high school	6	3	37 (35)	37 (34)
High school graduate	19	28	21 (29)	28 (37)
Some college	12	28	9 (10)	9 (9)
College graduate	38	28	10 (9)	6 (6)
Graduate degree	24	9	...	...
Nonresponse	1	4	...	...
Total	100	100	100	100
Income§				
Less than $3,000	6	33	30	65
$ 3,000–5,999	18	22	24	26
$ 6,000–9,999	35	31	30	7
$10,000–14,999	29	10	11	1
$15,000 or more	7	...	5	1
Nonresponse	5	4	...	...
Total	100	100	100	100
X̄	$8,860	$4,436	$6,159	$2,601

* For the United States as a whole, data from U.S. Bureau of the Census, 1957.
† For the United States as a whole, figures for Head of Family are listed under "Male." Data for 1960. U.S. Bureau of the Census, 1963.
‡ Figures for the United States for ages 25–34 are given in parentheses for comparison. Data for 1960. U.S. Bureau of the Census, 1960, Table 173.
§ For the United States, data from U.S. Bureau of the Census, 1967.

By any of the three measures of socioeconomic status shown in Table 3 these childless couples are clearly of higher status than the United States population in general. The occupational score used here is a measure computed by using standardized scores of income and education associated with each occupation in the United States. If we compare the husbands of the childless couples to the heads of U.S. families in 1960 (a not entirely comparable group) it can be seen that the childless husbands are much more likely to be in the highest status occupations (62%) than are the U.S. family heads (14%). Even the childless wives have higher occupations overall than do U.S. family heads.

The educational attainment comparison is even more striking. Fully 62% of the childless husbands have a college degree or more, while only 10% of the male U.S. population could claim such an educational attainment in 1960. It is only fair to point out, however, that since the childless couples are largely below 30, their educational attainment is likely to be higher than that for the entire U.S. population. Table 3 also gives the educational attainment distribution for males and females age 25–34 years in the United States in 1960. Still, the voluntarily childless couples show a much higher educational attainment.

The distribution of income follows this same pattern. The mean income of the childless husbands is $8,860 while that same figure for U.S. males in 1967 was $6,159. Similarly with females there is nearly a $2,000 differential in the income of these childless wives and U.S. females in 1967.

Table 4 gives the contraceptive and pregnancy histories of these couples. The great majority of them (89%) were contracepting at the time they requested sterilization and had been doing so for a number of years. Eight per cent had used some form of contraception previously but were not now doing so. Three per cent of them had never contracepted.

Since most of the couples mentioned using various methods of contraception, the percentages in this column do not add to 100 and multiple responses are included. Oral contraceptives were by far the most frequent method of contraception used. Condoms and diaphragms were less frequently used by these couples, and other methods shown in Table 4 were not often mentioned.

The mean number of years these couples had been contracepting, by whatever method, is 4.3. The largest group of them had contracepted for five or more years, with one couple reporting they had been practicing birth control for 18 years. Apparently the decision to be sterilized is not often a quick one made in reaction to the inconvenience of contracepting. A disappointingly large percentage of these couples did not report these data, most probably due to the actual wording of the question, which asked them to specify when they began using contraceptives. It could be

TABLE 4 Contraceptive and pregnancy histories of childless couples requesting voluntary sterilization.

Use of contraception	
Previously, not now	8
Previously and now	89
Never used	3
Total	100
Methods used*	
Diaphragm	32
Condom	42
Suppository	3
Jelly	18
Oral	68
Other	18
How long contracepting	
Less than one year	4
1 to 2 years	17
3 to 4 years	19
Five or more years	24
Nonresponse	36
Total	100
$\overline{X}$	4.3
Miscarriages and abortions	
1 or more miscarriages	7
1 or more abortions	4
1 or more of both	2
Neither	71
Nonresponse	16
Total	100

* The percentages here do not add to 100 since several couples mentioned using several different methods.

that they could not remember or that they did not feel these data were relevant to AVS.

Finally, Table 4 gives the pregnancy history of these couples. Apparently 71% of them have never been pregnant, since they are presently childless and have had neither miscarriages nor abortions. Another option exists—to bear a child and then give it up by adoption—and these data would not show how many couples have done so. Six per cent of the couples have had abortions, and 9% have had miscarriages, which may or may not have been deliberately inflicted.

Table 5 shows the reasons these couples gave on their applications for wanting to be sterilized. Unfortunately, 24% of the applicants said simply that they did not wish to have any children—making them unusable for an analysis which tries to tap reasons for not wanting children. Table 5 gives both the first reason given by the couples in making their applica-

TABLE 5   Percentage distribution of the first reasons given and total reasons given for wanting to be sterilized by childless couples.

Reason	First mention	Total mentions*
Population concern	15	28
Health	16	25
Career	10	17
Too old	11	11
Dislike for children	7	12
Economic	3	12
Fear of pregnancy	1	8
World conditions	. . .	7
Intend to adopt	4	12
Don't want children	24	24
Other	8	22
Total	99	. . .

* The percentages in this column do not add to 100 since respondents were permitted to cite multiple reasons and often did so.

tion and the total reasons mentioned by the couples. The most common reason given by these couples was some concern for the world or national population problem. The theoretical question this finding raises is whether this is a true reason which motivates these couples or whether this is a socially acceptable reason they have seized upon with the advent of population propaganda in order to justify a decision they have already made. These data do not provide answers to questions of this sort.

Health reasons were also important in leading to this decision to seek sterilization. Included here were heart conditions, blood problems, or other physical conditions, particularly of the wives, which would make childbearing difficult at best. These are presumably conditions out of the direct control of these couples and might not qualify them as strictly voluntarily childless.

Several of the couples mentioned deep or time-consuming involvement with careers which would make child rearing inconvenient. Typical of this kind of comment, made by 17% of the sample, is the following:

Before my wife and I were married seven years ago, we both expressed our desires to have no children, so that we could do justice to our work, unhindered. I am a writer. My wife is deeply involved in sculpturing. We both have jobs and come home at night to our hobbies.

Eleven per cent of the sample simply stated that they were too old to begin their families now. In some cases these couples married late, but in others no reason is given for not starting the family at an earlier age.

A plain dislike for children was given as a reason for wanting to remain childless by 12% of the sample. Typical of this kind of response are the following:

> Both of us are too familiar with the smell of sour pablum, diaper pails, and baby "b.m.'s" and we find equally nauseating the sound of crying, screaming, and infant temper tantrums. These so called "joys of parenthood" are definitely not for us.

Or the couple who said:

> We are unable to tolerate the presence of children for any appreciable length of time and cannot imagine any circumstances in which either of us would ever want children of our own.

Some of the couples mentioned economic problems which they felt prohibited them from having children. Examples of these couples' comments include:

> We are unable to afford the expenses of pregnancy, child birth, child raising and subsequent family illnesses . . . . An accidental pregnancy now would keep us living in cheap apartments for the rest of our lives.

One of the wives wrote:

> Another reason we do not want children are our financial problems. My husband never finished school, and his low paying job doesn't really meet our needs, with the high cost of living. It pays the bills and there is none left over for saving. There is no real future in his job. . . . We live in a one bedroom 8' by 31' house-trailer and it's really too crowded for the two of us. It will be several years, if ever, before we can hope to do better. A new car must come first, as our 14 year old Chevrolet won't stand up much longer without falling apart.

Other reasons given by fairly small proportions of the sample include some mention of a preferred style of life, other than professional ambitions, which would be inhibited by children. Included here are couples who intend to travel or who enjoy solitude for its own sake. World conditions, other than overpopulation, were mentioned by 7% of this group. These respondents were concerned about war, pollution, crime, etc., and did not feel such a world was a good place to bring up children. Finally, nine of the couples intend to adopt children, which, of course, does not make them voluntarily childless at all.

Included in the category labeled "Other" reasons were a smattering of couples who were mentally retarded, who thought such an operation would improve their sexual life, or who said only that they were frankly untrusting of the birth-control methods available to them, for health or effectiveness reasons.

SUMMARY AND CONCLUSIONS

This has indeed been a cursory look at a select population of couples who, with the exception of nine potential adopters, intend to be permanently childless. With such limited data and given such a population, the most we can hope to do is pick up a few leads as to what sorts of characteristics persons with negative fertility attitudes are likely to have and what they perceive as some of the reasons behind this attitude. Our data show that an average couple in this group is likely to be living in a large metropolitan area and to have been married an average of about five years. They are likely to be about thirty years of age, to say they have no religion, and to be of generally high socioeconomic status. Most all of them have used some method of birth control, usually the pill, have been contracepting for a number of years, and are not likely to have had a miscarriage or abortion. Such a profile of the average person in our sample, of course, obscures as much as it enlightens.

Finally, in looking at the reasons for wanting to remain childless, population concerns and health considerations are the two most mentioned reasons and if truly a reflection of the couple's rationale are not "selfish" reasons which may be ascribed to childless couples by society in general. Reasons which might be more reasonably associated with hedonism include career commitments, style of life, or economic desires. Disliking children and fear of pregnancy might be classified as "hang-ups" which may or may not be associated with selfish pursuits.

In future research on the voluntarily childless couple, the strategy that might be taken in locating these couples is not clearly indicated by these data. It is clear from the small percentage of the population which they comprise that random samples of the population, unless quite large, are not likely to unearth sufficient numbers of them to do detailed tabulations. An availability sampling technique might be tried in large communities— with no hope of representativeness. These authors tried, prior to receiving these data from AVS, to search out such couples in several ways, including surveying couples in apartments known to be one-bedroom or smaller where the presence of children was unlikely. This method of course turns up mostly couples who are postponing their childbearing, a few single people, and several pregnant wives. Further, even among the couples found who claim to be permanently and voluntarily childless, some of them will no doubt experience an accidental pregnancy in the future and keep the child. It is possible to place ads in various newspapers and other community publications asking childless couples to volunteer to answer a questionnaire. Such a method is plagued by the usual problems associated with using volunteers in any research.

Nevertheless, these two methods in concert, used over a period of time in a large community, might yield another select population like the one discussed here. Certainly any additional data would be useful, since as mentioned above, the literature on these special couples with negative fertility attitudes is so sparse.

ACKNOWLEDGMENTS

The authors wish to thank the Association for Voluntary Sterilization for their cooperation in furnishing us with these data. The analysis of the data was funded by the Research Committee of the University of Utah, to which the authors are indebted.

REFERENCES

U.S. BUREAU OF THE CENSUS. 1958. Current population reports, 1957. Series P–20, No. 79. Government Printing Office, Washington, D.C.

————. 1963. Methodology and scores of socioeconomic status. Working Paper 15. Government Printing Office, Washington, D.C.

————. 1963. Eighteenth census of the United States, 1960. Government Printing Office, Washington, D.C.

————. 1969. Income in 1967 of persons in the United States. Series P–60, No. 60. Government Printing Office, Washington, D.C.

————. 1969. Marriage, fertility, and childspacing: June 1965. Current Population Reports, Series P–20, No. 186. Government Printing Office, Washington, D.C.

————. 1971. Previous and prospective fertility: 1967. Current Population Reports, Series P–20, No. 211. Government Printing Office, Washington, D.C.

30 *Jerry J. Bigner*

Parent Education in Popular Literature: 1950-1970*

Content analyses of popular literature publications have been performed for data from 1820 to 1948. The purposes of the present study were to extend these analyses to present times and to describe what were advocated as "good" childbearing procedures over the past 20 years. Results indicated that during the years 1950 to 1970, the primary topics of interest in three women's magazines were socialization of children (24 percent), parent child relations (20 percent), and developmental stages (17 percent). Changes in advice-giving indicated a shift from encouraging parents to rear children to conform with anticipated adult life styles to rearing children to become self-actualizing individuals.

INTRODUCTION

Winch (1963) has noted that a characteristic of American parents is their uncertainty about how to raise children. As a consequence, there has been a response to this uncertainty in terms of advice-giving ranging from folklore to "expert" syndicated columnists and from government pamphlets to popular literature publications.

Information from magazines has constituted a primary source for analysis and description of trends in child care. Advice-giving in popular literature has been traced to 1820. (Sunley, 1955) In the period preceding the Civil War, Sunley reported that contradictory advice was prevalent with some authors advocating indulgent treatment (demand feeding, etc.) and others prescribing stern discipline (breaking the child's will, etc.) as

Jerry J. Bigner, "Parent Education in Popular Literature: 1950-1970," from *The Family Coordinator*, July, 1972, pp. 313-319. Reprinted with permission.
* The author wishes to express appreciation to Mrs. Kay Tudor for assistance in data collection.

the best method for rearing children. With the exception of a 30 year gap (1860–1890), content analyses have been performed for data through about 1950. (Escalona, 1949; Stendler, 1950; Bruch, 1952; Vincent, 1953; Wolfenstein, 1953; Senn, 1955) Stendler performed a detailed analysis of popular women's literature appearing from 1890 to 1948. Describing trends in advice-giving during each decade of the period under investigation, she concluded that there appeared to be a cycle of advocated "best" childrearing procedures, and that by the 1940s there appeared to be a return to similar attitudes and guidance expressed in the 1890s concerning methods of childrearing.

The value of these historical surveys lies not in evaluating the effectiveness of mass media approaches in parent education but in describing the evolution of this particular facet of the parent education movement. Thus, the primary purpose of the present survey was to extend the analyses of Stendler (1950), Sunley (1955), and others to the present time. In addition, by examining the content of popular magazine articles to determine changes in types of topics mentioned over the past two decades, it would be possible to ascertain what were advocated as "good" childrearing procedures.

The data of the present study were collected from three popular women's magazines: *Ladies' Home Journal, Good Housekeeping,* and *Redbook.* These magazines, with the exception of *Redbook,* were used by Stendler (1950) in her content analysis and were chosen in order to provide a measure of continuity with her data. Beginning in 1950, each issue of these magazines was examined in each biennial year, e.g., 1950, 1952, etc. through 1970. A content analysis was performed for articles dealing with selected parent education topics. These topics were patterned after those used by Stendler (1950) and included the areas of specific behavior problems, personality development, parent-child relations, socialization practices, developmental stages, health care, and pregnancy. A checklist was prepared for use in collecting the data.[1]

ADVICE-GIVING: 1950–1970

It is possible to view the years 1950 to 1970 as a period during which the popular literature was concerned primarily with the topics of socialization of children, parent-child relations, and developmental stages. During these decades, 24 percent of the topics dealt in one way or another with a "how-to" approach to the primary task of parenthood: socialization of children to societal-familial values, attitudes, behavior, etc. It was expected that the articles dealing with socialization would in some way include the topic of parent-child relations since these two topics were interrelated in

many aspects. This assumption was largely supported in that 20 percent
of the information available to parents over the 20 year period dealt with
ways to improve or to understand the parental role in relation to childrearing responsibilities. It was somewhat surprising to note that seventeen
percent of the total topics surveyed dealt with developmental stages since
there has been a tendency to place less emphasis in teaching child development via developmental norms in recent years. These data are presented in
Table 1 which also presents the results of the content analysis by biennial
year.

TABLE 1   Percentage of parent education topics in three popular women's
magazines: 1950–1970.

Topics	% 1950	% 1952	% 1954	% 1956	% 1958	% 1960
Specific Behavior Problems	3	4	6	9	8	15
Personality Development	9	6	13	8	11	13
Socialization	21	19	27	31	26	22
Parent-Child Relations	19	20	17	19	16	20
Health Care	19	19	14	6	11	8
Pregnancy	2	4	3	2	5	3
Developmental Stages	22	20	19	21	16	15
Miscellaneous	5	8	1	4	7	4
Total Topics	149	142	162	160	122	144
Total Articles	72	81	73	78	59	68

Topics	% 1962	% 1964	% 1966	% 1968	% 1970	— X%
Specific Behavior Problems	11	9	16	13	15	10
Personality Development	12	8	11	10	10	10
Socialization	24	23	26	23	23	24
Parent-Child Relations	23	17	20	22	21	20
Health Care	12	15	3	7	4	11
Pregnancy	2	14	9	6	8	5
Developmental Stages	12	10	12	17	18	17
Miscellaneous	3	4	3	2	1	3
Total Topics	129	111	148	190	196	
Total Articles	76	60	83	89	94	

A difficult problem that faced Stendler as well as the present investigator in the collection of the data was that of recognizing the overlapping of
topics within a single article. Many writers were likely to discuss several
topics within one article, e.g., socialization and developmental stages.
Thus, the number of topics listed in the final analysis was greater than the
actual number of articles surveyed. The total topics was the base for determining percentages for each year.

It was interesting to note that the majority of topics examined provided information which focused on the early childhood years (42 percent), followed by the middle childhood years (32 percent), adolescence (15 percent), and infancy (11 percent). This finding appears to indicate that the early childhood years continue to be a time of considerable importance for providing information to new parents.

THE PARENTAL ROLE

Vincent (1953) described the period 1935–1945 as the "baby's decade" since mothers were urged to make their interests and authority "become secondary to . . . baby's demands." By a similar analogy, results of the present study suggest that the period from 1950 to 1970 may be described as the parent's era—a time during which the parent was urged to recognize his own individuality within his role in shaping a child's development. A primary proponent of this attitude was Dr. Benjamin Spock. Over this 20 year period, Dr. Spock contributed heavily to two magazines used in the present study, *Ladies' Home Journal* and *Redbook*. He appeared to lend great significance to the role of the parent in shaping his child's development. A recurrent theme of his articles was that of bolstering parents' confidence in handling their relationship with the child. Time and time again, Dr. Spock emphasized the need for parents to give children consistent, firm but loving guidance. An example of his advice was: "A child needs to feel that his father and mother, however agreeable, still have their rights, and know how to be *firm*. He likes them better that way." (Spock, 1954, 156) Another example of Spock's advice to parents was: "Parents have to be reasonably consistent; have to feel and speak and act as if they expected to be obeyed. Firm guidance which springs from devotion is not only good for children—they love it." (Spock, 1956a, 20) His emphasis on building parents' confidence can be illustrated by the following example:

> There's a further complication that makes parents' jobs unpredictable. All children are born with somewhat different temperaments . . . yet, parents have to put up with what they receive in the way of children: it's a great credit to them that they get along at least reasonably well with most of their children. (Spock, 1966, 26)

The controversy over Dr. Spock in relation to his purported advocacy of permissive childrearing was not supported by a survey of his advice-giving over the 20-year period. In an article written in 1960, he stated his objective in giving advice to parents:

My aim is to help parents who are wasting valuable patience and energy in excessive deference to their children's whims and moods and minor misbehavior. Will he grow to dislike his mother if she is strict about mealtime manners? That depends on how she disciplines him. But he will be miserable if she lets him go on churning up commotions in the household. (Spock, 1960, 24)

Spock specifically denied any advocacy of permissive childrearing in 1968: "I never believed in permissive childrearing. A child is not only better adjusted, but happier when his parents know just what to expect of him in the way of behavior and make this quite clear to him." (Spock, 1968a, 48)

The period between 1950 and 1970 appeared to reflect significant changes in expectations regarding the role of the father. The view appearing in 1950 was that there was not too much that could be expected from a father with regard to participation in childrearing activities:

Actually, about all a woman can ask of her husband during the first few weeks of living with a new baby is that he be reassuring, patient, tolerant, and careful not to roll over when she's changing the baby on the bed. Beyond that, anything he does is whimsey and not to be counted on for steady employment. (Jackson, 1950, 112)

In 1954, fathers were being encouraged to participate more actively in their role: "Doing for his child is the quickest way for a man to be inducted into true fatherhood, and the whole family benefits." (Bundesend, 1954, 72) Spock, as usual, took a stand on the matter and explained the misconceptions surrounding fatherhood: "Some fathers have been brought up to think that the care of babies and children is the mother's job entirely. This is the wrong idea." (Spock, 1956b, 50) By 1970, the general consensus in articles appeared to emphasize that a father was expected to participate as much as possible in childrearing responsibilities along with the mother, the net result being better personality development for children.

In line with Stendler's (1950) findings, advice-giving to parents of infants emphasized a great deal of handling and a less rigid enforcement of schedules. Parents were advised:

Babies, even small ones, are tougher than you think. They are also sociable little creatures who love having people around and literally thrive on attention. Therefore, almost as soon as the little head stops wobbling, the DO NOT TOUCH sign should come down. In the long run, it is far better for the baby to have to endure unskillful handling than to be so closely guarded that he may feel shut out and resentful. (Anon., 1960a, 26)

The emphasis on less rigid scheduling was a much discussed topic as illustrated by the following article which appeared in 1952:

> Diaper days last longer than they used to. We have gotten away from the idea of forcing early training, and what a relief this is, especially to those conscientious ones who used to judge their success or failure as mothers by whether or not the baby kept dry. By far, the most sweeping of the new ideas is the "relax and enjoy your baby" attitude. Freedom and comfort (for both generations) is the key to modern baby care. (Montgomery, 1952, 45)

Parents of infants were advised to be less restrictive of their children as illustrated by a discussion of the use of the playpen:

> Overuse of the playpen quite literally keeps them (the infants) from attaining the fullest physical and mental development of which they are capable. This may sound like an extreme statement, but consider that a baby learns the properties of the world by constant touching and tasting. The baby who shows that he is fed up with captivity should be let out. (Black, 1952, 75)

Dr. Spock is on record for encouraging toilet-training before eighteen months: "Ease in training depends a great deal on a mother's recognizing and taking advantage of the different stages of her child's readiness." (Spock, 1968b, 22) In addition, the use of the pacifier, an instrument highly scorned before 1950, was encouraged. Primarily, the use of the pacifier was recommended in helping infants to overcome fretfulness and in preventing the onset of thumbsucking.

THE PARENT AS "EXPERT"

A popular theme during the 1960s could be described as a reaction formation to all types of advice given previously. There was a rash of articles with a common theme of "experts don't know any more about raising children than I (the parent) do." An example of this view is illustrated as follows:

> I have come to only one certain conclusion in my study of the history of child care. There is no single "right" way to rear children; therefore, stick to the "expert" who fits you best. No advice is infallible . . . but will be good advice if we select and apply it with the three types of sense every parent needs: Common Sense, a Sense of Humor, and a Sense of Perspective. (Geddes, 1965, 146)

In 1966, a regular column began to be featured in *Ladies' Home Journal*. This column had as part of its masthead the following:

> The greatest child care experts in the world are mothers, because they alone know the special joys and daily headaches of bringing up children. To tap this natural resource of experience, we asked our readers to share with each other their best solutions to their everyday problems in living with children. (Anon., 1966, 11)

This type of article perhaps recognized a growing sense of personal autonomy of parents in their belief that they could freely exercise their role without fear of greatly damaging their children in the process. It should be noted that this same approach was being presented simultaneously by Dr. Spock. Hence, it is possible to view the 20 year period as a time during which parents were encouraged to discover their abilities to participate actively in their role without fear.

DISCIPLINE

The subject of discipline received the greatest amount of attention with regard to advice-giving. Forms of advice represented numerous points of view on this subject. One approach was to provide information via developmental stage of the child: "Reasoning will get you nowhere when a three-year-old says, 'I won't;' " and "No need to get tough with a two-year-old when diversions work miracles." (Anon., 1960b; Anon., 1966)

The primary approach in advice-giving concerning discipline was to urge parents to avoid the use of physical punishment. Such viewpoints stressed that rather than using these techniques, parents should encourage a child to become self-reliant; hence, the need for physical punishment would not be necessary. One author in particular stressed that physical punishment should be avoided for the following reasons: "(1) It never worked. (2) It was stupid, primitive, and cruel. (3) It was based on a social philosophy that permitted Papa to be a household emperor if that was his inclination." (Black, 1954a, 12) Catchy little phrases were used also to emphasize the point that physical punishment was harmful for children: "Remember then to restrain with love; if you do, the chances are that your children will love without restraint." (Black, 1954b, 78) The apparent attitude toward corporal punishment was best summarized by Redl (1968): "Spanking is not a means of communication. By itself, it carries no message except that big people aren't afraid to hit little people." (Redl, 1968, 164)

As long ago as 1950, authors were emphasizing what has come to be known today as behavior modification as an alternative to physical punishment. One author provided a step by step account of his principles of child training under this aegis:

> (1) It can be easily demonstrated that a child holds on to any pattern of behavior that is rewarded. (2) Refusal to reward a pattern of behavior causes that pattern of behavior to disappear. (3) Children will go to almost any lengths to get rewards. (Hohman, 1950, 112)

The Spock viewpoint was to provide *firm* guidance. This seemed to be the magic formula for parents to follow in obtaining consistent, obedient behavior from their children. On the other hand, the viewpoint as expressed by Haim Ginott, seemed to provide a different and somewhat unique way to provide guidance and discipline for children:

> We parents need to learn to express anger in nondamaging ways. This lesson is difficult because we have a lot to unlearn. Anger without insult is most helpful; it gives sound to fury without causing damage, it brings relief to parents, insights to children, and no harmful side effects to either. When parents are angry, children are attentive. They listen to what we say. We have a unique opportunity for teaching good English. We can express our anger with one limitation; no matter how angry we get, we do not attack a child's personality or character, e.g., "When I ask a question and get no answer, I feel ignored. It is very annoying. That noise you're making makes me feel uncomfortable. Your behavior (not you) makes me feel angry." (Ginott, 1968, 139)

ADVOCATED "GOOD" CHILDREARING PRACTICES: 1950–1970

The content analysis performed on articles appearing in three popular women's magazines between 1950 and 1970 indicated that the following points were advocated as "good" childrearing procedures:

1. A primary responsibility of the parent was to train the child for self-reliance by being *honest* and *frank*. By being untruthful, a parent would breed mistrust on the part of the child.
2. The parent could best aid the child's intellectual development by providing him with a sense of security by loving him. This would enable him to feel free to explore and be curious about his environment.
3. The parent had a right to privacy. He should not have to answer every question or provide answers for everything.

4. The best start for every baby was breast-feeding and a delivery by natural childbirth methods.

5. Parents, it was indicated, should always be in firm control of all situations involving their children. Parents should not let children manipulate them by their cute behavior; rather, the parent should show the child who is the "boss."

6. In providing sex education, the facts were not enough. However, parents should not go into too much detail, but protect their own modesty and privacy, and call a "spade a spade."

7. The parent was advised not to try to be a perfect parent since this was impossible; mistakes should be expected to be made without causing irreparable harm to the child.

8. The parent was expected to recognize the child as a person of worth and aid in the development of his self-concept by encouraging independent actions and efforts.

9. The parent was encouraged to use and trust his own common sense. Expert advice was often conflicting, confusing, not necessarily workable for one's child, or always correct. The parent was advised to use whatever worked best for himself and for his child.

10. As a childrearing practice, the authoritative pattern was recommended. This pattern attempts to strike a happy medium between authoritarian and permissive childrearing practices. It encourages parents to set limits within reason, and to use power and shaping by positive reinforcement to achieve objectives. (Baumrind, 1966)

11. Discipline was viewed as important in affecting later adult behavior. Punishment in the form of spanking was considered to be a good parental action in the early 1950s according to some authors, but later became an action to be assiduously avoided by the 1960s. Psychological punishment was the advocated form. Behaviors of children which induced sharp reactions from parents were cited as being the three D's: Disobedience, Dawdling, and Defiance.

12. The most important functions of the parent were seen as loving the child, letting him know it both physically and psychologically; thinking of him as an individual person; appreciating what he does; trusting him and telling him so; and above all letting him know he is wanted.

IMPLICATIONS

Various trends over the past 20 years in parent education—at least as it is represented in popular women's literature—were discovered in this study. Perhaps some of the origins of events and behaviors that have led to the development of contemporary "youth culture" with its "new" morality, drugs, etc., are reflected in these trends. However, pointing to the popular literature as a prime agent leading to these developments is an over simplification at best. Rather, the present findings indicate specifically that 20 years ago parents were advised to rear children according to conformity with anticipated future adult life styles, whereas more recent advice appears to suggest that parents should rear a child to be a person and an individual in the crowd. Furthermore, it appears that more recently parents were encouraged to discover their own rights as individuals and to trust their own "common sense" more than the advice of an "expert." Yet, the impact of "expert" opinion is far from ended as evidenced by the popularity of such individuals as Dr. Benjamin Spock, Dr. Bruno Bettelheim, and Dr. Haim Ginott. It is through the influence of such experts that it becomes possible to see the impact of modern behavioral science on the general public, particularly with regard to the role of the parent and to the advocated methods of handling discipline.

By and large, the findings of the present analysis appear to lend support to Winch's (1963) contention that mass media advice has replaced the grandmother as a resource of wisdom concerning the rearing of children. The present results appear to suggest that this form of communication has conveyed a large body of information in the areas of socialization and parent-child relations over the past 20 years, thereby signifying a transfer to some degree of a former family function to other agents in society.

Most important, it should be noted that the publications examined may be assumed to be middle-class in orientation with regard to the values, attitudes, and expectations of behavior of children expressed by the authors. This limitation would imply that the results of the present survey perhaps reflect changes in the literature serving the middle class population in general.

ENDNOTES

1. A more detailed discussion of methods and quantitative analysis of data may be obtained by writing the author.

REFERENCES

Anon., Discipline for Danny. *Good Housekeeping*, 1960a, 151 (3), 30–31.

Anon., Betsy Comes Around. *Good Housekeeping*, 1960b, 151 (4), 26.

Anon., If It Were My Child. *Ladies' Home Journal*, 1966, 84 (7), 11.

Baumrind, Diana. Effects of Authoritative Parental Control on Child Behavior. *Child Development*, 1966, 37, 887–908.

Black, Irma. Don't Fence Me In. *Redbook*, 1952, 99 (4), 73.

Black, Irma. Spare the Rod. *Redbook*, 1954a, 102 (3), 12.

Black, Irma. What Makes Children Destructive? *Redbook*, 1954b 103 (3), 78.

Bruch, H. Psychiatric Aspects of Changes in Infant and Child Care. *Pediatrics*, 1952, 10, 575–579.

Bundesend, Harold. Getting Father into the Act. *Ladies' Home Journal*, 1954, 71 (7), 72.

Escalona, Sybil. A Commentary upon Some Recent Changes in Childrearing Practices. *Child Development*, 1949, 20, 157–163.

Geddes, Jane. Bringing up Baby: A History of Completely Contradictory Advice. *Redbook*, 1966, 125 (4), 141–146.

Ginott, Haim. How To Be an Angry Mother. *Redbook*, 1968, 131 (2), 139–140.

Hohman, L. B. My Child Won't Obey. *Ladies' Home Journal*, 1950, 68 (7), 112–113.

Jackson, Susan. How to Make a Husband a Father. *Redbook*, 1950, 95 (5), 112.

Montgomery, Charlotte. When Baby Makes Three. *Redbook*, 1952, 98 (6), 45.

Redl, Fritz. A Psychiatrist's Guide to Discipline. *Redbook*, 1968, 132 (1), 164.

Senn, Milton. Changing Concepts on Child Care: A Historical Review. *March of Medicine.* New York Academy of Medicine Lectures to the Laity, No. 17. New York: International Universities Press, 1955, 83–103.

Spock, Benjamin. What Spoils a Child and Why? *Ladies' Home Journal*, 1954, 71 (12), 156.

Spock, Benjamin. How Do I Make Him Mind? *Ladies' Home Journal*, 1956a, 73 (10), 20.

Spock, Benjamin. However Good a Child's Intentions, He's Still a Child. *Ladies' Home Journal*, 1956b, 73 (11), 50.

Spock, Benjamin. Are American Parents Overpermissive? *Ladies' Home Journal*, 1960, 77 (11), 24.

Spock, Benjamin. Do Parents Cause Children's Emotional Problems? *Redbook*, 1966, 127 (2), 26.

Spock, Benjamin. Toilet-Training before 18 Months. *Redbook*, 1968a, 131 (2), 22.

Spock, Benjamin. The Fuss over Baby Care. *Redbook*, 1968b, 131 (6), 48.

Stendler, Cecilia. Sixty Years of Child Training Practices. *Journal of Pediatrics*, 1950, 36, 122–134.

Sunley, Robert. Early Nineteenth Century American Literature on Child Rearing. In M. Mead and M. Wolfenstein (Eds.), *Childhood in Contemporary Cultures*. Chicago: University of Chicago Press, 1955, 150–167.

Vincent, Clark. Trends in Infant Care Ideas. *Child Development*, 1953, 22, 199–209.

Winch, Robert. Rearing by the Book. In R. Winch, *The Modern Family*, New York: Holt, Rinehart, Winston, 1963, 447–471.

Wolfenstein, Martha. Trends in Infant Care. *American Journal of Orthopsychiatry*, 1953, 23, 120–130

31 *Benjamin Schlesinger*

The One-Parent Family: An Overview

According to the 1960 Census, the United States had 44.2 million families, while Canada counted 4.15 million families. Statistics also show that 12.5 percent of these families in the United States were classified as one-parent families, and in Canada 8.5 percent of the families were classified as one-parent families. At that time the United States had 181,252,000 people; and Canada had a population of 18,250,000. Thus one could state that Canada is about one-tenth the size of the United States in relation to general family statistics.

William N. Stephens defines the "family" as "a social arrangement based on marriage and the marriage contract, including recognition of the rights and duties of parenthood, common residence for husband, wife, and children, and reciprocal economic obligations between husband and wife" (Stephens, 1963, p. 8). This definition rests on four subsidiary terms: "marriage and the marriage contract," "reciprocal economic obligations between husband and wife," "common residence," and "rights and duties of parenthood."

A normal family is considered to be the "immediate group of father, mother, and children living together." This may be more specifically defined as a "nuclear family" (Berelson and Steiner, 1964, p. 297). The problem of the single parent is related to the fact that today society is dominated by the idea of the nuclear family.

The United States Census in 1960 defines the one-parent family as a "Parent-Child group" and states that this group consists of "parent and

Benjamin Schlesinger, "The One-Parent Family: An Overview." *The Family Life Coordinator*, Vol. 15, No. 4 (October 1966), pp. 133–138. Reprinted by permission.

The material contained in the article has been adapted from an address given at the Groves Conference on Marriage and the Family in Philadelphia, Pennsylvania, on April 26, 1965.

one or more own single sons or daughters under 18 years of age living together." The charter of the organization "Parents Without Partners" defines the one-parent family as "consisting of one parent who is caring for his or her children, in his or her home, and who is a single parent due to widowhood, divorce, separation, or who is unmarried" (Grills, 1963). The terms used by the community such as "single parent," "parent without partner," "only parent," "broken home," and "mother centered home" shed some light on the marginal status of the one-parent family in society.

Family statistics show that about 90 percent of one-parent families are headed by a mother. In most divorce actions, the custody of the children is given to the mother; in cases of desertion, it is usually the father who has left; and in case of death, statistics show that most women outlive their spouses. In the case of the unmarried mother who keeps her child, it would be a very rare court that would award the child to an unmarried father. Thus, most one-parent families in Canada and the United States are the "matriarchal type."

The literature on one-parent families in North American books is of the popular variety. There are books which give advice to widows (Champagne, 1964) and attempt to help the single parent raise his or her children (Arnstein, 1964). The single comprehensive book directed at "parents without partners" is by the Eglesons (Egleson, 1961). A search of the literature in professional journals revealed only two papers on the one-parent family (Freudenthal, 1959, and Ilgenfritz, 1961) and twenty-five related articles which dealt with the absent father and the effects of desertion on family life. Two unpublished studies are in the process of publication in American journals. On this continent sociologists and psychologists have looked predominantly at divorce (Despert, 1962, Goode, 1956, and Ostrosky, 1962) and remarriage (Bernard, 1956, and Smith, 1953) but have not begun to examine the one-parent family in research context. A beginning was recently made when the Groves Conference on Marriage and the Family chose as their theme "The One-Parent Family in the United States."

The types of one-parent families in society might be ranked in the following order of acceptance by society at large:

1. Widowed
2. Divorced
3. Separated
4. Unmarried

Thus the one-parent family who is widowed feels relatively secure in her environment, while the one-parent unmarried family feels rejection by society.

In the United States 1960 Census, there were 2,093,073 widows who formed 50 percent of all female family heads. These one-parent families had 1,870,307 related children under 18 living with them (64.8 percent of these children were classified as own children, 35.2 as other children). In Canada the widowed one-parent population, according to the 1961 Census, amounted to 213,657 of which 42,154 were families headed by a male. The families headed by a female had 181,874 children under 18, and those headed by a male had 34,283 children under 18 living in their homes.

Quite often the widow is unprepared for sudden death. A period of grief and mourning is followed by the realistic fact that she is now a one-parent head of the family with economic and social changes which may be frightening. She faces many problems, as one widow stated:

"I found managing the household finances difficult, as my husband had looked after them. Household repairs were another problem. I had difficulty deciding if I was making the right decisions as we had always decided everything together. I relied completely on my husband. We did everything together. Suddenly I had to do everything alone" (Grills et al., 1963).

Emotionally, the first and most intense feeling is loneliness.

"I still haven't got used to it. You can be alone in a big crowd. However, I am now beginning to come out of it. A year ago if you had come for this survey, I wouldn't have been able to talk about it. It has affected my work to some extent" (Grills et al., 1963).

Another thirty-five year old widow echoes this emotional upset.

"The most difficult problem was loneliness—living in the house alone without him. I was very upset, and although I was a very healthy woman, I lost weight and my blood count went way down for the first six months after his death. I was just dumb. I didn't realize I was sick" (Grills et al., 1963).

Other adjustments have to be made because of the changing financial situation of the family. Some widows have to move in with their own parents.

"Coming back home to my parents made life most difficult. They tended to pity me and be angry about my predicament. You get used to thinking and saying 'we' . . . and it was hard to say merely 'I' again. This took some time. Income is not a problem because I earn nearly as much as my husband did before he died. I only have to pay a small amount toward housekeeping expenses. Loneliness was a real problem, with other people trying to be kind only making things worse" (Grills et al., 1963).

Pity on the part of many well-meaning persons can drive a widowed parent into apathy, despair, and isolation. Society can accept the widow and look upon her as the poor unfortunate mother left all alone with her children. Usually a widow would prefer a less gloomy approach to her situation and would prefer not to be the companion to married women who have been left at home for a few days while their "husbands are away on business."

If the late husband has provided well for them, the widowed one-parent family is able to manage quite well. In too many cases, though, inadequate preparations have been made and thus the widow has to assume a full time position in order to help her family.

The divorce rates in the United States and Canada are measured by relating marriages to divorces. In 1964, the American divorce rate was 1.7, and the Canadian rate was 1.2. In Canada the only legal "reason" for obtaining a divorce is adultery, and this may account for the lower rate.

In most cases of divorce there has been adequate warning or even preparation that a one-parent family will develop. During the waiting period there may be a separation and children are frequently involved in the quarrels, discriminations, and accusations of the parents. The parents often use the children as pawns in their own need to hurt or to revenge.

After the separation, the children in divorced families face difficulties such as the questions of visitation, dual loyalties, and frequently two families if the other parent has remarried. When a divorced one-parent mother has to work full time to support her family, the children become acutely aware of losing her companionship. One mother sums this up: "The children try to cram everything into the evenings. They are always so happy when it's Saturday and I'm home."

The divorcee, as a one-parent head of the family, finds herself an easy sexual prey. One mother stated, "You can't find the odd man you can trust." The stereotype of a divorcee in our society is that she is an easy target for sexual advances, and that it is safe to approach her since her status is such that she has broken all former marital ties.

The divorced mother finds that in her social life it is the wives who fear her most. One divorcee said, "When I enter a social gathering, I feel that instinctively the wives hold on to the arms of their husbands as if to protect them from the she devil."

In the separated family a leading factor of separation is marital discord over financial matters. Very often one partner feels the spouse is immature in dealing with money. Low earning, poor money management, exorbitant credit buying, and other similar inadequacies are all examples of reasons given for incompatibility.

The separated woman finds herself in a vacuum as far as our society is concerned. In her social life, most separated mothers feel uncomfortable because they are neither single, nor married, nor legally free to marry again.

"I am in an anomalous position; I don't belong to anybody; I am a social misfit. It weighs heavily against meeting anyone with a view to re-marriage. I am not anything. I am just a woman that is not living with her husband. The separation paper is not worth anything—only an agreement. I would like to be finished and be free of him. I am nowhere and I don't see getting out of it. He does not want a divorce; he does not want to remarry."

The parent who remains in the home tends to have feelings of hostility, guilt, and confusion. Many wives find it difficult to understand why she must remain in the home while her husband can just walk away. For this reason many separated mothers seek work. For many separated wives it is necessary financially. Many others seek work in order to seek satisfaction outside the home.

The children in separated homes are usually unprepared for the separation when it occurs. Although they are almost always aware of a strain in the home, most parents fail to explain the separation to the children before it happens. It is understandable, then, that most of this group of one-parent heads find that the children are negatively affected by the separation. Most of the separated group find great difficulty in explaining the separation to the children and in handling questions and attitudes about the absent parent. This causes the children to experience confusion about the absent parent, difficulty in school, and to experience health difficulties. Many of these children feel humiliated at being abandoned by their parent. The fact that most of them do not know the reason for the separation adds to their anxieties, and they become embarrassed when asked about their absent parent.

The number of one-parent unmarried families in a country is related to the number of illegitimate births in that country. In 1960 there were 200,000 illegitimate children born in the United States and 20,000 in Canada. Clark E. Vincent estimates that in 1964, 275,000 children will be born out of wedlock in the United States. Vincent also points out that only 29.2 percent of all children born out of wedlock in 1960 were adopted (Vincent, 1964, pp. 513–520). To have some picture of the magnitude of the unmarried one-parent family, the percentage of the children kept by the unmarried mothers must be defined.

Adams and Gallagher, in reviewing a Bureau of Family Services Report of 1960, state (Adams and Gallagher, 1963, pp. 43–49):

"Of an estimated 2.5 million children under 18 in the United States who had been born out of wedlock, 31 percent had been adopted, 13 percent were receiving aid to dependent children, and 1 percent were in foster care. Little is known about the remaining 55 percent. This large group, which included over three-quarters of the nonwhite children and one-fifth of the white children under 18 years of age born out of wedlock, suggests that the majority of unmarried mothers who keep their children continue to manage in some way through subsequent marriage, employment, or support of their children by relatives, friends, or other means, but we know very little about the kinds of homes in which their children are growing up" (Adams and Gallagher, 1963, p. 47).

In a study of 227 unmarried mothers at Mount Sinai Hospital in New York (Rashbaum and Rehr, 1963, pp. 11–16), the investigators found that:

"Adoption was the primary plan among the white women, but only one Puerto Rican and one Negro woman planned adoption. The ethnic distribution in the Mount Sinai Study was almost a 4-3-3 ratio among Negro, white and Puerto Rican women respectively. The dearth of community services for the Negro or Puerto Rican child may be a factor in the fact that these children were kept by their mothers."

In Cincinnati, Ohio, a study of 118 unmarried mothers who kept their babies was carried out by the Y.W.C.A. (Reed, 1965, pp. 118–119). A sample of the study, obtained through social agencies, showed it to be two-thirds white and one-third Negro women. This sample also showed that the reasons the mothers kept their children were emotional reasons rather than realistic considerations for the welfare of the children.

The unmarried one-parent family is in a most peculiar position in society. Most social agencies still work towards the release of the child for adoption, especially if the child is healthy and white. Thus we overtly admit that the unmarried one-parent family is dysfunctional as a family unit.

With a statistical fact that 29 percent of children born out of wedlock are adopted, we may have to take a closer look at our present approach to unmarried mothers. We may have to begin encouraging and supporting unmarried mothers to keep their children; since in many cases, for this one-parent unit, this may be the best solution for family life.

PARENTS WITHOUT PARTNERS AS AN ORGANIZATION

In 1957, the idea of an organization for "Parents Without Partners" was born. From a small nucleus, the organization has grown to approximately 16,000 members in 145 chapters in the United States and Canada. A regular periodical, *The Journal,* is published by the organization.

"Parents Without Partners" is a predominantly white, middle class, non-sectarian group which has been able to obtain favorable publicity in the mass media and has spread all over the continent. In a statement, which appears in each issue of *The Journal,* the organization has outlined their purpose of existence.

As conscientious single parents, it is our primary endeavor to bring our children to healthy maturity, with the full sense of being loved and accepted as persons, and with the same prospects for normal adulthood as children who mature with their two parents together.

From the divorce or separation which divides a family, or the loss of a parent by death, it is the child who suffers most. For children in such circumstances to grow unscarred requires the utmost in love, understanding, and sound guidance. To provide these is a responsibility inherent in parenthood. It does not end with separation or divorce, for either parent.

The single parent in our society is isolated to some degree. The difficulties of providing both for ourselves and our children a reasonable equivalent of normal family life is increased by that isolation. The established pattern of community life lacks both means of communication and institutions to enable us to resolve our special problems, and find normal fulfillment.

Therefore, in the conviction that we can achieve this and through working together, through the exchange of ideas, and through the mutual understanding help and companionship which we find with one another, we have established "PARENTS WITHOUT PARTNERS, Inc." to further our common welfare and the well-being of our children.

The program differs from chapter to chapter and, as of today, the research element has not yet been built into the organization. If research projects could be developed by interested parties, the members of this group would greatly help in filling in many of the unknowns about the one-parent family.

The organization demonstrates to the newly divorced, separated, or widowed parent that he is not unique. He or she learns that he shares with many the distrait feelings of confusion, helplessness, guilt, indecision, doubt—the lost feeling of being a displaced person.

Most recently a new dimension has been added to the organization with the formation of the Fathers-at-Large committee. The committee seeks to bring male companionship to children who have lost their fathers or who have not seen their fathers for a period of at least six months. Men accompany groups of fatherless boys and girls on a variety of outings. The New York committee, which now numbers about 50 members, has taken children to a parachute jump expedition, a big league baseball game, and an excursion to a cavern.

In a recent article, Arthur Stillman (Stillman, 1965, pp. 4–8) discussed the leadership of the organization.

P.W.P. starts with a membership of followers who are troubled, unhappy, deprived, confused, often depressed and hurt. The purposes of P.W.P. are to overcome these painful states by various means, and to strive toward happier, healthier, and better adjusted adults. And indirectly through better-adjusted adults, strive to provide a more untroubled atmosphere for children with single parents. It then must follow that leadership in P.W.P. must include, the first and foremost, the ability to accept the fact that every new member must be led from sickness to health, from unhappiness to more happiness, from feelings of being lost to feelings of direction and purpose.

Dr. Stillman goes on to point out that P.W.P. is a "permanent organization of transients." He compares it to a college wherein the staff changes, the student body changes, but the organization goes on.

THE NEEDS OF ONE-PARENT FAMILIES

One-parent families in the United States and Canada have many complex needs. Common to most of the one-parent families are problems of financing, childrearing, maintaining a satisfying social life, and emotional problems of adjustment to single parenthood.

There is need of community services regarding financial assistance other than public assistance, and less costly legal services. The community needs to offer help to one-parent families who do not know of existing services or do not understand their nature.

Since many single parents use doctors, lawyers, and clergy appropriately to help solve their problems, close contacts between these professions and social services would be beneficial. More helpful use of community resources should be made at an earlier stage in marital disharmony to help repair an unhappy marriage or to carry out a separation on a more positive and constructive basis. Other services required by one-parent families are adequate day-care services, counseling of the one-parent and his children, father substitutes like a Big Brother for the children, a matrimonial bureau, and after school care for school aged children.

The special vulnerability of children in separated homes indicates the need for more explanation and interpretation to the children in preparation for the separation. Because of the difficulties involved in this area, many of the parents need professional help themselves in interpreting a separation. Most of the mothers in the separated group recognize the need of male companionship for their children and try to do something about it. But, again, many need help themselves in this area, especially early in the separation.

Parents Without Partners has been, on the whole, very useful and satisfying to most of the members. Possible consideration might be given to the formation of a clearing house for information on community services. Perhaps a booklet of services could be listed, and perhaps information about obtaining the services of a professional social worker for referral purposes, and for work with the program of the group could be included.

For single parents who do not join such a group because of social class, race, religion, or for other reasons, it might be wise to think of setting up counseling groups or family life education which would include a social-recreational aspect in some of our community centers. Such an arrangement might attract many of the single parents and their children who could benefit from such a program.

CONCLUSION

When a marriage has ended, whether by death, separation, desertion or divorce, the now-single parent must face a complete reorientation in his life. He now makes all major decisions, virtually on his own, with no partner to present another viewpoint. A woman may have great financial problems. Many young husbands fail to provide sufficient life insurance protection; consequently, the widow must care for herself, her children, and the household on a less-than-adequate budget. Most divorcees have to stretch a meager child-support check beyond its breaking point. In this stage of affairs, the woman must make a decision about returning to work. Can she provide a loving mother substitute for her child during those hours she will be on the job? Should she try to wait until all the children are in school? In addition to the financial aspect, many women prefer holding a job for the increased contacts and satisfactions it offers, while for others, the daily domestic routine is sufficiently fulfilling.

Divorced persons feel a strong sense of failure and shame of having fallen short of what so many people successfully attain. The widowed persons experience an engulfing grief and loss that even close family members cannot fully understand. Parents without partners must struggle with these enormous personal difficulties and must also be a stabilizing influence for their children.

And what of the children? When the marriage has ended, what kinds of adjustments must they make? Parents without partners list their children's fear of being different, of being left out of the main stream, as the largest problem. Many children cannot communicate their deep anxieties even to their parents. For those who retreat into themselves and brood, the parents have to work very hard to bring them back to full participation in school, clubs, sports, or any group activities that will de-emphasize the children's difference from their peer group.

Because some children feel the difference so keenly, they are anxious for their parent to remarry, so that they, too, can be part of a two-parent family. Often they will pressure the parent with such obvious remarks as, "Is he going to be my new daddy?"

Despite their uncertain, not-married-and-not-unmarried status, the one-parent heads of families are conscientious parents striving to bring their children to healthy maturity with as much capability for finding happiness as if they had both father and mother in an intact family. Their job is lonely and endless. It goes on twenty-four hours a day and requires countless decisions, large and small. Seldom is there anyone from whom single parents can expect moral and emotional support, advice, encouragement, praise, or even fault finding. Isolation from normal community life to some degree is the fate of parents without partners—whether they are divorced mothers who have custody of their children, fathers who are struggling to build normal relations with their children when they have visitation privileges only a few hours a month, or widows or widowers with children. They don't seem to fit any of the normal social patterns. They are the self-styled "fifth wheels" of society.

We who are concerned with family life in all of its manifold aspects, must pay closer attention to the one-parent family. It is true that more research is needed, but let us not get hung up on that magic formula of "research" to solve all of our social problems. Let us begin to include material on the one-parent family in our courses on the family; let us work in our communities to help the one-parent family re-enter the normal stream of life.

REFERENCES

Adams, Hanna M. and Ursula M. Gallagher, "Some Facts and Observations about Illegitimacy," *Children*, 10 (2, March–April, 1963), pp. 43–49.

Arnstein, Helen S., *What to Tell Your Child About Birth, Death, Illness, and Other Crises*, New York: Pocket Books, 1964.

Bell, Robert F., "The One-Parent Mother in the Negro Lower-Class," *Social Forces*, 43 (4, May, 1965), pp. 493–501.

Berelson, Bernard and Gary A. Steiner, *Human Behavior; An Inventory of Scientific Findings*, New York: Harcourt, Brace and World, 1964.

Bernard, Jessie, *Remarriage*, New York: Dryden Press, 1956.

Census of Canada: 1961. *Households and Families*, Series 2:1, Bulletin 2, pp. 1–7, Ottawa: Dominion Bureau of Statistics, 1964.

Champagne, Marion, *Facing Life Alone*, New York: Bobbs-Merrill, 1964.

Despert, J. Louise, *Children of Divorce*, New York: Dolphin Books, 1962.

Dickinson, Louise, *Only Parent*, Philadelphia: J. B. Lippincott, 1953.

Egleson, Jim and Janet, *Parents Without Partners*, New York: E. P. Dutton, 1961.

Freudenthal, Kurt, "Problems of the One-Parent Family," *Social Work*, 4 (1, January, 1959), pp. 44–48.

Goode, William J., *After Divorce*, Glencoe, Illinois: Free Press, 1956.

Grills, G., B. Hansen, H. Heilbron, D. Moore, J. Tapp. "Parents Without Partners," unpublished Master's Thesis, School of Social Work, University of Toronto, 1963.

Ilgenfritz, Marjorie, "Mothers on Their Own—Widows and Divorcees," *Marriage and Family Living*, 23 (1, February, 1961), pp. 38–41.

Jackson, E., *Understanding Grief*, New York: Abingdon Press, 1957.

Jones, Eva, *Raising Your Child in a Fatherless Home*, Glencoe, Illinois, Free Press, 1963.

Langer, Marion, *Learning to Live as a Widow*, New York: Julian Messner, 1957.

Marris, Peter, *Widows and Their Families*, London: Routledge and Kegan Paul, 1958.

Ostrovsky, Everett S., *Children Without Men*, New York: Collier Books, 1962.

Parents Without Partners, Inc., 80 Fifth Ave., New York, N.Y. 10011. Excerpts from Constitution, in publicity pamphlet, 1962.

Rashbaum, William, Helen Rehr, Janice Paneth, Martin Greenbert, "Use of Social Services by Unmarried Mothers," *Children*, 10 (1, January–February, 1963), pp. 11–16.

Reed, Ellery F., "Unmarried Mothers Who Kept Their Babies," *Children*, 12 (3, May–June, 1965), pp. 118–119.

Simon, Anne, *Stepchild in the Family*, New York: Odyssey Press, 1964.

Smith, William C., *The Stepchild*, Chicago: University of Chicago Press, 1953.

Stephens, William N., *The Family in Cross-Cultural Perspective*, New York: Holt, Rinehart and Winston, 1963.

Stillman, Arthur, "Leadership: P.W.P.'s Permanent Crisis," *The Journal*, 7 (2, February–March, 1965), pp. 4–8.

United States Bureau of the Census: *Current Population Reports: Population Characteristics*, Series p. 20, No. 100, April 13, 1960, pp. 4–5.

Vincent, Clark E., "Illegitimacy in the Next Decade: Trends and Implications," *Child Welfare*, 43 (10, December, 1964), pp. 43–49.

Wynn, Margaret, *Fatherless Families*, London: Michael Joseph, 1964.

32 *Geraldine M. Devor*

Children as Agents in Socializing Parents

When the lay person hears the word "agent," more than likely he visualizes a somewhat shadowy figure dealing in foreign intrigue. The sociologist, on the other hand, may readily recognize the word as an abbreviation for the sociological concept "agent of socialization." The connotations may have some degree of similarity but the contexts in which the concepts function are worlds apart.

An agent of socialization is most frequently defined in terms of a force acting upon the individual causing him to adjust his attitudes, values, or mode of living. In the relevant literature, for example, the parent almost universally is described as the major agent of socialization for the child. (Bossard and Boll, 1966; Havighurst, 1962; Hollingshead, 1961; Ritchie and Koller, 1964; and Tyler, 1967) Indeed, the most important function of parenthood is that of preparing children to become competent members of society. It is primarily through parents that children learn the culture, e.g., language, behavior, attitudes, values, and standards of the society to which they belong. The child also receives from his parents other more subtle kinds of education, perhaps even more influential in the development of his personality. Among these learnings are the child's particular perception of the world in which he lives, his characteristic mode of emotional response to stimuli from that world, and an individual mental "set" for coping with problems that come his way.

The term "socialization" is considered here as a dynamic, ongoing process. Inasmuch as culture itself is constantly in a state of change, an individual is never completely socialized to a culture. Furthermore, there are many forces or agents acting upon the individual with different times, e.g., family, other significant people in his life, mass media, and institu-

Geraldine M. Devor, "Children as Agents in Socializing Parents." *The Family Coordinator*, Vol. 19, No. 3 (July 1970), pp. 208–212. Reprinted by permission.

tions such as government and education. In other words, when one speaks of a person becoming socialized, he does not mean that the person has achieved a particular state which he retains the remainder of his life.

PURPOSE

The idea explored in this study was that the child acts as a socializing agent for the parent as well. This possibility had been suggested as an area of research for the future in the more recent professional journals and books.

> Probably one of the most obvious controlling influences within the family upon the parent has been most neglected in parent education. This is the influence of the child upon the parent, arising from the fact that the child himself has rights and legitimate modes of control regarding his relations with his parents. Each parent-child relation is different, and in the course of interaction over time certain norms arise which determine what is legitimate behavior on the part of *both* parent and child. . . . But beyond a given age, probably age two, the parent is influenced by the child's receptivity to changes which the parent attempts to introduce into his child-rearing practice. (Brim, 1959, 68)

What follows in this paper is the report of a preliminary investigation designed to examine the ways in which parents perceive themselves being socialized by their children.

METHOD

SUBJECTS

This research was conducted in conjunction with a larger study using the same subjects and their children. The subjects in this study were 107 mothers enrolled in 25 Child Observation Classes sponsored by the Los Angeles City Board of Education. The classes consisted of two sections: the first, in which the preschool children participated in planned nursery school activities while the mothers observed them; and, the second, where the mothers met in planned parent education discussion groups to relate what they had observed and learned in class to their own children, to child development patterns, and to their own family living.

The subjects were divided into four groups on the basis of social class and race. (See Table 1.) The middle class groups, Caucasian middle class

TABLE 1 Distribution of subjects by race and social class.

	Caucasian	Negro	Totals
Middle class	43	10	53
Lower class	33	21	54
Totals	76	31	107

(CM) and Negro middle class (NM), lived in neighborhoods identified as middle to upper middle class and the primary occupations of the fathers were professional and managerial. The lower class groups, Caucasian lower class (CL) and Negro lower class (NL), lived primarily in neighborhoods identified as disadvantaged and the fathers were predominantly engaged in unskilled or semi-skilled occupations.

PROCEDURE

In the larger study of which this research was a part, the investigator had occasion to question the mothers individually regarding their children's ages, periods of attendance in the class, fathers' occupation, etc. The situation was structured so that it was necessary for each mother to wait a brief period of time for her child to complete another task in an adjoining area. During this interval, the researcher engaged in casual, informal conversation with the parent. After some preliminary social remarks, the researcher asked each parent if she could think of any way her attitudes or way of living may have been changed because of her children. To assure spontaneous opinions, no attempt was made to elicit complete responses. The answers to the questions were recorded after the parents left the room.

RESULTS

RESPONSE CATEGORIES

Perhaps the greatest difficulty in analyzing the wealth of data obtained was in classifying the variety of responses into discrete categories. For the purpose of this study, six areas of children's influence on parents were selected: child-rearing attitudes, parental personality, husband-wife relationships, recreation, miscellaneous, and no change.

Twenty-one of the total of 107 mothers indicated modification of child-rearing attitudes resulting from interaction with their children. These are illustrated by remarks as: ". . . relaxing my idea of discipline;" "My child doesn't *always* need to obey me;" "I gave my child more opportunities for independence;" "I'm stricter than I thought I would be;" "I'm beginning to like children;" and "I don't want any more children."

Changes occurring in their own personalities which they attributed to the influence of their children was perceived by seventeen mothers. Some of the comments included: "I'm more social;" ". . . gave me confidence;" "I'm learning to hold my own;" "I'm more energetic;" ". . . more efficient;" and "I'm more confused."

Six parents interviewed noted an effect on their relationships with their husbands because of the presence of children in the home: "We don't fight in front of the children;" "We're trying to have a more democratic family life;" and "We have more in common, the children."

Contrary to expectation, the influence of children on family recreation was less salient. The responses of five mothers included: "No more nightclubbing;" "We read different things;" "We enjoy watching 'Lassie' on TV;" and "Our taste in music seems to be changing."

The most frequent response listed under the miscellaneous category was: "Many ways, can't put my finger on any one thing." Others included in this category were: "Can't work any more;" and "The kids made us change the church we went to."

Forty mothers did not perceive any changes in themselves or their mode of living resulting from the influence of children. Table 2 shows the breakdown of this category by socio-racial groupings as well as the other selected categories of perceived influence by children.

TABLE 2 Number of responses indicating children's influence by various categories and by socio-ethnic groupings.

	CM	CL	NM	NL	Totals
Child-rearing Attitudes	6	8	4	3	21
Parental Personality	10	3	0	4	17
Husband-wife Relationship	2	1	2	1	6
Recreation	1	3	1	0	5
Miscellaneous	12	4	0	2	18
No Change	12	14	3	11	40

DATA ANALYSES

Chi square was used as the non-parametric statistic to test the relationships between socio-racial group position and parental perception of children's socializing influence upon them. Specifically, comparisons were made between middle and lower class Caucasians and middle and lower class Negroes. The analyses of data of this method revealed no significant difference between the four socio-racial groupings relative to the amount of influence wielded by children from these families. Other analyses dealing solely with the race variable (classes combined) and with the social class variable (races combined), also, revealed no significant differences.

One may conclude, therefore, from the total population of mothers interviewed, that there is a tendency for parents to perceive of their children as agents of socialization for them. Middle class mothers of both races were particularly conscious of this influence.

DISCUSSION

As one would expect, a pilot study of this broad nature raises many more questions than it answers. For example, the investigator was careful to define the socialization process as that which was "perceived" by the parents. Pertinent questions which may have affected the findings include: the awareness of parents of their children's influence, i.e., the child may influence the parent without the parent realizing it; the willingness of parents to admit to these influences; the casual structure of the interview; and, the limited amount of time for thought before the mothers responded.

Another limitation to the study was the age level of children whose mothers were questioned. An hypothesis that children older than two-and-one-half to five years would be stronger agents of socialization in the family would appear to be reasonable. As the child matures and moves away from the nuclear family, he acquires new repertories of behavior and attitudes which furnish him with the ammunition to express his individuality and, thus, enhance his attempts to influence his family.

> Although the attitudes and knowledge that the child gains from the family often aid him in making the transition into other systems, his roles in these other systems may require much more of him . . . he may find that participation in non-family social systems impose strange, new and conflicting demands upon him. Whatever his social background, as the child moves into these new situations, his values, attitudes, knowledge and skills are almost certain to be modified and enlarged. (Ritchie and Koller, 1964, 43)

Relevant at this point, also, is the discussion by Schiller and Leik (1963) of family role adjustment in terms of the acquisition of universals of society. These universals are defined as entities that become a frame of reference within which the person views the situation or object. The number of universals varies with societies and is acquired through experiences of the individual. Therefore, the more experience the person has, the more universals he may acquire. The "bargaining power" of children in the society is increased and their influences as socializing agents enhanced because they are part of a "youth culture" as well as an "adult culture;" they have more opportunities to learn universals and, consequently, a greater range of role patterns at their disposal.

Differences in social class appear to be a factor in the receptivity of the family to their children's efforts to effect change. This conclusion is supported by studies reported by Strodtbeck (1964) and Maas (1951). The essence of the hidden curriculum in the middle class home, according to Strodtbeck, may lie in the interaction within a democratic atmosphere occurring between child and parent which brings about consensus. "The patent familiarity of this process sometimes hides the recognition that very complicated social behavior is involved." (Strodtbeck, 1964, 12) Although the greater power of middle class parents is recognized, it is only in rare circumstances that full mobilization of power is required. Some inferences which may be drawn from these conclusions are that middle class parents are more secure in their roles in the culture, thus allowing for openness and flexibility. Furthermore, this flexibility could facilitate the socializing influence of the child on the parent.

In a study proposing a reinterpretation of some social behavioral patterns of pre-adolescents and early adolescents in lower class and core-culture families, Maas concludes that middle class children experience a more flexible and open parent relationship. Lower class children, on the contrary, reported a closed and quite rigid relationship with their parents. Because lower class parents are particularly vulnerable to unpredictable threat, the power of the child in a social interaction situation is minimized. One, therefore, may conclude from this analysis that the lower class child is in a weaker position than the middle class child to serve as an agent of socialization for the parent.

Bronfenbrenner (1961), however, suggests that social class may be becoming a less salient variable in this kind of research. After an extensive review of the literature over the past 20 years, he drew the conclusion that the gap between social classes in patterns of child-rearing is narrowing. The most important causes of this development are mass communication and increasing mobility of the society. Another factor may be the effect of the middle class schoolroom on the lower class child and its subsequent influence in the parent-child interaction situation.

IMPLICATIONS

In conclusion, this pilot study demonstrates that the socializing influence of children upon parents is, indeed, a promising area for further study.

With the results obtained from this investigation, guideposts which give tentative direction to further research have been suggested. Parent educators, particularly, will be interested to learn more of the ramifications of the parent-child interaction situation. Certainly, the more sensitive the parents are to the influence of their child-agents, the better they will be equipped to fulfill their roles as mothers and fathers. On the other hand, an awareness by parent educators of the potential influence of children on parents will increase their understanding of family structure and functioning as well as enhance their effectiveness as counselors.

The influence of classroom teachers as socializing agents may reach into the home by way of children. This influence can be seen as a positive force in the society in areas such as attitudes toward minority groups, sources of factual information which may clarify the issues of the day and, in general, reinforcers of the society's standards and values. Although this increases the responsibility of the teacher, it enhances that role in society by recognizing teachers as figures of authority.

REFERENCES

Bossard, J. H. and E. S. Boll. *The Sociology of Child Development.* New York: Harper & Row, 1966.

Brim, O. G. *Education for Child-Rearing.* New York: Russell Sage Foundation, 1959.

Bronfenbrenner, U. The Changing American Child—A Speculative Analysis. *Merrill-Palmer Quarterly,* 1961, 7, 2, 73–84.

Havighurst, R. J. and B. Neugarten. *Society and Education.* Boston: Allyn & Bacon, 1962.

Hollingshead, A. B. *Elmtown's Youth.* New York: John Wiley, 1961.

Maas, H. S. Some Social Class Differences in the Family Systems and Group Relations of Pre- and Early Adolescents. *Child Development,* 1951, 22, 145–152.

Ritchie, O. W. and M. R. Koller. *Sociology of Childhood.* New York: Appleton-Century-Crofts, 1964.

Schiller, J. A. and R. K. Leik. Symbolic Interaction and Family Role Adjustment. *The Pacific Sociological Review,* 1963, 6, 1, 30–36.

Strodtbeck, F. L. The Hidden Curriculum in The Middle Class Home. Paper from The Social Psychology Laboratory, University of Chicago, September, 1964.

Tyler, L. E. *The Psychology of Human Differences.* New York: Appleton-Century-Crofts, 1956.

33

E. E. LeMasters

Counseling with Parents

In his book, *Games People Play*, Berne makes the following statement: "Raising children," he writes, "is primarily a matter of teaching them what games to play."[1]

In this chapter on counseling with parents we are adopting a stance somewhat similar to that of Berne: counseling with parents is primarily a matter of helping them see explicitly what parental model they have been using; examining that model with the parents to see how well it fits them and their children; suggesting alternate models that might work better for them; and, finally, teaching the parent (or parents) how to implement the model decided on. The rest of this chapter will attempt to explain how this counseling system works.

THE ATTITUDE OF THE COUNSELOR

Before proceeding to parental models and their implementation, a few words need to be said about attitudes that social workers, teachers, ministers, judges, psychologists, and psychiatrists tend to have toward parents.

Parents are often assumed to be guilty before they even get a hearing with the counselor.[2] The child has been doing something wrong, therefore the parents have been doing something wrong. The professional counselors forget that parents are *amateurs*—very few of them ever had any training for the parental role. This means that the professional counselor[3] is usually using professional norms to assess the performance of nonprofessionals.

Counselors who have never been parents tend to underestimate the

E. E. LeMasters, "Counseling with Parents." From *Parents in Modern America* (Homewood, Illinois: The Dorsey Press, 1970), Chapter 12, pp. 210–225. Reprinted by permission.

complexity and hazards of being a parent in our society—they are too willing to condemn parents if a child is having difficulty.[4]

Almost all counselors, including this writer, have feelings and attitudes from their own family experience that sometimes intrude on the counseling situation—appropriately or inappropriately. Some of these attitudes and feelings may be conscious but others are subconscious or unconscious.

Brim makes it clear that most workers in the family life education field reflect a built-in middle-class bias.[5] It seems likely that parent counselors have the same bias.

Most American parents seen by counselors are already suffering from a deep feeling of inadequacy. Regardless of how hard they may have tried, the results of their parental efforts have not been satisfactory. Therefore, it does not seem appropriate or desirable for the counselor to add to this crushing weight of failure. It may help the counselor if he remembers that even unsuccessful parents have often tried hard to rear their children properly—their efforts have simply not paid off.

Finally, parent counselors need to watch that they do not become "child worshippers"—people who seem to be willing to do almost anything to parents "if it will help the child." Parents are people too, and they have as much right to consideration as children have.

With this background let us examine various parent models and attempt to see how better knowledge of them might help parents.

PARENT MODELS

Whether they realize it or not all parents adopt one parent model or another. In the rest of this chapter we wish to examine some of these models to see what their essential characteristics are and to discuss how parent counselors can use the models in working with parents.

THE MARTYR MODEL

Many parents, without realizing it, adopt the martyr model. "Nothing is too good for my children," they will say, or "I would do *anything* for my child."

The following characteristics are usually found in this model.

Parental guilt. For some reason these parents usually exhibit guilt and the counselor needs to explore this with them.

Overprotection. Guilt is often accompanied by overprotection. The parent is afraid that something will happen to the child and attempts to set up a "supersafe" world for the child. This, of course, almost invariably produces problems for all parties concerned—parents as well as children.

It is our impression that divorced parents, or those whose marriage has failed even though it is still intact, are especially subject to the guilt-overprotection syndrome. Parents with handicapped children will often exhibit this pattern also.

It hardly needs to be said that these martyr parents spoil their children. They cannot set realistic goals for their children, or if they do, the goals are not adhered to.

Revolt or meek submission by the child. A healthy reaction by children living under this parental model is that of revolt—they almost instinctively reach out for a normal life and this inevitably brings them into conflict with the parent or parents. At this point the martyred parent assumes the posture—"look what you are doing to me—and after all I have done for you." Berne analyzes this game as it is enacted between marital partners.[6]

A child that does *not* revolt against the martyr model is a sick child—he will be crippled for life if he does not revolt. This might not be true in some societies but it is certainly true in the open-class, competitive, impersonal society American children will graduate into.

As a youngster the writer grew up with a boy who submitted to a mother who had adopted the model of the martyr.

George was an only child—not unusual in this model—and his father had died when this boy was about 10 years old. The boy did not participate in male peer group activities, and later on in high school he never dated. As soon as school was out he would hurry home so that his mother "wouldn't worry" about him.

After high school graduation, George never moved into the open adult society. During the economic boom of World War II he did not enter the labor market but remained at home with his mother.

When the writer was visiting his home community several years ago this "boy" (now about 50 years old) was to be seen on the front porch of the family home, with his mother sitting nearby.

This case is not presented as being typical of what happens when parents adopt the martyr model, but it does illustrate how severe the crippling of the child can become.[7]

Hostility and resentment by the child toward the parent. In the event of revolt this will be open and obvious. In cases of submission it will be covert and repressed. Martyr parents can never understand this reaction by their children: "Look at that attitude after all I have done for them."

It is the writer's belief that the martyr model is perhaps the most destructive one found in American parents. In some ways it is even more destructive than the model of parent neglect—the neglected child is at least free and has a chance of finding a substitute parent.

On an ethical level it is simply not right that a parent should serve as a martyr for a child: it denies the parent his right to a life of his own as an adult; furthermore, it places the child in the inevitable role of the ungrateful offspring.

Some of the most difficult counseling situations in working with martyr parents are found when one parent adheres to the martyr model while the other one rejects it. This can be described as a "split model" situation. When this is found the counselor has to be careful not to be seduced by the martyred parent, and to see the split as an asset—it means that conflict is present and out of this conflict change can be generated.

The best strategy in dealing with martyr parents is to be honest and direct: unless they can be made to see what they are doing to themselves as well as their children the prognosis is not pleasant. These parents have thick defenses and the counselor will often need to be provocative and/or aggressive to get any movement.

THE BUDDY OR PAL MODEL

A certain number of parents in modern America seem to have adopted the buddy or pal model—they apparently feel that this is a solution to the gap between the generations.

Some students of the family have been rather caustic in their comments on this model. Bell, for example, has this to say:

> The middle-class belief that a parent should be a "pal" to his children reflects a social value which gives importance to a common world for parents and children. The belief in a common world has developed around notions of democracy between parents and children and implies they are equals socially, psychologically, and intellectually. If this is true, it is a devastating picture of the parents because it implies that they are still teenagers.[8]

Bell goes on to point out that the pal approach to parenthood is not the only area in which the lines between generations have been blurred in our society.[9]

In a sense the parents who adopt the buddy or pal models are following the old saying, "if you can't beat 'em, join 'em." They are trying to infiltrate the youth peer group and work from within. In some ways they resemble the social workers assigned to work with juvenile gangs on the streets of our large cities.[10] These social workers have no authority: they simply attempt to influence the gang leadership. This is not only a difficult role but also a dangerous one—and the writer has a hunch it is no easier for parents.

It is possible that the pal or buddy model received its impetus from the rush of early marriages that followed the end of World War II. The

writer interviewed a mother of 20 a few years ago who was taking care
of her two preschool children. She just laughed when we asked her if she
felt mature enough to be rearing a family.

"Nobody is grown up in this house," she said. "My husband is 20
also and he certainly isn't very grown up."

After a pause she looked at her two children and said: *"I guess we're
all growing up together."*

It struck us that her generation—at least some of them—do not accept
the traditional idea that you have to be grown up to get married. On the
contrary, all you need is somebody who wants to grow up with you. The
writer does not know how many young parents in America subscribe to
this point of view, but for those that do the pal model may be functional:
they would only be kidding themselves if they pretended to be mature
adults rearing a family.

Another impetus for the pal or buddy model may have come from
the rejection of middle age or old age in our society. Americans do not
revere the older person, or assume that he has any great store of wisdom
to offer young people. If anything, we tend to pity the older person—and
by older the society means anybody over 40. Thus, by the time American
parents are dealing with adolescents, they are near (or over) the dividing
line between youth and old age. Many of them are tempted to conclude
that they might as well pretend to be a pal or buddy because there is
nothing to gain by acting your age. Millions of women in our society use
this strategy (with some success) and some parents apparently use it also.

The writer happens to believe that the pal or buddy model of parenthood is difficult and risky. Its major problems follow.

It is extremely unrealistic. Our society holds that parents are responsible for the rearing and guidance of their minor children. Parents can be
imprisoned for neglect or mistreatment of their children. They can also
have their parental rights terminated under certain circumstances.

In view of the "generation gap" in our society it seems unlikely that
any children are going to be fooled by the pal model of parenthood.[11]
They know who the enemy is—and their motto seems to be: "never trust
anybody over 30."

As we pointed out earlier in this chapter, the pal or buddy model may
be realistic for some teen-age parents who are still children themselves,
but the model hardly fits the vast majority of American parents.

The roles called for in the model are quite complex. Few of us can
cross generation lines effectively and convincingly enough to make this
model work. One has to penetrate or infiltrate the youth peer group, understand its subculture, and be accepted by the group. Pal parents cannot
fall back on parental authority when the going gets tough—they have to
sustain the pal role consistently if the model is to work. Very few parents
can achieve this level of role performance.

The pal model requires superior parents to make it work. In World War II we had an opportunity to study at close range two types of officers in the U.S. Naval Air Corps.[12] The traditional officer maintained considerable social distance between himself and his enlisted men—a model that the Navy has found to be effective over the years. This traditional model was well defined and made no great demands on the imagination or creativity of the officer. All he had to do was to follow the rules and not much could happen to him. In the bomber air groups, however, with their long missions and close physical proximity, some officers abandoned the traditional model and adopted a pal or buddy model—their enlisted men did not have to salute officers, first names were used, regulation clothing was not insisted on, and so forth.

It was the writer's impression, based on three years of participant-observation, that only the *superior* officers could adopt the buddy model and get away with it. If the officer was average or below average in ability the flight crew soon deteriorated and order had to be restored by some subordinate, such as a chief petty officer, if the crew was to function properly.

It is our belief that the same conditions hold for parents: only the superior parent can play the buddy game with his or her children without losing their respect and their obedience.

The pal or buddy model involves considerable risk. This was quite clear in the Naval Air Corps in the opinion of the writer. Several tragic plane and crew losses might have been avoided in the writer's air group if crews had been held under more strict discipline.

We have the impression that the pal model is equally risky for parents: if things don't go well they have to retreat to a more formal, authoritarian parent model—and this retreat or shift in role is extremely difficult to manage without damaging the parent's image in the eyes of his children.

A professor known to us had been using the buddy model with a graduate seminar. Among other things he told the class that they didn't have to come to class if they didn't want to. One day this professor went to class and found only one student out of fifteen present. He was furious and immediately posted a notice that attendance would be compulsory in the future. The class reacted with resentment and the semester was completed in the atmosphere of an armed truce.

One of the advantages of the traditional authoritarian parent model is that it allows the father or mother to relax the rules occasionally without damaging the relationship with the children—in fact the relationship should be enhanced. This is not the case when the pal model has been adopted.

It should be clear to the reader by now that the writer has grave reservations about the workability of the pal or buddy parent model. The counselor should explore with the parents the complexity and hazards of the model and help them consider other models that appear to be less complex and less hazardous.

THE POLICEMAN OR DRILL SERGEANT
MODEL OF PARENTHOOD

Some parents seem to conceptualize their role as that of the policeman or drill sergeant. They are alert to punish the child for the most minor offense, making sure that he obeys the rules at all times. These parents seem to believe that this system of parenthood will keep their children from getting into trouble.

In some ways this policeman model is a foolproof defense system for the parents: if the child does get into difficulty the parents can always say—"we told him not to do it."

In our opinion this model will not work for most parents in the United States for the following reasons.

Americans tend to be "cop haters." Almost any book on police in the United States, or even casual reading of the daily newspaper, will reveal how unenviable the position of the policeman is in our society.[13] Except on television shows the police are the bad guys. In a recent incident in the Midwest a group of citizens stood by while a patrolman was beaten up by several men who had been creating a disturbance. Not one citizen offered to help the police officer.[14]

Vacancies in almost every urban police department testify to the reluctance of most Americans to assume this role.

In the armed forces the drill sergeants are no more popular than are policemen in the civilian community.

From the earliest colonial days Americans have been allergic to authority, and the allergy seems to be increasing, not decreasing.

The adolescent peer group is too powerful. Parents may get away with the policeman model while their children are quite young, but eventually the parents will be confronted by the adolescent peer group— and as we have seen in earlier chapters, this is a formidable opponent in modern America.

In some ways the policeman and drill sergeant have an advantage over parents: the legal structure is usually on their side. Parents are not always sure of a friendly reception in court—most judges and social workers will identify with the "helpless child." As Lerner says, there are no "bad children in our society—only bad parents."[15] In this sort of atmosphere it is difficult, if not impossible, for the extremely strict or harsh parent to win in our society.

A great deal of love is needed to make the policeman model work.

If the parent can achieve the image of the "benevolent despot," strict or even harsh discipline will be tolerated by many children. But warmth and love have to be so obvious and plentiful that the child can never doubt that the parent has the child's best interests at heart.

It is our impression that many parents who adopt the policeman or drill sergeant model simply do not have enough love for the child to make the severe discipline tolerable. Or if they do have the love it does not get communicated to the child.

Parenthetically, it can be said that much of the open hostility of the poor and minority groups in our society toward the police stems from the fact that these people are convinced that the police do not have their best interests at heart—they view the police as their enemy, not their friend.[16] It appears that many American parents who adopt the policeman model are viewed in a similar way by their children.

The pluralistic nature of our society, discussed in earlier chapters, also poses problems for parents using the policeman model—the norms are not that clear or that specific; there are often divergent or competing norms of behavior, and the child may challenge the right of the parent to select a particular norm to be enforced. Here, again, the policeman and drill sergeant have an advantage over parents—the laws governing communities and the regulations in the armed forces are more specific than those that parents operate with.

This model is not functional in our society. If the United States is actually an open-class, competitive society, then a premium would be placed on parental models that emphasize such qualities as initiative, aggression, and competitiveness—qualities that appear to be minimized in the policeman or drill sergeant model. It needs to be remembered that the police and the armed forces are primarily concerned with maintaining order and discipline, hence the model is functional for those systems. But to the extent that America is still an open-class, competitive society the model is dysfunctional for parents; it would not meet the basic needs of either the society or the child.

It is possible, however, to view the situation in an entirely different light—that America has become primarily a socioeconomic system of large bureaucratic organizations, both public and private, and that these systems maximize obedience, discipline, reliability, and conformity, qualities that appear to be attainable with the policeman or drill sergeant model.

Miller and Swanson found that the middle and lower class parents in their sample appear to be preparing their children to "fit into" large bureaucratic organizations.[17] When one remembers that the most expansive sector of the U.S. economy in recent decades has been that of public employment, these parents may be preparing their children very realistically for the America of today and tomorrow.

In reading Riesman and Whyte one gets the same message—American parents are preparing their children to live and work harmoniously in a tightly organized mass society.[18] Whyte does not like what he sees—nor does Riesman—but the picture they report is quite clear: American society today has more room for the conformist than it has for the innovator.

It may well be that the policeman or drill sergeant parental model is functional for the lower class and most of the middle class in our society, but that it is dysfunctional for other groups. This appears to be the finding of Miller and Swanson.[19]

The writer believes that the policeman or drill sergeant model has limitations that are not necessary. This will be seen later in the chapter when the fifth and last parental model is analyzed. But before that let us look at the fourth model, the teacher-counselor.

THE TEACHER-COUNSELOR PARENT MODEL

This is the developmental model.[20] The child is conceptualized as an extremely plastic organism with almost unlimited potential for growth and development. The limits to this growth and development are seen as the limits of the parent (and other teachers) to tap the rich potential of the child. Parents themselves are regarded as expendable—only "the child" counts. Discipline may be firm but never harsh—and punishment should be psychological, not physical or corporal.

The model presumes that the parent (as teacher-counselor) knows all the right answers—the only problem is to motivate the child to find out what they are.

The good teacher-counselor (parent) always puts the need of the child first—within the tolerance limits of the classroom or the school system itself.

This model has deep historical roots in our society—Christ is usually presented as a teacher or counselor; Benjamin Franklin and Abraham Lincoln, both folk heroes in America, reflect some of the teacher-counselor image. The dedicated (and underpaid) school teacher is a warm symbol in the United States, and in these days of social work and psychiatry the image of the counselor casts its shadow across the land.

This model reflects the progressive school era inspired by John Dewey, also the psychiatric viewpoint pioneered by Sigmund Freud. The child is seen as fragile and plastic but capable of infinite growth and development if enough parental love and guidance are applied. The uniqueness of each child is stressed—not his similarity with other children.

At the middle-class level this model has probably been dominant in the United States in recent decades. While it has many fine features the writer believes it also poses the following problems.

Parents are not viewed as ends in themselves. In this system the needs of the child are always paramount. Parents are expected to sacrifice themselves gladly for the welfare of "our children." Such a value system, in the opinion of the writer, can have devastating effects on fathers, mothers, marriages, society, and even the child himself. It is a great burden in later life for a son or daughter to be told—"I sacrificed everything for you." This takes us back to the martyr model discussed earlier in this chapter.

This model is often too permissive. American parents are often accused of "spoiling" their children.[21] This is easy to do in the teacher-counselor model because of the great stress placed on the uniqueness of each child and his needs—relatively little is said about the needs of the parent or the needs of society. Thus the child may get the impression that he is the center of the universe.

The model tends to produce anxiety and guilt in parents. Middle-class parents in modern America appear to be afflicted with anxiety and guilt. Lerner doubts that *any* human society has ever produced parents as anxious and threatened as those in our society.[22] Some of the reasons for this have been explored in earlier chapters in this book. Brim argues that one of the chief products of the massive parent education program in the United States has been parental guilt.[23]

The writer believes that most American parents are reasonably conscientious and competent in their parental role and holds the teacher-counselor model partly responsible for these fathers and mothers being made to feel guilty and inadequate.

The model tends to view parents as experts. Parents are *not* experts. Most of them have never had any formal training or education for their parental role—and by the time they have learned enough from their experience as parents to feel like experts their children are grown up and they are on the sidelines watching other young couples struggling with the same problems they struggled with.

When parents try to become experts they are courting trouble—they can never really learn all of the mystique known to the psychiatrist, the psychologist, the home economist, or the social worker, and if anything goes wrong they will be told, "but that's not what we said. You misunderstood us." In a very real sense a little knowledge is a dangerous thing.

What also happens is that the professionals (the designated experts) begin to judge parents by professional standards—parents should know this or that or something else.

This model does not adequately present the needs of the society. Since the model focuses primarily on the needs and development of the individual, the requirements of the community and the larger society are necessarily downgraded. This has been one of the factors that has produced a generation which displays relatively little respect for parents or other representatives of the social order.

It would seem that in any society a balance must be struck between the imperatives of the society and the needs of the individual—and it is our judgment that this parent model fails to pass this test.

THE ATHLETIC COACH MODEL

It seems to the writer that some of the most successful parents in our society employ a model derived from the role of the athletic coach. As we have analyzed this model it appears to have the following characteristics.[24]

Physical fitness. The players must be physically fit for the contest. This involves not only vigorous physical activity but also abstention or moderation in smoking, drinking, late hours, and so on.

Mental fitness. The athlete must be psychologically fit—that is, he must have confidence in his ability and a feeling that he can compete successfully.

Knowledge of the game. The player must know the rules of the game and the penalty for violating them. At times he may knowingly and deliberately violate the rules—but only after calculating the chances of getting caught and the potential gain if he is not caught.

Basic skills and techniques must be painfully learned. There are no "born" star athletes—they may be born with potential but only hard work will permit them to realize that potential. A player that refuses to practice, no matter how gifted, will not be tolerated on the squad.

The player must have stamina. He must not give up or reduce his effort—even when he is tired. As Woody Hayes, coach of the Ohio State football team, once said: "Victory in football means getting up one more time than your opponent does."[25]

Aggressiveness and competitive spirit. The athlete must desire to compete and to win. There are no "happy losers" among first-rate athletes or their coaches.

The player must accept strict discipline. Regardless of his status on the team—star or substitute—each player must submit to strict discipline. Violation of basic regulations usually results in suspension or dismissal from the squad.

Subordination of self to the success of the team. Each player is expected to put the success of the team ahead of his personal glory. Failure to do this not only brings repercussions from the coach but also from the other players.

The coach is expected to have the welfare of his players in mind at all times. In order for the tight discipline system in this model to work the coach must never order a player to do anything that might threaten his welfare—an injured player, for example, no matter how essential to the team, must never be ordered to play if his future may be jeopardized. Most coaches would not even permit a boy to play—even though he requested permission—if further injury at this time could result in permanent damage.

The coach cannot play the game—this must be done by the player. The coach's position here is quite analogous to that of parents: once the game has begun it is up to the players to win or lose it. The coach has some advantages over parents—he can send in players and he can substitute one player for another. But he faces the same prospect as parents of sitting on the sidelines and watching players make mistakes that may prove disastrous.

DISCUSSION OF
THE ATHLETIC COACH MODEL

The writer submits that this model has much to recommend it to American parents. The overwhelming popularity of competitive sports in our society seems to indicate general acceptance of the model among large numbers of youth as well as by the general population.

The model seems to contain a nice balance of aggression, competitiveness, and cooperation. The developmental theme is included in the expectation that each player will realize his full potential. The model emphasizes success but the players, as well as the coach, must also learn how to live with defeat.

The model has some limitations, however, due to the fact that the role of parent is not exactly the same as that of an athletic coach. Some of these limitations are as follows: (1) the coach has had professional preparation for his role—most parents have not. (2) The coach can select his players from a pool of talent—parents have to work with the children they have, talent or not. (3) The coach can substitute one player for another. Parents cannot. (4) The athletic contest for which the coach is preparing his team is more specific than "the game of life" for which parents are preparing their children. The athletic contest is less subject to deep social change than is the society for which parents are training their children. The time span is shorter for the coach also. He does not have to wait 20 years to see whether his efforts paid off. (5) The coach can quit if the situation seems hopeless—parents are not supposed to resign their roles as father or mother. Coaches can also be discharged or fired—something that is legally possible for parents but not common.

(6) Coaches are expected to like or at least respect their players—but parents are supposed to love their children.

In an interesting passage Brim says that "if a social role *requires* characteristics such as friendliness or love, it is almost self-defeating."[26] He goes on to say that "certain acts might be required in a role . . . but that love and similar expressions of feeling cannot be deliberate or contrived."[27] In this respect the athletic coach has an advantage over parents.

With all of these limitations it still seems to the writer that the athletic coach model has much to recommend it to American parents.

THE USE OF THESE MODELS IN COUNSELING PARENTS

It would seem that these models can be used by counselors to help parents see what they are doing. The technique is similar to that used in the client-centered counseling system developed by Rogers—the counselor reflects back to the parents the model they are using.[28] At an appropriate time the counselor should point out that several parent models are available in our society and that perhaps this father and/or mother might do better using another model.

It is recognized that this approach assumes that the parents desire to improve their role performance and are willing to consider modification of their behavior. If this proves not to be the case, then the counselor would have to explore other problems that would seem to be blocking the treatment.

OTHER FUNCTIONS OF THE PARENT COUNSELOR

As we said earlier in this chapter, it is important that the counselor approach parents with the right attitude—they should not be judged guilty without a fair hearing. Even the most inept parents have often tried hard to live up to their obligations as fathers and mothers.

It is also essential that the counselor use reasonable expectations in dealing with parents. Most of them have had to function under adverse conditions; most of them had no preparation for their role as parent; they are not social workers or clinical psychologists or psychiatrists. The fact that they could conceive and produce a child did not automatically endow them with any insight into themselves, their child, or their world. There is really no social test for parenthood in our society—only a biological test.[29]

It is the writer's conviction that marital conflict is a basic factor preventing good parent performance in the two-parent family. If this is true the counselor will often need to focus on the husband-wife relationship rather than the parent-child relationship.[30]

Inadequate and/or distorted communication networks are typical of families in which parents are not functioning well. Indeed, recent trends in marriage and family counseling, as represented by Satir and Haley,[31] indicate that improvement of communication is one of the most important functions of the marriage and/or family counselor.

It needs to be understood that improved communication does not necessarily resolve husband-wife or parent-child conflicts—but it does sharpen and clarify these conflicts so that they can be dealt with more effectively.

Some fathers and mothers will need some type of psychotherapy. It needs to be remembered, however, that there are "sick families" in which the various individuals themselves are not sick—the pathology is not intrapsychic but interpersonal.[32] This is often obvious in counseling with married couples, but it is not so obvious in parent-child counseling.

The writer has found that it often helps to explore the parent's childhood and how his parents handled him or her. We are all apt to forget or repress our own childhood—or to romanticize it. The writer has always been impressed, for example, with the inability of parents who grew up in the 1920's or the 1930's to remember any serious necking or petting— yet the sexual revolution in our society was well along by then. Parents need to be reminded of some of the things they did as young people. This should make them somewhat more tolerant of the current generation.

In view of the great burden of guilt and anxiety carried by most American parents it is hoped that the counselor will not add unnecessarily to this load. It may be that some parents could benefit from being made to feel guilty, but the writer believes these to be a small minority.

Finally, there is much to be said for counseling parents in groups.[33] They often have quite similar problems; some parents feel more comfortable in a group counseling situation; they get perspective on their problems by listening to other parents; and they can learn from each other.

SUMMARY AND CONCLUSION

In this chapter five parent models were presented and analyzed with the hope that these might be useful to counselors working with parents. Ideas from Berne and Rogers were utilized in the analysis. Our hypothesis has been that parents follow a certain system of performing their parental role whether they realize it or not. One of the basic functions of the counselor, as we see it, is to help parents understand what model or system they are using.

The chapter concluded with a brief statement of several other functions of the parent counselor.

ENDNOTES

1. Eric Berne, *Games People Play* (New York: Grove Press, Inc., 1964), p. 171.
2. Orville G. Brim, Jr., *Education for Child Rearing* (New York: Russell Sage Foundation, 1959). See especially chap. 9, "Aims of Parent Education."
3. The term *counselor* is being used generically here to denote any member of the helping professions who works with parents.
4. This observation is based on contacts with graduate students who are not yet parents in a school of social work.
5. Brim, *op. cit., passim.*
6. Berne, *op. cit.*, pp. 104–107.
7. In another case studied by the writer a woman of 65, in good physical health, entered a home for the aged because both of her parents were now deceased and she could not face the world alone.
8. Robert R. Bell, *Marriage and Family Interaction* (rev. ed.; Homewood, Ill.: The Dorsey Press, 1967), p. 431.
9. *Ibid.*
10. Some of these problems are reviewed in Richard A. Cloward and Lloyd E. Ohlin, *Delinquency and Opportunity: A Theory of Delinquent Gangs* (New York: The Free Press, 1964).
11. For an interesting analysis of the generation gap see Richard Lorber and Ernest Fladell, *The Gap* (New York: McGraw-Hill Book Co., 1968).
12. The observations on officer models in the U.S. Naval Air Corps are based on three years service during World War II.
13. See, for example, Arthur Neiderhoffer, *Behind the Shield: The Police in Urban Society* (New York: Doubleday & Co., 1967).
14. In a university city in which the writer was teaching, a group of young people watched passively while a patrolman was beaten up by three men he had tried to arrest for creating a disturbance.
15. Max Lerner, *America as a Civilization* (New York: Simon and Schuster, 1967), pp. 560–570.
16. One of the major findings of the *U.S. Riot Commission Report* (New York: Bantam Books, 1968), was the feeling of hostility (if not

hatred) that the urban racial minorities have toward the police. See chap. 11, "The Police and the Community."

17. Daniel R. Miller and Guy E. Swanson, *The Changing American Parent* (New York: John Wiley & Sons, 1958), chap. 4, "Child Training in Entrepreneurial and Bureaucratic Families."

18. On conformity in our society see David Riesman et al., *The Lonely Crowd* (New Haven, Conn.: Yale University Press, 1961), *passim;* also William H. Whyte, Jr., *The Organization Man* (New York: Doubleday & Co., 1957), especially Pt. 1, "The Ideology of Organization Man."

19. For a discussion of the functionality of the two systems of child rearing analyzed in their study, see Miller and Swanson, *op. cit.,* pp. 109–118.

20. For a delineation of the child development parent model, see Evelyn Duvall, "Conceptions of Parenthood," *American Journal of Sociology,* 52 (1946), pp. 193–203.

21. See Lerner, *op. cit.,* pp. 562–568 for a discussion of spoiling children by American parents.

22. *Ibid.,* pp. 562–563.

23. On the production of guilt in parents see Brim, *op. cit., passim.*

24. The athletic coach model used here was derived from several weeks the writer once spent with a group of coaches at Ohio State University. This group included two men who later became nationally famous for their winning teams—Paul Brown and Woody Hayes.

25. Athletic banquet speech reported in the *Milwaukee Journal,* November 14, 1965.

26. Brim, *op. cit.,* p. 98.

27. *Ibid.*

28. See Carl Rogers, *Client-Centered Therapy* (Boston: Houghton Mifflin Co., 1951). For a good analysis of the Rogerian counseling system, see Calvin S. Hall and Gardner Lindzey, *Theories of Personality* (New York: John Wiley & Sons, 1957), pp. 467–502.

29. There is a "social competence" test for adoptive and foster parents. This is why the writer believes that in some ways these parents have an advantage over biological parents.

30. For a statement of the functions of the marriage counselor see Gerald Leslie, "The Field of Marriage Counseling," in Harold T. Christensen (ed.), *Handbook of Marriage and the Family* (Chicago: Rand McNally & Co., 1964).

31. See Virginia Satir, *Conjoint Family Therapy* (Palo Alto, Calif.: Science and Behavior Books, 1964), and Jay Haley, *Strategies of Psychotherapy* (New York: Grune & Stratton, 1963).

32. Nathan Ackerman, *The Psychodynamics of Family Life* (New York: Basic Books, 1958), chap. 8, "Behavioral Disturbances."

33. See Satir, *op. cit., passim.*

WHAT DO YOU THINK?

Greg and Georgia have two children, a boy and a girl. They decided this is ideal and do not want a larger family because they prefer to give these children their time and attention; quality is more important to them than quantity. Greg's father keeps after him, telling him a "real man" should have many children, for they can work and take care of him in his old age. Greg's father is a bit ashamed of his son for not wanting a large family but secretly blames that modern young woman Greg married. Women used to want many children and gained status from having them.

Why does a man like Greg seem like a piker to his father?

If Greg makes enough money to feed and clothe a large family, why should he and his wife stop at two children?

What changed the attitudes of women like Georgia about having more children?

How does having many children affect the male ego?

Irving and Irene have two children and are struggling along, just coming out even on their income. They agreed that they cannot afford any more children but cannot agree on control methods. Irving thinks she should use contraceptives because she is the one who would get pregnant, and thus it is her responsibility. Irene resents this and tells him he has just as much to do with this problem as she has. She wants them to study the good and bad aspects of various kinds of contraceptives, but he will not talk about it.

What are the merits of Irving's and Irene's positions?

Would Irving be a better husband if he accepted more responsibility for birth control? What could he do about this?

What happens to men if they expect the women to take all the precautions as well as the blame if something goes wrong?

Jacob and Jenny had been married a year but were having trouble getting along together. Many little things annoyed each of them. Jacob decided the marriage was a mistake and wanted a divorce. Jenny did not like some things about Jacob but decided a child would save the marriage and change both of them. She quit taking her pills but did not tell Jacob. He likes children and so does she.

What are the pro and con factors of having a child to save a marriage?

How have women gained control over having or not having children?

How can Jacob and Jenny get out of this trap?

Kevin's family moved often and did not celebrate anything much. When he married Karen, she insisted on celebrating their birthdays as well as those of other members of their families. When the children were small, she added their birthdays, and gradually these became important events in their lives. There was always a cake with candles, there were gifts, and other ways of making the day important. They always let the honored one select the menu for dinner. The family had some odd food combinations when the children were small but laughed about this. Later, things got better. Kevin learned with the children that such affairs take on a feeling of rightness, of *family*. Even when his business took him out of town, he came back for the celebration because he realized this meant a lot to the children, and that he had missed such evidence of devotion in his own family.

What kinds of rituals did you experience when you were growing up?

Which of the rituals you experienced will you take into your own marriage?

Little Billy did not want to go to bed at the usual time. Then his father took him on a piggyback ride and deposited him on his bed. Both of them were laughing because this was fun, and Billy was now content to get into bed. The next evening, he had some excuse again but was elated when the same kind of ride was forthcoming. This went on for six months, then all of a sudden he just said "Goodnight" and went off to his room alone.

Why does ritual mean so much to children?

What does Billy's new attitude mean?

Is it better to have the children set up rituals, or should parents do this?